The Social Psychology of Language 1

General editor: Howard Giles

D0877719

Attitudes towards Language Variation

Social and Applied Contexts

Edited by Ellen Bouchard Ryan and
Howard Giles

Edward Arnold

© Edward Arnold 1982

First published 1982 by
Edward Arnold (Publishers) Ltd
41 Bedford Square, London WC1B 3DQ

British Library Cataloguing in Publication Data

Attitudes towards language variation.—(Social
  psychology of language series)
  1. Sociolinguistics
  I. Ryan, Ellen Bouchard   II. Giles, Howard
  III. Series
  401.9   ~~P40~~

ISBN 0-7131-6195-7

Text set in 10/11pt Times Compugraphic
by Colset Private Limited.
Printed and bound in Great Britain
by Richard Clay (The Chaucer Press) Ltd,
Bungay, Suffolk

Contents

Preface

Those fascinated by the importance and complexities of language in social life might look to psychology and especially social psychology for some insights. After all, much of an individual's behaviour occurs in a social context, is manifest linguistically, and mediated by cognitive processes. While language figures prominently in many areas of psychological inquiry such as cognition and development (albeit predictably asocial and acommunicative in the former case), detailed exploration of the dynamics of language and communication within social psychology are conspicuous by their absence. Although there are admittedly important exceptions by way of certain individuals, a few books and a couple of research topics, an examination of mainstream journals and influential texts in social psychology suggests that language and communication hold at the most a peripheral status within the discipline. This is not however to suggest that important research has not been documented. Yet it does exist – as a perusal of the present volume's bibliography will show – across an extremely wide set of outlets in the social and communication sciences. Our potential enthusiasts then are liable to be soon disappointed at the apparent dearth of mainstream interest in social psychology for the topic, and understandably reluctant to invest much effort in discovering the inevitably rich stores of information actually available.

They are more likely to be attracted by the equally important but far more accessible perspectives in other disciplines such as philosophy, sociology and anthropology which not only have long-serving labels for their endeavours (i.e. the sociology of language) but can justifiably display their wares proudly. One obvious venue for our language enthusiasts, apart from communication science (which in the interpersonal domain has an active social psychological perspective especially in methodology), is sociolinguistics. This, for many, is a healthy multidisciplinary field examining the relationships between language and society from (to name a few) political, demographic, economic and linguistic perspectives. It has in fact generated the most impressive array of interesting and societally important findings. And once again, understandable in terms of the above, neglects a coherent social psychological approach; again, there are important exceptions particularly with regard to the study of bilingualism and forms of address.

We might then ask: what *is* this social psychological approach that is so lamentably missing from language studies? It lies in two domains. First, language and society are viewed as *interdependent* not as dichotomies as reflected in much traditional sociolinguistics; it is tremendously difficult to separate linguistic and social processes in many instances. Thus, not only do speakers' language behaviours reflect the norms of the situation as perceived by them but that very language behaviour itself can often act creatively to define, and subsequently redefine, the nature of the situation for the participants involved. Second, attention is drawn to the fact that language behaviour is likely to be dependent upon how speakers cognitively represent their social and psychological characteristics and subjectively define the situation in terms of its norms and their goals as is any objective classification of that situation imposed from without (e.g. by investigators). In this sense, *cognitive representations* are seen to be important mediators between language and social context. Given that social psychological theories – as well as their methodologies – are all about the complexities and dynamics of cognitive organization and representation of the social world, it is felt that this perspective can broaden the explanatory scope of the study of language.

Notwithstanding the reasons why a social psychological approach to language and communication has never really gelled – apart from in the early days of its history and in certain national contexts such as Canada – suffice it to say that there are many indications now that it has 'arrived'. For instance, some sociolinguists are beginning to acknowledge the contributions that social psychologists of language are making toward predicting and explaining linguistic variation in social contexts, and the former are themselves integrating speakers' feelings, values, attitudes and perceptions into their research designs. Indeed, research activity in the last five or more years has grown enormously. This is evident in the advent of a number of books on social psychological aspects of language in the 1970s, the emergence of two International Conferences on this perspective (at Bristol) in 1979 and 1983 attracting enthusiastic participation world-wide, as well as the establishment of the *Journal of Language and Social Psychology* as a coherent forum for this speciality. Obviously, it is timely to promote the coherence of the approach by means of a Monograph Series of interest to those in social psychology on the one hand and language and communication on the other. In this way, we can resurrect language and communication ultimately to its rightful place as a mainstream concern in social psychology as well as concurrently continuing to promote a social psychological perspective to the study of language and communication as an essential one comparable in impact to its linguistic, sociological and anthropological counterparts. In this vein, authors and editors to this Series are being asked to expend considerable energy on taking into account the cross-disciplinary nature of the potential readership. In other words, the Utopian aim is to have volumes which are not only appealing to experienced researchers in the social psychology of language but are also compelling reading for students of linguistics having little social psychological background and for social psychological students having little linguistics background. The choice of 'language attitudes' to be the first topic in this Series may be particularly appropriate (dedicated as it is to the pioneering work and inspiration of Wallace E. Lambert). For instance, many commentators have viewed social psychology as basically the study of attitudes; certainly, it is a core construct in virtually all social psychological theorizing. Because of this ubiquity, attitudes always have been used as explanatory concepts in sociolinguistic investigations probably more so than any other social psychological entities. Moreover, the field of language attitudes arguably accounts for more empirical investigations than any other single topic under the rubric of the social psychology of language. Indeed, probably as many linguists have conducted language attitude studies and adopted the attending methodologies as social psychologists themselves. The topic as addressed herein shows the tremendous potential for applications of the approach to language studies in terms of policy making as well as in theory. It also highlights to social psychologists the fundamental importance of language variables in moulding people's social lives. Finally, the present volume demonstrates well two of the major themes of paramount importance to the social psychology of language as indicated above and therefore to the Series as a whole. That is, not only is speech behaviour in important social settings influenced by a complex set of cognitive mechanisms but also these very same speech behaviours can influence (sometimes change and othertimes even determine) one's own and others' attitudes and cognitions as well. It will be apparent from this and succeeding volumes that social psychologists of language can be highly self-critical on many levels with respect to what has been achieved. However, while it seems important to develop more wide-ranging and sensitive methods, more precise concepts and sophisticated theory, contributors to this Series will be at pains to stress that we do not see a social psychological approach as any more than an important *complement* to other equally important perspectives in language and communication; many of us are actually interdisciplinarians at heart.

Howard Giles
Bristol, May 1982

Notes on Contributors

Richard Y. Von Bourhis was born in Montreal and was educated in both French and English. After a BSc in Psychology at McGill University, he obtained his PhD in Social Psychology at the University of Bristol, England. His main academic interests are the social psychology of intergroup relations and conflict, and problems of communication in multilingual communities. Through his collaboration with numerous colleagues, Bourhis has conducted research in Wales, England, Belgium, Switzerland and Australia. Current research is concerned with language use in communications between Anglophones and Francophones in Quebec, Ontario and Acadia. Other research interests also include the investigation of the impact of language planning on language attitudes and language behaviours in multilingual settings. Dr Bourhis is presently editing a volume entitled, 'Conflict and language planning in Quebec' on the impact of the *Charter of the French Language* (Bill 101) in Quebec scheduled to appear in 1983. Dr Bourhis joined the Psychology Department at McMaster University as an Assistant Professor in July 1978.

James J. Bradac obtained his PhD in 1970 from Northwestern University. He taught at the University of Iowa for 10 years prior to moving to the University of California, Santa Barbara, where he is Professor of Communication Studies. His publications include the articles, 'Reciprocal disclosures and language intensity: Attributional consequences' (with L. Hosman and C. Tardy) and 'Three language variables in communication research: Intensity, immediacy and diversity' (with J. Bowers and J. Courtright), both of which won outstanding research awards from the Speech Communication Association. He is co-author (with Charles Berger) of *Language and social knowledge: Uncertainty in interpersonal relations* which will be the second volume in the present Edward Arnold Series, the Social psychology of language.

John T. Cacioppo is an Associate Professor of Psychology at the University of Iowa. He received his PhD from Ohio State University and has co-authored with Richard Petty numerous articles that have appeared in the *American Psychologist, Journal of Personality and Social Psychology, Journal of Experimental Social Psychology, Personality and Social Psychology Bulletin, Psychophysiology*, and others. They have co-authored books entitled *Attitudes and Persuasion: Classic and Contemporary Approaches* and *Attitude Change: Central and Peripheral Routes to Persuasion*, co-edited books entitled *Perspectives in Cardiovascular Psychophysiology* and *Social Psychophysiology: A Sourcebook*, and along with Robert Cialdini have authored the chapter on attitudes and attitude change in the 1981 edition of the *Annual Review of Psychology*.

Miguel A. Carranza (PhD in Sociology, University of Notre Dame) is Associate Professor of Sociology and Ethnic Studies at the University of Nebraska. For the past ten years he has been conducting research into language attitudes of Hispanics and is preparing a monograph on language issues in the Hispanic community in the United States. His other interests are social gerontolgy and minority relations in the United States.

Richard R. Day received his doctorate in linguistics in 1972 from the University of Hawaii. He is an associate professor and chairman of the Department of English as a Second Language. In addition to his interests in language attitudes and pidgin and creole languages, he has conducted research on native speaker–nonnative speaker discourse, and also done extensive research on the relationship between minority languages and educational achievement. His major publications include editing *Issues in Pidgins and Creoles: Papers from the 1975 Hawaii Conference* (1980); 'The acquisition and maintenance of language by minority children,' *Language Learning* (1979); 'The development of linguistic attitudes and preferences,' *TESOL Quarterly* (1980); and 'The ultimate inequality: Linguistic genocide' in *Language of Inequality* edited by J. Manes and N. Wolfson (forthcoming).

John Edwards (PhD, McGill) is Associate Professor in the psychology department at St Francis Xavier University, Antigonish, Nova Scotia. He was formerly Research Fellow at the Educational Research Centre, St Patrick's College, Dublin. His major interests include the linguistic aspects of 'disadvantage', bilingual education and its social implications, and ethnicity; he has published articles and chapters on these and other topics. He is the author of *Language and Disadvantage* (London: Edward Arnold, 1979) and *The Irish Language* (New York: Garland, 1982), and the editor of *The Social Psychology of Reading* (Silver Spring, Maryland: Institute of Modern Languages, 1981). Dr Edwards is currently editing a book dealing with linguistic minorities and their treatment in educational and other spheres, and is writing another on the relationship between language and identity.

Robert C. Gardner is Professor of Psychology at the University of Western Ontario, London, Canada. For more than two decades, beginning with his graduate training at McGill University, he has conducted research on second language learning in Canada, the United States, and the Philippines. He is co-editor of a book entitled *A Canadian Social Psychology of Ethnic Relations* (Methuen, 1981) and is editor of the *Canadian Journal of Behavioural Science*, a publication of the Canadian Psychological Association.

Howard Giles obtained his PhD in 1971 at the University of Bristol. His first teaching appointment was at University College, Cardiff and then he moved back to the University of Bristol where he is now Reader in Social Psychology. His major academic interests revolve around the development of the social psychology of language and communication with a very strong emphasis on theory-building. In this vein, he is co-organizer of the first two International Conferences on Social Psychology and Language (1979 and 1983) at Bristol and is the founding Editor of the *Journal of Language & Social Psychology*. He has published eight books and numerous articles on language attitudes; speech accommodation; language, situations and social categories; and the role of language in interethnic relations in a wide range of multicultural settings. In 1978, he was awarded the British Psychological Society's 'Spearman Medal'. His most recent research interests are in second language acquisition and the application of social psychological studies of language and communication in many areas including the educational and clinical spheres and especially with regard to speech abnormalities.

Robert Hopper (PhD, University of Wisconsin, 1970) is Professor of Speech Communication at the University of Texas at Austin. He has written 20 scholarly articles focusing on the concerns of 'linguistic underdogs' including women, children and members of ethnic minority groups. His major concerns are linguistic stereotyping, how people 'take things for granted', and the teaching of communication skills (he is author of half a dozen college textbooks).

Rudolf Kalin is Professor of Psychology at Queen's University, Kingston, Canada. He has done extensive research on ethnic relations in Canada, in which context he has conducted studies on evaluative reactions to varied accents. Another major interest has been sex bias in social evaluations.

Cheris Kramarae is Associate Professor of Speech Communication at the University of Illinois, Urbana, Illinois, USA where she teaches courses in sociolinguistics (language and gender; language and power) and interpersonal communication. Her publications include *Voices and Words of Women and Men*, ed. (1980), *Women and Men Speaking* (1981), and *For Alma Mater: Essays on the Nature of Feminist Scholarship*, co-ed. (in press). She is currently co-editing a feminist thesaurus.

Richard E. Petty is an Associate Professor of Psychology at the University of Missouri-Columbia. Since receiving his PhD at Ohio State University, his programme of research with John T. Cacioppo has focused on the cognitive, physiological, and behavioural antecedents and consequents of attitude change. They have co-authored two books entitled *Attitudes and persuasion: Classic and contemporary approaches* and *Attitude change: Central and peripheral routes to persuasion*; co-edited two books entitled *Perspectives in cardiovascular psychophysiology* and *Social psychophysiology: A sourcebook*; and contributed numerous articles to journals including the *Journal of Personality and Social Psychology, Journal of Experimental Social Psychology, Personality and Social Psychology Bulletin*, and *Psychophysiology*.

Ellen Bouchard Ryan obtained an MA in Linguistics from Brown University and a PhD in Psycholinguistics from the University of Michigan. She has held visiting faculty positions at the Universities of Guelph and Waterloo and at the Modern Language Centre in Ontario and is Professor and Chairman of the Department of Psychology at the University of Notre Dame. Her research interests focus especially on bilingualism, language minorities and first and second language learning.

Robert N. St Clair works in the Interdisciplinary Program in Linguistics at the University of Louisville, Kentucky.

Richard J. Sebastian received his graduate training from the University of

Wisconsin-Madison, served on the faculty of the University of Notre Dame, and is currently a Postdoctoral Research Fellow in the Family Violence Research Program at the University of New Hampshire. His major research interests are human aggression and prejudice and stereotyping. His publications include 'Immediate and delayed effects of victim suffering on the attacker's aggression' and 'Dynamics of hostile aggression: Influence of anger, hurt instructions, and victim pain feedback' both of which appeared in the *Journal of Research in Personality*.

Richard L. Street, Jr is an Assistant Professor in Speech Communication at Texas Tech University. His research interests entail the investigation of factors influencing the social evaluation and production of speech behaviour. His major publications are in *Language and Communication, Human Communication Research, Communication Quarterly*, as well as in several edited book volumes.

1

An integrative perspective for the study of attitudes toward language variation

Ellen Bouchard Ryan, Howard Giles and Richard J. Sebastian

Whether speaking one or five languages, all individuals belong to at least one speech community, a community all of whose members share at least a single speech variety and the norms for its appropriate use. Language variation within and between speech communities can involve different languages or only contrasting styles of one language. In every society the differential power of particular social groups is reflected in language variation and in attitudes toward those variations. Typically, the dominant group promotes its patterns of language use as the model required for social advancement; and use of a lower prestige language, dialect, or accent by minority group members reduces their opportunities for success in the society as a whole. Minority group members are often faced with difficult decisions regarding whether to gain social mobility by adopting the language patterns of the dominant group or to maintain their group identity by retaining their native speech style.

The dilemma facing minority group members is exemplified in a compelling personal essay by Rodriguez (1975), a college teacher who writes regretfully and self-questioningly of abandoning his Spanish–Mexican heritage in order to succeed in school and in the broader American society represented by the school.

> The change came gradually but early. When I was beginning grade school, I noted to myself the fact that the classroom environment was so different in its styles and assumptions from my own family environment that survival would essentially entail a choice between both worlds. When I became a student, I was literally 'remade'; neither I nor my teachers considered anything I had known before as relevant. I had to forget most of what my culture had provided, because to remember it was a disadvantage. The past and its cultural values became detachable, like a piece of clothing grown heavy on a warm day and finally put away. . . .
>
> I remember when, 20 years ago, two grammar-school* nuns visited my childhood home. They had come to suggest . . . that we make a greater effort to speak as much English around the house as possible. The nuns realized that my brothers and I led solitary lives largely because we were the only Spanish-speaking students. My mother and father complied as best they could. Heroically, they gave up speaking to us in Spanish – the language that formed so much of the family's sense of intimacy in an alien world – and began to speak a broken English. Instead of Spanish sounds, I began hearing sounds that were new, harder, less friendly. . . . The bonds their voices once secured were loosened by the new tongue. (p. 46)

The choice facing minority group members is complicated by several facts. It must

---

* Grade school, ages 6 to 14.

be made over and over again, in major decisions like whether to move to a region where one's language is attributed higher status and in perhaps less major, more frequent decisions like which code to use in an employment interview. The choice of speech style is, furthermore, not a simple dichotomous one. For example, even within the dominant language one can convey identification with a particular social group by pronunciation, intonation, or vocabulary.

Whereas the range of speech-style choices available is typically greater for members of minority groups, all speakers make choices regarding their speech along a variety of dimensions. In general, speech cues can be used by listeners to make inferences regarding an individual's personal characteristics (e.g. age, sex, intelligence), social group memberships (e.g. regional, ethnic, class, occupational), and psychological states (e.g. need for social approval, interest in continuing an interaction, anxiety, depression). Selection of a particular speech style and subsequent evaluations by listeners depend upon the specific situation and upon the symbolic values associated with the selected style as it contrasts with relevant alternatives.

The views of speech community members toward the contrasting language varieties characteristic of their society have been examined from several disciplinary perspectives. Within a sociological framework, the symbolic values of language are viewed within societal and situational contexts. Thus, according to Fishman (1971, 1),

> Language is not merely a carrier of content, whether latent or manifest. Language itself is content, a referent for loyalties and animosities, an indicator of social statuses and personal relationships, a marker of situations and topics as well as of the societal goals and the large-scale value-laden arenas of interaction that typify every speech community.

Sociological studies tend to utilize the questionnaire or interview method to elicit attitudes. In addition, content analyses are conducted of historical developments within society and of particular aspects of social treatment of the target language varieties. From a sociolinguistic perspective, research following the lead of Labov (1966, 1972) has focused upon two main problems: (1) understanding the association between specific linguistic features (e.g. phonological variants, lexical patterns, and grammatical contrasts) and characteristics of the societal, social group, and situational contexts in which they occur; and (2) understanding the inferences listeners make about these associations. From social psychological and communication perspectives, emphasis is upon the individual and his/her display of attitudes toward ingroup and outgroup members as elicited by language and as reflected in its use. Most of the research conducted within social psychological or communication traditions has followed the lead of Lambert (1967) and has involved the elicitation of evaluative reactions toward speakers using contrasting language varieties. Attitudes toward particular varieties are then taken to be attitudes toward speakers of those varieties. Since this book is part of a series on social psychology, the primary focus is upon studies of the speaker-evaluation type, but important themes from the sociological and sociolinguistic approaches also flow throughout the volume.

An organizational framework

In the following section, we provide a general framework within which to consider the language attitude studies reviewed in the present volume. Given the lack of theory in this area (see Giles and Ryan, this volume: ch. 13), we present a number of critical dimensions along which to compare language attitude studies conducted in different language settings. First the sociostructural determinants underlying the development and expression of language attitudes are discussed in terms of two dimensions, standardization and vitality. Second, the three types of measurement technique (content analysis, direct and indirect) are outlined. Finally, status and ingroup solidarity are presented as the two primary evaluative dimensions of language attitudes and their relationship with the sociostructural determinants described. The identification of the primary determinants of language attitudes and their integration with a set of prototypical language attitude patterns is intended to assist the reader in fitting together the various contributions to this book.

Determinants

Researchers (Fishman 1971; Giles, Bourhis and Taylor 1977; Stewart 1968) have identified several attributes of language varieties which relate to how they are viewed within a given speech community or within any larger social group (e.g. a nation). From among the possibilities, the two critical sociostructural determinants appear to be standardization and vitality. Whereas standardization represents the codification of the status quo, vitality more directly reflects the forces for shifts in language use and in symbolic values. For both these attributes, it is important to distinguish between the actual characteristics of a language variety and that variety's characteristics as perceived by members of the relevant speech communities.

Standardization. The primary distinction among varieties is based upon the extent to which they have been standardized. According to Fishman (1971), a language variety is said to be standardized if a set of norms defining 'correct' usage has been codified and accepted within a speech community. Typically, these codified norms are available in the form of dictionaries, grammars, style manuals and prototype texts. The acceptance of the codified form of a language variety is normally advanced by the power elites of a society (see St Clair, this volume: ch. 10) and confirmed via social institutions such as government, schools and the mass media. The standard variety then comes to be associated with these formal institutions, the kinds of interactions which normally occur within them and the sets of values they represent. Variants which are used in written communication are much more likely to be standardized than those which are used solely in the oral modality. Not every language has a standard variety, nor does the same variety necessarily survive across time as the recognized standard of a speech community. For example, it was only in the nineteenth century that American English achieved separate status as a standard for the United States, and discussions continue regarding whether Quebec should recognize France's French or a distinct Québecois variant as its standard (see Bourhis, this volume: ch. 3). Standardization, then, is a characteristic of the social treatment of a variety, not a property of the language variant itself.

Two other aspects of standardization concern the autonomy and historical roots of language varieties (Giles and Johnson 1981; Ullrich 1971; Wolff 1959). Where two language varieties are very similar to each other, efforts can occur by one or both speech communities to increase their independence. One common type of solution is separate standardization, which is often achieved via the creation of political boundaries (e.g. the development of Dutch as a separate language from German). An important step in the process of increased autonomy is typically the establishment of distinct written versions (e.g. as in the creation of writing systems for the many distinct indigenous languages in the western hemisphere) and the use of the written language more frequently in more formal situations (e.g. Catalan in Spain); conversely, abandoning the use of one of the written varieties typically promotes convergence of the two variants. As Garvin (1964) pointed out, a standard language serves a unifying function for the speech communities which share it at the same time that it serves a separatist function by creating a boundary between these speech communities and their neighbours. The relationship between full standardization and autonomy is bidirectional in that separate standardization leads to enhanced autonomy, while standardization is not probable unless a variety can be viewed as capable of standing alone. Another aspect of standardization rests on the recognition given to the variety by past generations. For some variants, the claim of development from respectable ancestors is easily supported by written records. Historicity, however, can also be promulgated through new emphasis upon evolution from some ancient language. For example, it has been important for the status of Black English to trace its roots to Africa rather than to emphasize its development within the setting of American slavery (Dillard 1973).

Vitality. The second sociostructural determinant of language attitudes concerns the degree to which a variety has visible vitality (i.e. interaction networks that actually employ it natively for one or more essential functions). The more numerous and more important the functions served by the variety for the greater number of individuals the greater is its vitality. According to Fishman (1971), the status of a language variety rises and falls according to the range and importance of the symbolic functions it serves. Thus, French can be considered as more vital for Québecois French Canadians who use the language for all their daily interactions than for those French Americans who use it only in the home and with relatives. One's ethnic language is much more likely to survive emigration from the mother country if it continues to be used across most situations, with most interlocutors, within most role relationships. Stable bilingualism (or bidialectalism) is most likely to occur within speech communities characterized by diglossia (Ferguson 1959). In diglossic societies, one language variety (known as the high variety) serves the functions of outgroup and formal communications while another variant (known as the low variety) is used for ingroup, informal, intimate interactions. Through functional specialization, diglossic speech communities have imposed autonomy on their two varieties as well as useful social boundaries between them.

Additional aspects of so-called 'ethnolinguistic vitality' have been discussed by Giles, Bourhis and Taylor (1977) and Giles and Johnson (1981): Status, demographic strength and institutional support. Status refers to the economic, social, political and sociohistorical power wielded by the speakers of the language variety. In terms of demography, the vitality of a variant depends upon the number and distribution of its speakers within the speech community as well as upon the diversity and power of other speech communities who employ it. Relevant to the stability of the demographic picture is the extent to which users of the language variety are separated from communities of non-users (Giles 1979a). For example, the native tongue in an immigrant community typically undergoes substantial change as its members become more and more bilingual, and its very survival is threatened to the extent that its speakers can easily merge into the dominant culture. The degree of institutional support for a language variety provides an important index of its current and future vitality. Institutional support, in turn, consists of a number of factors: whether the variety is recognized as an official language by regional and/or national governments; whether it is used in monolingual or bilingual educational programmes at some or all age levels; whether it is employed in society-wide and/or ingroup business transactions; whether it is used in society-wide and/or ingroup publications, radio/television and community organizations.

As one would expect, standardization contributes substantially to the vitality of a language variety while strong vitality enhances its potential for achieving standardization. Yet, as exemplified in the two-dimensional model presented in Figure 1.1, there are contexts in which increasing vitality occurs for nonstandard varieties as well as situations in which standard varieties lose vitality. It should be noted that the standard–nonstandard dimension is a relatively static, readily documentable determinant of language attitudes whereas the extent to which a particular language variety is increasing or decreasing in vitality is much more variable across time and location as well as more difficult to assess comprehensively. Furthermore, the influence of standardization and vitality upon language attitudes is mediated by respondents' perceptions of these two sociostructural factors. Clearly, then, *perception* of these attributes is more important for attitudes than their actual existence (see Giles and Johnson 1981; Street and Hopper, this volume: ch. 11). Greenbaum (1977a) provides an illustration of assessments of perceived standardization and autonomy; and the development and value of a subjective vitality questionnaire is discussed by Bourhis (this volume, ch. 3). Future language attitude research would be enhanced considerably by the inclusion of both objective and subjective measures of the sociostructural support for the varieties contrasted.

The value of the two-dimensional model can perhaps best be understood by comparing some of the language settings presented in Figure 1.1. Since the exact location within the model for any setting could only be established after serious empirical research focused directly on these dimensions, these examples are to be taken as illustrative rather than definitive. French (see Bourhis, this volume: ch. 3), for example, has been moving toward greater use and acceptance in Canada during the last two decades. Indeed, within Quebec the advances for French have been impressive while the momentum there toward English, still the first language of Canada as a whole, has essentially been reversed. A consequence of this increase in vitality has been some greater recognition for Québecois as a legitimate (even standard) form of French. In contrast, French has lost its status as the official language in Southern Asia, and many former French colonies in Africa are struggling to identify ways of reducing the European influence in their young nations. Most regional languages and dialects as well as most immigrant and indigenous languages in nations across the world have been declining in vitality over the years as the pressures for homogeneity and unity have increased. Yet, as Carranza (this volume: ch. 4) reports, Catalan in Spain and Guarani in Paraguay are also reversing the trend toward universal use of the national language. For both of these languages, increased vitality has led to greater standardization, which in turn has enhanced their vitality. In the United States, Spanish seems to be the

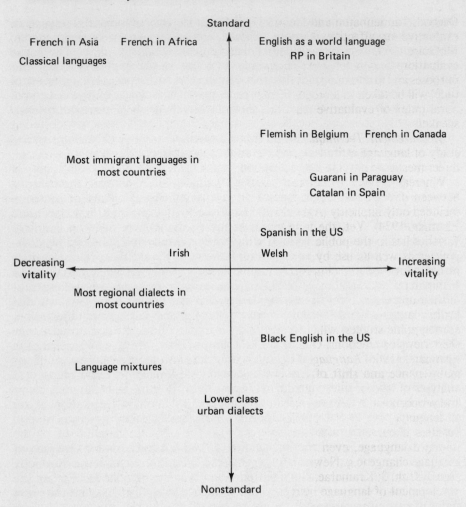

Fig. 1.1 The two primary sociostructural factors affecting language attitudes: standardization and vitality.

single non-English language whose speakers and functions are increasing. As a result of the Black Power Movement, the ingroup values of Black English in the US today are well recognized; and blacks are less willing now than 30 years ago to give up their dialect (Hoover 1978). Finally, the decline in use of the classical languages illustrates the fact that standardization does not guarantee survival across the years.

Measuring language attitudes

Numerous theoretical and operational definitions of 'attitude' have been employed in the past. Although a number of researchers (see Fishbein and Ajzen 1975;

Osgood, Tannenbaum and Suci 1957; Oskamp 1977) would limit the term to an evaluative or affective response, another common concept of attitude (see McGuire 1969) includes two additional components: belief (cognitive basis for the evaluation) and behaviour (observable reflection of the evaluation). For our purposes and in common with the other contributors to this volume, 'language attitude' will be taken in a broad, flexible sense as any affective, cognitive or behavioural index of evaluative reactions toward different language varieties or their speakers.

   Measurement Techniques. The three assessment techniques relevant to the study of language attitudes can be termed content analysis of societal treatment, direct measurement and indirect measurement.

   Whereas previous reviews of language attitudes have addressed the contrast between direct and indirect measures, analysis of societal treatment has been included only implicitly (Agheyisi and Fishman 1970; Cooper 1975a; Cooper and Fishman 1974). Yet, the first source of information about views on language varieties lies in the public ways in which they are treated (i.e. official language policies as well as use by various social groups in government, business, mass media, education and church). Actually, the approaches termed by Agheyisi and Fishman (1970) as autobiographical, observational and case study, as well as most of their unclassified studies, can be considered under this category. Also included in this category would be other types of research (e.g. participant–observation, ethnographic studies) which do not involve explicit requests to respondents for their views or reactions. One of the best illustrations of this type of approach is Fishman's (1966) *Language Loyalty in the United States* in which trends in the maintenance and shift of ethnic languages are examined in terms of detailed analyses of laws/policies regarding language use, the numbers of language users and proportions of language use in various domains. Within a language, analyses of language use in the public domain (press, broadcasting, government and business documents, and literature) provide the basis for descriptions of the standard language, even for dictionaries, as well as the basis for critiques of language change (e.g. Newman 1974; Orwell 1949b). Three chapters in this book (Bourhis, ch. 3; Kramarae, ch. 5; St Clair, ch. 10) aim to describe and explain the development of language policies within society and the consequent differential status of particular varieties.

   A major method for observing language attitudes involves the use of a series of direct questions, either presented in written form to large groups or in individual interviews. The kinds of questions that have been asked have concerned language evaluation (e.g. how favourably a variety is viewed), language preference (e.g. which of two languages or varieties is preferred for certain purposes in certain situations), desirability and reasons for learning a particular language, evaluation of social groups who use a particular variety, self-reports concerning language use, desirability of bilingualism and bilingual education, and opinions concerning shifting or maintaining language policies. Although this method tends to focus upon beliefs, some instruments emphasize affect as well. Moreover, behavioural intentions (e.g. planning to study Spanish the following year or planning not to teach one's children the native tongue) and actual behaviours (e.g. how many years of Spanish are studied, degree of proficiency attained and use of it in various situations) have occasionally been incorporated into direct attitude studies (e.g. Fishman *et al.* 1971) and could well be included more regularly. The direct method of eliciting attitudes is considered primarily in chapters 4 and 8 by Carranza and Gardner respectively.

The indirect method, inferring language attitudes from evaluations of speakers of two or more language varieties, was introduced by Lambert, Hodgson, Gardner and Fillenbaum (1960). Lambert's (1967) review of a series of matched-guise studies, in which the same speakers are heard using the contrasting varieties, provided the impetus for the many indirect studies which have been conducted in language-contact settings across the world. Speaker evaluation studies are reviewed throughout this volume, as they form the foundation of the social psychological perspective on language attitudes (see Giles and Powesland 1975). Although most of these investigations have obtained only evaluative reactions to the speakers presented, some projects have also obtained behavioural indices of attitude, either in the form of a listener's accommodations of his/her own speech style in response to a speaker or in the form of non-speech behaviours such as attitude change, attendance at a meeting, or completion of a questionnaire. As Edwards (this volume: ch. 2) argues, it would be valuable within this paradigm to distinguish carefully between assessment of listeners' affective responses and their beliefs about the speaker (e.g. intentions, social group memberships, attitudes on vital topics). Other important issues (see Cooper 1975a) concern the possible discrepancies between directly measured attitudes toward language varieties and attitudes toward their speakers (Edwards, this volume: ch. 2) as well as the distinction between evaluations of a variety as representative of a reference group and attitudes toward the speech characteristics themselves as correct, beautiful, musical, inarticulate or improper.

Evaluative dimensions. With regard to the structure of attitudes toward contrasting language varieties, the two major dimensions along which views vary can be termed social status and group solidarity (Brown and Gilman 1960; Fishman 1971; Ryan 1979). These evaluative dimensions relate to the sociostructural determinants in that the distinction of standard/nonstandard primarily reflects the relative social status or power of the groups of speakers and the factors contributing to the solidarity value of a variety are precisely those forces responsible for its vitality. Moreover, standardness and status are much more stable than vitality and solidarity with regard to diachronic changes across time as well as synchronic variations across speech communities, subgroups within speech communities and situations.

As denoted by the terms 'high' and 'low' in the description of diglossia above, the variant reserved by a speech community for informal uses within ingroup interactions enjoys less social prestige than the variant appropriate for formal and outgroup occasions. Aspirations for social mobility are supported by increased use of the high variety (Weinreich 1963). In terms of social status, the relative degree of standardization of and institutional support for variants leads to differential associations with their speakers (see the notion of class standard, in Giles and Powesland 1975). Moreover, the socioeconomic status of the native speakers of each variant significantly influences perceptions of their relative prestige. Associated with ascriptions of high social class (including education and wealth) are additional status attributions for 'high' variety speakers of associated competence characteristics such as intelligence, expertise, ambition and confidence (Giles 1971b; Lambert 1967; Mulac 1976a; Williams *et al.* 1976).

The important symbolic dimension operating orthogonal to status is that of ingroup solidarity or language loyalty. Although this dimension has been addressed less frequently, it reflects the social pressures which operate to maintain language varieties, even in the absence of social prestige. The language or dialect of one's family life, intimate friendships and informal interactions acquires vital social meanings and comes to represent the social group with which one identifies. One's native language typically elicits feelings of attraction, appreciation and belongingness. In situations where a group's identity is threatened, the variety with which it is associated can become a key symbol of the group's culture and identity (Bourhis, this volume: ch. 3; Carranza, this volume: ch. 4; Weinreich 1963). As discussed in Giles and Ryan (this volume: ch. 13), an important aspect of solidarity (i.e. with an intergroup emphasis *vs* the usual interpersonal emphasis) has been virtually unexamined as yet in speaker evaluation studies.

Types of language preference patterns. In Table 1.1 are presented four of the primary types of language preference patterns that can be found in social contexts around the world. The patterns contrast in terms of whether the ingroup and outgroup judgements are similar or different and in terms of whether judgements along the status dimension coincide with those along the group solidarity dimension. Although few studies have been conducted in which data have been gathered on both dimensions from both groups, the pattern types can be illustrated in a tentative manner with published language-attitude investigations. Further research aimed at filling in the gaps within this schema would be of substantial empirical and theoretical significance. Indeed, since the types of pattern highlighted here are dependent upon the scales used and the cultures examined, different patterns may emerge in the future.

Table 1.1: Distinctive patterns of language preference for two contrasting language varieties (LV1 and LV2)

| Type of preference | Judges | | | |
	LV1 speakers		LV2 speakers	
	Status	Solidarity	Status	Solidarity
A. Majority group	LV1	LV1	LV1	LV1
B. Majority group for Status/ingroup for solidarity	LV1	LV1	LV1	LV2
C. Ingroup	LV1	LV1	LV2	LV2
D. Majority group for status/ minority group for solidarity	LV1	LV2	LV1	LV2

Pattern A represents what can be termed 'majority group preference' in which speakers of both varieties acknowledge the superiority of the dominant group's language variety (LV1) with regard to social power as well as for group solidarity values. Within this category are at least two interesting subtypes. First, the minority group speakers of the subordinate group's language variety (LV2) can exhibit an inferiority complex by showing even stronger preferences (on both dimensions) for the 'high' variety than majority group members (e.g. English Canadian *vs* French Canadian, Lambert *et al.* 1960; many second generation immigrants). Second, the minority speakers might go along with the majority group in preference but not as strongly. Hence, minority speakers might show a weaker preference for LV1 in terms of solidarity than status (e.g. English *vs*

Spanish, Carranza and Ryan 1975; standard *vs* accented English, Ryan and Carranza 1975), and they might show a weaker preference overall for LV1 than do LV1 speakers (e.g. standard *vs* accented English, Ryan and Carranza 1975).

Pattern B, which can be termed 'majority status, ingroup solidarity', refers to situations in which minority speakers prefer their own variety along the group solidarity dimension but not on status. Assessing the views in Peru of minority speakers only, Wölck (1973) found that Quechua judges preferred Spanish on status but preferred their own speech in terms of the solidarity-related characteristics of social attractiveness and integrity. Likewise, among Newfoundlanders Clarke (1981) found that the low-status regional varieties of English were rated much more favourably on solidarity traits than the high-status standard British and Canadian varieties.

Pattern C, which can be termed 'ingroup preference', represents situations in which each group prefers its own speech. This pattern can arise in two very different contexts. On the one hand, distinct groups of equal status would provide such a pattern (e.g. respondents from Spain and Italy each rating standard Spanish and Italian speakers). On the other hand, language loyalty among LV2 speakers might yield this pattern even when objective measures suggest that LV1 enjoys the distinctly higher status in the society (e.g. Southern black speakers' reactions to Southern white speech in Tucker and Lambert 1969; young French Canadian monolinguals in Anisfeld and Lambert 1964; the Chicano subgroup of Mexican Americans in Flores and Hopper 1975). Mild or stable language loyalty would yield a pattern in which LV1 preference for its own speech would be stronger than that of the minority group, at least on the status dimension. Fierce or resurging language loyalty would give rise to stronger LV2 preferences than the LV1 preferences. This type of language loyalty would probably be found among political activists (e.g. Black Power Movement, Chicano Movement, Basque Liberation Movement). The symbolic return to Irish Gaelic by the IRA in its conflict with the British regime in Northern Ireland illustrates the resurgence of loyalty to a language of distinctiveness.

Finally, Pattern D, which can be termed 'majority group status, minority group solidarity', refers to the situation in which the widely recognized high-status variety does not elicit feelings of attraction from its speakers (e.g. RP in Britain, see Edwards, this volume: ch 2). This pattern would also be expected for standard languages which are not spoken as a vernacular by any group (e.g. High German, Classical Arabic).

Figure 1.2 below is a speculative attempt to show how language attitude profile-type can be meshed within the two-dimensional model presented in Figure 1.1. Cross-cultural comparisons become more viable within this type of framework since the sociostructural factors responsible for the attitude pattern are pinpointed. For example, if the sociostructural context underlying Pattern A changed to the one underlying Pattern B, the language attitudes would come to fit Pattern B. A social psychological consequence of increasing vitality for a nonstandard variety is that its speakers (and sometimes speakers of the standard as well) begin to see cognitive alternatives to the power structure within the society (Giles 1979a). Pattern A, then, appears to result when neither the high nor low-status group perceives any alternatives to their relative power. Pattern B occurs when members of the low-status group begin to be aware of alternatives, while Pattern C reflects the sense (whether realistic or not) of equal status. Pattern D indicates that both groups have become aware of alternatives to the status quo. The main forces for change in language attitude patterns appear to be the psychological consequences of the increasing or decreasing vitality of contrasting varieties. In chapter 13 (Giles and Ryan), we will add to this framework by arguing for the importance of the measurement context as another determinant of the language attitude pattern observed.

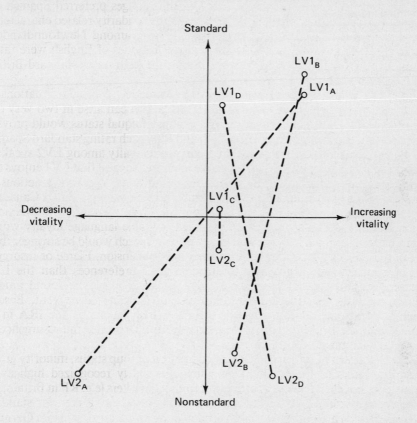

Fig. 1.2 Schematic illustration of the relationship between sociostructural factors and status/solidarity evaluations of majority (LVI) and minority (LV2) group speakers.

Summary. Within this organizational framework, it should be possible to see many interrelations among the individual chapters that follow. Even though the discussion of determinants, evaluative dimensions, and attitudinal patterns has been in terms of language and dialect differences, variations related to social class and other social groups (e.g. men *vs* women) can also be interpreted within this model. The characterization of the sociocultural determinants presented in Figure 1.1 and the contrasting language attitude patterns in Table 1.1 and Figure 1.2 ought to be especially useful to readers. These themes will be further elaborated and numerous other issues developed in the final chapter.

Overview of the volume

The chapters in this volume address language attitudes from a variety of perspectives, primarily social psychological and sociolinguistic. The general themes were
selected by the editors, who then invited contributors with relevant expertise to
discuss each one. The book is intended to provide a broad, up-to-date coverage of
the diverse language attitude literature in ways and under headings not so far
presented in published form. Important integrative works already published on this
topic include: Lambert's (1967) 'A social psychology of bilingualism'; Agheyisi and
Fishman's (1970) 'Language attitude studies: A brief survey of methodological
approaches'; Shuy and Fasold's (1973) *Language Attitudes: Trends and Prospects*;
Cooper's (1974, 1975b) two special issues of the *International Journal of the
Sociology of Language*; Ford's (1974) 'Language attitude studies: A review of
selected research'; Giles and Powesland's (1975) *Speech Style and Social
Evaluation*; Williams *et al.*'s (1976) *Explorations of the Linguistic Attitudes of
Teachers*, and Edwards's (1979b) *Language and Disadvantage*. The present
volume focuses attention upon the area anew, reviews recent findings, continues
the discussion of old issues, and raises new issues critical to the eventual development of theories of language attitudes.

Following this introductory chapter, the next three chapters each focus on the
language diversity, attitudes and policies for a major world language. The three
languages selected (English, French, and Spanish) have been the central concern of
most of the research on language attitudes.[1] Whereas English has been the focus of
most of the earlier reviews, the Francophone and Hispanic chapters are the first
worldwide reviews of attitudes toward regional, ethnic, and social class variants of
these languages. The subsequent two chapters examine gender-related speech and
lexical variation, respectively, as important bases for evaluation which cut across
the more traditional ethnic and class considerations. Next, the development of
language attitudes among majority and minority group children is addressed. Since
attitudes toward language variation can exert strong influences in many real-world
situations, their role in several applied settings (educational, second language
learning, medical, legal and occupational) is a major theme of three chapters
(including chapter 2). The four final chapters propose various theoretical
frameworks which might guide our interpretations of existing findings regarding

---

[1] Clearly, our focus on three languages has led to the omission of relevant language-attitude research
from other regions of the world: Switzerland (e.g. Weinreich 1963); Netherlands (e.g. Deprez and de
Schutter 1980; Ebertowski 1978); Germany (e.g. Ammon 1977, 1979; Politzer 1978; Ris 1979; Steinig
1976, 1978, 1980); Austria (e.g. Braunstein, Köberl and Stuckler 1979; Gal 1978; Priestly, 1981);
Scandinavia (e.g. Blom and Gumperz 1972; Kleiven 1979; Loman 1976); Italy (e.g. Grassi 1977; Mioni
and Arnuzzo-Lanzweert 1979); Belgium (e.g. Verdoodt 1978); Wales (e.g. Lewis 1975; Roberts and
Williams 1980); Scotland (e.g. Dorian 1980; MacKinnon 1977); Ireland (e.g. Edwards, in press a;
Macnamara 1971; Report of the Committee on Irish Language Attitudes Research 1975); Middle East
(e.g. Cooper and Fishman 1977; Cučeloglu and Slobin 1976; El-Dash and Tucker 1975; Ferguson
1959); Africa (e.g. Fishman, Ferguson and Das Gupta 1968; Hofman 1977; Kotey and Der-Houssikian
1977; Vorster and Proctor 1976; Wolff 1959); and Southern Asia (e.g. Gumperz 1958; Lyczak, Fu and
Ho 1976). Moreover, several other communication varieties (e.g. sign language, gestures, slang and
technical jargon), as well as a number of important social contexts (e.g. Church, football grounds, pubs
and bars, dinner-time) have been omitted from discussion; yet with few exceptions (e.g. Woll and
Lawson in press), they tend to constitute isolated investigations in terms of the language attitudes
paradigm. The findings reported in these projects from across the globe fit rather well into the overall
framework presented in this volume.

language attitudes as well as motivate systematic lines of future research. In the subsequent paragraphs, we will elaborate upon the main points of each chapter.

Edwards (chapter 2) reviews the extensive body of research concerning attitudes toward regional, social class and ethnic varieties of English. Although most of these studies have been conducted in Great Britain or in North America, the Australian, New Zealand, and Middle East investigations cited are important reminders of the wealth of other English language settings available for study. The most consistent finding is that the standard variety elicits attributions of competence and high social status from all social groups. While nonstandard regional and ethnic variants in Britain tend to be evaluated more favourably than the standard on characteristics related to integrity/social attractiveness and group solidarity, the standard in both North America and Australia seems to be viewed favourably on these aspects as well. Continued examination of the conditions under which and the evaluative dimensions along which nonstandard variants are viewed more favourably is clearly needed. Of critical importance for education are the affective reactions of teachers toward their pupils' speech and the extent to which those reactions affect teachers' behaviours and pupils' achievement. Edwards reviews the studies examining whether teachers believe that disadvantaged speech is deficient or simply different and discusses their implications for the education of minority children. Findings in both North America and Britain of covert prestige for nonstandard variants lead Edwards to raise the issue of whether typical methodologies might only be tapping an individual's public views towards language varieties. Relatedly, Edwards calls for more research to be conducted outside the laboratory in naturalistic settings; for more attention to the distinctions between beliefs, feelings and reasons for both; and more cooperation between sociolinguists and social psychologists in the search for appropriate methodologies and conceptualizations.

Bourhis (chapter 3) examines the development of the unquestioned assumption in France of one correct French and the spreading of this view to all the French cultures across the world. Language policies in France have been very protective of Parisian French for more than three centuries, and regional variants are rarely viewed as favourably as the universal standard. Bourhis looks at Francophone cultures in other European countries, Africa, Asia, the Caribbean, and North America. Former French colonies in southeast Asia have been the first to return to the use of native languages for government, and movements in this direction are apparent in various countries in Africa. Distinctive regional variations of French have developed (e.g. Québécois, Belgian, Flemish-accented, Senegalese, Congolese, North African, Vietnamese), but in most cases their speakers would still rate Parisian French speakers more favourably. Among France's former colonies, Haitian Creole and Québécois French are the most autonomous and most likely to achieve local status equivalent to the universal standard. It is in Quebec where the original speaker evaluation studies were conducted; social psychological research in Quebec concerning French–English contrasts as well as regional and class variants of French continues to be empirically and theoretically important. Yet, very little research concerning French language attitudes has been conducted outside Canada. Hence, much of Bourhis's review is based on language policies and other aspects of the social treatment of contrasting language varieties. This thorough sociocultural analysis of the highly varied Francophone situations lays the groundwork for empirical tests of the numerous specific hypotheses presented. Bourhis argues that language attitude research ought to include assessments of respondents' views of the sociocultural factors affecting the language varieties being studied. Moreover, distinguishing between formal and informal domains of language usage is critical since standard French has remained the prestige form for formal settings in many regions of the world while nonstandard variants and indigenous languages are emerging as symbols of group solidarity in informal settings.

In chapter 4, Carranza examines language attitudes within the Hispanic world, in a wide variety of cultural and geographical settings from Spain and Latin America (where standard Spanish enjoys high status in contrast to local languages and dialects) to the United States (where Spanish must struggle against English-only pressures for survival and respect). In Spain, the official national language is Castilian, which is necessary for economic and social advancement in most regional areas of the country. Yet, not only have several regional languages persisted for centuries, but also one of these, Catalan, is undergoing a dramatic revival as a prestige language. In Latin America, the primary language issue has been the relative status and appropriate domains for Spanish and indigenous languages. Most of the Hispanic language attitude research has been conducted in the US, where Hispanics constitute the second largest majority group and will soon overtake the black minority in numbers. In the US, studies have considered attitudes toward English *vs* Spanish, bilingualism as a gift or a handicap, contrasts between standard English and Hispanic variants, contrasts between standard Spanish and Anglicized variants, and code-switching. Complementing the perspectives of the other chapters, Carranza emphasizes the value of direct attitude measures and the need to integrate the use of these along with speaker evaluation paradigms. Contextual factors such as formality and domain of interaction are of particular concern for future Hispanic research since the relative values associated with contrasting varieties are intimately tied to context.

In chapter 5, Kramarae focuses upon the distinction between men's and women's speech, a fundamental social distinction relevant to some extent in any society. The term 'gender' is used, rather than sex, in order to emphasize that it is a social construct, not a simple direct consequence of biological differences. Kramarae provides a unique illustration of how social treatment of speech styles can be revealed through examination of the popular media (i.e. proverbs, advice books, public records, newspapers). Her historical analysis of these public expressions of attitudes shows clearly that the appropriate functions and allowable forms for women's speech have traditionally been quite limited. The review of actual and expected gender-related speech differences in the Anglophone world reveals that the perceived differences are much larger than the actual ones. Moreover, the traits typically associated with women's speech (e.g. frequent use of intensifiers, hedges, questioning intonation and tag questions) tend to be evaluated unfavourably for both male and female speakers and may be primarily reflective of the traditionally powerless social status of women. Indeed, the overlap discussed by the author between gender-related and class-related speech characteristics as well as stereotypes is quite striking. Relatedly, evaluations of women's speech are seen to depend importantly upon the situation, especially the role relationships involved. Future research directions include continued examination of the effects of situation and other social information (e.g. social status, group identities, political ideologies) on reactions toward women's and men's speech, clarification of the reasons why similar speech behaviour is differentially evaluated for men and women, and exploration of the differences in amounts and types of accommodation men and women make toward the speech of their interlocutors. The chapter concludes with a discussion of the cognitive organizational and identity-maintenance functions of maintaining actual and stereotyped differences between men's and women's speech.

In chapter 6, another aspect of within-language variation is addressed. Bradac examines the antecedents and consequences of between-group, within-group, and intra-individual variations in lexical usage. Dimensions of lexical choice and lexical patterning are outlined, with special attention given to the more extensively studied variables of intensity, immediacy, diversity and power. In terms of lexical usage, researchers have been primarily concerned with sociological sources of variation (i.e. group memberships and situational contexts), on the one hand, and psychological sources of variation (e.g. motivational and personality variables), on the other hand. In terms of evaluative connotations, listeners tend to react to particular patterns of lexical usage along two basic dimensions, speaker competence and speaker/listener similarity. No simple generalization can be offered regarding the relationship between lexical variables and these dimensions because speech variations interact significantly with characteristics of the speaker, listener and message. As well, both the contexts within which lexical variants are presented and listener inferences regarding the reasons for their use have important effects upon how they are interpreted. Like Edwards, Bradac believes more research in naturalistic settings is necessary. Moreover, he argues for systematic examination of listener perceptions of situations (including changing perceptions of the changing situation over the course of an interaction) and the impact of variability in situation perception on evaluative reactions toward speakers and consequent behaviours.

In chapter 7, Day discusses the important developmental issue of how children come to share the attitudes toward language variation of their parents. Language attitudes are viewed as an integral component of children's developing communicative competence. That is, they form part of the social knowledge required for producing and interpreting messages appropriately within one's environment. The first issue addressed concerns the age at which children initially become aware of language and dialect differences and their evaluative connotations. Research with preschoolers shows that the contrast between two dialects of the same language is recognized by children as young as age four, and children between the ages of four and six years have been shown to differentiate between contrasting speech varieties with social evaluations that look much like those of the adults in their speech communities. The second issue concerns the relative evaluations of high-status standard and lower-status nonstandard varieties of majority group children who speak the standard and minority group children who speak the nonstandard variants. As with the adults, there is a tendency among minority children across a variety ·of sociocultural settings (e.g. black children in the US, speakers of Hawaiian Creole English in Hawaii and regional dialect speakers in Italy) to be more favourable toward the standard than their own variety. Moreover, some evidence exists to suggest that this tendency to prefer the standard increases across the early school years. At any given age, the standard language preference, where it exists, is weaker for minority children than for majority group children. Finally, the similarity between the racial/ethnic attitudes and language attitudes of children is discussed. The patterns are similar, except that tolerance for outgroup members increases with age for majority group children in the former type of study but not the latter. Day concludes his chapter by arguing that children's attitudes toward the relevant language varieties within their speech community cannot be assessed accurately without going beyond the school setting, where the influence of the standard language and culture is so strong. Since every speech community values its native language/dialect at least for some purposes, investigations should be mounted to identify the positive features associated with that variety and to determine when children first come to appreciate them.

Gardner, in chapter 8, examines the role of language attitudes in second language learning, an applied setting of considerable importance to most societies in today's world. Correlational studies conducted in Canada have established that aptitude and attitude contribute separately to achievement in foreign language classrooms and that attitude is more consistently related to achievement than is aptitude. Similar studies conducted outside Canada have not shown such consistent results, but methodological problems and the fact that they are more concerned with acquisition of the majority language by minority group individuals limit their comparability with the Canadian studies. Attitudes have been shown to relate to perseverance in language study as well as to classroom behaviour. The expected positive effects of second language achievement upon attitudes have been more difficult to demonstrate. Gardner suggests the use of cross-lagged panel designs and path analysis for testing the causal relations underlying the correlational data. Furthermore, he proposes a socioeducational model of second language learning which states that attitudes (both integrativeness and attitude toward the specific language learning situation) affect achievement via mediational effects upon motivation. Aptitude, as assessed by standardized tests, is viewed to be much more important in formal learning situations than in informal situations. Moreover, for minority individuals learning the majority language, motivation becomes a very critical determinant of achievement. Attitudes toward the target language and one's own language become both more important and more complex since there is often pressure to give up one for the other. According to Gardner, future research ought to be directed toward generalizing the links between attitudes and achievement, perseverance, and classroom behaviour to areas outside Canada; examining the effects of informal *vs* formal language learning situations upon the links between attitude, motivation and achievement; identifying additional motivational variables which might be related to second language achievement; and attempting to confirm the prediction that second language learning will lead to more positive attitudes toward the target language and its speakers.

Extending coverage to additional applied contexts, Kalin (chapter 9) examines evaluative reactions toward contrasting speech styles in medical, legal and occupational situations. Within the medical setting, the focus has been on the doctor–patient relationship and the ways in which high social status and situational power are conveyed by physicians through speech, the extent to which diagnoses may be affected by inferences based upon patients' speech characteristics, and the extent to which compliance with physicians' advice is affected by speech cues accompanying the advice. Within the legal context, communication accuracy, credibility, and social influence are particularly important. Whether or not a person is comprehended, believed, and heeded depends upon fluency with the standard language, vocal cues, pronunciations, lexical choices and lexical patterning. Although more studies have been conducted within an employment context than in the other domains, all of these have focused on the personnel interview (which is just one aspect of the work arena) where first impressions are so very important. Although some studies have not found discrimination against nonstandard speakers in simulated hiring situations, most of the data are consistent with other speaker-evaluation studies in demonstrating the downgrading of nonstandard speech. In fact, social class inferences following from speech cues have been shown to be powerful enough in some situations to lead to double discrimination (i.e. high-status speakers are favoured for high-level positions while low-status speakers are favoured for low-level positions). The possibilities for research in these important domains have just begun to be explored. Kalin suggests that future studies use both experimental and correlational designs, use a larger number of exemplars from each speech community, assess a greater variety of behavioural outcomes, and examine a greater variety of situations within each domain.

The final section of the book, beginning with chapter 10 by St Clair, consists of four integrative perspectives upon language attitude research. In order to achieve a complete understanding of how language attitudes develop within a particular sociocultural context, it is necessary to examine how social and political forces have operated in the past as well as how they continue to operate. St Clair discusses the rationale within societies for 'the standard language' from such a sociohistorical point of view. The establishment and maintenance of the standard language is viewed as part of a political socialization process in which a powerful elite claims its language is THE language, a group of public-minded civil servants enforce acceptance of that view and victims' attempts to gain access into the system are therefore blocked. This pattern is exemplified in this chapter by a detailed description of the rise of linguistic prescriptivism in the United States during the nineteenth century. The attitude that only speakers of standard English were true, worthy Americans was only one aspect of an ideological movement in which the powerful discriminated against the powerless by not accepting as legitimate any deviations from their own language, culture, religion and race. The author also discusses how the earlier chapters by Bourhis and Kramarae illustrate important aspects of the sociohistorical perspective. In concluding, St Clair argues for integrating the social psychological speech-accommodation theory (Giles and Powesland, 1975) with this social historical approach in order to explain more fully the converging and diverging speech behaviours (and their interpretations) of individuals within both powerful and powerless groups.

Street and Hopper (chapter 11) propose a mediational model of speech evaluation. Their model incorporates variations at all levels of speech, from the paralinguistic level (i.e. non-linguistic vocal level) to pronunciation, vocabulary, and syntax to conversational style and language choice. The first stage of this model, how the actual message is perceived by the listener, is affected by two classes of variables: perceptual biases and listener goals. Evaluation, the second process, depends upon traditionally conceived language attitudes as well as perceived similarity, age and sex stereotypes and judgements of paralinguistic variables. Since the influence of paralinguistic cues is not reviewed elsewhere in this volume, the topic receives special attention from Street and Hopper. For example, speech rate has been found to be linearly related to competence ratings while a curvilinear relationship exists between rate and benevolence ratings such that a moderate rate is preferred. Other vocal cues linked to evaluative consequences include pauses, pitch, intensity and vocal quality. The third component of the model concerns the connection between evaluative judgements and the extent to which the original listener accommodates his or her own speech (i.e. converges toward or diverges from) that of the original speaker. Hence, the typical speaker-evaluation paradigm is expanded here by the measurement of perceived aspects of the message and the assessment of a behavioural response following from the evaluation (i.e. selecting the characteristics of the return message). The authors argue for research that integrates these three components while examining several speech cues simultaneously. The benefits of such ambitious designs are well exemplified by Street's own empirical research.

Cacioppo and Petty (chapter 12) survey the major approaches within experimental social psychology to attitudes and persuasion (i.e. conditioning/modelling, message learning, perceptual judgement, cognitive consistency, attribution, combination, and self-persuasion) and examine the implications of these theoretical perspectives for language attitude research. It is clear that language attitude investigators have only taken advantage of a few of these approaches and only in a limited manner. The authors focus upon the mechanisms that underlie attitudes and attitude changes and seek where possible to examine attitudes in terms of behavioural measures beyond self-report ratings. Although the approaches vary widely in their explanations for attitude change, they tend to address one of two general processes, which Cacioppo and Petty have termed 'central' and 'peripheral' routes to persuasion. They propose that the manner in which speech characteristics affect persuasion be conceptualized in terms of these two processes. Speech cues affect persuasion via the central route (which leads to enduring changes and predictable behaviours) when they increase the amount of thinking about issue-relevant information. Alternatively, speech cues yield attitude change via the peripheral route (which leads only to a temporary change which is not highly related to subsequent behaviour) when they induce the recipient to move toward agreement without thinking. For example, speech cues reflecting expertise affect thoughtful processing of the message whereas speaker/listener similarity is more likely to induce superficial agreement. A recent study conducted by the authors illustrates this distinction between thoughtful and thoughtless persuasion effects as well as the role of issue-involvement in determining the route which is taken. The use of rhetorical questions within a persuasive message enhanced thinking about the arguments when subjects were not naturally motivated to engage in much thought about the target issue, but distracted highly involved subjects from thinking about them.

All chapters in this volume are characterized, as can be gleaned from our overview of them, by their distinct concern for the future development of language attitude studies. Throughout, we are provided with many compelling and insightful proposals at the empirical, methodological and theoretical levels. The final contribution, chapter 13 by Giles and Ryan, is an attempt to integrate some of the constructive criticisms made in the foregoing as well as to introduce some additional ones based on contemporary research into social cognition and intergroup relations. These authors discuss the major limitations of traditional language attitude studies in terms of four interrelated problem areas: (1) that speech variables are usually manipulated in a social, psychological and linguistic vacuum; (2) that listener-judges feature almost as cognitive nonentities; (3) that aspects of the social context are socially and subjectively sterile; and (4) that language attitudes are devised and measured without recourse to their situational, functional and behavioural implications. Under these rubrics, specific research proposals and hypotheses are introduced as well as a model relating perceived situation to the evaluative dimensions of status and solidarity. It is argued that programmatic research following such suggestions would yield data fruitful enough ultimately so as to prepare the ground for a viable social psychological theory of language attitudes. In this vein, the more sophisticated language attitude study of the future, it is proposed, should (1) comment on the socio-structural context of the language situation investigated in such a way as to make it comparable to other situations (perhaps as discussed earlier in this prologue), (2) consider the constraints on generality imposed by the use of particular independent variables and ideally individuate the speakers by specific linguistic, social and psychological attributes, and (3) take care with the selection of dependent variables and determine their relationships to anticipated behaviours, listener-judges' cognitive mechanisms and subjective contextual definitions. Caution is also advocated in this chapter against overly cognitive individualism at the expense of exploring the social functions of various language attitudes in the context of specific social milieus and socio-structural climates.

While the focus of this future-oriented epilogue is social psychological, as indeed befits a contribution to the Series of which it is the inaugural volume, it is stressed throughout that an interdisciplinary approach which has social policy implications is the ultimate goal; the whole tenor of this book substantiates our commitment in that direction. Finally, while our eyes are naturally enough on exciting theoretical prospects for the future, it is to be hoped that the substantial empirical gains already achieved in this area which are clearly and extensively reviewed in this volume will not only fascinate readers but also make them understand more clearly the tremendous social implications of language variation in everyday life.

2

Language attitudes and their implications among English speakers[1]

John R. Edwards

The concept of attitude, though widespread in social psychology, is not one about which there has been universal agreement; examination of any text on social psychology will demonstrate that. At a general level, however, one might agree with Sarnoff (1970) who views attitude as 'a disposition to react favourably or unfavourably to a class of objects' (p. 279). This disposition is often taken to comprise three components: feelings (affective element), thoughts (cognitive element) and predispositions to act (behavioural element) (see, e.g. Secord and Backman 1964). That is, one knows or believes something, has some emotional reaction to it and, therefore, may be assumed to act on this basis. Two points may be made here. The first is that there often exists inconsistency between assessed attitudes and actions presumably related to these attitudes (language attitudes, however, have perhaps not fared too badly in this respect: see Bourhis and Giles 1976; Giles and Farrar 1979; and Giles and Ryan, this volume: ch. 13). The second is that there is sometimes confusion between belief and attitude; this is particularly so in the domain of language attitudes. *Attitude* includes *belief* as one of its components. Thus, a subject's response to, 'Is a knowledge of French important for your children, yes or no?' indicates a belief. To gauge attitude one would require further enquiry into the respondent's *feeling* about his expressed belief. For example, he might believe that French is important for his children's career success; yet, he may loathe the language. Many 'attitude' questionnaires are, in fact, 'belief' questionnaires, at least in part.

With regard to sociolinguistics in particular, attitudes have traditionally been of considerable importance. This is because people's reactions to language varieties reveal much of their perception of the speakers of these varieties. Useful reviews of this topic in general may be found in Agheyisi and Fishman (1970), Cooper and Fishman (1974) and Giles and Powesland (1975). These writers also discuss the methods used to elicit and assess language attitudes. In the main, these consist of questionnaires, interviews, scaling techniques and various indirect methods – of which the 'matched-guise technique' (see below) is perhaps the best known and most used. Since each of these has both strengths and weaknesses, it is apparent that the most useful assessment of language attitudes would be one based upon some eclectic approach. As will be seen, however, such an approach is less used than one might hope.

[1] I should like to thank Ellen Bouchard Ryan and Howard Giles for kindly providing me with material relevant to this chapter.

One important use to which language attitude information has been applied is in connection with subjects' learning of a second language. I shall not discuss this in detail since it is a narrower and more specialized topic than that of chief concern here. It has been, and continues to be, an area attracting considerable research attention (see Gardner, this volume: ch. 8). The general view here is that, *ceteris paribus*, positive attitudes are likely to facilitate the learning of another language.[2] Variations in the context of second language learning, and in the perceived functions of that language for the learner, may, however, interact significantly with the importance and type of positive attitude or motivation (see, e.g., Carroll 1978; Macnamara 1973).

My major interest in this chapter is to consider the findings of language attitude studies among English speakers and, in addition, to attempt an evaluation and a synthesis of them. Three closely related issues are of concern here: the knowledge that we gain by such studies of the language variety itself, of the speakers of that variety, and of those who provide the attitudinal judgements. At the heart of it all, then, are the processes and patterns of social interaction – especially across class and ethnic group lines – which may reveal themselves through language.

The social nature of language evaluation

It is important, before turning to consider studies of language attitudes themselves, to understand the general basis of these evaluations. There are three broad possibilities here. Evaluations of language varieties may reflect intrinsic linguistic inferiorities/superiorities, intrinsic aesthetic differences or social convention and preference. In fact, the first two possibilities are unlikely. A considerable amount of effort has gone into the demonstration that languages, and language varieties, although clearly differing from one another, cannot reasonably be described in terms like 'better' or 'worse', 'correct' or 'incorrect', 'logical' or 'illogical' (see Edwards 1979b for a review of this). Similarly, aesthetic judgements made of language varieties do not appear to be based upon any inherent qualities of pleasantness or unpleasantness. Two studies by Giles and his colleagues (Giles, Bourhis and Davies 1979; Giles, Bourhis, Trudgill and Lewis 1974) demonstrated that when listeners heard unfamiliar language varieties which differed sharply in perceived aesthetic and status qualities within their own speech communities, they did not make discriminations on these grounds. The studies suggest that judgements of the quality and prestige of language varieties are dependent upon a knowledge of the social connotations which they possess for those familiar with them (see also Trudgill 1975a). Thus, we are on a fairly safe footing if we consider that evaluations of language varieties – dialects and accents – do not reflect either linguistic or aesthetic quality *per se*, but rather are expressions of social convention and preference which, in turn, reflect an awareness of the status and prestige accorded to the speakers of these varieties.

In many studies of attitudes towards language, we see revealed differential evaluations of standard and nonstandard dialects. A standard dialect is one spoken by educated members of society, used in writing and in the media, and supported

---

[2] As, indeed, they may well do for *any* subject under study. Language, however, is often considered rather a special case, since it is perceived as having a potentially greater extra-academic significance for those studying it.

and encouraged at school. Its particular form is often due to historical chance; if York had become the centre of the royal court, for example, rather than London, Standard English would today be quite different. Standards are the dialects of those who dominate (see St Clair, this volume: ch. 10). As a dialect, there is nothing intrinsic, either linguistically or aesthetically, which gives Standard English special status. As a marker of power and dominance, however, it is in some sense *primus inter pares*. In comparisons with other varieties, therefore, it is often evaluated more favourably.

In the next section I shall deal with language attitudes in general, as these have been studied in Britain, North America and elsewhere. I turn then to the influence of attitudes in the educational context. Although these two sections are not mutually exclusive in any theoretical sense, it is worthwhile to treat them separately; thus, the first sets the general tone, while the following one looks somewhat more closely at a specific aspect of the topic. In fact, the educational setting represents perhaps the single most important subdivision of the area, for reasons which shall be mentioned below.

Language attitudes

Twenty years ago, Lambert, Hodgson, Gardner and Fillenbaum (1960) introduced the 'matched-guise' technique as a means of assessing language attitudes. Judges evaluate – on a number of dimensions – a tape-recorded speaker's personality after hearing him or her read the same passage in each of two or more language varieties. That the speaker is, for all 'guises', the same person is not revealed to the evaluators and, typically, they do not guess this. Their judgements are then considered to represent stereotyped reactions to the given language varieties, since potentially confounding elements are constant across guises. While the matched-guise technique has been criticized, mainly for its alleged artificiality (e.g. Agheyisi and Fishman 1970; Lee 1971; Robinson 1972; and, in response, Giles and Bourhis 1973, 1976b; Giles and Powesland 1975), it does seem to provide useful information which can be confirmed by other means (e.g. by questionnaire, or by ratings of actual speakers *not* adopting guises; see below). In general, the matched-guise technique provides to the listener samples of speech which are thought to act as identifiers, allowing the expression of social stereotypes. That is, it is not the speech *per se* which is evaluated, but rather the speaker. Most studies of language attitudes, in fact, would be more accurately termed studies of attitudes towards speakers of language varieties.

The study of Lambert *et al.* (1960) considered reactions towards French and English guises in Montreal. The English-speaking judges in the study generally reacted more favourably to English than to French guises. More interestingly, French-speaking judges *also* rated English guises more positively. Lambert and his colleagues concluded that the findings demonstrated not only favourable reactions from members of the high-status group towards their own speech, but also that these reactions had been adopted by members of the lower-status group. This 'minority group reaction' is a revealing comment on the power of social stereotypes in general, and on the way in which these may be assumed by those who are themselves the objects of unfavourable stereotypes. Further work on language studies in Montreal and Quebec may be consulted in Bourhis (this volume: ch. 3), Lambert (1967), Gardner and Lambert (1972) and Lambert and Tucker (1972).

Since this mainly concerns francophone language attitudes, or attitudes with regard to second language learning, I shall not deal with it further here.

Lambert's techniques, however, were soon seen to be applicable in other contexts. Thus, Strongman and Woosley (1967) presented English psychology undergraduates with two speakers, each of whom read the same passage with a Yorkshire and a London accent. Half of the student judges were southerners, half northerners (from counties north of Staffordshire). The results indicated that, with northerners and southerners evaluating northern and southern accents, no large differences were found. Thus, 'both groups of Ss tended to hold the same stereotyped attitude towards each accent group but did not regard either of them particularly more favourably than the other' (p. 164). Strongman and Woosley attributed the outcome to the fact that, unlike earlier studies (e.g. Lambert *et al.* 1960), neither group here could easily be classed as minority or majority, and hence no 'minority group reaction' would have been expected.

In another study, Cheyne (1970) employed the matched-guise technique to investigate reactions to Scottish and English regional accents, finding generally that both Scottish and English raters tended to view Scottish speakers as somewhat lower in status than the English ones. There were, however, some anomalies; for example, some (Scottish) subjects rated male Scottish speakers more favourably than English ones on personality dimensions suggesting 'warmth', and both groups of judges evaluated them as being more 'friendly'.

A study by Giles (1970) investigated reactions of British secondary school children to a variety of accents, including the non-regional RP (Received Pronunciation – sometimes characterized as 'BBC English' or 'the Queen's English'), Irish, German and West Indian. In terms of status, aesthetic quality and communicative content (a measure of the perceived ease of interaction with the speaker), RP was rated most favourably, regional accents (e.g. South Welsh and Somerset) were in the middle ranks, and urban accents (e.g. Cockney, Birmingham) were at or near the bottom of the scale. These results largely agree with an earlier suggestion by Wilkinson (1965) that there exists in Britain a tripartite accent prestige hierarchy. At the top is RP (and some foreign accents), then come various regional accents and, at the lower end of the continuum, accents associated with heavily urbanized areas (see also Trudgill 1975a). As with Cheyne's study, however, Giles's work revealed that various anomalies exist in accent rating. For example, his Irish accent was generally perceived as higher in aesthetic quality than German, but lower in status. North American was higher in status than Northern England but lower in aesthetic terms, and so on.[3]

Slightly earlier than these studies, Lambert (1967) had introduced a refinement which seems able to account for some of these anomalies. He categorized the many personality dimensions on which judges typically rate speech and speakers into three groups. Thus, some are seen to reflect a speaker's *competence* (e.g. intelligence and industriousness), some *personal integrity* (e.g. helpfulness and trustworthiness), and some *social attractiveness* (e.g. friendliness and sense of humour).

A further study by Giles (1971b) considered reactions to RP, South Welsh and Somerset accents along these lines. Although RP received the highest ratings in terms of *competence*, the other two were perceived more favourably on *integrity*

[3] The reader, of course, will understand that descriptions like 'Irish' and 'North American' leave a lot to be desired in terms of specificity. For Giles's purposes, however, and given his subject sample, they seem to have sufficed (see also the work of Milroy and McClenaghan, discussed below).

and *attractiveness*. These evaluations were made by judges who were themselves from either South Wales or Somerset. In a later study, Giles (1973b) presented the same three accents, plus a Birmingham variety, to groups of South Welsh and Somerset school children whose views on capital punishment had earlier been ascertained. The guises in this study all presented arguments against capital punishment. Giles was interested to assess both the children's views of the quality of the arguments thus presented, and any changes in their stance on capital punishment. It was found that the higher the status of an accent, the more favourable were the ratings of the quality of the argument presented via that accent. However, in terms of attitude change (i.e. in the children's views on capital punishment), only the regional accents proved effective. The study thus suggests that messages may be seen as high in quality without necessarily being more persuasive; or, to use Lambert's terminology, accents judged as reflecting high speaker *competence* need not always have greater influence upon listeners than regional varieties seen to reflect more speaker *integrity* and *attractiveness* (see also Giles and Powesland 1975, and the notion of *solidarity*, below).

A study by Edwards (1977a) provided further evidence that accent evaluations are not uni-dimensional. Irish secondary school children judged five regional guises – representing Galway, Cork, Cavan, Dublin and Donegal – on a number of personality traits. The Donegal speaker was perceived most positively on dimensions reflecting *competence*, but not on those underlying *social attractiveness* or *personal integrity*. The Dublin guise, lowest in terms of *competence*, was highest in *attractiveness*. These results were discussed in relation to stereotypes currently existing in segments of Irish society. In general, the Donegal accent appears to operate in this context as the received variety, with the others constituting nonstandard regional variants. While this takes into account some longstanding historical views, it clearly does *not* relate to the status of the so-called 'Ascendancy' accent – which, because of its non-regional nature, is perhaps the best Irish analogy to the British RP (Bliss 1979).

Another Irish study is that of Milroy and McClenaghan (1977). Fifteen Belfast undergraduates listened to four stimulus speakers possessing Scottish, Southern Irish, RP and Ulster accents. Overall, the RP speaker was evaluated most favourably, especially so on dimensions reflecting *competence*; on *personal integrity* and *attractiveness*, however, the RP speaker was viewed somewhat less positively than the Scot and the Ulsterman. Evaluations of the Southern Irish speaker were generally favourable in terms of *competence*, but were the lowest on the other two broad scales (it is unfortunate that the authors did not specify more closely their 'Southern Irish' variety). Milroy and McClenaghan relate their findings to the Ulster–Republic interaction in general and, more particularly, to the fact that 13 of their 15 judges were Protestant. It is interesting that the high *competence* ratings accorded to northerners (Donegal speakers – still 'southern' Irish, however) in the Edwards (1977a) study noted above were not found here, where Northern Irish judges were evaluating northerners (Ulstermen) – but where, of course, an RP speaker was included among the stimuli.

Milroy and McClenaghan remark on the consistency of their results, even across judges who *misidentified* accents.[4] They note:

---

[4] In this study, judges were asked to say where each speaker came from; this is not done in all such studies.

It has been widely assumed that an accent acts as a cue identifying a speaker's group membership. Perhaps this identification takes place below the level of conscious awareness. . . . Presumably by hearing similar accents very frequently [one learns] to associate them with their reference groups. In other words, accents with which people are familiar may *directly* evoke stereotyped responses without the listener first consciously assigning the speaker to a particular reference group (pp. 8–9).

An analogous possibility has been suggested by Robinson (1979), with regard to the identification of socioeconomic status through speech cues. In any event, these remarks throw interesting light upon the suggestion made earlier by Robinson (1972) that, since attitude studies typically conceive of the speech sample as a cue evoking a stereotype of the speaker's group, other identifiers might do just as well – including perhaps simple written descriptions of the speaker. If it is the case that, sometimes at least, evaluations are made on the basis suggested by Milroy and McClenaghan (above), then provision of, say, written descriptions might not elicit quite the same sorts of reactions (see, however, Giles 1970; see also Ball 1980; Shuy and Williams 1973).

Overall, these British (and Irish) studies of accent evaluation show that speech samples may evoke stereotyped reactions reflecting differential views of social groups. Standard accents usually connote high status and competence; regional accents may be seen to reflect greater integrity and attractiveness. These findings seem fairly consistent when judges are themselves regionally accented speakers; there is also evidence that similar results occur when evaluators possess standard accents (see Edwards 1977a; Powesland and Giles 1975). The trust and liking apparently associated with regional varieties may be related to conceptions of ingroup solidarity (see below). However, the common downgrading of non-standard varieties in terms of prestige and competence – dimensions which may outweigh those of integrity and attractiveness in many contexts – remains an important consideration.

We might also refer here to information from another English-speaking setting – Australia. There is some agreement, in this context, over three general points on an Australian accent continuum; these are Broad, General and Cultivated Australian (Baker 1966; Mitchell and Delbridge 1965). Berechree and Ball (1979) investigated the reactions of student judges to these speech styles, and found that competence and attractiveness (but not confidence – integrity) were associated with more cultivated speech. If we were to consider *non*-cultivated Australian speech as roughly equivalent to nonstandard British accents/dialects, then the social attractiveness associated here with *cultivated* speech would seem anomalous. However, as the authors themselves acknowledge, the Australian continuum may not be analogous to the standard–nonstandard spectrum found elsewhere. If it *is* roughly analogous, then the attractiveness associated with a high prestige variety invites further investigation. Eltis (1980) *has* suggested that the cultivated Australian accent conforms generally to the British RP and, in a study of teachers' reactions to pupils, demonstrated that cultivated accents were perceived most favourably (and the broad Australian least so). This finding, of course, is strongly reminiscent of those elsewhere. Finally, we may note that the results of some research recently conducted in New Zealand (Huygens and Vaughan 1983) appear to support the association between prestige and RP in that context as well.

American studies are also important here. Carranza and Ryan (1975) investigated the reactions of Mexican-American and Anglo-American students to speakers of Spanish and English. Although the topic discussed by speakers had some influence upon the ratings, English was generally rated more favourably than Spanish on both status-related *and* solidarity (i.e. integrity and attractiveness) traits (see Carranza, this volume: ch. 4). This association of attractiveness with high-status varieties is interesting, in that it tends to support Berechree and Ball's (1979) Australian findings noted above; and it rather goes against those from British studies. I shall return to this matter again. In any event, in the Carranza and Ryan study being discussed here, Spanish *was* seen more positively on the solidarity than on the status dimensions. Again, therefore, one observes a tendency for a variety possessing lower prestige to have somewhat more favourable connotations along other lines. Again, as well, the results were obtained from both lower-status and more middle-class judges.

Similar results were found in a study by Ryan and Carranza (1975) in which evaluations of Standard English and Spanish-accented English were made by Mexican-Americans, blacks and Anglos (i.e. white English speakers). Arthur, Farrar and Bradford (1974) found that white Californian college students downgraded the so-called 'Chicano' English on several personality dimensions. Ryan, Carranza and Moffie (1977) also have shown that the *degree* of accent may affect evaluations. As Spanish-American accentedness increased across speakers, the reactions of English-speaking students became less favourable (see also Brennan and Brennan 1981a, b; Ryan and Carranza 1977). A final note: a study by Flores and Hopper (1975) found some preference for the speech styles of Mexican-Americans among those Mexican-American listeners who referred to themselves as Chicanos. Since, however, the term 'Chicano' is associated with cultural and linguistic pride and since the judges were themselves Mexican-American, this finding is probably of limited generality. That is, apart from demonstrating that *within*-group perceptions can and do change, the study unfortunately does not permit us to assume much change in the perceptions of the larger mainstream society in which Mexican-American and other minorities must exist.

Studies involving black speakers in the United States have also shown that language attitude investigations reveal social perceptions. Tucker and Lambert (1969) presented a number of American English dialect varieties to northern white, southern white and southern black college students. All groups rated 'Network' speakers most favourably (Network English being roughly equivalent to British RP); black speakers and others were downgraded (see also Fraser 1973). Irwin (1977) found that white judges perceived black college students less favourably than their white counterparts on the dimensions of voice quality, fluency and confidence. We might also note here the work of V. K. Edwards (1979), since her studies of evaluations of black speakers in Britain show a similar pattern – both teachers and West Indian adolescents perceived West Indian speakers less favourably than working-class and middle-class English speakers.

These studies, then, can be seen to support the European findings. Speech patterns of regional speakers, ethnic group members and lower-class populations (all three descriptions often applying to the same group) evoke unfavourable reactions, at least in terms of status and prestige, from judges who may or may not be standard speakers themselves. It is important, however, to remember in all this that the social context in which speaker evaluations occur is not itself a static entity. As it changes, one should expect to see changes in evaluation patterns too;

in fact, these may be employed as useful indicators of larger adjustments in social perceptions. The resurgence of interest in ethnicity and 'roots' in the United States, the new-found political clout of nationalistic French Canadians in Quebec, the contemporary interest in regional devolution in the United Kingdom, and the increasing group militancy and pride among American blacks and Spanish speakers – all these phenomena will no doubt cause changes in patterns of reaction to language varieties. Already, for example, Lambert, Giles and Picard (1975) have reported less downgrading of local speech patterns among French speakers in Maine; Bourhis, Giles and Tajfel (1973) provided some evidence that bilingual speakers in Wales may be seen more favourably than RP-accented ones.

Nevertheless, the process by which speakers of nonstandard varieties adopt the stereotyped views of the majority continues (see Edwards 1979b). Still, we do not observe the large-scale defection from these varieties to which this might be considered to lead. In this connection, we should recall the bonding or solidarity function often associated with nonstandard speech (see above) and reflected in evaluations along integrity and social attractiveness dimensions. There are also penalties involved in attempts to leave one language group and join another; regrettably, this is a topic which cannot be further pursued here (see Carranza and Ryan 1975; Edwards 1979b; Ryan 1979). One related point should, however, be made. Labov (1966, 1972) and Trudgill (1974a, 1974b, 1975b) have commented on the association, in both America and Britain, between lower-class speech patterns and masculinity. This, it is proposed, may constitute a 'covert prestige' in which nonstandard speech forms possess more status than standard variants. The phenomenon seems to cross class lines; middle-class speakers often report using *more* nonstandard forms than they actually do (Trudgill 1975b). This would clearly seem to be something of greater relevance for males than for females; however, there is some suggestion that covert prestige may influence females as well (Trudgill 1975b; see also Kramarae, this volume: ch. 5; O'Kane 1977; for recent sociolinguistic work investigating the relationships between sex and class, see Elyan, Smith, Giles and Bourhis 1978; Giles, Smith, Ford, Condor and Thakerar 1980). The implication from studies of covert prestige is that attitudes towards language varieties may be more subtle than had hitherto been thought; in particular, overt downgrading of nonstandard varieties may coexist with more latent, positive connotations.

Language attitudes in education[5]

We have now looked at language attitudes in general terms. It is in the educational setting, however, where such attitudes may have the greatest importance. Schools represent the single most important point of contact between speakers of different language varieties. In particular, the school encourages and reflects Standard English practices and, consequently, the way in which it deals with those whose dialect is nonstandard may be of some relevance – both during the school years and afterwards (see Day, this volume: ch. 7).

Since teachers are people first, we should not be surprised that they too have the sorts of language attitudes discussed generally above. In particular, we should expect them to hold less than completely favourable views of varieties other than

---

[5] More detail on matters discussed in this section will be found in Edwards (1979b).

their own in many cases. Gumperz and Hernandez-Chavez note here that 'regardless of overtly expressed attitudes . . . teachers are quite likely to be influenced by what they perceive as deviant speech . . . thus potentially inhibiting the students' desire to learn' (1972, 105). Trudgill (1975a) has stated that teachers have not been averse to verbalizing their views; thus, teachers have labelled children's speech as being 'wrong', 'bad', 'careless' and even 'gibberish'. Trudgill goes on to note that the influence of Bernstein's views has been particularly harmful here. That is, Bernstein's conception of 'elaborated' and 'restricted' codes (see, e.g. Bernstein 1971) has commonly been taken to refer to standard and nonstandard varieties respectively, with the further implication that the latter are essentially inferior variants. Although Labov (e.g. 1973) and others have done much to demonstrate that nonstandard forms are *not* inferior forms, the impact of Bernstein's work remains. Not only have teachers in Britain and America been affected, but those elsewhere as well – e.g. in Germany (Shafer and Shafer 1975) and in Australia (Thomson 1977).

Teachers, like the rest of the population, are prone to make and hold generalized expectations. The controversial work of Rosenthal and Jacobson (1968) claimed to demonstrate, in fact, that teachers' expectations could be easily manipulated by providing them with false information about pupil's capabilities. Their research prompted a considerable response (for an overview, see Dusek 1975). However, whatever the verdict on such *induced* expectations, there is little doubt that, in regular classroom settings, teachers do form judgements of pupils; this is surely not a controversial statement. Further, in many instances one may well suppose that the judgements made by persons familiar with and concerned for children are effective and accurate shorthand devices. Given what has already been discussed, however, we might concern ourselves here with cases in which expectations and evaluations may be inaccurate. The importance is obvious – such views may unfairly hinder children in their school life and beyond (see also Rist 1970).

A useful study to begin with here is that of Seligman, Tucker and Lambert (1972). Judges were provided with more than voice samples; in addition, photographs of children, drawings by them and written compositions were collected. The authors selected and combined these elements from third-grade Montreal boys such that the work of eight 'hypothetical' children could be presented to the student-teacher judges. All possible combinations of 'good' and 'poor' voices, photographs and drawings/compositions were represented in the eight composites. The findings revealed that all types of information influenced the ratings given to these 'hypothetical' children. Boys having better voices, who were seen to look intelligent, and who had produced good work were judged as more intelligent, better students, etc. When considering the *interaction* among the types of information, the authors noted that speech style 'was an important cue to the teachers in their evaluations of students. Even when combined with other cues, its effect did not diminish' (p. 141; see also Eltis 1980).

Choy and Dodd (1976) provide further evidence that teachers' assessments of pupils may be related to the latter's speech style. Evaluations of Standard English and Hawaiian English speakers consistently favoured the former (fifth-grade pupils, here). They were seen as being more confident, better in school, less disruptive in class and likely to achieve greater academic and social success. In fact, teachers were willing to make quite far-reaching judgements of children – of, for example, how happy their marriages would be likely to be (see also Edwards

1979a). Day (1980, this volume: ch. 7) has provided some supplementary information here concerning the development of linguistic attitudes among young Hawaiian children themselves.

Granger, Mathews, Quay and Verner (1977) report similar results from a study of reactions to black children's speech in the United States. Speech samples were obtained by having children describe a picture; it was hoped that this method would allow children some spontaneity while still retaining some comparability across children. Teachers' ratings of such samples displayed a social class and racial bias when compared with their ratings of white children. Granger *et al.* suggest that 'teachers were attending less to *what* a child said than to *how* he said it' (p. 795). This is exactly, of course, the danger to which stereotypic perceptions may lead.

Two studies conducted in Dublin also demonstrated that teachers' judgements may be affected by speech cues. Edwards (1977b) asked five middle-class judges to evaluate 20 working-class and 20 middle-class primary school boys on the basis of speech samples. All children were, on the information of their teachers, average students. On all the dimensions evaluated, the working-class children were seen less favourably than their middle-class colleagues. Some of the ratings – e.g. those of fluency and communicative ability – might, in fact, reflect actually 'poorer' performance if middle-class norms were taken into account. Judgements of voice quality and intelligence, however, would seem to be much more subjective and are harder to link to intrinsic elements in the speech samples. A further investigation was that of Edwards (1979a). Here, both boys and girls provided speech samples, and the evaluators were student teachers. On 17 scales, working-class children were perceived less favourably than middle-class pupils. Factor analysis of the results indicated only one underlying factor (labelled, simply, 'disadvantage-nondisadvantage'); this suggests the validity of the notion that teachers' reactions derive from an overall elicited stereotype (further details are reported in Edwards 1979b).

Williams (1976) has summarized the results of a research programme in America that began in the late 1960s. In studies of white, black and Mexican-American children, he and his associates have investigated the reactions of teachers to pupils. Factor analyses of results have consistently revealed two underlying factors. One of these, labelled by Williams 'confidence/eagerness', reflects such things as perceived confidence and social status. The other, also associated with judgements of social status, relates as well to perceptions of ethnicity and nonstandardness/standardness of speech. As noted above with regard to the Edwards (1979a) study, this two-factor structure of attitudes suggests a strong stereotyping process. Two underlying dimensions, after all, are not much more diverse than one. In fact, given that ethnicity is not a factor of significance in the Irish context studied by Edwards (1979a), the similarity between Edwards's and Williams's findings is considerable.

We should also note here that not *every* study shows that teachers uniformly downgrade nonstandard speakers on every dimension that researchers can think up. Crowll and Nurss (1976), for example, found that among black and white teachers in the southern United States speech samples from black boys were judged more favourably than those of their white counterparts. The authors suggest that 'the relationship between speech characteristics exhibited by speakers of different ethnic groups and listener behaviour is more complex than previous work has indicated' (p. 238). Taylor (1973) surveyed black and white teachers across the United States; they were asked their views on several aspects of Black English. The results demonstrated interesting interactions among types of teachers and aspects of Black English evaluated. In general, though, Taylor reported considerable positive reaction towards Black English and language variation in general.

These cautionary notes apart, however, it appears that teachers – like other members of the population – do maintain stereotyped and often negative views of certain language varieties and their speakers. In one sense, then, the information presented in this section simply adds to that presented previously. Teachers' perceptions are rather special, however. They, more than other individuals, are in a position directly to hinder a child's early success if they hold and act upon overly generalized views. It also follows, of course, that teachers are well placed to help children overcome the negative evaluations made of them by others and, in some cases, by themselves (see Day, this volume: ch. 7). This is why it is particularly necessary for the topic under discussion here to be fully presented to teachers. If we wish teachers to alter their views, we should give them evidence that they are right to do so.

Conclusions

The conclusions to be made here are, in essence, quite straightforward. First, language varieties which diverge from Standard English are liable to be viewed, even by speakers of those varieties themselves, less favourably than the Standard. This is especially so when evaluations are being made of traits relating to a speaker's *competence*. Regional and class varieties may be seen to reflect more friendliness and warmth, however, and may serve a bonding or solidarity function. We should recall here that some of the Australian data (Berechree and Ball 1979), and some results reported by Carranza and Ryan (1975) have shown that solidarity and attractiveness dimensions may also be attributed to more standard speakers. This suggests further research. It may be that there are conditions in which high-prestige speech styles also connote attractiveness; it would be valuable to discover what the relevant criteria are for this. On the other hand, it may also be that, in some instances, the relatively clear standard–nonstandard distinctions found in, say, the British context are not exactly analogous to speech continua elsewhere. Again, further investigation is implied.

Second, unfavourable linguistic attitudes cannot reasonably be said to reflect any inherent linguistic or aesthetic inferiorities in the varieties concerned. Rather, they represent social judgements, ones of taste, preference and convention. To say so is, however, to do no more than to clear the air. For social judgements are not only endemic and powerful, they are also by their nature singularly resistant to change. It would be naive, for example, to suppose that dissemination of the currently available psychological and linguistic evidence would rapidly alter them among the population at large. Related to this is the fact that many who make these social evaluations are convinced that they are expressing *more* than conventional preference. This is particularly dangerous, of course, in settings in which evaluators have some direct power over those judged. The school is the prime example here. If teachers feel that their judgements reflect pupils' cognitive and intellectual capabilities, and if there is reason to suppose that the judgements have, at least in part, a stereotypic basis, then it is not difficult to see that unfair burdens may be placed upon children (who, in many instances, have quite enough to deal with outside the school; see Edwards 1979b).

When researchers who deal with language varieties and their speakers have the opportunity to do so, it would be salutary to emphasize one major point. While individual preferences and attitudes will continue to colour our views of speakers, we should try to remember that they are just that – preferences and attitudes. We are quite entitled to find given dialects and accents more or less pleasant; we are not entitled to draw conclusions from these perceptions alone concerning speakers' basic skills.

Some more general observations are also in order here. As noted in the introduction, increased attention to the assessment of attitudes *per se* would repay the effort. It would, first of all, be useful if language attitude studies showed greater awareness of the attitude-belief distinction – most studies involve a great deal of *belief* assessment. If one had to describe a typical study, one would probably mention the collection of speech samples, presentation of these to raters, and raters' evaluations of speakers along a number of dimensions. Thus, a judge may indicate that speaker A sounds more intelligent than speaker B, and so on. Such ratings are reflections of judges' beliefs, and not of their attitudes. This distinction, it may be argued, is a rather minor point. Nevertheless, there are at least two reasons why it is not entirely valueless. First, attention paid to the attitude-belief distinction might help the cause of creating common ground between socio-linguists and social psychologists – the latter having traditionally viewed such matters with some importance. Secondly, such attention might open up new possibilities in terms of understanding *why* judges' evaluations take the forms they do. Consider, for example, a case in which speaker A sounds more intelligent to judges than does speaker B. Might it not be valuable to probe further, to attempt to find out something of the reasons for the choice, to try and add the affective element to the belief component already assessed? Surely the time has come – given the state of the current research effort – to move in this direction. I am not unaware that efforts *have* been made here (see, e.g., Sebastian and Ryan, in press); my point is that greater clarity concerning what is being elicited in speaker evaluation studies will expedite the process (see Giles and Ryan, this volume: ch. 13)

Future research along these lines would not be wholly original; it could profitably draw upon earlier work. For example, the view that nonstandard varieties evoke less favourable reaction has typically been discussed in terms of speakers' differential status or prestige. It would be useful to confirm this, from the *judges'* point of view, by asking them the bases for their evaluations. This is especially interesting given the indication that nonstandard varieties do elicit positive ratings along some dimensions, and that more standard varieties sometimes are viewed positively in terms of solidarity and attractiveness (Berechree and Ball 1979; Carranza and Ryan 1975). Also of interest here is the phenomenon of covert prestige (noted above; Trudgill 1975b). These seeming anomalies might well be dealt with by further probing along the attitude-belief continuum. After all, it is surely sensible to gather as much information as we can from the actual judges in language studies, as well as imposing theoretical interpretations upon their responses.

I should also stress here the concern, mentioned in the introduction, for eclecticism (and the lack of it) in language attitude studies (see also Carranza, this volume:

ch. 4). Most of the work discussed in this chapter has employed one methodological approach – usually an assessment of disembodied speech in less than entirely natural surroundings. While such reasonable efforts have revealed a considerable degree of similarity of results, this does not in itself guarantee accuracy; artifacts of experimentation may themselves be quite consistent. Investigators should thus be urged to consider new ways of proceeding in sociolinguistic studies; some, of course, have already done so. It could be argued that, of all aspects of human behaviour, speech is the most rapid to change when attention is focused upon it. Thus, the problem of relating empirical findings to natural behaviour – while hardly unique to language attitude theorists – should be of some particular concern.

There is, in fact, considerable scope in the area of language attitudes for linking experimental findings to real-life settings, and for finding in the latter confirmation of more detached study. Although somewhat peripheral to the main emphasis of this chapter, we might consider the work reported in Fishman, Cooper and Conrad (1977) on the spread of English (see also Fishman, Cooper and Rosenbaum 1977 – especially the section on language attitudes by Cooper and Fishman 1977). Here, a study of attitudes towards English held by high-school students in Jerusalem was conducted in an educational context in which usage and proficiency were also examined. Another area, the attitudes of immigrants towards English, is also relevant here. It has been argued, for example, that current desires for cultural pluralism and 'maintenance' bilingual education in the United States do not, in fact, correspond well with the attitudes of immigrants themselves towards the English-speaking mainstream. In this case, the patterns of assimilation provide a rather good, real-life substantiation of linguistic and other attitudes (see Edwards 1980, in press-a, in press-b). We should also bear in mind, generally, the position of English as a world language when considering linguistic attitudes. A language of great scope, dominance and prestige will obviously evoke attitudes different from those related to 'smaller' languages. Useful comparative studies could be done in this area which, again, points to the necessity of linking experimental observations to natural contexts.

Given these observations, it is apparent that the increased unity now being called for (see, e.g., Giles 1979b; Smith, Giles and Hewstone 1980) between sociolinguistics and social psychology in general will benefit from some heightened awareness on each side. The social psychologist, upon considering sociolinguistic efforts such as those reviewed here, should appreciate that to relegate language and speech to a minor or peripheral position in his theoretical scheme of things is unwarranted. The interrelationship of speech styles with many other socially significant phenomena can no longer be (nor should it have ever been) denied. Similarly, the student of language attitudes should not be ignorant of the potentially useful efforts within social psychology. Perhaps the most general and important aspect here has to do with the broader scope of social psychology – this could have the useful effect of being a constant reminder of how speech studies form but a part of the larger social picture.

However, before they achieve some glorious oneness, both sociolinguistics and social psychology should take care to ensure that they are participating in something of value. Perhaps since social psychology is the superordinate category here, it is the sociolinguists who should be most on their guard. There are many (e.g. D. Robinson 1979) who feel that social psychology's net contribution to human understanding has, as yet, been negligible. While this is hardly the place to debate such matters, it is a pleasant thought for sociolinguists to bear in mind that they may have the opportunity to inject new life, by their participation, into a larger field of study.

3

Language policies and language attitudes: le monde de la francophonie[1]

Richard Y. Bourhis

Attitudes towards the French language in 'le monde de la francophonie' have been deeply influenced by language policies developed in France since the seventeenth century. Through vigorous and sometimes brutal language planning programmes, multilingual France emerged in this century as a unilingual French state. In addition to legislating against non-French languages, policy makers in France insured that only the 'Ile de France' dialect emerged as the prestige standard form of the language. By virtue of its population and cultural vitality, France today can still be considered the heart of the francophone world. Consequently, it seems appropriate to devote the first part of this chapter to the development of language attitudes in France.

Social psychological research has already shown that a prestige standard form of a language has no *inherent* aesthetic or linguistic advantage over nonstandard varieties of this or other languages. Rather, the prestige ascribed to the standard form of a language is usually the product of culture-bound stereotypes passed on from one generation of speakers to the other (Edwards 1979b; Giles, Bourhis and Davies 1979; Giles, Bourhis, Trudgill and Lewis 1974; Giles and Powesland 1975; Trudgill 1975a). In France, the history of language planning efforts in favour of the Ile de France dialect demonstrates that the prestige attained by a standard form of a language may not be just the product of a cultural accident favouring its use, but the result of centuries of systematic efforts to impose *one* variety as the prestige norm to the exclusion of all other varieties.

The second part of this chapter will consist of an overview of language attitudes in the francophone world *beyond France*. Coverage of French language attitudes in countries other than France will proceed by zones of French language influence, as one moves progressively further geographically from France. Beginning with western Europe, language attitudes in francophone parts of Belgium and Switzerland will be discussed. Following the path of the French colonial presence in North Africa, language attitudes in Algeria, Tunisia and Morocco will be examined followed by a discussion of the special language situations in Lebanon and Southeast Asia. French colonial power was at its proudest during the time of the French African empire. As the French presence imposed a uniform rule on its African territories the current language situation in African nations/states will be discussed under a common rubric. Moving to island communities we will examine

[1] I would like to express my gratitude to E. B. Ryan, H. Giles, B. Weinstein, B. Saint-Jacques, I. Sachdev, R. Clément, M. Daly and R. Day for their useful comments on earlier drafts of this chapter. I also wish to thank Beverly Pitt for her cheerful patience in typing various versions of this chapter.

language attitudes in Haiti, Martinique and Guadeloupe. After reviewing the French language situation in the USA, language attitudes towards French in English Canada and in francophone Quebec will be surveyed. Smaller francophone communities will not be covered in this overview. Excluded from the discussion will be French-ruled overseas territories such as La Réunion, Tahiti and Saint Pierre et Miquelon, as well as other small francophone communities such as Luxembourg, Monaco, the Aoste valley in Italy and French Guiana.

Three major points emerge from this overview. First, as in France, very little *empirical* data exist on attitudes towards the French language in le monde de la francophonie. The notable exception to this state of affairs is the situation in Quebec, which remains the most active centre for the investigation of language attitudes in the Francophone world (Douaud 1979).[2] Indeed, much of the techniques and knowledge developed for the social psychological investigation of language attitudes was generated in the Quebec setting (Lambert 1967; Giles and Powesland 1975; Giles and Bourhis 1976b). One aim of this chapter is to provide a sociohistorical context for broadening empirical work on language attitudes to all parts of the francophone world.

The second point that emerges from the overview is that from existing anecdotal evidence and secondary sources, it seems that relative to indigenous speech varieties, standard French remains the prestige norm for many francophones across the world. Indeed, diglossia (Ferguson 1959; Fishman 1967) seems to be an important legacy of the French colonial presence in the francophone world. Contributing to this state of affairs is the fact that France imposed standard French as the only language of civilization throughout its empire. Also, the ruling elites of many francophone states have been trained in France where standard French has long been the prestige norm in educational circles. To this day, economic, cultural and educational activities in France promote the use of standard French as the prestige norm across the world. Finally, standard French remains the target norm taught to those learning French as a second language in most parts of the world. These four sociostructural factors help account for the maintenance of standard French as the prestige norm across the francophone world.

The third point to emerge is that though 75 million people still speak French in the world today, French language usage seems to have decreased in former French colonies. Many third-world countries whose own language was displaced by French during colonial days today reassert their identity by replacing French with

---

[2] It is worthwhile to note that l'Office de la Langue Française (OLF) recently published two useful analytical bibliographies of the world literature on language and society. The bibliography by Sabourin and Petit (1979) covers over 5000 recent titles in sociolinguistics, language policies and language planning, linguistic demography, and the sociology of language. The bibliography by Sabourin and Lamarche (1979) covers over 3300 titles on Québécois French research alone. Both of these publications can be obtained from: L'Office de la Langue Française, CP. 316, Tour de la Bourse, Montréal, Canada, H42 1G8. Additional sociolinguistic work is regularly published by the International Center for Research on Bilingualism. A list of available publications can be obtained from: Centre International de Recherche sur le Bilinguisme, Pavillon Casault, 6e sud, Université Laval, Québec, Canada G1K-7P4. Finally the Ontario Institute for Studies in Education regularly publishes sociolinguistic research on Franco-Ontarians and other linguistic minorities in Canada. A recent compendium of sociolinguistic research on Franco-Ontarians has been compiled by Mougeon (1979) and can be obtained from: Centre d'études franco-ontariennes, Ontario Institute for Studies in Education, 252 Bloor Street West, Toronto, Ontario, M5S 1V6.

a modernized version of their own language. For such countries the reintroduction of a strong ancestral language as a symbol of identity is seen to have the advantage of promoting the group solidarity necessary for successful nation building (Deutsch 1953; Fishman 1977).

In spite of the lack of empirical data, an attempt will be made to assess language attitude towards varieties of French in each francophone country reviewed in this chapter. Existing secondary sources and anecdotal evidence will be used as a basis for these assessments of language attitudes (Giles, Bourhis and Taylor 1977). It is hoped that these assessments will be tested in future empirical studies across 'le monde de la francophonie'.

Language attitudes in France

Current attitudes towards the French language in 'Le monde de la francophonie' have been shaped by the notion of 'le bon usage' developed in Paris in the seventeenth century. This notion was introduced by Claude Favre de Vaugelas in his work entitled 'Les remarques sur la Langue Française' published in 1647. Vaugelas maintained that there was only one correct way of speaking the French language. 'Le bon usage' could only consist of the French spoken by esteemed members of the King's Court. Vaugelas expected the best authors of the day to enshrine the best forms of courtly French in their writing. According to Vaugelas, reading the best authors was not sufficient to guarantee appropriate usage, as correct French pronunciation could only be acquired through regular attendance at the Court. Since the King's Court was established in Le Palais du Louvre, the Ile de France dialect spoken by the King and his entourage became the prestige form of the language to the exclusion of other French dialects spoken in other parts of France.

Vaugelas was also an influential member of l'Académie Française (its 40 members called les Immortels). Established in 1637 by Cardinal Richelieu, l'Académie Française had the task of purifying and perpetuating correct French usage as rendered by the Court and esteemed authors. Vaugelas fully expected that the elite constituting Les Immortels would guarantee the harmonious development of correct French through the ages. It was during the reign of Louis XIV, whose cultural policy encouraged the great French literary masters, that the French language was standardized. The literary works of Corneille, Molière and Racine became the models of good style and correct spoken French.

In the eighteenth century the myth of French as a classical language blessed with unique virtues such as clarity, purity, rationality and discipline was widely accepted and propagated by the French ruling elites throughout Europe (Gordon 1978). To this elite, changing aspects of French vocabulary and grammar, or adopting foreign borrowings could only lead to the corruption of the French language (Calvet 1974). More importantly, it was felt that only the Ile de France dialect could be considered as the vehicle of French civilization. All other forms of French spoken in France were dismissed as 'degenerate patois' best left to the abuse of the 'common people'. By the end of the eighteenth century the test of whether a person could be classed as belonging to 'les honnêtes gens' came to depend on the quality of his or her spoken French (Gordon 1978).

Nation building in France was facilitated by language legislation promoting French *language* unilingualism. As early as 1539, François I decreed French as the only official language of France. This decree banned the use of the Latin, Breton,

Basque and Occitan languages from the courts and enshrined French in texts of laws. Until the French revolution no systematic attempt was made by the monarchy or ruling elites to impose 'le bon usage' on the common people. But, with the French Revolution in 1793 France disposed of the monarchy as a unifying symbol. It is during this period that standard French emerged as a potentially unifying symbol to inspire the nationalism of the new Republic. The victorious bourgeoisie needed to suppress existing regional commercial and language barriers to establish its economic control across France. The Ile de France dialect adopted by the Parisian bourgeoisie was seen as a tool to suppress competing regional, economic and language interests in the name of the new Republic (Balibar and Laporte 1974). Simultaneously, Parisian proletarian elements associated strong regional language groups in the provinces with feudalism and the counter-revolution (Marcellesi 1979). Therefore, bourgeois and proletarian interests converged to favour a strong centralized nation state cemented by the imposition of French unilingualism in all the regions of France. In 1793 Abbé Grégoire was commissioned by the National Convention to undertake a language survey aimed at determining the number of French speakers in France. Grégoire was forced to report that out of a population of 26 million in France, only 3 million inhabitants could speak the Ile de France dialect fluently (Barbeau 1970; Calvet 1974). In his report, Grégoire identified patriotism with the speaking of French while non-French speakers were viewed as potential traitors to the revolution and a threat to the political unity of the emerging French Republic. As advocacy for French unilingualism the title of Grégoire's Report is revealing: 'Report on the needs and means to destroy the "patois" and to universalize the use of the French language'.

Between 1793 and 1794 the National Convention passed a series of laws which made the teaching of French compulsory in primary school and proclaimed French unilingualism in all parts of France including Brittany, the Basque country, Alsace, Corsica and the whole of southern France known as l'Occitanie. This first attempt at language planning resulted in a complete failure for linguistic unity in France (Calvet 1974). By late 1794, faced with the strength of regional languages and a desperate lack of French teachers, the National Convention was compelled to pass a law allowing bilingual education in primary schools.

After the revolution of 1830 a law was passed requiring clerks and administrators seeking public office in any region of France to demonstrate mastery of written French. For the aspiring middle classes of the regions this law meant that access to civil service positions could only be achieved through mastery of French. By 1850 numerous French dictionaries served the needs of the upwardly mobile, eager to learn the standard Ile de France dialect as enshrined by the prescriptions of l'Academie Française (Caput 1972).

Between 1881–4 the laws of Jules Ferry successfully entrenched French unilingualism in France. As primary education became compulsory, so was the teaching of all disciplines to be made exclusively in the medium of French. This time an adequate number of teachers had been made available through 'les Ecoles normales'. These institutions trained elementary school teachers to become proficient language teachers in standard literary French. For the ruling elites and the growing middle class, French was the language of civilization destined to replace not only the Occitant and Breton languages in France but also to replace Arab and African languages in the expanding French colonies (Calvet 1974). The contempt for non-French languages in France was epitomized in Brittany, Occitanie, Alsace and Corsica where students caught speaking their non-French mother tongue on school premises were punished by being forced to wear the infamous signum or Token. Pupils wearing the Token at the end of the school day were severely punished by the teacher. A pupil could only dispose of the Token by catching another student using the patois and reporting him to the teacher before the end of the school day (Calvet 1974; Marcellesi 1979). Such practices fostered distrust between non-French speakers and made school children ashamed of using their parents' language both at school and at home. Compulsory military service in the French army also contributed to the decline of non-French languages in France. During the 1914–18 war, recruits from linguistically diverse regions of France were systematically assigned to regiments where only French could serve as a lingua franca (Calvet 1974). At the end of the first world war, non-French languages were in decline while the linguistic unification of France was well under-way. Indeed, by the late 1960s, Pottier (1968) noted that apart from the German/French bilinguals in Alsace and migrant workers throughout France, 95 per cent of the 53 million inhabitants in France were of French mother tongue.

Language standardization in favour of the Ile de France *dialect* was always viewed as a way of promoting linguistic unity in France. From the revolution onwards attempts were made in the school system to insure that no other dialect of French be taught than the standard Ile de France variety. In the French educational system, official attitudes towards nonstandard dialects were generally hostile. For instance, official directives issued by the Ministry of Education from the 1920s to the 1970s emphasized the teachers' duty of fostering correct oral and written French to offset the 'debasing influence of ordinary usage' (Marks 1976, 212). More recent directives for preschool education assumed that the mother tongue of the preschool years only meant the Ile de France standard. Lentin (1973) pointed out that only 20–30 per cent of preschool pupils in France came from homes where the standard form of French was the mother tongue. Lentin maintained that for 70–80 per cent of preschoolers using German, Arabic or French nonstandard dialects, the teacher's standard dialect constituted an almost foreign language. Lentin noted that for many of these nonstandard speakers, the disadvantage was further increased by teachers who judged the correctness of the child's language by reference to the norms of standard French.

In 1972 a series of recommendations for French language teaching in elementary school was proposed in Le Plan Rouchette. This government-sponsored document pointed out that over 50 per cent of elementary school pupils (mostly working class) spoke nonstandard dialects, which made learning to read and write standard French as difficult as learning a second language (Marks 1976). With evidence that over 50 per cent of French children left elementary school only bordering on literacy, Le Plan Rouchette recommended that French be taught in elementary school using *second* language techniques. The Plan Rouchette was vehemently attacked by numerous academics, politicians and members of l'Académie Française who felt that the new methods of teaching French would fail and thus threaten the very existence of the French language. To cool the debate a new Ministry of Education document was quickly published recommending a compromise between the traditional and new approaches to mother-tongue instruction in the primary school system. It is clear that to this day French educational policies are aimed at promoting language standardization in favour of the Ile de France dialect. Government guidelines remain designed to discourage nonstandard pronunciation in the school setting (Marks 1976).

Indications are that the repressive policies and attitudes towards nonstandard usage take their toll in the French educational system as is evident from the high proportion of failures in the school system (Marks 1976). It is probable that non-standard speakers experience a considerable degree of linguistic insecurity by the time they have completed their education. Goosse (1970) remarks that many secondary school leavers 'feel paralysed by the fear of making a mistake in their written or oral French' (p. 99). Anecdotal evidence reported by Laks (1977) also supports this observation. Using techniques developed by Labov (1972), Laks compared the ability of middle-class *vs* working-class French pupils to switch from colloquial French to the prestige Ile de France pronunciation. Laks (1977) reported a considerable amount of linguistic insecurity, especially amongst working-class respondents who were aware of their inability to switch to the prestige pronuncia-tion. Laks quotes a working-class pupil named Jean Pierre as saying:

'Il faut savoir quand même ton français, si c'est du français arabe t'es dedans. A l'école je suis nul, alors je suis dedans' (p. 124).

Jean Pierre refers to his nonstandard French as being as bad as 'français Arabe', an allusion to the low status ascribed to Arab-accented migrant workers in France. Feeling useless in school, speaking as bad as 'français Arabe', Jean Pierre considers himself 'out of it' with little hope of 'ever making it'.

The imposition of standard French and the chastising of nonstandard speech styles was not limited to the educational system. Since the introduction of radio and television in France the prestige and diffusion of the Ile de France dialect has increased to the detriment of nonstandard dialects and non-official languages. As Bourdieu (1977) points out, even in university texts such as those of Guiraud (1956, 1965, 1968), colloquial French, regional and urban accents and dialects are often described using derogatory and value-laden terms. For instance, Guiraud (1965, 7th edition 1976) unleashes his most vehement attacks on nonstandard speakers when he describes the special vocabulary of the Parisian proletariat (known as '*l'Argot*') in the following terms:[3]

. . . the vocabulary of the vulgar Parisian is almost exclusively concrete . . . it is based on a narrow reality devoid of culture and literature . . . the degradation of its sentimental values is only matched by the degradation of its aesthetic values. The masses have few words to express beauty. . . . In any event, the materialism and obscenity of the vulgar Parisian glares in the vocabulary of these masses. (p. 42–6)

Guiraud (1968) distinguished between accent deviations from the norm which could be tolerated and those which he felt must be stamped out. On this issue Goosse (1970) is less rigid and concedes that it is illusionary to attempt the elimina-tion of all nonstandard accents in France or elsewhere. Instead he proposes 'to correct the most visible and shocking departures' while noting that amongst those who have been 'better educated', many have succeeded in 'correcting their faulty pronunciation' (p. 100). The eminent French linguist, Martinet (1969) expressed most tolerance by pointing out that a French speaker should never be denigrated on the basis of accent or dialect as long as he/she 'uses impeccable syntax and vocabulary' (p. 124). In fairness to the above scholars, it must be pointed out that in more recent times French linguists have adopted a more socio-

---

[3] All translations into English are mine and have been phrased so as to capture the flavour of the originals.

linguistic approach to the study of dialectal diversity in France.

From this overview it seems that to this day a majority of academics, educators, policy makers and mass media specialists favour one standard norm of French which happens to be the Ile de France dialect (Rey 1978). Nonstandard dialects and accents are not much tolerated as these are viewed as a threat to both the linguistic unity of France and to the purity and universality of the French language. No study of the type reviewed in Giles and Powesland (1975) has investigated empirically the impact of the above policies and views on attitudes towards standard and nonstandard speech styles in France. Indeed, J. Ross (1979) pointed out that:

> little systematic work, apart from dialect studies, has been done on nonnormative descriptions of French . . . and, indeed, in nonlinguistic circles there is still a tendency towards a folklore denying the existence of socially conditioned or status-indicative variants of French . . . but the tradition of one France, one French seems unreasonable and can be refuted on endless anecdotal grounds. (p. 233)

Thus, one might expect that on a prestige (high–low status) and evaluative (good–bad) continuum of speech styles in France, the Ile de France standard would be rated very favourably by both standard and nonstandard speakers. Conversely, one could expect regional accents and dialects to be rated below the Ile de France style, while urban nonstandard and ethnic speech styles would be rated even lower on this prestige and evaluative continuum. Finally the Parisian Argot and the foreign ethnic-accented French of migrant workers from North Africa and Eastern Europe would most probably receive the lowest ratings on this continuum. On the other hand, one might also expect each of the above nonstandard varieties of French to be rated favourably in their respective milieus for usage in informal settings. The above speculations are necessarily subject to empirical verification using survey and experimental procedures of the type developed by Lambert (1967), Giles and Bourhis (1976b) and Bourhis (1981).

Not all nonstandard speakers in France could be expected to denigrate their own speech style in favour of the standard norm. Loyalty to nonstandard speech styles could be expected amongst cultural nationalists and urban activists in numerous parts of France. Intellectuals such as Lafont (1973), Person (1973) and Calvet (1974) have argued that the history of language and cultural policies in France amounts to a linguistic and cultural genocide against most dialect and language groups other than the Ile de France elite. Since the Second World War, reactions against the government's centralist linguistic, cultural and economic policies culminated in numerous ethnic revival movements. Regionalist demands were so great after the war that a law called 'Loi Deixonne' was passed in 1951 allowing for the teaching of regional languages such as Breton, Occitant, Catalan and Basque as second languages in schools of these respective regions. By 1970, Corsican was allowed to be taught as a second language in Corsica, while Flemish and German were allowed in their respective regions as 'foreign languages' (Marcellisi 1979). However, the 'Loi Deixonne' is seen by many as too limited since these second language classes are only optional, often scheduled at inconvenient times and are assigned to teachers who lack proper second language training skills (Marcellisi 1975). Today, ethnic revival movements can be found in Occitanie with its *langues d'oc* made up of numerous dialects including Gascon, Provençal, Limousin and Auvergnat (Bazalgue 1973; Bec 1973; Schlieben-Lange 1977). Other movements emerged in Britany around the Breton language (Mayo 1974; Piriou 1973; Roudaut 1973; Van Eerde 1979); in the Basque Country with the Basque language (Davant 1973; Mayo 1974) in Catalogna with the Catalan language (Bernardo and Rieu 1973); in Corsica with the Italian dialect (Ettori 1975); in Alsace with German (Marc 1975; Cole 1975); and in French Flanders with Flemish (Dupas 1975; Woods 1980). As in Wales (Bourhis, Giles and Tajfel 1973; Bourhis and Giles 1977) and other parts of the world (Fishman 1977; Giles *et al.* 1977; J. A. Ross 1979), these cultural nationalists and regional activitists reject standard French in favour of their own distinctive accent, dialect or language which they use as symbols of group identity. Though no empirical study has yet addressed this issue in France, evidence suggests that loyalty to nonstandard languages and dialects persists in the above regions of France. Finally, as was observed by Léon (1973), one should also find working-class nonstandard speakers maintaining their loyalty to working-class speech styles as a symbol of group identity and/or class solidarity.

Though loyalty to nonstandard speech styles exists in certain regions of France, it is likely that such loyalties are seriously undermined as institutional support in favour of the Ile de France standard grows more overwhelming for each new generation of Frenchmen. To many a Frenchman, attachment to standard French has grown deep as a symbol of the unity, prestige and vitality of French culture in the world. In this respect, it seems that language policies aimed at the linguistic unification of France have been so successful that the future of nonstandard accents, dialects and languages is bleak in France (Tabouret-Keller 1981).

The French language beyond France

In the eighteenth century the prestige of standard French as a universal language and culture was well established amongst the elites in both France and across Europe (Gordon 1978; Viatte 1969). In the nineteenth century, the French colonial empire guaranteed the spread of standard French as the language of civilization beyond Europe. In each of its new colonies, standard French was established as the language of administration and the linguistic tool needed by local elites to share in the 'universality' of French civilization. As in France, non-French languages encountered in the colonies were usually dismissed as mere patois or vulgar vernaculars best left to the 'unassimilable masses'. By the beginning of the First World War, France's colonial empire was second only to that of Britain. On the eve of the Second World War the French colonial empire stretched across five continents, with Paris still considered the cultural capital of the world.

It is not surprising then, to find that long after decolonization standard French still commands much prestige in the world. To this day, the Ile de France dialect remains the prestige norm against which francophone speakers across the world are most likely judged. Indeed Goosse (1970), a Belgian linguist, reiterated the necessity of maintaining the Ile de France dialect as the universal standard for French by concluding that:

> the history of the French language, the numerical importance of the French in France and the cultural role of France virtually dictates no other choice but that of standard French as the universal norm for French. (p. 96)

To this day, much emphasis has been placed on teaching standard French rather than local varieties of French to pupils in schools across the world. The rest of this chapter will deal with how standardization and status planning in metropolitan France has combined with indigenous sociocultural and demographic factors to affect language attitudes in 'le monde de la francophonie' beyond France.

Language attitudes in Belgium

In Belgium, the long history of language conflict between francophones and Flemish has resulted in the establishment of three autonomous linguistic territories (Bourhis, Giles, Leyens and Tajfel 1979; Lorwin 1972). These territories are namely unilingual French Wallonia in the south (pop. 3.2 million), unilingual Flemish Flanders in the north (pop. 5.5 million) and the officially bilingual capital of Belgium (pop. 1 million) situated in Flanders. Brussels is comprised of 80 per cent francophones and 20 per cent Flemish and, as a predominantly French city on Flemish soil, it remains the source of the current linguistic conflict in Belgium. There is agreement amongst linguists that on most linguistic dimensions the French spoken in Belgium is distinct from standard French spoken in France (Beardsmore 1971). Piron (1970) identified two main styles of Belgian French: the French spoken in Wallonia and the French spoken in Brussels. According to Piron (1970) the distinctive pronunciation of French dialects in Wallonia has been influenced by Belgo-roman patois that go back to the twelfth century. In Brussels, phonetic interference from the Flemish language has shaped the distinctive French working-class Brussels accent. Beardmore (1971) identifies a third style of Belgian French which he documents as being typical of French-Flemish bilinguals.

Francophone Belgians have long felt strong cultural affinities with France. For instance, after the Second World War, the economic and demographic decline of Wallonia spurred some Walloons to seek economic and political union with France. With French used as one of the international languages of the EEC based in Brussels and with numerous francophone Belgians considering Paris as their cultural and intellectual capital, standard French persists as the prestige form for many francophones in Belgium. Through the pervasive influences of the school and the mass media it seems that standard French remains the ultimate criterion for judging correct usage in Belgium. As late as 1970, Piron referred to distinctive patterns of Walloon pronunciation as 'regional flaws' while referring to the working-class Brussels accent as being the most 'aberrant' of Belgian speech styles.

But recently, the intensification of the community conflict between francophones and Flemish has contributed to the emergence of a more self-conscious Walloon identity that takes pride in its distinctive Walloon dialect (Lefevre 1979). Indeed, recent survey results obtained by Lefevre (1978) showed that Walloons not only identified themselves as Walloons rather than as francophones or Belgians, but also reported facility in using the Walloon dialect and enjoyed speaking it. However, these survey results indicated that while Walloon respondents reported using their Walloon dialect in informal situations, they limited its use in formal situations where standard French usage was seen as more appropriate.

The above considerations suggests that on a prestige and evaluative continuum francophone Belgians would grant standard French their most favourable rating while Walloon regional accents would receive intermediate ratings. The working-class Brussels accent would probably receive the lowest ratings. As with most diglossic situations, one would expect standard French to be viewed as most appropriate in formal situations while Belgian regional styles could be viewed as most appropriate for informal settings.

The long history of ethnic conflict in Belgium suggests that francophone Belgians could be expected to display a considerable degree of loyalty to their own Belgian speech style especially when these are contrasted with outgroup Flemish interlocutors (Bourhis *et al.* 1979). Finally, as in most western European countries one would expect the foreign-accented French of migrant workers in Belgium to receive the lowest prestige and evaluative ratings from francophone Belgians.

Language attitudes in Switzerland

Of Switzerland's six million population, one million are Francophones, known as francophone Romands. French is the official language of the Cantons of Geneva, Vaud, Neuchatel and recently of the truncated Jura. Francophones are also in a numerical majority in the cantons of Fribourg and Valais. According to Gordon (1978) the francophones of Switzerland always remained loyal to the Swiss federation, never questioned its traditional neutrality and never sought any special links with France. The majority of francophone Romands are Protestants and according to Gordon (1978):

> tended to see France as a nation of Catholics or pagans, a frivolous people, monarchical by instinct. The Romands' generally moralistic, introspective nature – as the stereotype would have it – was reflected in their language . . . not a medium for literature perhaps, but a symbol of an identity that was clearly Swiss and not French. (p. 112)

Such cultural differences may help explain why standard French does not seem to be viewed as the absolute prestige norm for francophone Romands. Instead of using unilingualism and radical centralization as the sole basis of nation building, as was done in France, Switzerland evolved on the premise that national identity could be sustained on the basis of small particularized cantons each enjoying a substantial degree of autonomy. Political decentralization and the geographic isolation of speech communities also help account for the rich diversity of francophone speech styles in Switzerland. Most cantons and big cities (Geneva, Neuchatel, Lausanne) have their distinctive accents of which speakers can be quite proud. For instance, Doise, Sinclair and Bourhis (1976) described Vaudois and Valaisan-accented speakers as follows:

> Vaudois and Valaisan accents are very strong indeed. For both groups, accent is an important part of their social identity: it is the only way one can recognize members of these groups. Perhaps for this reason, accent is often emphasized (particularly on radio and TV) and both groups are somewhat proud of their accents. Jokes, imitations, etc. about accent are frequent . . . both groups claim the other group has a strong or peculiar or typical accent. (p. 248–9)

Loyalty to canton and urban speech styles appears strong in Switzerland. A distinctive standard Swiss radio accent also seems to have gained the favour of francophone Romands as a prestige norm on equal footing with the French standard. Evidence of accent loyalty on the part of Lausanne-based Vaudois-accented respondents was obtained in a study by Doise *et al.* (1976). In this study, Vaudois listeners rated Vaudois and Valaisan-accented speakers heard attenuating or accentuating their distinctive speech style during cooperative or competitive intergroup encounters. Results showed that Vaudois listeners rated an ingroup

Vaudois speaker more favourably when he *accentuated* his Vaudois accent than when he *attenuated* it in the competitive situation. Similar patterns of ratings showing accent loyalty could probably be obtained in other francophone cantons of Switzerland.

On a prestige and evaluative continuum one would expect francophone Romands to perceive the standard Swiss radio accent at least as favourably as the French standard. Regional and urban speech styles should be perceived favourably by local ingroup listeners for most domains of language use, whereas the foreign accented French of migrant workers should be perceived least favourably by most francophone Romands. As with the situation in France and Belgium the patterns proposed for Switzerland remain to be verified through further empirical studies.

Language attitudes in North Africa

Algeria (pop. 18 million), Tunisia (pop. 6 million) and Morocco (pop. 18 million) are former French colonies and make up francophone North Africa. Unlike the situation in Black Africa where no one African language could compete with the arrival of the French language, Arabic in North Africa had already displaced numerous indigenous languages and was emerging as the symbol of Arab identity. As in France with non-French languages, French colonialism in North Africa denigrated the Arab language and culture and imposed standard French as the only language of civilization and advancement. Much of the resistance to colonialism in North Africa centred around the desire to restore Arabic as the sacred language of the Muslim population. Once independence was achieved, these three North African nations were confronted with the task of introducing language reforms promoting Arab authenticity through Arabization while also aiming for industrialization and modernization. To this day the influence of the French language and culture has been so enormous in North Africa that language reform in favour of Arabic has had to proceed very gradually through a phase of French/Arab bilingualism.

Gordon (1978) summarizes the effect of two decades of Arab nation building on the status of the French language in North Africa as follows:

> In 1975, then, the French linguistic presence was strong in Tunisia by choice, in Morocco, partly through inertia, and in Algeria, if only provisionally. In all three French was becoming a language of the masses through the universalization of education. . . . this deep French cultural presence continued . . . to give North Africa a different personality from the other Arab states. (p. 172)

Gordon (1978) argues that despite the bitter experience of French colonialism, by the time independence was achieved, standard French had become the language of modernization, education and international communication for North African states. By the mid 1960s, classical Arabic had been sufficently adapted for purposes of modernization in the Middle East. However, in North Africa, *dialectal* Arabic was more widely spoken and due to lack of standardization was not as suited as a language of modernization (Gordon 1978). Also, decades of colonial French unilingualism had created an Arab French elite proud of its French education and culture and interested in maintaining its priviledged position within state and private institutions. Thus, even today the knowledge of standard French in North Africa remains the key to desirable governmental, business and educational positions. French is only slowly being replaced by Arabic in the primary and secondary school systems of these countries, while standard French remains the primary language of higher education and University (Gordon 1978). For many, French remains more important than Arabic as the language of personal advancement although Arabic remains indispensable for informal usage.

North African identity seems torn between a desire for Arab authenticity and the cosmopolitan appeal of European French. This dilemma was recently observed by Stevens (1980) to be particularly salient for the bilingual elite of Tunisia. Also this dilemma is a recurrent theme in the work of North African intellectuals such as Albert Memmi, Driss Chraibi, Mohammed Khan-Eddine. Since 1973 the growing power of the oil producing OPEC nations, of which Algeria is an active member, favours Arabic authenticity in North Africa. Nevertheless, influential thinkers maintain that the nation states of North Africa can benefit from a dual identity combining the best of Arab and French civilization (Gordon 1978).

Though little empirical data (see however Bentahila 1981) are available it would seem that to this day standard French could still receive high prestige ratings from the majority of speakers in Algeria, Morocco and Tunisia. Amongst sectors of the population that strongly identify with the Islamic movement, classical Arabic should also receive very high prestige ratings. Lanly (1971) identified a distinctive North African accent in French which results from the linguistic interference of Arabic on French pronunciation. This is the style of French most often spoken by numerous North Africans whose mother tongue is Arabic and who have conventional schooling. One would expect North African-accented French to receive intermediate ratings on the prestige continuum while dialectal Arabic might receive lower prestige ratings. Loyalty to dialectal Arabic and North African-accented French may be more likely to emerge for usage in informal settings than for formal situations. It must be noted that in France, the North African-accented French of Algerian, Tunisian and Moroccan migrant workers is probably the most denigrated variety of French spoken in France today. This reflects the plight of North Africans who are the frequent target of racist attacks in western Europe.

Language attitudes in Lebanon

Though Lebanon achieved its independence from France in 1945, the French language and culture has remained very much part of Lebanese identity. This has been the case especially for the economically and politically powerful Christian Lebanese who, usually bilingual themselves, felt that Lebanon could serve as a bridge between East and West by maintaining a dual identity through French/Arab bilingualism. This view has not usually been shared by the predominantly working-class Muslim population who maintain that Lebanese identity is essentially Arabic speaking and Islamic. Though consisting of a rich multitude of cultures and religions, Lebanon's 2.5 million population can be viewed as made up of Christians in the north and of Muslims in the south with numbers from both groups living in different parts of Beirut (Viatte 1969).

With independence, Arabic was made the official national language of Lebanon. The constitution also promoted Lebanon's multi-cultural identity through the establishment of French/English private foreign schools. Very soon after independence the state successfully provided primary and secondary education in Arabic. The University of Lebanon was founded in 1953 and was officially Arabic with French rather than English as the main foreign language. In addition to the availability of Arabic, as many as 95 per cent of Lebanese students had the opportunity to learn standard French in primary and secondary school (Gordon 1978). Higher education in the French language was available in numerous lycées and at a francophone University. The international role of Beirut as the banking capital of the Middle East has long promoted French and English language usage even though Arabic remains the language of the majority. By 1970, it was estimated that 45 per cent of the population in Beirut knew French as a second language while 26 per cent knew English. But by 1972 the French presence in Lebanon was put in question by Muslim Arabists who argued that the predominance of French in higher education reinforced social inequality in favour of francophile Christians. The delicate balance between Arabic Muslims and francophile Christians maintained in Lebanon since independence was disintegrating by the early 1970s and finally developed into the civil war still raging today. With Beirut's banking system severely crippled, the vital role of French as a language of commerce is in jeopardy in Lebanon.

No empirical study exists on attitudes towards varieties of French in Lebanon. With standard French being taught as the correct variety in the educational system it is likely that standard French would receive the highest prestige ratings from francophone Lebanese. There is also a Lebanese-accented French influenced by linguistic interferences from Arabic which could rank in an intermediate position on the prestige continuum amongst Lebanese francophiles. For some Lebanese francophiles, this Lebanese accented French may serve as a badge of francophone Lebanese identity and may be favourably perceived especially for informal usage. A dialect known as Francobanais also emerged amongst French-educated Lebanese. Francobanais is a variety of French where Arab words are mixed with French. Although this variety of French seems popular in casual conversation among francophone Lebanese, it would probably be rated low in prestige by most Lebanese francophiles. As for Muslims who have often deplored the teaching of French as a threat to the Muslim and Arabic character of Lebanon, attitudes towards any variety of French cannot be expected to be particularly favourable in peace time, let alone during the present civil war.

As for the prestige of French in other Middle Eastern countries such as Egypt, Syria, Turkey and Iran, Gordon (1978) concludes that after independence French quickly lost its appeal for the ruling elites both as a dimension of national identity and as a tool of international communication.

Language attitudes in Southeast Asia

Cambodia (pop. 7.5 million), Laos (pop. 3.6 million) and Vietnam (pop. 4.8 million) are the three countries in Asia where the French language had an important cultural and political role to play. In Cambodia (now Kampuchea) and Laos, French lost its influence during the American involvement in Vietnam. In Vietnam, French ceased to have an important role immediately after the French military debacle of 1954.

Both Cambodia and Laos became French Protectorates in the latter part of the nineteenth century. From this period through Independence, numerous French schools and lycées were created to serve the urban elites of both countries. French culture and education was so highly valued by the ruling elites of Laos and

Cambodia that both countries adopted French as their national language along with Laotian and Khmer respectively (Gordon 1978). In the primary schools of Laos and Cambodia, French along with Laotian or Khmer remained obligatory until the late 1960s and French was used almost exclusively in secondary and higher education. France maintained close diplomatic and commercial ties with both countries by sending numerous 'coopérants' as technical advisers and French teachers who taught standard French in various sectors of the Laotian and Cambodian educational system. The prestige of standard French was felt mostly in urban centres and amongst the ruling elites who sent their children to finishing schools in France. The rural majority in each country usually remained unilingual in Laotian or Khmer respectively. By the late 1960s, the prestige of standard French seems to have been at its greatest in both Laos and Cambodia (Viatte 1969).

By the early 1970s the neutrality of Cambodia and Laos in the Vietnam War was compromised and resulted in the overthrow of francophile westernized elites by popular liberation movements. The Khmer language in Cambodia and the Lao language in Laos became the voices of identity and national liberation while the French language lost most of its influence.

French involvement in Vietnam goes back to the latter part of the nineteenth century when France occupied and took under its Protectorate formerly Vietnamese territories. From 1915 to 1949 standard French became the language of the civil service and of the urban ruling elite, while the majority of the population in rural areas remained unilingual in their native Vietnamese language. From the 1920s to 1950 the prestige of standard French was felt most strongly amongst the Vietnamese urban elites (Gordon 1978). But by the late 1940s the desire for Vietnamese authenticity was strongly felt. By 1949 in Hanoi and 1951 in Saigon, French was replaced by Vietnamese as the language of primary and secondary education. French colonial presence in Vietnam ended with the military defeat at Dien Bien Phu. Vietnamese was declared the national language of North Vietnam and later of South Vietnam (Viatte 1969). English became more important than French as a foreign language during the US involvement in South Vietnam. By 1975 North and South Vietnam were reunited with Vietnamese enshrined as the national language.

It is clear that the status of French in Cambodia, Laos and Vietnam decreased as national liberation movements replaced westernized elites and reinstated their respective ancestral tongues as the only national language. The richness of the cultures embodied by these ancestral languages, the geographical and ideological distance separating France from these three countries, as well as the substantial turmoil generated by the ferocious national liberation wars waged in each of these countries contributed to the end of French language influence in Southeast Asia. Relative to their national languages today, standard French probably rates only as one of the prestige foreign languages useful for international communication. For all intents and purposes, Southeast Asia is one place where the French language has ceased to exist as a vital language of communication for its elites and the vast majority of the population.

Language attitudes in African states

By virtue of the fact that the 24 francophone states in Africa share a common historical experience of having been part of the French African Empire, the language situation in these countries is somewhat similar and can be discussed under a common rubric. African states under the French African Empire shared a number of experiences with African states under the British and Portuguese African Empire (Deutsch 1953; Schermerhorn 1970). Through colonial wars, conquests, pacts and allegiances the traditional homelands of African-language tribal and cultural groups have often been divided or enlarged to suit the needs of European empires. Often, the divisions and amalgamations of African territories were militarily engineered by Europeans to eliminate or neutralize troublesome groups within more convenient and governable administrative units. With the decolonization struggles of black Africa in the post WWII years, newly independent African states were confronted with populations that were linguistically, culturally and tribally heterogeneous. While the black elites of these new nations had been educated in the capitals of Europe where they learned either French, English or Portuguese, the African masses spoke an impressive array of diverse languages and dialects, none of which on its own could compete with the European colonial languages. Various linguists estimate the number of languages and dialects spoken in Africa to be between 800 and 1,140. Influenced by the European model of nation state, the black elites of post-colonial Africa believed that nation building could be best achieved through the adoption of a single national language. Ironically, the adoption of the colonial language as the official language of these emerging nation-states had the double advantage of avoiding potential inter-ethnic conflict while facilitating modernization through technology and international communication.

In the French African empire, the imposition of standard French as the only language of civilization and advancement during colonial days had the effect of placing African languages in a subordinate status position. Indeed, only standard French was allowed in government, business and education. As with nonstandard French dialects and non-French languages in France, African languages in the colonies were dismissed as primitive patois and dialects. Also, French was taught in school as if it were the mother tongue of African children rather than as a second language. As in France, primary schools in Dakar and elsewhere in francophone Africa used the infamous Token to discourage the use of non-French languages and dialects.

Since independence, most of these African states have had the difficult decision of either adopting French or an African language as their official national language. For most of these countries the solution to nation building, national mobilization and modernization was the adoption of French as the official or national language. These decisions had the effect of perpetuating a situation in which standard French was viewed as the prestige language while African indigenous languages were perceived as having lower prestige. Ironically, the prestige of standard French was further enhanced by virtue of its association with African national independence. Indeed, Gordon (1978) noted that:

> the French language . . . had become in several parts of Africa, the language of national identification, as it had become, before independence, the language of revolt and of the quest for African authenticity. . . . To 1975 at least, the general pattern among the states to emerge from the French African empire, was to seek identification in French and to consider, or to pretend to consider the French language their own heritage. (p. 176–7)

Today, standard French remains the official language of former French colonies such as Chad (pop. 4.4 million), Congo-Brazzaville (pop. 1.4 million), Ivory Coast (pop. 7 million), Gabon (pop. 8 million), Mali (pop. 6 million), Senegal (pop. 5.3 million), Togo (pop. 2.3 million), and Upper Volta (pop. 6.4 million). (For a full listing see Gordon 1978). But the percentage of scholarization in these countries varies greatly such that French is often known only by a minority of the population while the vast majority of these populations speak their respective African indigenous languages. The choice of French as the national language of most former French colonies in Africa was also determined by the lingering influence of France (Weinstein 1980). France largely financed French Universities in Africa and still supports numerous student exchange programmes. Standard French is taught in African universities and lycées by a large contingent of French 'coopérants' sent as aid from France. Despite the institutional support it receives in education, government, business and the media, standard French remains best known by the ruling westernized elite who stand to gain most from the maintenance of standard French as the prestige national language of these countries. To this day many elites in these African states believe the French language and French civilization to be superior to African languages and cultures and support the use of French in world affairs such as in the United Nations. Weinstein (1980) also notes that numerous African intellectuals and government officials who joined the 'francophonie' movement proposed that French should remain the sole written language of African society.

The above considerations lead one to expect that attitudes towards standard French in francophone Africa should be quite favourable while attitudes towards African languages should be less favourable. This may still be the case for the majority of black elites leading many of today's francophone African states. But Weinstein (1980) has identified a number of factors which may have changed language attitudes in Africa in the late 1970s:

A loosening of economic and military ties, disappointments with development programmes, the advent of new leaders on both sides of the Mediterranean . . . have coincided with an evolution in attitudes. More leaders and intellectuals speak about the value of African languages. In almost all countries, African languages are no longer dismissed as dialects, patois, or vernaculars. Political and cultural leaders as well as the masses refer to them as languages. . . . Everywhere they are increasingly perceived as part of a cultural heritage of which Africans are justly proud. Concomitantly French is being labelled foreign and a second language . . . this should affect teaching techniques – no longer teaching French as if it were a mother tongue and the introducing of African languages into schools at least as subjects. (p. 62)

It would seem that a movement in favour of indigenous languages and cultures is having an impact on educational policies such that bilingual education is considered more seriously in numerous African nations. Recently, Weinstein (1980) pointed to mounting evidence that the teaching of standard French in African states has failed to produce literate populations, while even access to primary school instruction remains problematic. The obvious failure of unilingual French schooling in much of Africa has spurred the creation of experimental programmes where African languages are taught as media of instruction in primary school. Such programmes exist in the Central African Republic, Senegal, Niger, Togo,

Madagascar, Mauritania and Mali. The aim of such programmes is to use the African language in the first year of school and then to switch gradually to French. But Weinstein (1980) documents how the use of African languages in the school system has already led to ethnic conflict. This seems to be the case especially when the language of one ethnic group is introduced more rapidly than the language of another ethnic group. Whatever trend prevails, conflict over the appropriate language of instruction in primary and secondary schools is imminent in francophone Africa. For the moment, the majority believe that better jobs are obtained with French than without it. Though increasingly proud of their African culture, many Africans still perceive French to be more useful than any African language. An interesting trend to emerge in the last few years is a pride in local African-accented varieties of French. This new trend is often coupled with the derogation of standard French as taught in classrooms across Africa. As Kwofie (1977) has shown, there exists a wide range of African-influenced varieties of French in Francophone Africa. Distinctive African-accented French varieties have been identified in the Ivory Coast, Senegal, the Congo and in the Central African Republic. Perhaps a greater tolerance for African nonstandard varieties of French on the part of educators and francophile elites could allow African-accented French to emerge as a symbol of African ethnic identity while remaining a useful language of communication across francophone parts of Africa.

On a prestige continuum one could still expect standard French to be very favourably perceived in francophone Africa, perhaps closely followed by African-accented French. African languages may receive lower prestige ratings than French while loyalty to African languages for use in informal settings seems to prevail in most African states.

Language attitudes in the French West Indies

The French West Indies consist of Haiti, Martinique and Guadeloupe. An overview of language attitudes in each of these islands will begin with a discussion of the situation in Haiti.

Haiti declared its dependence from France in 1804. Until 1918 French was taken for granted as the language of the government, administration, justice and education. With the threat of anglicization from the adjoining Dominican Republic the government declared French as the only official language of Haiti in 1918. French became obligatory in all public services in spite of the fact that 90 per cent of the 5 million population was and remains unilingual in the Haitian French-based Creole (Viatte 1969). Indeed, French is the minority language of the ruling dictatorship and the aspiring middle class. As of 1968 only 2 per cent of the Haitian population was unilingual French while 5 to 8 per cent of the population was bilingual in French and Creole. Though French is the language of the schools, only 16 per cent of the eligible population had access to formal education in 1968 (Pompilus 1969).

The Haitian bourgeoisie has long held the Haitian creole and its culture to be inferior to the French language and its civilization (Valdman 1976a). But intellectuals such as Price-Mars have contributed to an ethnic revival movement which revitalized the Creole language and its culture. Price-Mars and others argued that only the Creole spoken by the vast majority of the Haitian population could express the true cultural identity of Haitian. Furthermore, Survélor argued that the Creole was not a form of deformed French but rather:

> a vernacular language which robs French of its potency. Through Creole, Blacks maintain their integrity while mocking the language of their masters. (cited in Valdman 1976a p. 167)

Indeed, Haitian intellectuals have argued that like American Black English, the Haitian Creole can be used as a tool of linguistic inversion (Holt 1973) to resist the abuses of the dominant bourgeoisie. Throughout the 1940s and 1950s an impressive Creole literature and poetry flourished, demonstrating that the Creole had the capacity of expressing as vast a range of sentiment as the French language (Valdman 1976b). Pompilus (1969) also pointed out that the clergy contributed to this revival by producing Creole versions of the bible and of religious songs. By 1964 the Haitian Constitution was amended to allow the use of the Creole in cases where such usage could facilitate citizens' dealings with government services. Nevertheless as of today, French remains the only official language of administration and education in Haiti. Valdman (1976b) has argued that the standardization of the various forms of Haitian Creole for literary use is the only hope of introducing Creole as an official language in the education system, in government services and ultimately as the national language of Haiti. According to Valdman (1976b) there is little chance that such a trend will emerge for Creole in the foreseeable future.

It would seem that standard French remains the prestige form in Haiti. Though perceived low in prestige, Creole is probably evaluated favourably as the informal ingroup speech style for the majority of Creole speakers. But it appears that the more French forms are retained in the rendering of Creole, the more favourably it is perceived by Creole speakers. Indeed, Orjala (1970) documents how rural Creole speakers attempt to gallicize their speech when faced with urban Creole speakers whose Creole sounds more French and thus more prestigious than the rural Creole.

Both Martinique and Guadeloupe were French colonies until they were fully integrated administratively under direct rule from France as 'départements d'outremer' soon after the Second World War. In both Martinique (pop. 330,000) and Guadeloupe (pop. 310,000) a French-based Creole spoken by the vast majority of the population coexists with French. By virtue of their political link with France, French rather than Creole remains the only official language of Martinique and Guadeloupe. On both islands, French is the only official language of administration, business, education, politics and the mass media. In both settings, the ruling elites are fully French in education and culture (Lefebvre 1974, 1976).

Prior to the First World War, education in French was limited to the privileged whites (béké) and a few mulattos. Afterwards, France made it compulsory for children in the colonies to attend primary school and learn French. According to Lefebvre (1974), the opening of the schools to Blacks has been an important factor in promoting upward mobility in the French West Indies. Today the majority of people in Martinique and Guadeloupe either know or understand French in addition to speaking their mother tongue Creole. Perhaps as a result of the political link with France the Martinique and Guadeloupe Creole has not developed into a written language with a distinctive literature as was the case in independent Haiti.

52   *Richard Y. Bourhis*

Indeed, renowned intellectual figures from Guadeloupe and Martinique such as Saint-Jean Perse, Gay Tirohen, Aimé-Césaire and Frantz Fanon have made their distinctive contributions on 'négritude' in the medium of French.

The pressures to learn French are very great in the French West Indies. Lefebvre (1974) points out that French is the only language in which one can be educated. Indeed parents at home try to speak French rather than Creole to improve their child's chances at school where the use of Creole is discouraged. Lefebvre (1974) reports that in Martinique, Creole parents with no knowledge of French speak Creole to their children but require their children to respond in French. Nevertheless, the spontaneous use of Creole for everyday functions such as informal conversation, parties and carnivals usually results in children learning Creole faster than French.

Lefebvre (1974) identifies French and Creole as two distinct varieties of speech in Martinique. The French speech styles consist of standard French and Creole-accented French, while the Creole speech styles consist of the stabilized Creole proper and a French-influenced Creole. From her field studies Lefebvre (1974) points out that:

> the varieties of French are labelled in terms of good and bad, reflecting a normative view of the language. . . . It should be noted that this normative view is widely shared among Martinicans . . . and is not limited to teachers. (p. 69)

Evaluations of the different styles of Creole reported by Lefebvre (1974) are particularly interesting:

> As the informant pointed out, you cannot speak of a good or bad Creole. Anyone who is born in Martinique speaks Creole well. Creole is the language that everybody speaks. It is the way we speak. (p. 69)

The result of standardization and status planning in Metropolitan France can be clearly seen in the above example from Martinique. For the Martiniquais, Creole varieties can be seen as *different but equal* while French varieties are perceived as *different but unequal*.

In both Martinique and Guadeloupe one could expect standard French to receive very favourable prestige ratings. Creole-accented French could be expected to receive intermediate prestige ratings while French-influenced Creole and Creole proper could receive the lowest ratings. For informal usages, Creole-accented French and Creole should be favourably perceived.

Since the 1960s and early 1970s important ethnic revival movements have emerged in Martinique and Guadeloupe. These movements favour autonomy from France and the establishment of Creole as the national language of each island (Gordon 1978). Influential intellectuals such as Aimé Césaire have argued that metropolitan France exploited Martinique as a colony while the poet Daniel Boukman has demanded total independence for Martinique. Whatever the outcome of these ethnic revival movements, it is likely that Creole speakers imbued with a new pride in their distinctive culture might display some loyalty towards Creole for usage in an increasing range of informal and formal settings. Again, the above considerations remain to be verified empirically.

Language attitudes in the United States of America

Unlike its role in other former French colonies, French in North America was the native language for Francophone minorities who were descendants of immigrants from France. The bulk of the French presence in the USA today can still be found in Louisiana and in the New England states of Maine, New Hampshire, Vermont, Rhode Island, Connecticut and Massachusetts (Casanova 1975). Many of the Francophones in Louisiána (now known as 'les Cajuns') are descendants of the Acadians deported by the British from Acadie in 1755 and of exiles from France following the French Revolution. Today's francophones of the New England states came mostly from Quebec in search of jobs and better opportunities between 1840 and 1930 (Dugas 1976).

Many of the first Acadians to arrive in Louisiana in 1764 were given land grants and they established numerous francophone villages in southern Louisiana. In 1803, France sold Louisiana to the United States, and the Acadians as well as Catholic Blacks who spoke a French Creole known as Gumbo became American citizens (Leich 1977). By 1846, private Catholic schools in French were available for those francophones who could afford it. French village life continued unperturbed and until 1864 most governors of Louisiana had been Francophone Catholics. Louisiana was officially bilingual until 1864 when English was declared the only official language (Kloss 1971). By 1898 subsidized public schools made education available to all, but schooling was only in English with no French allowed in classes or in schoolyards. Bradley (1976) reports that:

> many local residents recall being punished at school for speaking French on the playground. The Acadian who attended school became bilingual as he learned English in addition to his native French, a language which he never learned to read or write. Because the Acadian became literate only in English, that language has become the prestige language. Parents, knowing that their children would be required to speak English in school, were inclined to speak English at home resulting in the fact that fewer and fewer of the educated Acadians in this generation speak French. (p. 63)

Indeed, by 1940, only 300,000 Cajuns still claimed French as their first language while 1.1 million claimed French as a second language. Young Cajun recruits were also anglicized through their service in the US army during World War II. The pattern of assimilation to English continued after World War II, when the oil and gas industry brought an influx of Anglo-Americans amongst traditionally Francophone communities and when English-language television became popular in the early 1950s.

In 1968, the need to ensure literacy for non-English American populations prompted the US Congress to pass the Bilingual Education Act. This act aimed to provide primary education in languages other than English in regions of the US such as Louisiana where a high proportion of the population spoke languages other than English. In 1968, the state legislature declared Louisiana officially bilingual and passed Public Law 409 establishing the Council for the Development of French in Louisiana (CODOFIL). CODOFIL had the objective of preserving and developing the use of French in Louisiana and of benefiting the state culturally and economically by encouraging international trade and tourism (Bradley 1976). As the president of CODOFIL, the Francophile James Domengeaux successfully lobbied the Louisiana, Quebec and French Governments to provide funds and teachers for the teaching of standard French as a first and/or second language in primary schools across Louisiana. In the late 1960s few students studied the French language in Louisiana public schools. Between 1972 and 1974 the number of students enrolled in French CODOFIL programmes increased substantially (Lobelle 1976). Through his efforts, Domengeaux imbued francophones with a renewed pride in the French language. Renewed interest in Cajun music, language and history emerged while the state Legislature provided partly bilingual television for francophone viewers. These events helped slow the trend towards anglicization in Louisiana, where in 1968 the bulk of francophone speakers were over 35 years of age with few under 30 able to speak French (Lobelle 1976). The main effect of the Bilingual Education Act and especially CODOFIL has been to introduce many anglicized Cajun youngsters to the French language. Today, the survival of French in Louisiana depends not only on bilingual education in schools but also on the broadening of French language usage in all spheres of cultural and economic activity (Gilbert, 1981).

It is probable that in the pre-1968 years Cajun French, with its lexical and grammatical borrowings from English and its distinctive accent, was unfavourably perceived relative to both standard French and the English language. Evaluative reactions to Cajun French may be more favourable today as a result of renewed pride in Cajun identity and the introduction of Cajun French alongside standard French in audio-visual material used for language teaching. Empirical verification of the above considerations would be welcome at this critical phase of the Cajun ethnic revival movement.

In the New England States of the 1940s, approximately 1.1 million Americans of French origin still claimed French to be their first language. After World War II Americans of French origin were eager to be assimilated into the American melting pot and anglicization progressed rapidly (Dugas 1976). The widespread distribution of Franco-Americans across the six New England states and the breakdown of Franco-American parishes and schools fostered a faster rate of assimilation in New England than in Louisiana. By 1976 new questions in the US Survey of Income and Education allowed Veltman (1979) to estimate that the historical anglicization of Franco-Americans in New England states was as high as 53 per cent (Franco-Americans who no longer use French at home). In 1976, Paris summarized the position of Franco-Americans in New England States as: 'a minority on the way to complete linguistic and cultural assimilation'. But the Bilingual Education Act and the creation of CODOFINE programmes in New England States gave renewed hope for the survival of Franco-American minorities in New England States. According to Paris (1976) the creation of French primary schools has had a positive impact on Franco-American identity and French language usage amongst younger Franco-Americans. The optimism expressed by Paris (1976) seems to be borne out in a number of recent empirical studies. Using multidimensional scaling, Giles, Taylor, Lambert and Albert (1976) found that 16-year-old Franco-American bilinguals in northern Maine considered the French language the most salient dimension of their ethnic identity. In another study carried out in northern Maine, Lambert, Giles and Picard (1975) found that 17-year-old Franco-American students rated Franco-American-accented French speakers as favourably as standard French and American English speakers (see also Lambert, Giles and Albert 1976). It would be interesting to check if such favourable reactions to Franco-American French could be obtained in New

England states not adjoining the francophone Quebec border. Though bilingual schooling could contribute to favourable attitudes towards French language usage, Dugas (1976) remarked that French teachers in Franco-American schools of the early 1970s still denigrated Franco-American accented speech relative to standard French.

As with the Cajuns in Louisiana, the survival of Franco-American minorities in New England depends on the expansion of French language usage to all aspects of cultural and economic activities. Unlike the Cajuns who are concentrated in southern Louisiana, Franco-Americans have the numerical disadvantage of being thinly distributed across the six New England States. In both Louisiana and New England states there is little evidence of accrued institutional support in favour of the French language scheduled for the 1980s.

Language attitudes in English Canada

Since Lord Durham's Report of 1839 which advocated the full assimilation of Francophones to the English culture, French Canadians have usually been a minority everywhere in Canada except Quebec. Both before and after the British North American Act (BNA) of 1867, French Canadians from Quebec settled in English Canada seeking better jobs as labourers, farmers and small entrepreneurs. The French linguistic presence in English Canada has been most important in Ontario and New Brunswick. According to Canadian Census figures of 1971, 9.6 per cent of the Ontario population was of francophone origin while in New Brunswick 37 per cent of the population was of French background. In the other English provinces, French Canadians have not been so numerous and assimilation to the English majority has been predicted to be close to complete in the near future (FFHQ 1978; Joy 1972, 1978).

Across English Canada, French Canadian assimilation has usually gone through a phase of individual French/English bilingualism followed by English unilingualism. Indeed, Stanley Lieberson (1970) in his now classic *Language and Ethnic Relations in Canada* concluded that:

> Patterns of bilingualism in recent decades in Canada have very much favoured the English language . . . there is little doubt that a French Canadian who becomes bilingual is increasingly likely to raise his children in English. (p. 222)

The Anglicization of French Canadians residing in English Canada has been facilitated by the omnipresence of English as the language of work, business, administration, mass media and leisure. Historically, assimilation has also been accelerated by English Canadian discrimination against French Canadians (Royal Commission on Bilingualism and Biculturalism, 1969) and by Public Education Acts banning French-medium schools in Ontario (Law 17, 1917) or laws banning the teaching of French as a second language in public schools such as those of Manitoba (1916) and Saskatchewan (1929). Indeed, a survey of language and education policies enacted in English Canada since the BNA act of 1867 shows that many of these laws contributed to the assimilation of Francophones in English Canada (FFHQ 1978).

Today, more tolerant language laws allow French-medium schools in Ontario (1968) and Manitoba (1980), while the Canadian Official Languages Act (1969) declared English and French the official languages of the Federal Parliament and

Government services. Nevertheless, the Canadian Census showed that the rate of anglicization of francophones (or language transfer in favour of English) in the nine English provinces was an impressive 27 per cent in 1971. Indeed, of the 1.4 million respondents who acknowledged their French Canadian origin (6.6 per cent) in English Canada, 65 per cent claimed French as their mother tongue while only 48 per cent claimed French was still the most often spoken language at home (FFHQ 1978). The census data also showed that language transfer in favour of English occurred mostly for francophones between the ages of 20 and 44, this age group having an anglicization rate of 35 per cent (Castonguay and Marion 1975). This latter trend suggests that francophone anglicization in English Canada may be even higher by the 1981 Canadian Census (FFHQ 1978).

Patterns of language use and francophone assimilation in English Canada suggest that French Canadian attitudes toward their own language may be less positive than those they have towards the English language. In addition, standard French rather than local-accented Canadian French has long been taught as the prestige form of French in both English and French-medium schools across English Canada. Consequently, one may expect both French and English Canadians to perceive standard French more favourably than local-accented Canadian French on prestige dimensions.

In Ontario, Mougeon and Canale (1979) identified Franco-Ontarian French as a linguistically distinctive dialect of French which they note is perceived negatively by most Anglo-Ontarians and numerous Franco-Ontarians. Indeed, survey results obtained by Léon (1976) showed that working class speakers of Franco-Ontarian French felt linguistically insecure relative to both standard French and the English language. Nevertheless, as the largest group of francophones outside Quebec. (pop. 737,360), Franco-Ontarians have recently emerged as culturally and politically more active in their defence of broader language rights in Ontario. This recent militancy on the part of Franco-Ontarians may herald more positive views towards Franco-Ontario French as a possible badge of Franco-Ontarian identity distinct from English Canadian and Québécois identity.

By virtue of their numbers (pop. 235,000) and their demographic concentration in the northern and eastern parts of New Brunswick known as Acadia (Williams 1977), French-speaking Acadians have not only resisted assimilation (only 7.7 per cent in 1971), but have recently emerged as an assertive ethnic group in eastern Canada (Daigle 1980; Griffiths 1973). Since the last decade, Acadians and English Canadians have clashed over language and cultural issues in Moncton and other parts of Acadia. The Acadian ethnic revival movement recently culminated in the creation of 'Le Parti Acadien' which seeks the establishment of Acadia as a new francophone province within the Canadian Confederation.

Acadians have long been made ashamed of their distinctive Acadian dialect both by teachers of standard French and by New Brunswick English Canadians (Boudreau-Nelson 1976). The struggle of the Acadians for fairer treatment fostered a resurgence of the distinctive Acadian cultural and linguistic identity. Pride in Acadian identity peaked in 1979 when Antonine Maillet received France's most prestigious literary award (le Prix Goncourt) for her recent novel written in the distinctive Acadian dialect. It now appears that amongst students and cultural nationalists at least, the Acadian accent and dialect (Chiac) has come to serve as a symbol of pride in Acadian identity and group solidarity. A study by Larimer (1970) in the late 1960s showed that amongst Acadian respondents, the

Acadian accent was evaluated as favourably as Canadian-accented English and more favourably than Québécois-accented French. Studies contrasting attitudes towards standard *vs* Acadian *vs* Québécois-accented French should reveal whether or not Acadian French has emerged as a symbol of positive identity for substantial portions of the Acadian population.

Language attitudes in Quebec

Beyond France, Quebec today represents the largest native French-speaking population in the world (5 million). Under the influence of the Catholic church, the French Canadian population in Quebec during the 90 years following the British conquest rose from 70 thousand in 1763 to a staggering 670 thousand by 1850. A prodigious birth rate and loyalty to both Catholicism and the French language are important factors which prevented the anglicization of French Canadians in Quebec. Unlike the situation in English Canada where the anglicization of dispersed French Canadians increased with each generation, French Canadians held their own as a majority concentrated in the province of Quebec.

Though a majority in Quebec (80 per cent of the population) French Canadians have been the economic underdogs in a province controlled by a powerful English Canadian minority (Rioux 1974). Studies such as the Royal Commission on Bilingualism and Biculturalism (1969) showed that French Canadians in Quebec have long been discriminated against by members of the English Canadian bourgeoisie. But the modernization of Quebec society in the 1960s gave rise to an ethnic revival movement which asserted the distinctiveness of the Québécois linguistic and cultural presence in North America. In the 1970s the Québécois nationalist movement fostered both democratic and para-military political movements which sought Quebec's independence from the rest of Canada. By 1976 the pro-independence Parti Québécois led by René Levesque was elected and promptly passed Bill 101 in 1977, making French the official language of Quebec. Essentially, Bill 101 was drafted with the aim of making Quebec a completely French-speaking society within North America (Corbeil 1980). From the evidence so far it seems that this linguistic legislation has been successful in reaching its immediate goals (d'Anglejan 1979).

As elsewhere in the Francophone world, has standard French emerged as the prestige form relative to the local Québécois style French? Following the defeat of the French army on the Plains of Abraham in 1760 the French population of Quebec was cut off from the influence of Metropolitan France. Consequently, French in Quebec developed for more than 200 years without the normalizing influence of the standard Ile de France dialect (Barbeau 1970). This led Spilka (1970) to note that:

> The French spoken in Quebec today by all but a small academic and professional elite differs at all levels of linguistic analysis from the accepted prestige form spoken in France. (p. 5)

Before the substantial impact of modernization, education and improved Franco-Quebec relations, it is likely that French Canadians had positive views towards their own style of Québécois French. But early efforts of Quebec language planners in the 1960s may have inadvertently denigrated Québécois-style French by introducing language planning favouring standard French (Chantefort 1970; Daoust 1980). This effect was also compounded by the negative views towards Québécois French held by some French Canadian elites (Daoust 1980) and by English Canadians (Lambert 1967). For instance a study by Bourhis, Giles and Lambert (1975), using a dialogue refinement of the matched-guise technique, showed that French Canadian listeners rated a French Canadian speaker to be more intelligent and educated when she switched to standard French than when she maintained or accentuated her Québécois-style French. Most studies up to 1975 contrasting attitudes towards standard French *vs* Québécois middle-class and working-class French showed that French Canadians downgraded their own mode of speaking relative to standard French (Aboud, Clément, and Taylor 1974; d'Anglejan and Tucker 1973; reviewed in Giles and Powesland 1975).

Political, cultural and linguistic events favouring the Québécois cause were expected to have an impact on the value attached to Québécois speech styles relative to standard French (d'Anglejan and Tucker 1973). Daoust (1982) reports the results of a yet unpublished study which indicates a:

> perceptible change in the attitudes of the French-speaking student population in favour of Quebec French. The preliminary analysis of part of the secondary school students' sample seems to reveal that Quebec French is perceived more favourably and that the group studied feels less need to fall into line with standard European French. . . . although we cannot draw any final conclusions, it is tempting to suppose that this apparent change in attitude is an indication of a trend toward an improved self-image. (p. 18–19)

Future language-attitude studies should help determine which styles of French French Canadians consider most appropriate for formal and informal usage in Quebec. From recently released language planning documents, there are indications that l'Office de la Langue Française in Quebec supports the re-evaluation of middle-class Québécois French relative to standard French (Boulanger 1980). Indeed, it would seem that of all the francophone communities beyond France, Quebec has the demographic and institutional means needed to imbue its own middle-class Québécois-style French with as much prestige as standard French. In this sense, the emerging strong position of Québécois French relative to standard French is becoming more similar to the strong position of American English relative to the British standard and to Mexican Spanish relative to the Castilian standard in Spain. In these three cases demographic and institutional support built up in favour of the New World renderings of these languages have grown to the point of matching the prestige ascribed to the Old World standards of these languages (see Edwards, this volume: ch. 2; Carranza, this volume: ch. 4).

As elsewhere in the francophone world it is noteworthy that local Québécois French must not only coexist with standard French but must also compete with the predominance of the English language in the North American continent (Heroux 1978). Traditionally in Quebec, the English language has dominated over the French language in prestige value and as the language of business and economic advancement (Gendron 1972; Joy 1972, 1978; Lieberson 1970). Language policies in Quebec favoured institutional French/English bilingualism until the passage of Bill 22 in 1974. As early as 1864 both English and French were declared the two official languages of Parliament and of the Legislature. In addition to providing bilingual civil services, Quebec, to this day, maintains two parallel government-financed systems of primary, secondary and higher education servicing both the French majority and the English minority. Freedom of choice for the language of education became an important political issue when the French Canadian birth rate dropped dramatically in the 1960s and when statistics showed that immigrants to Quebec chose English rather than French as language of adoption for themselves and their children. Both Bill 22 and Bill 101 addressed this issue by maintaining freedom of choice for the language of education of English Canadians but restricting the choice to French for recently landed migrants to Quebec.

The historically dominant position of English Canadians and the subordinate position of French Canadians in Quebec was reflected in Lambert's classic series of studies using the matched-guise technique (Lambert, Hodgson, Gardner and Fillenbaum 1960; Lambert 1967, 1979). The results of Lambert's studies and of others reviewed by Giles and Powesland (1975) showed that English Canadians in Quebec tended to evaluate English-speaking representative speakers of their own group more favourably than French Canadian speakers, while French Canadians showed the *same* tendency in a *more exaggerated* form, that is, they too rated English Canadian speakers more favourably than French Canadian speakers. In addition to showing that the English language had more prestige than French, these results were also interpreted as indicating that French Canadians had accepted for themselves the negative stereotypes English Canadians had of them in the context of French/English relations.

The Québécois nationalist movement of the 1970s was expected to have a positive effect on French Canadian identity in Quebec. Preliminary results to this effect were obtained in a study by Bourhis and Genesee (1980) using a dialogue refinement of the matched-guise technique (Bourhis *et al.* 1975). One of the patterns of results obtained in this recent study showed that instead of denigrating representative speakers of their own group, French Canadian students rated a speaker of their own group more favourably than an outgroup English Canadian speaker. Such results remain to be corroborated in further studies, but the general atmosphere in favour of French in Quebec seems to have raised the status of Québécois French relative to both the English language and standard French.

Conclusions

Some important methodological and conceptual points emerge from this overview. On a methodological note, future social psychological studies of language attitudes in the francophone world must take two important points into consideration. The first point is that social psychological research on language attitudes must distinguish empirically between formal and informal domains of language usage. In many francophone communities, standard French remains the accepted prestige form for usage in formal settings while nonstandard renderings of French and indigenous languages have often emerged as the voice of identity and group solidarity for informal usage. Since decolonization, language policies in new nation-states have sought to broaden the use of indigenous languages to more formal settings with mixed success. Throughout the francophone world there is a pressing need to assess the success or failure of such language planning efforts using the best possible sociolinguistic and social psychological techniques.

Though sociolinguistic surveys usually monitor attitudes towards language usage in both formal and informal settings, this has not always been the case for social psychological studies of language attitudes. For instance, it is no longer sufficient to design matched-guise studies (Lambert 1967) which ask listeners to rate stimulus speakers without specifying the setting for which the various speech styles are destined. At the very least, listeners must be asked to rate for which setting the speech style they heard is most appropriate. More interestingly perhaps, stimulus speakers can be presented for evaluations as they are heard code-switching (or not) in dialogues which are contextualized in terms of the social status of the interlocutors, the social role of the speakers and the setting in which their encounter takes place. Examples of cross-cultural studies which have taken some of these points into consideration through the development of dialogue refinements of the matched-guise technique include Bourhis *et al.* (1975) and Doise *et al.* (1976) for the evaluation of accent switches in Quebec, Wales and Switzerland and by Bourhis and Genesee (1980) for the evaluation of French/English language switches in Quebec. In such studies, paralinguistic cues such as speakers' voice quality are controlled by selecting stimulus speakers who are perfectly bilingual or bidialectal. Two or more such speakers then voice content-controlled dialogues which vary in terms of permutations of code switches across preset numbers of speaker turns. Attitudinal reactions to code-switching sequences can be obtained by asking listeners to rate repeatedly stimulus speakers who code-switch in the course of the dialogues. In addition to allowing the investigation of controversial and theoretically interesting code-switching permutations through the *creation* of realistic stimulus dialogues, the present technique has the advantage of revealing listeners' changing patterns of attitudinal reactions to code-switching sequences in conversations. Such a degree of control over stimulus dialogues and the sequential monitoring of attitudinal reactions to code-switching patterns is not usually obtained in anthropological studies of code switching such as those of Kimple, Cooper and Fishman (1969), Gumperz (1971, 1978), Scotton and Ury (1977) and Scotton (1976).

More dynamic matched-guise refinements (discussed in Giles and Bourhis 1976b) in which listeners' attitudes towards language usage are supplemented with listeners' actual verbal behaviour have been developed by Bourhis and Giles (1976, 1977) in Wales; Bourhis *et al.* (1979) in Belgium and Giles, Taylor and Bourhis (1973) in Quebec. Recently, Bourhis (1981) utilized a real-life refinement of the matched-guise technique (Giles, Baker and Fielding 1975) in conjunction with a sociolinguistic survey to assess the impact of Bill 101 on cross-cultural communication in Quebec. In this field study a perfectly bilingual experimenter addressed French Canadian and English Canadian pedestrians in either French or English in the streets of downtown Montreal. The language in which the pedestrians replied as well as answers they gave to the survey constituted the dependent measures used in this series of studies. Future studies must combine sociolinguistic surveys with such social psychological methods to monitor effectively the impact of language planning efforts on both language attitudes and actual language behaviour in multilingual communities (see Giles and Ryan, this volume: ch. 13).

The second methodological point that can be made in this conclusion is that language attitudes do not emerge in a sociostructural vacuum. The present chapter on 'Le monde de la francophonie' is an example 'par excellence' of how sociohistorical, demographic and institutional support factors can affect language attitudes in a wide range of speech communities across the world (see St Clair, this volume: ch. 10; Kramarae, this volume: ch. 5). Social psychological studies of language attitudes cannot ignore the sociostructural contexts which inevitably influence such attitudes. We have seen that in the absence of actual empirical data, an overview of sociostructural factors affecting ethnolinguistic groups can be a precious source of information for assessing language attitudes in target speech communities. Using sociostructural factors as secondary data sources group vitality was recently proposed as a framework for objectively categorizing speech communities in terms of their ability to behave as distinctive collective entities in intergroup settings (Giles *et al.* 1977). Objective accounts of group vitality using status, demographic and institutional support data gathered from secondary sources was proposed as a useful method for comparing ethnolinguistic groups in cross-cultural research. The method used in this chapter to arrive at an estimate of language attitudes in francophone communities using sociostructural factors was based on the vitality method proposed by Giles, Bourhis and Taylor. (1977). One assumption of this approach is that speech communities which have high vitality are in a better position to elevate their own style of speech as the prestige norm than speech communities that have low vitality. Throughout this overview we have seen how more powerful speech communities have succeeded through language planning efforts to impose their own style of speech as the dominant norm within and beyond the limits of their linguistic territories.

In addition, Bourhis, Giles and Rosenthal (1981) pointed out that ethnolinguistic group members' *subjective* assessment of their own group position on vitality dimensions may be as important in determining language attitudes and behaviours as the group's *objectively* assessed vitality. For instance, members of a speech community may be made to perceive (through the mass media and education) that their distinctive speech style has little intrinsic value or prestige and that assimilation to the dominant speech community is a preferable outcome. Bourhis *et al.* (1981) proposed a new questionnaire designed to assess how group members subjectively perceive their own group position relative to salient outgroups on important vitality dimensions. Future language attitude studies might well include the administration of the Subjective Vitality Questionnaire to better account for the effect of objective and subjective sociostructural variables on language attitudes and language behaviours (see Ryan, Giles and Sebastian, this volume: ch. 1, and Giles and Ryan, this volume: ch. 13).

Finally, three points have emerged from this overview: first, in France as well as beyond France, very little empirical data exist on attitudes towards the French language. Empirical work is needed to monitor changing trends in language attitudes in the francophone world. Secondly, one is struck by the importance language policies have had in promoting or restricting the use and prestige of linguistic varieties in the francophone world. More than three centuries of status planning in favour of the Ile de France dialect succeeded in elevating this style of French as the prestige standard in France and abroad. Thirdly, it is only recently, through decolonization and persistent ethnic revival movements, that speech varieties other than standard French have emerged as languages of identity and group solidarity. Future language-attitude research in the francophone world must monitor changes in the strength of movements in favour of nonstandard speech varieties relative to the forces in favour of maintaining standard French as the prestige norm. As such, the study of language attitudes belongs as much to the psychology of stereotyping as it does to the social psychology of social change and intergroup conflict.

4

Attitudinal research on Hispanic language varieties

Miguel A. Carranza

Language attitude research has received a great deal of attention within the past few years and has substantially contributed to the development of the field of sociolinguistics. In fact, language attitude as a research topic has been the major focus in many recent sociolinguistic studies (Cooper 1974, 1975b; Shuy and Fasold 1973). However, despite the number of recent studies, the field of language attitudes is still very much in a developmental stage (Agheyisi and Fishman 1970; Cooper and Fishman 1974). This state is in sharp contrast to the development of attitudinal research in other areas, such as race relations and political beliefs. There remains a critical need for the establishment of collaborative (and interdisciplinary) research related to language attitudes, which will yield the theoretical and methodological foundations for future research efforts.

Despite the developmental status of research on language attitudes, it is apparent that this phenomenon does indeed influence language behaviour. Language attitudes can contribute to sound changes, define speech communities, reflect intergroup communication, and help determine teachers' perceptions of students' abilities. It is evident that different language varieties occupy distinctive positions of perceived social status. Language varieties that are seen as less prestigious and are associated with the lower classes are usually downgraded in preference to other varieties. This differential evaluation is readily observable in a number of studies which have investigated reactions toward contrasting languages (Cohen 1974; Lewis 1975; Wölck 1973) and different varieties within a language (d'Anglejan and Tucker 1973; Anisfeld et al. 1962; Tucker and Lambert 1969). A comparison of language attitudes held by ingroup and outgroup individuals toward language varieties characteristic of specific language groups is one topic that needs further investigation.

The purpose of this chapter is to utilize the perspective developed in language attitude research and focus on a specific language group – Spanish speakers – Hispanics[1]. This overview will discuss the similarities and differences in experience among Spanish-speaking populations in the world. Although this review does not cover all Hispanic contexts, the author has attempted to include all those Hispanic groups with whom language attitudinal research has been conducted. This review will focus on the sociolinguistic research that addresses language attitudes toward Hispanic language varieties, both from majority and minority

[1] The term Hispanic is meant to include those language groups for which Spanish is seen as one language variety alternative. In this work it will refer to groups in Spain, Latin America, and three Spanish-speaking groups in the United States (Puerto Ricans, Cubans and Mexican Americans).

perspectives. Moreover, this chapter will investigate reactions toward different languages (e.g. English and Spanish; Spanish and Catalan), different varieties of the same language (e.g. English and accented English; Spanish and Guarani-Spanish), mixtures of two languages (e.g. Tex-Mex and Jopará), as well as bilingualism (e.g. Quechua/Spanish; Spanish/English).

Language attitude research focuses on the differential evaluation of language varieties. As such, this perspective indicates that the level of prestige accorded language varieties is heavily influenced by two important factors: social structure and cultural value systems (see Ryan, Sebastian, and Giles, this volume: ch. 1). The social structure is an important determinant of how a language is regarded by members of the society. For example, one language variety, usually the standard, is more often associated with a high socioeconomic status group while other non-standard varieties are usually associated with lower classes. Fishman (1971a) distinguishes between a 'high' and 'low' language, where the high language corresponds to status, high culture, and strong aspirations toward upward social mobility, while the low language is associated with solidarity, comradeship and intimacy by its speakers.

Closely associated with this social-class phenomenon is the fact that some ethnic groups are mainly concentrated within narrow social-class boundaries; and as a result, their language varieties are often equated with that social class. This 'class–ethnicity' relationship helps to illustrate the necessity for viewing another relevant factor: cultural values.

It is simply not the case that any one particular language variety (be it high or low) is evaluated similarly on various dimensions by all members of that society. For example, several researchers (Cheyne 1970; Giles 1971b; Strongman and Woosley 1967) have demonstrated that nonstandard regional language varieties in the United Kingdom tend to be favourably viewed by their speakers with regard to personal integrity and social attractiveness, but less favourably on competence. The recent movement to reinforce the speaking of Black English in the United States (Hoover 1978) reflects this same lack of consensus on a language variety often classified as a low language. These 'mixed' results demonstrate the inadequacy of a simple social-structure analysis and the necessity to include a cultural values perspective.

Cultural values play an integral role in the perpetuation of language differences, especially for those varieties most often seen as nonstandard. As shown by Hesbacher and Fishman (1965, p. 153), 'Language loyalty designates a state of mind in which a language . . . assumes a high position in a scale of values.' For a less prestigious language to be maintained, it must be associated with values that its speakers see as positive and with which they wish to identify.

The development of a sociocultural context is extremely important in understanding the dynamics involved in language attitude research with the Hispanic population (See Ryan, Giles and Sebastian, this volume: ch. 1). There are no set patterns where one language is always defined as the high language and all others as low languages. Given different sociocultural contexts a language may be seen as the high language in one instance and the low language in another (e.g. Spanish in Latin America *vs* the US). This review is intended not only to demonstrate the changing roles played by language varieties but more importantly to portray accurately the tremendous diversity within the Hispanic world. Various researchers have argued the case for sub-groups within the Hispanic population in the United States, but the case is even more emphatic when the entire Spanish-speaking population in the world is considered.

Hispanic contexts

Spain

Given the origins of the Spanish language and the fact that this chapter focuses on Hispanics, Spain is a quite natural starting point. It has often been erroneously assumed that everyone in Spain speaks Castilian Spanish and only Castilian. This review will attempt to demonstrate the substantial amount of language diversity that exists within the country of Spain.

The official national language of Spain has been and continues to be Castilian Spanish. Castilian is viewed as the language necessary for economic and social advancement and it receives strong institutional support from the national government. Due to the strong emphasis on linguistic ethnocentrism in Spain, learning Castilian most often has meant discarding any other language variety a person might happen to speak. Historically, bilingualism has not been encouraged and language policy has stressed Castilian at the expense of other regional varieties and dialects (Aracil 1973).

In view of this governmental programme solidly supporting Castilian as the standard language, it is somewhat surprising to find that other languages have existed in Spain for centuries. Primary regional languages that can currently be found are Catalan, Basque, Gascon and Galician. Although all four of these varieties are based in the northern provinces of Spain, there is considerable variation regarding the number of people who speak each language. Catalan is by far the most strongly preserved by some six million speakers, followed by Galician, which numbers a little more than two million speakers, Basque with some one-half million supporters, and finally Gascon with less than one-half million. It should also be mentioned at this time that there are several types of dialects that exist within these regional languages (Perez-Alonso 1979). However, the purpose here is not to discuss the regional varieties and dialects in detail, but to demonstrate the language diversity in Spain and highlight the factors which seemingly account for this multilingual context. In order to exemplify the minority language situation in Spain we will focus on the development of two of these regional varieties, Catalan and Galician. By exploring the different histories of these two languages and the people who speak them, we can gain some insight into the language attitude situation in Spain.

Between the Spanish government and the people of Catalonia there has been a long history of conflict centred around the use of the Catalan language. Catalonians have struggled for centuries to maintain their linguistic and cultural diversity. Since the early eighteenth century the people of Catalonia have lived in colonial oppression, including the suppression of their language. This linguistic ethnocentrism eventually resulted in Catalan being banned from public use in 1939 by the national government.

Since that time Catalan has undergone a revitalization as Catalonian people have begun to re-establish an ethnolinguistic vitality within their region. Although the people of Catalonia do not have political autonomy in Spain, they have indeed created a certain level of linguistic autonomy for the use of Catalan. There has developed a greater freedom for the use of Catalan in public arenas, even though Castilian is still considered the official language in the educational sector. The mere fact that people are writing about the various perspectives on bilingualism (especially Catalan and Castilian) is indeed a healthy sign (Aracil 1973; Badia i Margarit 1962; Ros and Giles 1979).

One factor that cannot be overestimated for its impact on this issue of language rights is the economic dimension. Catalonia is situated in the northern part of Spain in a thriving industrial area. As a result, the people who speak Catalan are primarily of the middle and upper socioeconomic classes. This economic strength has helped to force the issue of recognition and the use of Catalan in various domains. By the late 1960s the push for language autonomy was being led not only by the lower but also middle-class Catalonians. The open repression by the nationalistic government only served to reinforce the determination of the people to make Catalan an official language. In many ways Catalan did become the official language of workers, students, and politicians (Perez-Alonso 1979).

An example of the significant changes occurring related to language policy was the publication of a language survey conducted by Badia i Margarit in 1969. What made the study unique was that it focused on language use and was written in a minority language – Catalan! The survey itself, which was conducted in Barcelona in 1964–5, yielded extensive language data. More important than the quantitative aspects of the study was the role it played in creating an awareness among Catalonians of the present status of their own regional language (Robinson 1976).

Today the number of people speaking Catalan is steadily increasing. Catalan as a language of culture and vitality has been discussed by various authors (Aracil 1966; Badia i Margarit 1973). A growing ethnic consciousness has helped to strengthen the position of Catalan as a prestige language, even though it is still considered a minority language by national standards.

In contrast to Catalonia there is the northwestern province of Galicia. Historically, the Galician region has been the subject of benign neglect by the Spanish national government. In fact Galicians have been characterized by Macias (1979) as Spain's forgotten minority. Being oppressed or being neglected can have the same impact on a native language – relegation to secondary status. Galician was given this inferior position and Castilian was recognized as the standard language in Galicia. Educational institutions reaffirmed the lower status of Galician by teaching in Latin and Castilian. As further proof of this language dominance, Macias (1979) writes that the Church was also involved in perpetuating anti-Galician policy by often punishing seminarians for speaking Galician.[2]

In comparing the two language situations, Catalan and Galician, one difference is notable and merits further discussion. The speakers of these two languages are quite different when it comes to socioeconomic background. Whereas Catalan speakers have included the middle and upper classes, the Galicians were primarily

[2] There is a considerable degree of irony yet similarity between this situation and that of Mexican Americans in the United States. Galician seminarians were punished for speaking Galician instead of Castilian Spanish, whereas, as we will see later in the chapter, Mexican American youth were punished for using Spanish instead of English in the schools.

lower class. In fact, the general economic condition of Galicia has been significantly lower than that of Catalan. Governmental policy designated this region for agricultural and forest development, and this plan contributed greatly to the overall underdevelopment of Galicia. This lack of industrial development and accompanying accumulation of wealth has made it difficult for Galicians to effect changes in the governmental policy toward the use of Galician. One positive aspect of the underdevelopment of this region has been that the people are not seen as political or economic threats and are ignored. This invisibility gives the people an opportunity to develop an ethnolinguistic vitality without fear of reprisals.

As a result the revitalization of Galician has been much more covert and slower to develop than that of Catalan; however, the direction is the same. More and more support for Galician is developing in the region, including support from universities. Many new books are being written in the language. Most importantly this institutional support has encouraged many of the native speakers to continue speaking Galician and to resist complete assimilation.

Given the language diversity in Spain, language attitudinal research would seem to be well warranted. The descriptive work in volume I of Badia i Margarit's study (1969) needs to be complemented by the still to come volume II which deals more directly with the attitudinal information of the survey. This attitudinal research is limited by the fact that the survey was collected in 1964–5 and has become somewhat outdated. Ros and Giles (1979) have attempted to analyse the sociolinguistic situation in Valencia by means of a social psychological perspective. By viewing language in a bilingual context (Castilian and Catalan) on dimensions of status and solidarity a better understanding as to language choices in interpersonal and group interactions occurs. They suggested that speakers converged towards the dominant language of the high-prestige speaker and that this shift occurred even in informal contexts if the highest-status speaker was present. In one of the few traditional language attitude studies known to this author, Woolard (1980) investigated evaluative reactions toward Castilian and Catalan speakers. This exploratory study, by use of the matched-guise technique, had students at five schools rate speakers on fifteen different traits. Preliminary results indicated that the Catalan language does not suffer a loss of respect in the view of natives or immigrants. Group solidarity caused judges to feel friendlier toward those who used their own language, but only when the speakers were identifiable as native speakers. In addition, recent personal correspondence with researchers in Spain (e.g. L. V. Aracil, M. R. Garcia and M. Strubelli Trueta) indicates that language attitudinal research will continue to establish itself in the future.

Latin America

In general there has not been an abundance of sociolinguistic research conducted in Latin America. The traditional language surveys performed quite regularly in other countries have been the exception to the rule in Latin America (Alleyne 1975). On the surface the absence of such surveys seems ironic given the great linguistic diversity that exists in this region of the world. This diversity is apparent not only in comparing indigenous languages with the standard language (e.g. Quechua and Spanish), but also in the wide diversity of indigenous languages found in each of the countries (e.g. Peru, see Wölck 1973). It would seem that the official language policies of most governments in Latin America ignore the reality of the situation and instead promote the myth of the 'linguistic melting pot'. This would help to explain the absence of language surveys found in this corner of the world.

Despite this prevailing myth and reticence on behalf of many governments in Latin America, several studies focusing on language issues have been conducted. Two examples of these language surveys are the *El Simposio de Cartagena: Actas, Comunicaciones, Informes* conducted by the Instituto Caro y Cuervo (1965) and the *Proyecto Sociolinguistic del Instituto de Investigaciones Sociales* carried out by the Universidad Nacional Autonoma de Mexico (Villegas 1970). Although these do not specifically address language attitudes, the research data on language and dialect use do provide an excellent foundation for further sociolinguistic investigations.

Several studies have addressed the topic of bilingualism and, as a result, have had a more direct relationship to the area of language attitudes. Escobar (1976) and Elizaincin (1976) investigated the phenomenon of bilingualism as it related to dialectology both within a country (Peru) and on a border between countries (Brazil and Uruguay). In Mexico, it may be the case that increasing bilingualism actually strengthens the dominant position of Spanish over the many indigenous languages (Suarez 1978). Albo (1970) conducted a massive language survey on bilingualism in Bolivia. By looking at Quechua and Spanish, Albo collected a substantial amount of ethnographic data examining a basic sociolinguistic question, 'Who speaks what language to whom and why?' The major emphasis in this work, however, dealt with the techniques, instruments and methodology involved in the completion of the research project and, as a result, placed considerable attention on description rather than focusing specifically on attitudes.

The work of Wölck (1973) in Peru has proved very useful to the area of language attitudinal research. Wölck focused on the topic of bilingualism (Quechua and Spanish) in a multilingual setting. This bilingualism was investigated in light of two kinds of attitudes toward the language situation that existed in Peru: hispanicist and indigenist. The hispanicist position favours the speediest 'hispanicization' of the non-Spanish speaking population over retention of their indigenous language – Quechua. On the other hand, the indigenist position promotes the native language and culture by denying the usefulness or necessity of knowing and speaking Spanish. Several interesting results were found in this matched-guise study of bilingual listeners' evaluations of Spanish and Quechua speakers. Most notable was the relationship between language and social status, where Spanish speakers were rated more favourably on status-stressing dimensions, but Quechua speakers were judged more favourably on affective dimensions. It seems as though the recognition of Spanish as the language for social advancement was also accompanied by an affective loyalty to their native language. With regard to individual or subgroup differences, another interesting finding revealed that as the degree of bilingualism increased the perceived status differences between Spanish and Quechua decreased.

One country that has received more attention than most other countries in Latin America is Paraguay. This attention has largely developed since the late 1960s; in fact, it was not until 1967 that the indigenous language (Guarani) was officially recognized by the Paraguayan government. This is in spite of the fact that it is estimated that 92 per cent of the population speaks this native language and over 50 per cent are Spanish/Guarani bilinguals. Previously, Guarani had suffered the fate of most indigenous languages, that of being labelled an inferior tongue not to be spoken by high-status people. Spanish was the standard language and Guarani was not used in the educational system.

Fundamental to any official recognition of an indigenous language is a positive attitude toward the language by its speakers. This pride is essential to the development of an ethnolinguistic vitality regardless of any governmental actions. Since the recognition of Guarani as an official language in 1967 attitudes have continued to change. The official recognition has helped reinforce the realization that this indigenous language is not a lower-class variety to be discarded, but rather a language to be maintained within the society. The ethnolinguistic vitality of this indigenous population has been assisted immeasurably by the approval of the national government.

Several studies corroborate this positive attitude towards Guarani (Rhodes 1979, 1980; Rubin 1968). In a classic study of bilingualism in Paraguay Rubin (1968) investigated four factors: attitudes, stability, usage and acquisition and proficiency. Language attitudes were viewed on several characteristics: language loyalty, pride, rejection of the language, prestige and awareness of norms. Results indicated that Paraguayans exhibited a strong language loyalty toward Guarani but not Spanish. Guarani was frequently being attacked as an inferior language and as a result, people developed a strong loyalty to their native tongue. In regard to the attitude of pride, both Guarani and Spanish elicited a strong element of pride, but in quite different ways. Paraguayans felt pride in Guarani because it encompassed a strong feeling of intimacy, whereas pride in Spanish was most often thought of in terms of status and social advancement. As expected, prestige was most often directed towards Spanish and its value in being able to advance socially. Finally, the awareness of usage norms revealed that there were three occasions in which appropriate language usage was rigidly defined: (1) Guarani in rural areas (2) Spanish in the schools, and (3) Spanish on public formal occasions. Some 10 years later the work of Rhodes (1979, 1980) continues to support Rubin's findings. There still remains a high degree of bilingualism among Paraguayans. Most Paraguayans were very optimistic regarding the future of Guarani in their country, and they believed that Guarani should always be retained without being replaced by Spanish. Overall, it seems that Paraguayans do not deny the necessity for knowing Spanish to achieve upward social mobility. Yet, this does not automatically imply that their native tongue is of no value. In other words, knowing the standard language (Spanish) does not necessitate discarding the indigenous language (Guarani).

United States

In 1980 the number of persons of Spanish origin in the United States totalled some 13.2 million (US Bureau of the Census, 1981). Of this total, the three major Hispanic groups, Cubans, Puerto Ricans, and Mexican-Americans, comprised 6 per cent, 14 per cent and 60 per cent, respectively, of this total population. There exist many differences among these groups and that is the rationale for discussing each of them separately in regards to language attitude research.

Cubans. The Cuban population in the US numbers some 830,000 people. Cubans are predominantly an urban population that arrived in the United States in two major migrations, in the 1960s exodus from Cuba and the recent immigration of Cubans in the past couple of years. In comparison with Puerto Ricans and Mexican-Americans this group is slightly older, employed in higher occupations and have higher family incomes. There appears to be little sociolinguistic research concerning the Cuban population prior to the mid 1970s. The few writings that did exist were ethnographic and described the transition of Cubans coming to the United States. Very little emphasis was placed on the language dimension of the Cuban experience. For example, Smith (1968) writes of the Hispanic settlement, including Cubans, in Tampa, Florida but does not specifically investigate language issues. She does mention indirectly the importance of Spanish for traditionalism, and differences in the way Old Cubans (pre-Castro) and New Cubans speak Spanish. The work of Stevenson (1973) attempts to view the impact of assimilation on Cubans in Miami and what changes in national identity were necessary for social acceptance in US society. Most other studies addressing Cubans and their language have primarily been concerned with linguistic variations (e.g. phonological analysis).

Several recent studies have begun to address issues directly related to sociolinguistic research in general and language attitudes in particular. Brainard (1977) investigated the attitudes toward bilingual education held by Cuban, Mexican-American, Puerto Rican and Anglo parents. Specifically, Brainard looked at three dimensions: bilingual education, language loyalty and the teaching of culture. The Cuban parents scored highest on the dimensions of bilingual education and language loyalty. No differences were found on the teaching of culture. Although all groups were favourable toward bilingual education, length of residence was a significant factor, with those parents who had lived in the US the longest the least favourable toward bilingual education. Finally, parents who had children in a bilingual programme held more positive views toward bilingual education and showed more loyalty to the Spanish language.

Attitudes toward bilingual education were also the major focus of a study conducted by Cruz (1977). In this investigation, Cuban, Mexican-American and Puerto Rican parents were asked their views of bilingual education, language loyalty and ethnic affinity. Again, the majority of parents had favourable opinions of bilingual/bicultural education. In addition, several relationships with favourable views toward bilingual education were revealed. Parents with lower incomes, less education, strong Spanish language loyalty and positive perceptions of ethnic affinity held more favourable views of bilingual education.

Two studies have looked at language attitudes by investigating the reactions that people have to Cuban speech. Arnov (1978) utilized the matched-guise technique to elicit the evaluative reactions of Cuban-American and Anglo-American college students toward English and Spanish. The English and Spanish speech samples were recorded using Cuban-American bilinguals. Results showed that Anglo-American monolinguals held the strongest biases against the Spanish speakers, and, quite surprisingly, the Cuban-American students also demonstrated a bias against the Spanish speakers. Some support for the positive merits of bilingualism was found in the fact that the Anglo-American bilinguals showed a marked preference for the Spanish guises.

A study by Rey (1977) investigated another dimension of language attitudes, namely, how the way you talk affects your employability (see Kalin, this volume: ch. 9). Rey studied the reaction that employers have to Spanish-accented speakers. Speech samples were obtained from white Americans, black Americans, and

Cuban nationals, with the Cuban speakers divided into three groups: minimal, medium and heavy accent. Employers listened to a speech sample and then were asked to judge the speaker in terms of his suitability as a prospective employee. The white American speech was rated most positively black American speech and minimal accent next, medium accent less favourably, and heavy accent least favourably. Significant differences were found for all job categories utilized in the study.

Puerto Ricans. The island of Puerto Rico is a commonwealth country of the United States. It is estimated that some 3.4 million people live on the island of Puerto Rico and some 1.8 million Puerto Ricans live in the United States. The distinction is sometimes made between Puerto Rican 'islanders' and 'mainlanders', even though there is a considerable overlap between the two groups, as movement between Puerto Rico and the US is quite normal. The vast majority of sociolinguistic research has been conducted on Puerto Ricans residing in the US.

Since the 1950s, literature dealing with the Puerto Rican experience has usually included some reference to their language background. Most of these works, however, have made only general references to language in the light of some other major focus, e.g. community life or migration (Mills *et al.* 1950; Padilla 1958). Others began to integrate the language dimension into their work but still in a quite general fashion. Examples of this research orientation were studies concerning Puerto Rican children in the educational system (Leavitt 1969; Lennon 1963). Their results generally indicated that language was important for developmental factors such as educational achievement and social adjustment.

Sociolinguistic research on the Puerto Rican population received a tremendous boost with a major study conducted by Fishman *et al.* (1971b). This was a massive investigation of the Puerto Rican community in the New York City area that researched a wide variety of language issues relevant to this population. The study focused on several different Puerto Rican population areas: a complete Puerto Rican neighbourhood, Puerto Rican high-school students, and Puerto Rican intellectuals. Some of the topics studied were language behaviour (actual and reported), self-concepts (as Puerto Ricans and as Americans), language consciousness, and language attitudes. Methods utilized included participant observation, self-reporting, recorded interviews and performance testing. In addition, researchers conducted a content analysis of Spanish newspapers and Spanish radio programmes in the city for a six-month period.

This was indeed an ambitious and in-depth research project which served an excellent function in helping to focus on several sociolinguistic topics related to and including language attitudes. The results revealed a general feeling of language consciousness among Puerto Ricans, an awareness of the existence of different language varieties within the community and a sensitivity to these varieties, and an increased understanding of Puerto Rican identity. The work performed by Wolfram (1974) with Puerto Rican English in New York also served to further highlight the issue of language use in the United States with its social implications for the Puerto Rican community. Most recently, the Centro de Estudios Puertorriquenos at City University of New York has embarked on a large-scale research project dealing with language policy and the Puerto Rican community (1978). Primary efforts have been directed toward reviewing issues and alternatives involved in language policy and their relationship to the community, the practical implications of language policy, and the level of sociolinguistic knowledge related to the Puerto Rican speech community. As part of this major effort to formulate and implement language policy for Puerto Ricans in the United States, the Centro conducted a survey of language attitudes in a Puerto Rican community in New York (Attinasi 1979; Language Policy Task Force 1980). This study became part of the empirical portion of the tri-component (ethnographic-linguistic-attitudinal) project. The purpose of the language attitude survey was to ask questions related to key issues in the community: language choices, existing community resources, linguistic issues in education, and the role of language in cultural and national identity.

The findings of this study were very interesting. On the topic of national identity two items judged important for Puerto Rican identity were parents and pride. Surprisingly enough, language was not evaluated as being extremely important for Puertorican-ness, the implication being that a person does not have to speak Spanish to be a Puerto Rican. In addition, the majority did not feel that English was a threat to being Puerto Rican. These results seem to indicate that Puerto Rican identity can be expressed in English or Spanish, and American culture is compatible with the Spanish language.

In regard to Puerto Rican status most respondents felt they were a part of both the United States and Puerto Rico, and their nationality preferences reflected their participation in the two cultures (Puerto Rican, Nuyorican and Puerto Rican-American). However, it should be mentioned that the vast majority felt it was important for Puerto Ricans to retain their distinctiveness as a group. One group of these adults, the young adults, were particularly strong in their affirmation of Puerto Rican culture and desire to be bilingual. These young adults also rejected the idea of having to choose between isolation and assimilation, and instead found pride in being Puerto Rican and bilingual.

Strong support for maintenance of Spanish in the community was observed, and the majority felt that responsibility for this maintenance belonged in the home environment. In addition, the majority of the adults felt that children should acquire both Spanish and English initially. It goes without saying that the community favours bilingual education, even without knowing much about its purpose or usefulness and success of the current programmes.

In terms of language use the majority of the adults indicated they were speaking more English, whereas one-third reported using more Spanish than previously. Young adults reported an especially high increase in their use of English. Based on the findings of the ethnographic research component, it is clear that English is becoming more widespread, and the researchers predict that English will become the primary language of communication in the future.

The issues of language use and bilingual education have important implications for Puerto Rican youth, as indicated by the group of young adults mentioned in this last study. Kimple, Cooper, and Fishman. (1969) investigated language switching and its effects on interpretations of conversations among high-school students. Utilizing a multiple-choice questionnaire Puerto Rican high-school students listened to conversations and assessed them according to the following criteria: role relationships of the speakers, setting of the conversations, manifest content, social or latent content, and appropriateness. These bilingual students appeared to have internalized generally accepted norms regarding the appropriate use of Spanish and English. Shifts in use of language may not cause loss of comprehension but evidently produce feelings of language inappropriateness.

Giles, Llado, McKirnan and Taylor (1979) conducted a survey to examine the social identity of Puerto Rican high-school students living in Puerto Rico (islanders). By means of a card-sorting task they sought to discover dimensions relevant to the social identity of Puerto Rican youth. Three major dimensions emerged from their analysis: personal identity, language identity and economic wealth identity. Within the first dimension of personal identity the students strongly identified with their own parents, personality characteristics and 'good' Puerto Ricans as described by religion or skin colour. The second dimension, language identity, indicated that language was an important factor in their social identity. However, it must be emphasized that this is seen as being separate from their personal identity. The last dimension of economic wealth represented a contrast between wealth and political change; and again the high-school students did distinguish this type of identity from their own personal identity. In summary, the Puerto Rican students had a favourable image of themselves but did not necessarily identify their personal images with specific language or cultural groups.

Mexican-Americans. The Mexican-American population[3] comprises the largest group of Hispanics in the United States – approximately 8 million people. They are primarily an urban population residing in the southwest region of the United States. However, a sizable (10–15 per cent) and growing number of Mexican Americans reside in urban centres outside the southwest; Chicago, Illinois; Detroit, Michigan; and Omaha, Nebraska just to name a few (Cardenas 1977). Mexican-Americans primarily occupy the lower end of the socioeconomic ladder (Grebler, Moore and Guzman 1970); and, as a result, they are an economically, politically and socially powerless minority group in American society.

Sociolinguistic research has attempted to identify the exact role language plays in the process of subordination of this particular minority group. As early as the 1930s and 1940s, Barker (1947) was investigating the Mexican-American community in Tucson, Arizona. This work was a pioneering effort which addressed the social functions of Mexican-American language varieties and described patterns of language use in this bilingual/bicultural community. Recently, several authors have addressed themselves to the complexity involved in working in the area of Mexican-American sociolinguistics (Aguirre 1978; Berk-Seligson 1980; Penalosa 1980). It quickly becomes apparent that the field of Mexican-American sociolinguistics is indeed quite diverse and complex, but has not been researched to any great extent. This is in spite of the fact that the Mexican-American speech community is the largest non-English speaking population in the US.

The sociolinguistic research that does exist on Mexican-Americans has usually been of a descriptive nature and has dealt with issues such as patterns of language use, language loyalty, and language maintenance (Christian and Christian 1966; Fishman and Hofman 1966; Thompson 1974). Given the negative history of non-English language tolerance in the US (Fishman 1966), it is important to consider how the Mexican-American community views its own language varieties.[4] As stated by Penalosa, 'Language is used not only to communicate ideas,

---

[3] The term Mexican American used here refers to all people of Mexican descent residing in the United States. Two other terms often seen as interchangeable and used to refer to this same group are Mexican and Chicano. However, this author has chosen to use only one term for purposes of clarity.
[4] A brief review of the existing literature on attitudinal research towards Mexican American language varieties is presented here. For a more extensive and in-depth discussion of this research, please refer to Ryan and Carranza (1977).

feelings, and attitudes, it is also the object of ideas, feelings, and attitudes. Chicanos . . . have beliefs and attitudes about the way they and others talk or should talk' (1980, 180).

Several studies have attempted to research the interaction between Mexican-American language varieties. Politzer and Ramirez (1973a, 1973b) investigated the attitudes of Mexican-American and Anglo-American (grades 3, 6, 9, and 12) pupils toward English and Spanish guises. In the first study, Mexican-American students did not demonstrate different stereotypes for the two speech styles, while third and sixth grade Anglos upgraded English relative to Spanish. Several sub-groups rated Spanish more favourably (Mexican-Americans, females and older students). In the second study, ratings of third graders from a bilingual school were compared with third graders from a traditional monolingual English school. The upgrading of English by Anglo children in the bilingual school was less pronounced than those in the traditional school, while Spanish was rated more favourably by Mexican-American students in the bilingual programme.

Flores and Hopper (1975) asked Mexican-American adults and college students to evaluate speech samples (standard Spanish, standard English, Tex-Mex Spanish, and accented English). Although overall group ratings did not differ for standard Spanish and standard English, several subgroups showed a preference for Spanish. Those with 'Chicano' as preferred self-referent rated Tex-Mex Spanish higher than standard English, and individuals with low use of Spanish and those with at least some college education revealed a preference for standard Spanish over standard English.

Teitelbaum, Edwards and Hudson (1975) examined ethnic attitudes and second language acquisition by having university students perform a proficiency test and fill out a questionnaire designed to elicit attitudinal and demographic information. Results revealed very different patterns for students who were either of Spanish background (i.e. surnames, ancestry, mother tongue) or non-Spanish background. For the Spanish-background group, several factors were important: desire to study Spanish to preserve ethnic identity, expectation of using Spanish after completion of the course, positive attitudes toward Spanish language and culture, willingness to support Mexican-American culture and interest during the actual Spanish class. However, for the non-Spanish background group, the following factors were found: pro-American attitudes, favourable attitudes toward bilingualism and bilingual education, positive evaluation of Mexican-American traditions, and a desire to learn Spanish for travel and reasons of employment. Adorno (1973) interviewed Mexican-American parents regarding the importance of their children learning English and Spanish. Whereas English was considered important for practical reasons, Spanish was valued for idealistic and personal reasons. It seems as though the functional separation of Spanish and English was reflected in these parental attitudes.

To examine further the effects of the functional separation of English and Spanish, Carranza and Ryan (1975) elaborated the traditional evaluative reaction method by manipulating context (home *vs* school) as well as language (English *vs* Spanish). Adjective rating scales representing status- and solidarity-stressing dimensions were also employed (see Ryan, Giles, and Sebastian, this volume: ch. 1). The results for Anglo and Mexican-American high-school students revealed a preference by both groups for English in the school context and a slight preference for Spanish in the home context. While English was rated higher on both status and solidarity scales, the difference between English and Spanish was smaller for the solidarity ratings.

By the use of a mail questionnaire, Sole (1977) asked Mexican-American college students open-ended questions concerning language usage, language proficiency, and language attitudes. These students revealed high language loyalty toward Spanish. Most of them attributed greater expressiveness to Spanish than English for certain topics and situations. Spanish was considered more appropriate for cultural matters, intragroup interaction, and affective matters whereas English was deemed more appropriate for political, technical, academic, and occupational pursuits. The rationales in favour of Spanish are covered by three content categories: ideological, instrumental and affective. There were few overt negative responses to Spanish, and those were for pragmatic reasons – retarding effect on assimilation and lack of economic gains.

Ramirez, Arce-Torres and Politzer (1978) studied the attitudes of pupils and teachers toward various speech varieties (standard English, two types of hispanicized English, and code switching between Spanish and English). In general, (Anglo) teachers and (bilingual) pupils agreed in rating standard English higher than the other speech varieties. Teachers' attitudes were not changed by attendance at workshops, and pupils' evaluations of standard English over all others was positively related to pupils' achievement in reading and English (see Day, this volume: ch. 7).

Two studies have addressed language attitudes of Mexican-Americans by direct interview questions. Ryan and Carranza in an explanatory study in 1980 asked Mexican-American adolescents questions related to language attitudes and other cultural attitudes. Overall the students showed a slight preference for English, favourable attitude toward bilingualism, cultural allegiance favouring Mexico and a slight tendency toward authoritarianism. Although accentedness was seen as a slight handicap and the students revealed a certain degree of anomie, these findings were not statistically significant. In a more sophisticated second study (Carranza and Ryan, in press), the language attitudes and cultural attitudes of Mexican-American adults were investigated. The same three types of language attitude issues were addressed, but the language preference and attitude toward accentedness measures were elaborated in order to identify the distinct dimensions underlying each. Previous pilot work resulted in the following dimensions for language preference: affective, communicative, integrative and instrumental; and for attitude toward accentedness: general integrative, integrative, instrumental, and comfort (see Gardner, this volume: ch. 8). The adults revealed a slight preference for English, slight favourableness toward accentedness, strong support for bilingualism, slight cultural allegiance to Mexico, and high authoritarianism. Support for the multidimensionality of language preference and attitude toward accentedness was found, although not as pronounced for accentedness. More specifically, the adults made clear discriminations between various dimensions of language preference and also demonstrated positive attitudes toward accentedness without suffering feelings of alienation and personal disorganization.

In conclusion, it appears that the traditional abandonment of Spanish and preference for English among Mexican-Americans does not occur indiscriminately. These studies demonstrate that children, college students, and adults (including teachers) find occasions when Spanish is preferred rather than English. The use of a context variable also revealed preferences for Spanish on some occasions.

Language attitudes towards the Spanish spoken by Mexican-Americans have also been the topic of research efforts. This research has investigated the varieties of Spanish spoken and the role these varieties play in the development and maintenance of identity among Mexican-Americans. For example, Ornstein (1974) and Amastae and Elias-Olivares (1978) found that Mexican-American college students felt the Spanish spoken in the southwest was border slang. In another study Elias-Olivares (1976) also found a feeling of inferiority regarding their Spanish among older Mexican-Americans; yet younger Mexican-Americans typically regarded their way of speaking as a symbol of ethnic pride. The attempt to retain ingroup distinctiveness has been noted by Ramirez (1974) as a principal reason for the persistence of Mexican-American dialects. A pattern where Mexican-American college students showed greater appreciation for Spanish dialects is found in the work of Flores and Hopper (1975). Whereas the overall group of adults rated standard Spanish significantly more favourably than Tex-Mex, the college student subgroup (with 'Chicano' as their preferred self-referent) rated Tex-Mex higher than standard Spanish.

Utilizing an immigrant group with limited formal education, Cohen (1974) interviewed Mexican-American parents on attitudes toward Spanish. Clearly, the majority of the parents thought the best Spanish was spoken in Mexico, followed by Spain. A preference for Spanish as spoken in Europe was expressed most frequently by males, participants with higher socioeconomic levels, and by respondents with higher proficiency in Spanish and English. Although very few studies have been performed with reactions to Mexican-American Spanish, the 'mixed' results discussed here, especially with the younger population, merit further investigation.

In contrast to Mexican-American Spanish, Mexican-American English varieties have received much more attention in attitudinal research. Given the large numbers that speak some type of Mexican-American English, even native speakers of English, Ortego (1969) and Metcalf (1974) have argued for the recognition of Mexican-American English as a dialect. Recent studies lend support to such an argument. As Arthur, Farrar and Bradford (1974) have mentioned, the variety of English spoken by Mexican-Americans may not represent the unsuccessful attempt of native Spanish speakers to learn English, but rather the successful attempt of native English speakers to produce the English dialect of their community. In his analysis of 1970 census data Thompson (1974) examined language loyalty and noted a gradual shift in use from Spanish to English. As the shift progresses, Thompson suggested that the language problems of Mexican-American children may come from a Mexican-American English dialect rather than from Spanish interference.

The presence of an accent in speaking English has produced many reactions from those who speak it. Many Mexican-American parents do not want their children to be saddled with that handicap (Barker 1947; Krear 1969) and have made concerted efforts to discard their own Mexican accents (Tovar 1973). Ulibarri (1968) states that many feel an accent will be a stigma and vitally limit an individual's opportunities for social advancement. The diversity of attitudes toward accented speech is highlighted by Thompson (1975) in his study of Mexican-American male adults from Austin, Texas. Each adult's speech was analysed and placed in one of three categories: standard English, regional English, and Spanish-influenced English. The findings revealed that their English pronunciation was related to their attitude toward accent. Those who had a non-ethnic regional pronunciation believed that accent was of primary importance in obtaining employment, and most reported having consciously developed their accents. On the other hand, males with standard or Spanish-influenced English indicated that the criterion for job suitability was the ability to do the job, not accent.

In a comparison of standard and accented English, Politzer and Ramirez (1973a, 1973b) found that Mexican and Anglo-American children in both studies downgraded the accented speech relative to standard English. Brekke (1973) elicited attitudes toward standard and Mexican-American accented English from both adolescent and pre-adolescent Anglo and Mexican-American students. On speech scales, the older students strongly preferred standard English while the younger group, although still favouring the standard, rated the accented English as more correct, acceptable and valuable than the other groups. On speaker characteristics, the older group also placed more of a gap between the two speech styles. In addition the Mexican-American students rated accented English speakers significantly more favourably than did Anglo students. Wheeler, Wilson and Tarantola (1976) had grade-school children (grades 2, 4, and 6) listen to representatives of five language groups (white Southern, white standard, Arapahoe, black Southern, and Mexican-American). Findings revealed that dialect functions as an important cue in the judgement of others, and it appears that linguistic stereotyping begins quite early in a child's social development (see Day, this volume: ch. 7).

Attitudinal research among college students has also revealed negative reactions to speakers of accented English. Arthur *et al.* (1974) found that Anglo-American college students rated standard English speakers higher on status-related scores than Mexican-American English speakers, despite the fact that all the speakers were identified as being Mexican-Americans; and, as previously mentioned, Flores and Hopper (1975) discovered that every group rated standard English higher than Mexican-American accented English, except those who chose 'Chicano' as a self-referent.

Teachers' attitudes toward accented English can have quite an influence on the students in the classroom (Bailey and Galvan 1977; Edwards, this volume: ch. 2). Williams and associates (1976) have conducted considerable research focusing on teachers' language attitudes. Among the studies is one of particular interest in which in-service teachers (Anglo, black, Mexican American) evaluated videotapes representing Anglo, black, and Mexican American children from lower and middle classes. The teachers tended to give global evaluations of the language along the dimensions of ethnicity–nonstandardness and confidence–eagerness. Black teachers generally rated the minority children as less ethnic–nonstandard than did Anglo teachers. Anglo and Mexican American teachers both rated Anglo children as more confident and less ethnic-sounding and better in language arts and related subjects. The middle-status Mexican American children were rated as more confident and better students in all academic areas than the low-status Mexican American children. The social status differentiation was more important for evaluations of Mexican American than for Anglo children.

Despite the fact that ethnic speech serves as an ingroup symbol of pride and solidarity (Tovar 1973), Mexican American accented speech has still been associated with low social status. Given this contrast, Ryan and Carranza (1975) sought to find support for the functional separation of Mexican American speech styles. Anglo, Black, and Mexican American female high-school students rated male˙ speakers of standard English and Mexican American accented English. Contrasts of context (home–school) and rating scale (solidarity-stressing and status-stressing) were represented in the study. The standard English speakers received the more positive ratings in all cases; however, the differencs were greater in the school context and on status-stressing scales. Also, the Anglo students rated the accented speakers significantly lower on status scales than either the Black or Mexican American students. Findings revealed that the student raters reacted to the appropriateness of the speech style for the situation (home or school) and differentiated between types of rating scales (solidarity or status stressing).

Having found that standard English and Mexican American accented English elicit differential stereotyping, Ryan and associates then sought to discover whether reactions to varying degrees of accentedness are categorical or gradually shifting. A study on Black English (Baird 1969) revealed that even though the number of nonstandard features in the speech samples presented gradually increased, a minimum amount of non-standardness was sufficient to elicit the stereotype of a Black. It seems that the speech only served to identify and reinforce the ethnic background of the speakers. However, does this same situation exist for Mexican American speech?

An issue quite relevant to the relationship between evaluation reactions and accented speech is whether or not raters can detect varying degrees of accentedness. Brennan, Ryan and Dawson (1975) found that non-linguistically trained college students reliably rated variations in accentedness of Spanish-English bilinguals, and their ratings correlated significantly with the actual number of nonstandard features. A second study (Ryan, Carranza and Moffie 1977) used the same speech samples and further confirmed the reliability of the ratings. In addition, the college students made fine discriminations in rating a speaker's personality and speech characteristics on the basis of accentedness. More specifically, the Anglo students gave increasingly greater negative reactions to speakers as their accentedness also increased.

In an effort to contrast outgroup (Anglo) and ingroup (Mexican American) ratings, Ryan, Carranza and Moffie (1975) had Mexican American students rate Mexican American speakers, representing a wide range of accentedness. The results indicated that foreign-born students demonstrated a high level of agreement on accentedness ratings, but the native-born did not. The foreign-born rated the speakers more favourably as their accentedness increased, whereas, for the native-born students, more favourable reactions were accorded to the least accented speakers. Although most studies have shown a downgrading of nonstandard varieties, this upgrading by foreign-born students may partially be supported by the work of Dworkin (1965, 1971). He found that foreign-born Mexican Americans held a more positive self-image than many native-born (1965) and, in a second investigation, that the more time spent in the US by the foreign-born the less positive their self-image (1971). It may be the case that foreign-born, with a better self-image, have a more favourable and supportive view of accented speakers; and this support may decrease the longer the person stays in this country because of exposure to prejudice and discrimination against people of Mexican descent.

Several studies have provided further support for the work of Ryan and colleagues. Utilizing paired-comparison and criterion-referenced techniques to scale the speech of accented speakers Galvan, Pierce and Underwood (1975, 1976) asked teacher candidates to identify the degree of accentedness and assess stereotypes towards Mexican American accented speakers. Judgements were related to the degree of accentedness in the speaker, with the extreme speakers (most accented and least accented) receiving correspondingly extreme scores on both personality and speech scales. Brennan and Brennan (1981a, 1981b) explored the relationship between degree of accent and evaluative reactions of raters toward Mexican American speakers. An accentedness index score (based on linguists' scorings of selected nonstandard pronunciations) was previously collected for these speakers and had been established for each speaker. Anglo and Mexican American students estimated the degree of accentedness for each speaker and rated them on status and solidarity scales. Findings revealed that the accentedness index score, accent estimation scores and status ratings were all highly correlated. As the degree of accentedness increased, the student raters gave significantly lower status ratings. No relationship between accentedness and solidarity ratings occurred. It is indeed encouraging to discover that different methods for assessing degree of accentedness can be used and still yield comparable results when correlated with personality and speech characteristic scales.

In an extension of the studies heretofore mentioned, Ryan and associates have also attempted to view social judgements of accented speech by other significant social categories (e.g. social class). The idea that an accent may be downgraded largely because of social class assumptions extends the notion of the class-related standard developed by Giles and Powesland (1975). Ryan and Sebastian (1980) investigated the impact that social class and speech style have on evaluative reactions of accented speakers. Anglo American college students rated standard English and Spanish-accented speakers presented as either lower-class or middle-class individuals, on status, solidarity, stereotype, and speech characteristics, as well as social distance judgements. Lower-class accented speakers were perceived much less favourably than the lower-class standard speakers, while the differences associated with accented and standard middle-class speakers were smaller. The social class manipulation greatly influenced judgements toward the accented speakers.

Sebastian, Ryan, and Corso (in press) addressed several important questions related to the influence of social class: what assumptions do listeners actually make regarding Spanish-accented speakers when social class information is not provided?; and, is social class information associated with perceived belief and attitude similarity? In this study, Anglo college students listened to standard English and Spanish-accented English speakers, with the accented speakers being from three levels of accentedness (low, medium, and high). After listening to each speaker the students indicated the speaker's social class, evaluated his personality on several scales, indicated a perceived belief and attitude similarity and judged social distance relationships. The students then listened to a second random order of the speakers, rated each speaker's speech and identified him as either Mexican American or Anglo. Significant effects for speech style were found for every dependent measure, with the reactions generally becoming more negative as accentedness increased. Social class assumptions were important mediators of other judgements made regarding the speakers.

In another study attempting to understand the minority situation from an outgroup perspective, Sebastian, Ryan, Keogh and Schmidt (1980) introduced the concept of negative affect in speech style evaluations. Listening to speakers of non-standard languages arouses negative affect resulting from difficulty in basic under-standing, consequent difficulties in interpersonal communication, and/or task performance based on the nonstandard message. Thus, the speakers arouse negative affect and are consequently negatively evaluated. It should be noted that in this study the explicit purpose was one of communication, with a secondary purpose of evaluation of the speakers. There were two parts of this study and both were presented as colour-recognition studies. The results indicated that colour-recognition accuracy was significantly influenced by both noise and accent alone, as well as in combination. Speakers heard through a noisy background were down-graded suggesting that negative affect associated with a speaker leads to negative evaluation. Accented speakers received more negative responses than standard speakers on most measures, including several social evaluation scales. These findings suggest that serious attention be given to the negative affect mechanism involved in the social evaluation of nonstandard speech styles.

These later studies have uncovered an interesting area in language attitudinal research: the applied sociolinguistic setting. Whereas most previous Hispanic studies have only looked at the affective nature of nonstandard speech styles, this work makes important insights into the behavioural dimension (see Sebastian and Ryan, in press, for further discussion). Research of this type has important impli-cations in regard to how people behave given their language attitudes (see Giles and Powesland, 1975). This new research dimension helps in Hispanic language attitudes create a link between the traditional type of evaluative reaction research and the type focusing on the applied setting (see Giles and Ryan, this volume: ch. 13).

The majority of these research efforts on attitudes toward Mexican American English varieties have been primarily focused on the attitudes within the edu-cational domain (e.g., students, teachers, adults with children in school). However, Hopper and colleagues have sought to look at attitudes as they relate to another domain – work (see Kalin, this volume: ch. 9). In Hopper and Williams (1973) employment interviewers listened to tapes with four speech samples: standard English, Black English, Spanish-influenced English, and southern white dialect. These speakers answered questions representative of those used in job interviews without reference to particular job categories. After listening to the speech samples, the employment interviewers were asked to describe their reactions. From the descriptive terms included in the spontaneous reactions, evaluative scales were constructed. The ratings provided by another sample of employers were analysed into four factors: intelligence and competence; agreeableness; self-assurance; and Anglo-like non-Anglo-like. Seven job scales were developed and placed in a two-factor model: (1) executive–labourer composite and (2) clerical–technician occupations. Two trends seemed to merge: (1) the more a job involves executive or leadership skills the more important language attitudes are for predicting hiring decisions; and (2) ratings of intelligence –competence are the best predictors among the speech attitudes.

In a follow-up study (de la Zerda and Hopper 1979), employment interviewers at large businesses in San Antonio, Texas listened to English speech samples of Mexican American males simulating employment interviews. The speech samples were characterized by varying degrees of accentedness, and the interviewers were asked to indicate the likelihood of a speaker's being hired for each of three level positions (supervisor, skilled technician and semi-skilled worker). The higher the position level the more important were language attitudes in the hiring predictions. Standard speakers were favoured for supervisor and accented speakers favoured for semi-skilled worker.

There is another focus of attitudinal research on Mexican American speech that bears mentioning – the phenomenon of code-switching. Most studies that have included this variety have classified it either in terms of having a Spanish-base or English-base. Although a few authors have labelled this variety a separate dialect in itself (Coltharp 1975, Ramirez 1978), there seems to be little evidence at this time for such a decision. Perhaps future attitudinal research on Mexican American speech can help fill this void.

Critical issues and future directions

In this review of attitudes toward Hispanic language varieties, several core issues dealing with the topic become apparent. Most notable are the methodological considerations involved in conducting language attitude studies. In addition, the development of interdisciplinary models for explaining language attitudes must be a focus of future research.

Central to the methodological dimension is the question of which techniques are utilized to collect language attitudinal data. Many of the studies on Hispanics have utilized indirect measurement techniques. These indirect techniques can be in various forms, ranging from the matched-guise and verbal-guise strategies utilized in many of the speech style evaluation studies to the participant observation, content analysis, and case study approaches found in the Fishman *et al.* study of the Puerto Rican community (1971). In contrast to these indirect methods are the direct measurement techniques which involve questions that specifically address language attitudes. Excellent examples of this methodological strategy are the survey questionnaire and interview studies which have been conducted in Hispanic communities (Carranza 1977; Centro de Estudios Puertorriquenos 1978). A review of the techniques utilized in language attitude research on Hispanics reveals that indirect measurement has been primarily used in the United States and direct measurement has dominated outside the US. The use of both types of techniques when examining the same issues for the same population must be encouraged.

The recommendation to utilize both direct and indirect measures brings into focus the related methodological issue of triangulation. Triangulation is the process by which a social phenomenon is observed and measured by various techniques. An excellent example of the triangulation process is provided by the work of Fishman *et al.* (1971) who measured the language attitudes of Puerto Ricans with multiple methodological techniques, including interviews (direct), content analysis (indirect), and performance testing (indirect). Moreover, this project demonstrates a certain 'triangulation of expertise' since its research team was headed by a sociologist, a psychologist and a linguist. Given that the topic of language attitudes has been conceptualized and operationalized by researchers from various disciplines, it follows that measurement techniques should be developed from an interdisciplinary perspective in which the contributions of the different disciplines complement, rather than compete against each other.

Another methodological issue concerns the range of language variations examined. Most frequently, the focus has been upon two distinct languages (e.g. Spanish–English or Guarani–Spanish). Even when within-language contrasts have been investigated, seldom have studies incorporated more than two varieties for comparative purposes. It is important for future research to consider the whole continuum of speech alternatives available within a given speech community, rather than severely limiting the comparisons to two or three varieties. This expanded speech continuum would then include language varieties which are often seen as less prestigious (e.g. jibaro, calo, and jopara) and which are frequently overlooked in attitudinal research.

Speech style has also been somewhat narrowly viewed in that speakers have been most frequently asked to read the same brief passages in order to control for various confounding variables. However, some researchers (e.g. Williams *et al.* 1976) believe that casual spontaneous speech on a specified topic is preferable to readings because of the variability among individuals in oral reading ability. As well, reading naturally enhances attention to one's speech and inhibits use of less standard pronunciations. It would seem that future research in this field could indeed integrate wider varieties of speech style (e.g. reading, formal, casual, intimate).

In addition, the effects of context, topic, and domain have often been neglected. Many of the original evaluative reaction studies tended to use formal academic passages whereas most of the research on nonstandard Hispanic varieties has utlilized informal topics in order to elicit the maximum degree of nonstandardness from speakers. Ryan and Carranza (1977) have pointed out that choice of topic (as well as context and domain) may significantly alter listener reactions. Indeed, only studies which manipulate such situational variables will be able to observe accurate attitudinal reflections of the functional separation of Hispanic varieties.

Another important consideration is the selection of scales or dimensions along which speech varieties are evaluated. Since functional separation is such a critical aspect of many Hispanic speech communities, it is necessary that the scales or questions used allow the opportunity to examine the extent to which contrasting varieties reflect different values and different prototypical situations. Many of the studies reviewed in this chapter consider only the overall favourability of reactions (i.e. acceptable–unacceptable) while others consider each adjective scale separately (e.g., fluent–non fluent, good–bad, educated–uneducated). Williams and his associates (1976) selected a set of adjective scales presumed on the basis of pilot work to reflect the raters' natural framework for judgement and then employed a factor analytic approach to identify the major dimensions underlying those judgements: ethnic–nonstandard and confidence–eagerness. Some researchers have developed indices of status and solidarity with the belief that many ethnic and social groups tend to evaluate competing language varieties along these two sometimes-conflicting theoretical dimensions (see Ryan *et al.* and Giles and Ryan; this volume: chs. 1 and 13 respectively). Also, Carranza and Ryan (in press) illustrate how a greater variety of dimensions can be theoretically derived by considering the functions of particular languages for various groups. The search for a general multidimensional structure of language attitudes (e.g. one which would apply to all minority groups) as well as the examination of the specific structures relevant to specific groups must continue.

Another topic for discussion concerns the characteristics of the subjects involved in the attitudinal research. Most of the studies reviewed have involved students (in elementary and secondary schools as well as university), teachers, and parents of students. Even though both ingroup (Hispanic) and outgroup (non-Hispanic) perspectives have often been considered, it is time to go beyond this institutional bias and to examine language attitudes in non-educational settings. Investigations of the impact of language attitudes in the work domain (e.g. Hopper and Williams 1973; Rey 1977) are steps in the right direction. Another welcome addition is the characterization of the role of language attitudes in the process of psychotherapy (Marcos 1979, 1980; Marcos *et al.* 1977). These types of studies reinforce the idea that language attitudes do not only exist in an educational setting, but rather have far-reaching impact in other areas (see Kalin, this volume: ch. 9). Future work should begin to consider ignored areas, such as medicine, law and religion. It is important to know what attitudes professionals and policy makers have toward Hispanic language varieties since they influence the societal experiences of Hispanics on a day-to-day basis.

Accompanying this further investigation of outgroup research should be an expanded analysis of attitudinal variations within the ingroup population and of their correlates. The diversity found within the Hispanic population demands an increase in the amount of ingroup comparisons – not only on the national level (e.g. Cubans, Puerto Ricans, and Chicanos) but also on an international level (e.g. US and Spain). These extensions would complement the existing body of research in which some basic categories (e.g. rural *vs* urban, native-born *vs* foreign-born, long-term *vs* recent immigrants) have been used as well as some basic demographic characteristics (e.g. age, sex, educational level, income).

A final issue relates to theoretical implications. The field of language attitudes in general has been described in terms of its lack of theoretical development (Giles 1979a; Williams 1974), and Hispanic research does not provide an exception to this theoretical deficit (see Giles and Ryan; this volume: ch. 13). There is an urgent need to integrate methodological techniques with theoretical frameworks in order to explain our findings accurately and in order to advance the theoretical base of the field. As with the development of methodology, the integration of disciplinary perspectives into truly interdisciplinary explanatory models is essential.

Within the past decade, a significant number of studies concerning attitudes toward Hispanic language varieties have been conducted, and more are needed. One major research effort that has not been discussed in this review is the National Survey of People of Mexican Descent conducted in 1979 by the Institute of Social Research at the University of Michigan. It was a national sample of approximately 1,000 Mexican Americans, and the data collected included a section dealing with language attitudes. The results are currently being analysed and will undoubtedly add a considerable amount of information to a Hispanic language attitude data base.

In conclusion, this review has attempted to demonstrate the tremendous amount of diversity that exists within the Hispanic population in the world. It is hoped that this review will contribute to the further development of attitude research on Hispanic language varieties.

5

Gender: how she speaks[1]

Cheris Kramarae

'Attitudes toward women's speech' is merely a *topic* for some people, but a very present ingredient of life for many others.

In August 1975 Angela Rippon became the first woman to read the televised Nine O'clock News on BBC-1. The event was reported in newspapers throughout Great Britain. She said later that she had been very nervous: 'I was terribly conscious of reading the National News, in capitals, to about nine million people. I knew that if I made a hash of it no woman would be allowed another chance for at least five years' ([London] *Daily Telegraph* 8 Sept. 1975).

She was conscious of the restrictions on women's speech, and the evaluation of women's voices. And she knew broadcasting history. For example, while several women announcers were heard on the air in earlier years in what the BBC called 'experiments', BBC officials usually quickly labelled these experiments failures, and fired the women (except during WWII when women, needed as announcers, received good ratings in the press from BBC officials and the listening audience). Women in other countries have faced similar barriers.[2]

The reactions to women as possible and actual public speakers can most usefully be analysed through a general discussion of the attitudes toward women's voices. In the title of this chapter I call attention to the prevalent association of gender with female. No one would expect a chapter on gender and attitudes toward speech to focus on issues and research involving primarily attitudes toward male speech; females are more likely than are males to be considered biological beings.[3] Differing attitudes about the importance of this topic have resulted in research that is itself

---

[1] I thank Howard Giles, Ellen Bouchard Ryan and Lona Jean Turner for their comments on an earlier version. I am also appreciative of the help I received from the personnel of the BBC archives.

[2] See Strainchamps (1974), Baehr (1980), Butler and Paisley (1980). Gelfman (1976), Isber and Cantor (1975), and King and Scott (1977) for discussions of the types of arguments against women's on-air voices, and the news coverage of the relatively few women who are employed as news announcers. Angela Rippon is known as a careful, clear announcer. But several years after she began announcing, newspapers were still calling attention to her as an announcer to be judged and labelled in a different way than her male colleagues. She is called 'a popular lass', 'delectable', 'dishy Angie' – and 'Legs Rippon' or 'The Legs'. (Her picture, in a dance dress with a leg showing, was taken by a BBC employee from a film of a TV Christmas programme, sold without the permission of Rippon or BBC officials, and printed in the *Daily Mirror*. This event was widely publicized.)

[3] Social scientists usually prefer biological, rather than social, explanations for differences between females and males. Bart (1977), Unger (1979), and Rosaldo (1980), for example, write of researchers' preference for biological explanations, and of the consequences of that for social studies in general. I am using the term *gender* rather than *sex* to call attention to the social construction of the division female and male (see Kessler and McKenna 1978).

gender-linked. In most countries, the research on language and gender has been done primarily by women. However, the informal, non-scholarly discussion of language and gender issues in the popular media has been conducted primarily by men, who are much more likely to have access to public forums and to employment as columnists, editorial writers, and social critics. The content and intent of the two groups of researchers and writers appear to be quite different, and the inter-action between the two groups is itself a topic of study which can give us information about the creation and maintenance of stereotypes and the uses people make of their stereotypes (see Kramarae 1981; Martyna 1980a, 1980b).

I am defining *attitude* as an organization of motivational, emotional and judge-mental processes with respect to, in this case, the way women and men do and should speak, an organization which has a directive impact on what the individual sees and hears, thinks and does. (This definition follows those of Krech and Crutchfield 1948, and Allport 1966.) *Stereotypes* are defined as rigid attitudes about categories and objects which actually vary over time and situations – here, the attribution of fixed qualities to women and men and their speech. Included in this overview is material on attitudes about one's own language use and about the linguistic features stereotypically associated with females and males, and the impact of the attitudes on social interaction. I begin by mentioning the types of gender-related speech differences which have been found by British and North American researchers. This material provides a context for discussion of what follows – the types of stereotypes and evaluations of women's and men's speech as revealed through study of popular media and through empirical research; the connections of these stereotypes with other variables of social status; suggestions concerning some of the consequences of the attitudes toward women's and men's speech; and questions and analyses to guide our observations and research.

Gender-related linguistic differences

Women's speech, or men's speech, can not be defined apart from discussions of attitudes. The speech traits stereotypically associated with females are often posited as characteristics peculiar to them, and are often discussed as basic identi-fying characteristics of the social group female. However, as several scholars have recently emphasized (e.g. Smith 1979), there is no evidence for categorical speech differences between men and women. Brown and Levinson (1979) point out that most speech markers of gender either result from the hierarchical relationship between the genders, and thus are only indirect (although important) markers of gender, or result from the different social networks of women and men. The recent reviews of gender-related language research (e.g. Haas 1979; Kramer *et al.* 1978; Kramarae 1981; Philips 1980; Smith 1979) indicate what some of these markers are. For example, women are more likely to use standard (or 'correct') forms (Labov 1972; Trudgill 1975b). Nichols (1978), in her work in South Carolina Black communities, has found that differences between the men and women in their use of standard forms and of creole can be explained in terms of the speakers' different social mobility and job opportunities. If, for example, the good, accessible jobs for women are primarily in teaching or secretarial work and the jobs for men are in construction, women will be more likely than men to learn and use standard speech.

Pitch, which does distinguish most female and male voices, is seemingly a result of clear biological differences. Yet, cultural assumptions about what a 'man's voice' should sound like and what a 'woman's voice' should sound like probably influence a speaker's pitch – as well as other characteristics of speech style. Research from Great Britain and the US (see McConnell-Ginet 1978b; Smith 1979) indicates that women tend to use more rising tones and a wider pitch range than men do; these are culturally rather than biologically based differences. Most adults listening to short speech samples of pre-pubescent children are able to judge correctly the gender of each child (Edwards 1979c; Sachs 1975). That is, the adults were hearing vocal differences which could not be predicted solely from knowledge of the vocal tract size of each child. Adults and children listening to tapes can more often correctly identify the gender of a 7-year-old child than a 3-year-old, suggesting that girls and boys learn, during pre-and early-elementary school years, the speech rhythms associated with females and males (Fichtelius *et al.* 1980). This kind of communicative competence appears to be learned at an earlier age than children learn the syntax and lexical patterns stereotypically associated with men and women (Edelsky 1976).

The work on speech fluency, interruptions, verbosity, speaking time, topic and style is more limited in quantity, sometimes contradictory, but potentially very valuable in describing how social relationships among women and men are presently organized. Recently some researchers have analysed the *social functions* of the speech variants they are studying. For example, Fishman (1980), transcribing the conversations of three white, middle-class female/male couples, found that the women used 2 1/2 times more questions than did the men. Instead of explaining this difference in terms of gender identity and socialization, she considers the immediate context and the socially structured power relations. The women, she concludes, are speaking creatively, asking questions because of the conversational power of questions, in response to the problem they have of starting and keeping a conversation going with the men. Studying patterns of interruptions in male/female conversations from tapes made in several locations, Zimmerman and West (1975) found that males made almost all the interruptions, using them to control topics of conversation. Here and in other recent research the questions, hypotheses and explanations involved come from the current women's movement, but utilize some of the traditional disciplinary tools (McConnell-Ginet 1978a). (Some of the same questions and hypotheses were discussed by women [e.g. Gilman 1911; Parsons 1913] early in the century in the US and Great Britain, but these discussions were not recorded in the scholarly bibliographies and have only been recently rediscovered.) Increasingly, researchers examine the speech of men and women through a discussion of racial, economic and political structures. That is, they are attempting to provide a context which acknowledges and describes the particular situation and also the general social relationships of women and men and the ways they affect everyday interaction.[4]

We would expect to find gender-differences in language use because of men's and women's different social status, resources and opportunities. But much of the research, until very recently, was based on correlational study which, for example,

[4] A number of researchers (see *Signs: Journal of Women in Culture and Society* 5 (4), 1980; Goffman 1977) are discussing the manner in which the prevalent or dominant concepts about human sexuality and sex differences are diffused through many aspects of social experience.

looks for links between gender and a particular linguistic unit, without much consideration of the specific situation – including the relative status of the
speakers – or of the interaction variables such as topic shifts, agreement or
encouragement 'fillers', and interruption patterns. So we have formal evidence of
relatively few differences which seem to distinguish female and male speech. And
the differences which have been documented in, for example, intonation and pitch,
do not in themselves seem to justify the differing evaluation of women's and men's
speech. In the following sections I detail some of the attitudes and evaluations and
consider some explanations for their longevity and strength.

An historical perspective

Through an historical approach we can learn how our present attitudes toward
women's and men's speech were shaped (see St Clair, this volume: ch. 10, for the
value of the historical approach). This in turn encourages a study perspective more
open to consideration of the dynamics of speech and social structure, and change.
An initial inspection reveals that we have many more records detailing what men
have said about women's speech than vice versa. Our knowledge about women's
words on men's speech is increasing as more researchers become interested in
women's culture, but this information comes primarily from archives of letters and
diaries rather than from public records, sermons, advice books and school
materials. This historical material indicates that a serious effort to study attitudes
will include attention to the differences in social power between the genders, and
attention to the relative resources each gender has had available to influence the
speech of the other. This type of historical study has not yet been written, but we
do have access to some material which can guide our searches.

Proverbs

Some of the European and North American proverbs about women's and men's
speech apply to speakers regardless of gender. But the number of proverbs which
set forth men's wisdom on the qualities and quantity of women's speech is great.
Some express the disapproval of women who are heard as speaking manlike – for
example, 'crowing louder than the cock'. Many proverbs deal with women's noise
(e.g. 'Where there are women and geese there's noise'), unending speech (e.g. 'A
woman's tongue is the last thing about her that dies'), irrationality (e.g. 'Winter's
weather and women's words often change'), gossip (e.g. 'Tell nothing to a woman
unless you would have the world know'). A few proverbs deal with the possible
virtues of women's counsel (e.g. 'A woman's advice helps at a pinch'), but such
proverbs are few, and are usually qualified. (Written records of proverbs
concerning women's speech include Apperson 1929; Kin 1955; Tilley 1950.)

   These records do not tell us the amount of usage or impact of the proverbs. But
we can see the continuing popularity of the proverbs in many contemporary jokes
and cartoons, as we continue our study of the folk-linguistics of women's speech.

Advice Books

Proverbs, cartoons, indeed most records of a culture, only indirectly reflect the attitudes of a culture. The advice books, on the other hand, forthrightly declare the rights and wrongs of behaviour including speech. Advice books – from the courtesy books of the Middle Ages to the contemporary assertiveness-training volumes popular now, especially in the US – are intended to provide self-training for women and men who want to do and say what is proper and/or effective. From 1830 to 1876 more than 100 new guides appeared in the US – most of them written by Americans. Certainly not all social classes were equally interested in the books, but as one historian has pointed out, the etiquette rules 'far from being apart from life, are a veritable part of life, revealing [our] hopes, standards and striving' (Schlesinger 1946, vii).

A survey of more than 100 of these books published in the past 150 years reveals a striking similarity of advice on speech behaviour given through the years (Bornstein 1978; Eble 1976; Kramer 1975a). Most of the books and advice about speech are directed to women. While the books indicate that women are innately more modest and proper than men, evidently a lot of care must be taken by women and men to insure that these natural differences surface.

A very brief summary and some representative statements illustrate the concerns. Women are thought more likely to deserve the label gossiper. In *She-Manners* the author (Loeb 1959) in a chapter titled 'Gossip Not' warns that gossiping is not conversation but malice. His companion book *He-Manners* (1954) has no such chapter heading although he suggests that men should not make derogatory remarks or questionable jokes about others. This is one instance of many where behaviour by women is given one label while similar behaviour by men is called something else.

Women should learn about the topics favoured by men, while realizing that women will never be able to discuss these topics authoritatively with men. While mutual interests are hard for boys and girls to find, 'a safe subject is always the boy himself' (Witan 1940, 25). The problem of conversation between the sexes is made difficult because when girls are together they 'chatter' endlessly about clothes and dates, while boys together 'discuss' sports (Hertz 1950, 30). Women, naturally more modest and reticent, should take care that their control over their behaviour extends to their thinking. One of the Emily Post's etiquette editions states:

> The perfect secretary should forget that she is a human being, and be the most completely efficient aid at all times and on all subjects. . . . She should respond to [her boss's] requirements exactly as a machine responds to the touch of lever or accelerator. If he says 'Good morning,' she answers 'Good morning' with a smile and cheerfully. She does not volunteer a remark – unless she has messages of importance to give him. If he says nothing, she says nothing, and she does not even mentally notice that he has said nothing. (1945, 548)

Women are also cautioned to keep their voices low, soft, and agreeable. A number of the books advise women to avoid stating an opinion unless it is accompanied with a qualifying remark such as 'I think this is so.' (The use of qualifying remarks such as 'I think maybe' is judged by university students to make women seem less intelligent than men [Kramer 1974b; Siegler and Siegler 1976].) The directive is precise in a 1947 guidebook: 'Once during an evening is enough for a women to state a definite and unqualified opinion – and even then it should be something constructive or a defence of some one or something' (Wilson 1947, 206). This caution to women against making declarative statements appears related to the frequent discussions in the books about the ways women's thinking and speech deviates from men's: Women are said to be intuitive rather than analytical. One author adds that if 'by some freak of nature' a woman should shine at activities which take a logical mind, 'it will be found that she has a man's mind' (Wright 1936, 99, 101, 103).[5]

The advice books indicate that the types of beliefs and concerns about women's speech have remained much the same through the years. The recent assertiveness training books for women (e.g. Baer 1976; Phelps and Austin 1975) do advise them to be more independent in their speech, to speak up with confidence and honesty for what they want. However, the focus is still on the speech of the individual woman and on the changes she is to make, rather than on the institutional standards for, and particular restrictions on, women's actions. The recent discussions by men of the ways men can learn how to express emotions also focus on individual behaviour rather than on the inexpressiveness of men in terms of the social and sexual division of labour (Sattel 1976).

Public speaking

A study of other historical records leads to much the same conclusion about the longevity and consistency of men's complaints about women's speech. An initial examination of 150 years of women's attempts to win public speaking rights (Kramarae 1978) indicates that women today face some of the same opposition as did Lucy Stone and other nineteenth-century female reform workers. One of Stone's lectures was announced with criticism of a woman's 'manlike' speech activity similar to that contained in many proverbs: 'I am requested to say that a hen will undertake to crow like a cock in the town hall this afternoon at five o'clock.' (See O'Connor 1954 for a discussion of the struggles of some of the nineteenth-century reform leaders in the US. Some of the women wrote their speeches, and sat silent on the platform while male relatives or friends read the manuscript.)

The public statements about women's on-air voices, made by officials of radio and TV companies in the US and Great Britain, demonstrate that contemporary attitudes of the relative merits of women's and men's speech are not an aberration of history, but a continuation. Public discussions of the limitations of women's voices for announcing began in the early days of radio. For example, in 1926 British newspapers carried reports that BBC officials had decided not to employ women as announcers. One news report of the decision began, 'That women would be hopeless as broadcast announcers is the considered opinion of a number of officials of the BBC'. One official was quoted as saying that women 'are not suitable, especially for the reading of news bulletins'.

A study of English broadcasting officials' restrictions and pronouncements on women's speech through the 1970s provides a series of statements on some of the perceived limitations of women's speech as compared to men's, and also illustrates the complexity of the issues involved in discussions of attitudes toward women's

[5] The advice in these books is supported with the advice in many other printed and spoken instructions to women. An illustrative advertisement in the March 1980 issue of *Working Woman* advises, 'Look, all it takes to make your point is to keep your message short and your lashes long' and adds, 'Don't You Love Being a Woman? Max Factor'.

and men's speech. While women as a group were thought to have inadequate announcing voices, men of the 'wrong' class or educational background were also turned down as announcers during much of the BBC history. Further, the general economic situation and the specific economic policies of the government have had an impact on where and when women could talk without immediate criticism. In what they called an 'experiment', in 1933 BBC officials employed a woman announcer at Broadcasting House in London. She began her job amid a great deal of media discussion. While newspapers columnists and the listeners they interviewed immediately after her voice was first heard on air admired her 'cool, business-like, commanding . . . authoritative' tone (*News Chronicle* 29 July 1933), several months later she was fired; the 'experiment' had failed. Initially BBC officials said the problems were 'technical', but later they were quoted as saying that they had received thousands of complaints, stating that the woman should not be receiving a large, government salary because she was the wife of a pensioned naval officer (*Daily Express* 7 March 1934). The salary, unlike that of her male colleagues, had been widely reported in newspapers at the beginning of the experiment. During the Depression in Great Britain many women, if they married, were compelled to resign government and private industry jobs. Other critics suggested that it had become clear to the BBC officials that, if she were to have a permanent announcing position, they would need to hire a second woman announcer to preserve the anonymity of announcers, a practice of the BBC at that time.

The study of the public expression of the attitudes toward women as on-air announcers (in the US as well as in Great Britain), combined with other historical material on the evaluation of and restrictions against women speaking not only the news but even just speaking, helps explain the support for and extent of the contemporary expressions of attitudes toward women's speech. This material also suggests the importance of studying the functions (apart from studying the effects) of official and 'popular' statements concerning women's speech, showing concerns with the goals (as they are perceived by women and by men) of the speakers and writers, as well as the interaction of attitudes toward men's and women's speech with economic variables, government policies, and various traditional supports for the policies.

Stereotypes and standards

We have evidence that females and males agree, generally, on the gender stereotypes of speech.[6] For example, college students, given cartoon captions but not the cartoons, assigned gender to the speakers of the captions with agreement for more than 75 per cent of the statements, and women and men in response to open-ended questions generally listed the same cues for their decisions (Kramer 1974a, 1974b).

---

[6] Studies based on questionnaires have shown similarities in the stereotypes women and men have of their speech. How much does it matter, however, that the latter have, during the past hundred years, controlled the printing presses which have disseminated primarily men's ideas about themselves and women? Recent feminist literature is providing a continuing and diversified discussion of the functions of women's speech for them (e.g. Jones 1980; Smith-Rosenberg 1975), discussions which, with the material reviewed here, reveal women's speech (and men's) as a complex social product. This new type of literature with topics and perspectives infrequently heard before has already had some slight impact on the topics or perspectives of, for example, newspaper features, and might be expected with time to affect the attitudes toward women's and men's speech.

Men's speech is stereotypically logical, concise, and deals with important topics; women's speech is emotional, flowery (many unnecessary adjectives and adverbs), confused, and wordy. Many of the students indicated, while giving the reasons for their decisions on whether a statement was made by a female or male, that stupid comments which revealed ignorance of men's important activities or which seemed indirect and hesitant (containing qualifiers) were cues that the speaker was female. The students did not know that the statements they assigned to either females or males were cartoon captions. But they did indicate that women's speech, but not men's, is thought by many to be a joke. Women as a group, but not men, are stereotypically silly speakers. This research, and other research more specifically on causal attributions of performance on various tasks (Deaux and Emswiller 1974), suggest that our understanding and evaluation of women's and men's speech will be affected by these general stereotypes about speech (see Hall and Braunwald 1981), with women's speech heard as more constrained by biological deficiencies, and men's speech heard as more attributable to clear reasoning skills.

Other studies provide additional elaboration of general (context un-specified) beliefs about gender differences. For example, in my study (Kramer 1977, 1978) white midwestern teenagers in the US rated 51 speech traits as to how characteristic the trait was for women and men; men's speech was rated significantly different from women's on 36 of the traits when scores from both men and women were combined. The following traits were rated as associated with male speech: demanding, deep, boastful, use of swear words, dominating, loud, shows anger, straight to point, militant, slang, authoritarian, forceful, aggressive, blunt, sense of humour, relaxed stance. The following traits were associated with female speakers: enunciate clearly, high pitch, hands and facial expression, gossip, concern for listener, gentle, fast, trivial topics, wide range in rate and pitch, friendly, talk a lot, emotional, many details, smooth, open, self-revealing, good grammar, polite, gibberish, smile a lot when talking. A comparison of male and female participants' ratings showed that they differed somewhat in their assignment of speech characteristics. Men to a greater extent than women thought males were more straight to the point, relaxed, and likely to have a sense of humour in their speech, and that females were most likely to use good grammar and pronunciation, friendly speech, gibberish, and to talk on trivial topics. Women to a greater extent than men rated female speech as involving hands and facial expressions, concern with listener, wide range of pitch and rate, and enthusiastic delivery. While men and women generally agreed in their stereotypic assignment of speech characteristics, they differed somewhat in this process for one-third of the stereotyped characteristics. However, in no cases were opposing ratings given by the women and men – who were asked to give their own true impressions, not what they thought others might believe (Kramer 1977). The women and men agreed on ratings for the 'ideal speaker' except that men rated deep voice as more important than did the women (Kramer 1978).

Using a questionnaire based on the same 36 characteristics above, Scott (1980) conducted a test with students in a southern US university and found that stereotypical female language characteristics were, in general, rated more socially desirable and closer to the ratings of 'competent speaker' than those characteristics associated with men's speech. The results of the survey did not provide documentation for the mostly negative folklinguistic statements about women's speech. Yet, we have little other supporting evidence to indicate that the strong negative attitudes toward women's speech through the past 100 years have been suddenly reversed. How then to explain this positive evaluation in these surveys? Possibly, Scott (1980) suggests, the evaluation of women's speech in general terms conceals the evaluation of speech in specific situations – speech which, according to research based on observation of interaction, differs from the stereotypes. The original questionnaire items for these studies were chosen on the basis of responses by other teenagers in the same population as the participants in the main investigation. But perhaps these traits are not the most salient traits used in judgements of their own and others' speech in actual interaction. Further, possibly the positive traits, such as good grammar and friendly speech, when heard to be combined with other traits, such as emotionality, may add up to speech perceived as ineffectual. Perhaps the raters were using 'ideal' and 'socially desirable' as near synonyms to 'proper'. We know that for women 'proper' is often not powerful. For example, female school teachers and secretaries are expected to talk and write properly, but those skills do not lead many of the women to more powerful and better paying administrative jobs. A look at the list of stereotypes suggests that women are perceived to have control over grammatical forms and to desire non-combative interaction, but men are perceived to have control in a more basic sense over the speech situation.

Related studies give some help in interpretation of the results. In another US study (Siegler and Siegler 1976), the syntactic forms associated with males were rated as more intelligent than those associated with females. The participants in a University of W. Ontario study gave ratings to taped female voices which indicated that the men and women listeners agreed on the characteristics of the female voices, but disagreed about which characteristics were the most important (Batstone and Tuomi 1981). The students were in general agreement in their perceptions of the female voices, identifying two clusters of characteristics in their ratings on 20 semantic differential scales selected by Batstone and Tuomi from the part of their experiment designed to find undergraduates' descriptions of the quality of 'sexiness' in young female voices. One cluster, labelled *passive* by the researchers, consisted of characteristics such as 'soft', 'gentle', 'sweet', and 'feminine'. The other, labelled *active*, consisted of such characteristics as 'lively', 'colourful', and 'interesting'. While both females and males identified the same characteristics as descriptive of the voices they heard, the factor analysis of the data suggests that for female listeners the *active* characteristics were more salient aspects of the voices; for male listeners, the *passive* characteristics were more important. The results are useful in indicating that women and men may generally agree on the traits which characterize female voices but not agree on the relative importance of those traits. However, this particular study does not reveal how useful listeners of differing ages and cultural background would find these scales – selected to measure the 'sexiness' of women's voices – in their general description and evaluation of the voices of women.

Another team of researchers (Erickson *et al.* 1978) worked with some other voice traits which Lakoff (1973) posits as more characteristic of female than male speech: frequent use of intensifiers, hedges, questioning intonation, and tag questions (e.g., This is silly, isn't it?). The Erickson *et al.* study was an imaginative attempt to determine whether these 'female' traits were evaluated differently depending upon whether the traits were exhibited by females or males.[7] In two experiments (one involving tape recorders and the second, court transcripts) listeners evaluated more negatively the 'witness' – whether female or male, who was using what the researchers labelled the 'powerless' style (i.e. the stereotypical features of women's speech). In this study it is not clear which characteristics or combination of characteristics were heard as contributing to this 'powerless' talk, nor whether any part of the judges' negative ratings of the 'powerless speech' stemmed from the association of the traits with female speech (see Bradac, this volume: ch. 6; Kalin, this volume: ch. 9).

Examining actual court transcripts O'Barr and Atkins (1980) found that while some women spoke in the way Lakoff describes, so did some men; frequent use of the so-called 'women's language' was most characteristic of those people who held subordinate, lower-status jobs or were unemployed. Since most jobs are gender-segregated and 'women's jobs' have relatively low status, autonomy and pay, we would expect that behaviour differences linked to status would coincide largely but not exclusively with gender differences. In another study of the evaluation of speakers who used 'women's language' Newcombe and Arnkoff (1979) found that listeners heard tag questions, qualifiers and compound requests (e.g., 'Won't you answer the phone?' rather than the simple request 'Answer the phone') as decreasing the assertiveness of speakers whether female or male (see Cacioppo and Petty, this volume: ch. 12). These investigators suggest that women and men might be able to change the way they are perceived by changing their speech style. That is, women who wish to be heard as assertive should just not use tag questions and compound requests, for example. However, this advice is perhaps too simplistic. To understand people's talk we need to consider what they feel they can say to make the best of their (differing) situations. In her study of corporations Kanter (1977) found that the behaviour of secretaries is not evaluated by the same criteria as is that of managers; the expectations for their behaviour differs. While the female and male speakers in the laboratory experiments might be evaluated in much the same way when they use the same speech features, the female secretary and the male manager on the job might not. Further, asymmetrical authority relationships mean that many secretaries have 'few weapons at their disposal to use in negotiating and bargaining' with their boss (p. 96). Kanter adds that many secretaries turn to the traditional ways subordinates try to gain what they want and need from the more powerful – use of assumed helplessness or uncertainty. Even within roles there are often differences in evaluation and thus in what verbal strategies women and men believe are effective and safe tactics. Kanter reports that token women in higher management positions are often treated in accordance with the traditional expectations of, and assumptions about, women. She writes that the women in her study often found it 'easier to accept stereotyped roles than to fight them, even if their acceptance meant limiting the tokens' range of expressions or demonstrations of task competence, because they offered a comfortable and certain position' (236). Future studies which consider speakers' understanding

---

[7] While US and European studies do not provide clear evidence that the kinds of characteristics Lakoff lists are actually more frequent in women's speech in particular, or even often present in anyone's speech, the list of supposed markers has been widely discussed and in some publications listed as the most important actual differences. The list is evidently consistent with the beliefs of many academicians at least – which alone makes the list interesting.

of the evaluations others make of speakers in various occupational, social-class, and gender categories, and consideration of what linguistic tactics they believe are safe and effective for themselves will help us clarify the uses speakers make of stereotypes about the ways women and men talk.

Bristol research

The material reviewed above indicates that the traits associated with men's speech or women's speech do not affect our evaluation of speakers in autonomous ways. We shall see that mediating the evaluation of female and male speakers are such factors as their social status, political affiliation and regional background, as perceived by listeners. Researchers from the University of Bristol have systematically, through a series of studies, worked toward an understanding of the interaction of these factors and gender stereotypes, and their effect on interaction. Some of the studies include use of matched-guise tests in which the speakers, each able to speak convincingly in several accents, are recorded and the tapes played to 'naive' judges who are led to believe that each speech sample is from a different speaker. This technique eliminates some of the idiosyncratic variations of speech and allows a focus on the speech characteristics of the particular study. In earlier tests male speakers of standard English were rated high on social competence and male speakers of nonstandard varieties were rated high on social attractiveness (Giles and Powesland 1975). Elyan *et al.* (1978) in a matched-guise study involving women found a similar pattern: The most prestigious, standard accent in Britain, Received Pronunciation (RP), when spoken by women, was rated higher in competence and occupational prestige and more feminine, while the nonstandard (in this case, Northern) female voices were heard as more likeable, sincere, less aggressive or self-centred. In a similar study, only involving the matched-guise voices of two females and two males using RP and South Welsh accents, the RP voices were rated higher in competence and status, but listeners heard the women's voices, whichever the accent, as more feminine and profeminist and the men as more masculine and having more occupational status (Giles and Marsh 1979).

A follow-up study was designed to elicit listeners' sex- and class-related stereotypes, to determine the amount of overlap between them; the researchers realized that the 'masculine' items chosen to characterize the RP speech might have been chosen by listeners primarily to make class attribution (in this case middle-class) to RP speakers. And in fact the researchers did find a great overlap between the gender-related and class-related stereotypes (Giles, Smith, Ford, Condor and Thakerar 1980). Working with a revised set of adjective scales so that the class and gender stereotypes could be separated, the research team found that RP speakers, female and male, were rated higher on middle-class stereotypic items with both 'masculine' (e.g. ambitious and enterprising) and 'feminine' (e.g. affected and charming) connotations. While females and males in general agree on the ratings given to standard and nonstandard speakers, Elyan *et al.* (1978) found that female judges heard greater distinctions than did the males. This finding is in line with other work which indicates that women are somewhat more sensitive to people's appearance and verbal and nonverbal behaviour (Henley 1977).

This work from researchers at the University of Bristol led to another set of studies, this time to determine if listeners could distinguish feminist and non-feminist speakers on the basis of vocal cues alone (Giles, Smith, Browne,

Whiteman and Williams 1980). In the first study, based on tapes of spontaneous but topic-controlled speech of feminists and non-feminists (as measured by the Spence and Helmreich (1972) Attitudes Toward Women Scale), judges rated feminists as more lucid, confident, intelligent, likeable and sincere, and less monotonous and superficial than non-feminists. In a follow-up study in which content was controlled, listeners still detected differences; feminist speakers were heard as less fluent, less precise in their enunciation and more 'masculine' than non-feminists in this study. However, given that their further studies found that similar perceived speech differences accrue for pro-feminist males as well, the researchers now suggest that the evaluation of the pro-feminist speakers is not unique to women who are actively working to change their status in society but is linked more generally to the speakers' liberal ideology (see Giles, Smith, Ford, Condor and Thakerar 1980 for an overview of these studies). On the basis of this series of studies, the researchers conclude that gender does not have a constant, dominant salience across all situations, that some speech traits stereotypically linked to females or to males likely overlap and interact on many occasions with other discriminators such as those related to age, class, race, political ideology, ethnic and regional background.

An overview of these historical and empirical studies indicates the following: Women's speech is judged, by women and men, as different from men's speech. Women's speech is almost always evaluated in relation to men's speech, and at least in the abstract has traditionally been positively evaluated by men only as it is heard as conforming to correctness principles, is friendly, soft and infrequent, and is heard in 'female' places. There is a great continuity over the years in the attitudes toward women's and men's speech, and the traditional attitudes continue to be supported by a network of reinforcing institutions. As a group, women, but not men, are advised to modify their speech and to continue to restrict the places their speech is heard by men. The specific reasons why they should do this differ depending on the source and year – but include reference to women's natural modesty and reticence, problems with their voice qualities, logic, intelligence and/or knowledge, their duties to families and society in general, and their past failures as speakers. While the *explicit* word from a variety of sources treats women's and men's speech as neatly dichotomous, the empirical studies of attitudes indicate that, when evaluating speech, listeners combine their knowledge of the stereotypes and perceptions of the situation. That is, the listeners consider the norms and expectations of the speakers as well as their political ideology, group alliances and identities, social status, goals, and the constraints of the particular situation (see Giles and Ryan, this volume: ch. 13).

As all this indicates, people's responses to and attitudes toward women's speech cannot be explained simply. The questions raised by the work on speech stereotypes are many. For example, how are the stereotypes related to speakers' understanding of the causes and meanings of their own behaviour and that of others, female and male? How do we use stereotypes – and in connection with what other indicators – in initial interaction and in long-term relationships? How do the stereotypes affect people's understanding of what is said by women and men in various situations? Do people have hierarchies of speech stereotypes and if so, how shared are the hierarchies? Do people link the stereotyped traits of males and females in specific ways: e.g. do listeners need to hear certain speech *patterns* before they evaluate speech as female-type rather than as, say, pleasant-person-type? Do some listeners hearing one of the stereotyped characteristics imagine they have also heard others?

Developing directions

In order to understand the effects of social judgements on women's and men's psychological states and behaviour, we need a theoretical approach which will deal with the relationships between women and men, including the pressures which have affected their values and which have brought relatively greater restrictions on women's speech; the origins, types and effects of prescriptive literature and other formal and informal regulations; a comparison of men's and women's opportunities to be heard in public and to influence public policy (including those policies which affect family and other 'private' interaction); their political and economic strength; and their goals and their strategies. (The material in Kramarae [1981] reviews some of the work toward that goal.)

The long tradition of inequality in the determination of the norms for language use for women and men does not mean that women are unable to provide any organization or direction to their same-gender and cross-gender interaction. We know that women use, as do men, available resources, including their knowledge of what people ought to – or often do – sound like, to work toward their goals (see Brown and Levinson 1978).

We need further discussion of receivers' interpretation of women's and men's speech in order to understand the reasons why, for example, in some situations women and men displaying similar behaviour may receive different evaluations. In a study using the taped voices of two females and two males who read a short passage many times, simulating seven voice qualities and different degrees of speech rate and pitch, Addington (1968) found that changes in the voice tone of males affected the listeners' evaluations of the speakers' personalities differently than did similar changes in female voices. For example, judges seem to hear increased breathiness in the speech of males as evidence of more youthful and artistic personality, while judges rate breathiness in the speech of females as indication of a more feminine, pretty, callow, highly strung, petite and effervescent personality. Aronovitch (1976) also explored the relationship of personality and paralinguistic variables, by measuring the speech rate, intensity, fundamental frequency, and sound–silence ratio of the taped-recorded speech of 25 men and 32 women, and by obtaining listeners' evaluation (on 10 personality traits scales) of the voices. He found that judges evidently used different voice cues to evaluate the personality traits of female and male speakers. For example, the male speakers were judged more extroverted, confident and bold when their voices showed higher variance of intensity and fundamental frequency, and faster rate; but female speakers were judged as more extroverted, confident and bold when their voices showed higher mean intensity, fewer pauses and faster rate. (See Street and Hopper, this volume: ch. 11.) As Scherer (1979a) points out, we cannot be certain that the voice cues measured by the researchers are the cues most utilized by the judges in evaluating the personality of the speakers. However, these results do give strong support for the argument made by language and gender researchers and others who deal with the ways social classifications are used by people to understand what they hear: we should not assume that our speech forms alone determine the way our speech is heard and evaluated. In part, our gender speaks our place and evaluation in social interaction.

Perhaps stereotypes form a template from which to view, interpret and evaluate the language behaviour of women and men (see Giles and Ryan, this volume, ch. 13). Working with this suggestion Giles, Scherer and Taylor (1979) offer the following: People organize what they hear according to their predetermined cognitive structures of how speakers ought to or do talk. If speakers do not confirm these beliefs by using the expected speech traits, listeners may hear what is not present or ignore what is not expected. Even repeated experiences of talk which does not conform to the stereotypes might not alter the perceptions if other sources (textbooks, proverbs, jokes, cartoons, etc.) continue to support the evaluative biases. Receivers may, hearing one trait stereotypically associated with women's speech, assume that other traits are present, or, Giles, Scherer and Taylor (1979) suggest, if not hearing the expected characteristics, explain away their absence in terms of the situational constraints. Comparison studies of actual (recorded and carefully measured) speech and receivers' perceptions of that speech can help us understand the way attitudes function in interaction (see Street and Hopper, this volume: ch. 11).

A patient–doctor interaction study by West and Guiffre (1980) illustrates the possibilities of this type of research. Physician–patient interaction is, as much research illustrates, usually asymmetrical with the physician controlling the questioning, and the length of utterances and of total interaction. Doctors have, of course, the higher status in the hospital interview. However, the West and Guiffre study involving male and female doctors found that gender apparently had primacy over job status or race. Male doctors initiated 69 per cent of all interruptions in their interaction with patients; female doctors initiated only 32 per cent of the interruptions in their interactions. The most nearly symmetrical interactions in terms of interruptions were those between women doctors and women patients. These findings are especially striking when we note that the women doctors were white and the women patients, black. We would need additional information about the interactions to know whether the male doctors discouraged in some way or prevented interruptions of their speech, and whether the female doctors 'allowed' interruptions. And then if we could add information from the patients about their reactions to the interactions (about, for example, which of the speakers, if any, were thought disrespectful), we would have valuable information on speakers' understanding of how attitudes about women's speech and men's speech work in interactions.

A related issue for future research is the question of whether there is a difference in the amounts and types of accommodation women and men make to the speech of the people with whom they interact. We would expect people's attitudes, knowledge of stereotypes and of power and status variables to mediate their language behaviour, guiding them in what they say and how they interpret speech. One important aspect of accommodation theory (Giles and Powesland 1975; Giles and Smith 1979) suggests a speaker will, when she or he wants to impress or please someone, use knowledge of the beliefs and values of the addressee and alter, for example, style, accent, pitch or rate to make the speech behaviour more acceptable to the person addressed. In a study of requests made by men and women for tickets at a train station in Amsterdam, Brouwer *et al.* (1979) found that while women were more likely to hesitate and to request information, no differences between men and women were found for the number of words spoken, use of diminutives or civilities. However, the researchers also found that gender of the person *addressed* played a prominent part in the travellers' choice of words. We need additional research focused on the variance accounted for by the gender of the listener.

One proposition of accommodation theory suggests that those desiring another's approval (e.g. members of subordinate power groups desiring recognition or acknowledging subordination for the purposes of the interaction) will adapt more to the speech of others than will those who do not need or want approval or do not feel the need to acknowledge subordination. Following accommodation theory and working with our knowledge of gender hierarchy, we would expect that females would accommodate more than would males. Women are 'supposed' to be more careful and caring in their speech. A study by Valdes-Fallis (1978) seems to provide an illustration of this accommodation. In her study of code-switching among bilingual Mexican-American women, she found that the women used more switches to the last language spoken when they were speaking to males than when they were speaking with other females. Accommodation can take many forms (e.g. matching of language varieties, pronunciation, pauses, and lexicon) and serve several purposes (e.g. showing subordination, showing concern for the other participants, and marking in-group relations). (See Giles 1979a; and Thakerar *et al.*, 1982, for discussion of theoretical and empirical work on the linguistic and psychological factors involved in speech accommodation work.) Further study of linguistic shifts, the speakers' motivations for shifts and their evaluations of the shifts – over the course of a conversation and of a relationship – should prove valuable to our analysis of the effects of the differing judgemental standards applied to women's and men's speech.

Finally, attitudes about women's speech may serve male identity maintenance in basic and complex ways. Research on women's speech usually explicitly recognizes the importance of considering attitudes toward that speech and their importance in assigning and maintaining the social category *female*. Research on men's speech (i.e. most communication research) seldom recognizes the importance, to the shaping of men's speech and men's identity, of the existence and evaluation of something called *women's speech*. In order to make links between abstractions of social structure and everyday interaction we may do well to consider men's speech as, in part, different from women's speech. This difference is vigorously maintained through, for example, literature and folklore, through hiring policies stated as being, or understood as being, based on differing evaluations of women's and men's communicative styles and speaking abilities, and through everyday interactions which explicitly or implicitly employ differing evaluations of women's and men's speech. Studying the folklinguistic and the empirical studies that deal with the attitudes toward women's and men's speech, along with attention to the relationships between language styles and social structure, will help us detail how gender is spoken.

6

A rose by another name: attitudinal consequences of lexical variation

James J. Bradac

As the previous chapters have shown, membership in particular social groups is often associated with correspondingly particular styles of speech. These style variations are a source of stereotypic inferences in listeners (or readers), especially in first-impression contexts. The paradigm case is that of regional variation in phonology, syntax, and semantics, which is frequently linked to differences in social class (Giles and Powesland 1975), but non-regional linguistic variations among groups are increasingly interesting to theorists and researchers, e.g. the 'dialects' of males and females (see Kramarae, this volume: ch. 5; Mulac and Lundell 1980). This chapter is concerned with variation which occurs *within* social groups as well as that which occurs between them. Both sorts of variation are importantly associated with variation in receivers' *attitudes*. More particularly, the primary focus of the chapter is on *lexical* varieties and their consequences for communicators. Lurking in the background of the early discussion is an issue which emerges boldly in the last major section of the chapter: Whose conceptualization of 'lexicon' (and 'context') is now most useful for theory construction and research? That of the expert linguist or psychologist? Or that of the naive communicator stumbling through everyday life?

An initial view of lexical variation

Consider the following strings:
   A. John hit the table.
   B. The table was hit by John.
   C. The table hit John.
Each of these is a perfectly acceptable/grammatical sentence of English (see, however, Martin, Bradac, and Elliott 1977; J. R. Ross 1979) but the three sentences differ in some interesting ways. First, although A and B are not lexically identical they mean the same thing, at least when we assume a particular context. Here the term 'meaning' is used in the sense of 'proposition' or 'relationship among concepts', not in the sense of 'connotation'. Thus A and B are identical at the level of meaning (but not lexicon) because the same abstract logical proposition underlies both sentences. In the terminology of generative-transformational linguistics, they have the same 'deep structure' (Chomsky 1957). Another way of saying this is that one cannot imagine a world in which A is true but B is not or vice versa.[1] On the

[1] This fact was offered to the author by Larry W. Martin of Data General Corporation, Westborough, Massachusetts.

other hand, the meaning of sentence C differs from that of A and B, even though A and C are lexically identical. This fact points to the interdependence of lexicon and syntax in the production of meanings.

Consider a fourth sentence:

D. John clobbered the table.

Does this have the same meaning as A and B? The answer hinges on the extent to which the lexical items 'hit' and 'clobbered' refer to the same act or, more particularly, the extent to which the phenomena they index share criterial attributes. Whether or not they share attributes (or a sufficient number of these) is completely dependent upon the perceptions of members of the speech community in which they are used. There is no objective standard by which to measure this kind of similarity or difference.

In everyday life the discovery of the meaning of a speaker's utterance is crucially influenced by situational context. (This truism masks some interesting complexities which will be discussed below.) It is easy to imagine situations in which lexically and syntactically identical sentences mean different things. For example, two persons are discussing a fist-fight. One speaker says initially: 'John was pushed by Fred'. Then he adds: 'John hit the table'. Compare this with the situation where two persons are discussing John's violent temper. The first speaker says: 'John was very angry and he was shouting obscenities'. Then he says: 'John hit the table'. The former sentence probably can be paraphrased accurately as 'John crashed into the table', whereas the latter can be rendered 'John clobbered the table'. This simple example suggests that one's knowledge of syntax and lexicon is insufficient for assigning valid meanings to sentences, a fact ignored by most contemporary linguists. The discovery of linguistic meanings is *necessarily* a social psychological process of making inferences in context (see Hudson 1980). This is even more clearly the case when the connotative aspect of meaning is considered. Inferences about a speaker's attitude toward his/her topic when using lexical variants such as 'woman', 'female', and 'girl' will vary radically as a function of context.

The main point of the preceding discussion is that, in a serious sense, one can say the same thing in different ways and different things in the same way (see Sandell 1977). Meaning and expression are conceptually separable. For this author (and for several of the other authors in this volume), this is a basic assumption. Of primary importance is the fact that variations in expression are often associated with variations in listeners' attitudes toward the message and its source.

More specifically, linguistic expression or form of utterance can vary in terms of the following aspects, among others: lexical choice, lexical patterning, phonology, rate, pitch, and volume. This chapter will examine the choice and patterning of lexical items exclusively. Of course the social significance of words and phrases is crucially affected by paralinguistic variation, but such variation is discussed elsewhere in this volume (see Street and Hopper, this volume: ch. 11).

Lexical choice and lexical patterning have been discussed by theorists of style for centuries under various headings, e.g. *to prepon*, diction, figures, schemes, and tropes (Aristotle 1932; Bede 1962; Erasmus 1963; Sherry 1961). Swift's definition of 'good' style embraces both of these general concepts: 'Proper words in proper places' (1898, p. 200–1). Both lexical choice and lexical patterning have been examined in recent studies of language attitudes. Each concept comprises several specific variables which have been investigated in terms of their consequences for communicators.

Dimensions of lexical choice

The following variables have been subjected to extensive theoretical analysis and, to a varying extent, empirical investigation.

Abstractness

Words vary along an abstract–concrete dimension. Concrete words refer to objects or actions, while abstract words refer to ideas, relationships, and concepts. This distinction has a commonsense appeal, but it is extremely difficult to maintain rigorously (see Brown 1958, pp. 82–109). Is 'rock' less abstract than 'idea'? Which rock? Which idea? (A green one?) Perhaps words which refer to a larger number of objects are more general or abstract than words which refer to a smaller array. Thus, 'house' is more abstract than 'Spanish condominium'. However, it is not at all clear how many objects or referents must distinguish two words before one word is considered more abstract than the other. More fundamentally, it is impossible to imagine a criterion which would in principle allow such a numerical distinction. In spite of these difficulties, it should be noted that the abstractness–concreteness distinction seems to have been at the heart of some influential (although cultish) movements, e.g. 'Basic English' (Ogden 1968) and 'General Semantics' (Korzybski 1933). Some interesting research has been stimulated by this distinction, e.g. work on the child's initial acquisition of words (Bruner 1975) and studies of verbal memory (Goss 1972); but the research has few clear implications for the area of language attitudes. Perhaps greater progress will be made if researchers define 'abstractness' subjectively in terms of the persons responding to linguistic stimuli. The variable 'stimulus complexity', which may be related to 'abstractness', has been operationalized in this way with interesting results. For example, Bradac, Desmond and Murdock (1977) may have obtained an inverse relationship between degree of linguistic complexity operationalized objectively in terms of sentence features and subjects' subjective judgements of degree of complexity, although the authors argue against this interpretation of their results.

Familiarity

Words may be more or less familiar to a listener or reader. It seems reasonable to distinguish roughly among three levels of familiarity: completely, somewhat, and not at all familiar. A word is completely familiar if a person is sure she knows what it means, somewhat familiar if she thinks she has heard it before and may know what it means, and not at all familiar if she has not heard it before and cannot guess at its meaning. (Perhaps degree of information-processing effort assumes an inverted-U shape in this case, with effort peaking for words that are somewhat familiar.) Little research has been done on the communicative consequences of lexical familiarity, unfortunately (see Bavendam 1980). In light of the interesting results of research on attitudinal consequences of familiarity of *non*-linguistic stimuli (Zajonc 1968), exploration of the communicative consequences of lexical familiarity appears promising. It may be the case, for example, that as listeners are exposed increasingly to an unfamiliar term, they may become increasingly positive toward it and its user. Perhaps this will occur even if the meaning of the term remains unclear.

The familiar/unfamiliar distinction refers more specifically to concepts such as slang, jargon and argot. Many social groups, e.g. surfers, drug addicts, and lawyers, develop'special words which are familiar to group members and unfamiliar to outsiders (see Brown and Fraser 1979). Such words probably have several functions including maximizing communication efficiency and 'mystifying' the uninitiated (Duncan 1962; Orwell 1949a). An especially interesting function may be to increase cohesion or solidarity by increasing members' perceptions of their group's distinctiveness (see Tajfel's theory of group distinctiveness, 1974; Drake 1980).

Goodness

'Linguistic taboos' abound in the sense that some words are 'bad' words because they are obscene or profane (Hudson 1980; Mulac 1976b.) Richard Nixon and his advisors apparently thought his use of particular words in private discussions would be judged negatively by the American public, so they deleted these from the 'Watergate' transcripts (Nixon and the Staff of the Washington Post 1974). Other words are 'good' – they are sacred, evoking extremely positive reactions. An example may be the word 'tax-cut' when used by politicians. A more exotic example is the *mantra*, a unique word given by masters to novice transcendental meditators. The sacred–obscene dichotomy is essentially the same as the distinction between 'god' and 'devil' terms offered by Weaver (1953) and Burke (1950). Related notions are politeness and appropriateness (Hosman 1978). That is, some words or phrases are associated with gentle or barbaric behaviour, good or bad conduct (see Goffman 1971).

It can be argued that sacred or 'god' terms, for example, are, in the jargon of learning theory, secondary positive reinforcers. They have acquired reward value through association with a primary source of reward. It has been shown, in fact, that persons' responses to words can be conditioned (Staats and Staats 1958). It is interesting that in a given culture some words are almost universally reinforcing, whether positively or negatively, across many contexts and speakers. Advertisers and agitators exploit this fact. Eiser has demonstrated that positively and negatively valued labels can, in fact, produce the kinds of attitudinal effects sought by propagandists (1975; Eiser and Pancer 1979). To some extent, an individual's attitude toward a social object can be influenced by the 'good' or 'bad' connotations of labels used to describe the object.

On the other hand, it is important to note that there is a strong, idiosyncratic aspect to lexical goodness or badness. For example, particular authors have their own favourite words and phrases, if frequency of occurrence is a valid measure of favour (Spurgeon 1970; Yule 1944). This is true for speakers in everyday life as well. Finally, the use of a given word in one context will invite judgements of lexical badness, whereas the same word may be judged positively elsewhere. For example, reactions to obscene language may vary according to the sex of the speaker, with males often having a high degree of impunity in this regard (Smith 1979).

Language intensity

Lexical items may be perceived as more or less intense (Bowers 1963). Intensity has been operationalized in various ways by researchers (Bradac, Bowers and Courtright 1980), but conceptually theorists and researchers agree that some nouns, adjectives and adverbs will be judged as indicating a more intense feeling or attitude on the part of a speaker than will others. For example, the qualifying phrase 'extremely devastating' will be perceived as more intense than 'sort of nasty' by most speakers of English. Many studies have been done on the attitudinal consequences of intensity. Generally, the research indicates that intensity interacts with communicator characteristics and other aspects of the situation in producing communicative consequences (Bradac, Schneider, Hemphill and Tardy 1980). For example, Burgoon, Jones and Stewart (1975) found that a female communicator using intense language produced less attitude change in receivers than did her linguistically intense male counterpart. Conversely, the female was more persuasive than the male when she used low-intensity language. Some evidence indicates that high-intensity language is more likely to be seen as an attribute of a powerful person than is low-intensity language (Bradac, Hosman and Tardy 1978; Burgoon *et al.* 1975; see the discussion of powerful and powerless speech styles below).

Observations about the lexical choice variables

Relationships among the four dimensions of lexical choice merit some brief discussion. First, the dimensions are not completely orthogonal. For example, goodness and intensity may overlap as in the case of obscenity. Further, it is clear that the degree of familiarity, goodness and intensity of specific lexical choices depends largely (perhaps completely) upon the judgements of the speakers–hearers in a communication episode. That is, a given word in isolation is not independently, objectively, inherently familiar, intense, or good. Inherent familiarity in this sense is even difficult to imagine. Inherent goodness seems far-fetched, but perhaps certain concepts when yoked to certain sounds produce universally positive or negative responses. Although the 'inherent value' hypothesis usually refers to aesthetic aspects of phonology only, it might be construed as supporting this position (Giles, Bourhis, Trudgill and Lewis 1974). This hypothesis might also be stretched to incorporate the notion of inherently intense language. Some have argued that the abstractness of words can be assessed objectively (Chase 1938), but perhaps it would be more useful to conceptualize abstractness too as a phenomenological·or subjective variable as suggested above – you have concrete images for a word, whereas he can only think of synonyms (see Paivio 1971).

Along a different line, the goodness and intensity dimensions of lexical choice reflect the three basic dimensions of connotative meaning discovered initially by Osgood, Suci and Tannenbaum (1957) and shown subsequently to underlie persons' judgements of objects across diverse cultures (Osgood, May and Miron 1975). The evaluative component of meaning is equivalent to 'goodness'. The potency and, less directly, activity components are related to intensity. Since, according to Osgood *et al.* (1975), *all* stimuli (including physical objects) are judged in terms of these three dimensions, it is not surprising that lexical items can be distinguished using these same dimensional criteria.

Dimensions of lexical patterning

The complexities escalate as the focus shifts to the *patterning* of lexical items. Three words can be arranged in six different ways (3!). However, in the normal use of natural language the mathematical possibilities of lexical combination are reduced drastically by syntactic constraints. Stylistic constraints on combination also exist, although these are generally less rigid and formalizable than syntactic ones. As in the case of lexical choice, the following linguistic features have been subjected to analysis and research. The most general aspect of patterning (syntax) will be discussed first, and this will be followed by a discussion of four more specific variables.

Syntax

Presumably the native speaker has a tacit knowledge of the syntactic rules of his or her language and this comprises a large part of 'linguistic competence' (Chomsky 1965a). To oversimplify somewhat, these rules are of two major types: constitutive and regulative (Searle 1969). Referring to constitutive rules as 'Rules$_c$' and regulative rules as 'Rules$_r$', Sanders and Martin write:

> Rules$_r$ are simply norms. . . . In that they are norms, the violation of Rules$_r$ elicits censure from others.
> Rules$_c$ are best understood in terms of what can be called a *frame of reference*. . . . Within any particular frame of reference, a rigidly circumscribed set of behaviours must occur; for instance, there are certain behaviours which must occur during a wedding ceremony in order for a wedding ceremony to have taken place. The statements that specify the behaviours which must occur . . . are the Rules$_c$ of that frame of reference. If a behaviour violates the Rules$_c$ of a frame of reference, then the behaviour makes no sense, is incoherent in that frame of reference (1975, 68).

In a sense, a constitutive rule is a definition, while a regulative rule is a command. With regard to language, a simple constitutive rule is: S — NP + VP: 'Tall children eat large apples.' The rule NP + NP does not generate an English sentence: *'Tall children the small dog.' Nor is a sentence represented by ART + ART + NP + VP: *'The the apple tree has leaves.' Violation of a constitutive linguistic rule should in theory lead a hearer to judge that the speaker is not in fact speaking the language. Of course, speakers often do perform ungrammatically. They commit syntactic errors. Often these will not even be noticed in the processing of speech in actual communication episodes. They amount to 'noise' which listeners are trained or even biologically programmed to ignore as they search for the speaker's intended meaning (McNeill 1970).

On the other hand, a linguistic regulative rule takes the form 'Say X' or 'Do not say X'. For example, do not say: 'The police are continuing stopping drinking on campus.' This sentence is coherent and is, in fact, technically grammatical; but it is judged unacceptable by many native speakers of English because there is a prohibition against 'doubl-ing' (Martin *et al.* 1977; Ross 1972). Violation of a regulative rule should lead to the judgement: the speaker is speaking the language *badly*. When normal communicators, i.e. non-linguists, use the terms 'ungrammatical' and 'bad grammar', they are probably referring to the regulative or normative aspect of syntax. There is some evidence that 'bad grammar' is in fact a potent determinant of impressions of speakers, a potent factor in the stigmatization of minority groups (Labov, 1966; Triandis, Loh and Levin 1966).

Power

This variable relates to language intensity. In fact it could have been discussed above because it has been operationalized in terms of both lexical choice and patterning. O'Barr and his associates initially explored powerful and powerless speech styles in the context of courtroom communication (Lind and O'Barr 1979). Their approach was empirical, involving scrutiny of the language behaviour of persons differing in social power, e.g. expert versus non-expert witnesses. They found that less powerful persons tended to use more polite forms ('That is correct, *sir*'), more hedges ('*Well*, it was'), more deictic phrases ('Like that picture *over there*'), and more intensifiers – this may be a misnomer – ('He *really* made me mad') than did more powerful persons. The less powerful speakers were also more hesitant and their responses tended to be somewhat longer. Subsequent experiments have demonstrated that normal untutored listeners *perceive* messages which are distinguished on the basis of these features as differing with regard to the power of their sources (Bradac, Hemphill and Tardy 1981). Also powerful styles are associated with receiver judgements of relatively great communicator credibility and attractiveness (Bradac, Hemphill and Tardy 1981; Lind and O'Barr 1979).

However, the 'powerful/powerless style' variable may not be a unitary entity in terms of its consequences for speakers. That is, although six features covaried in the performance of speakers studied by Lind and O'Barr, and although the simultaneous manipulation of all six features in experimental messages produced the anticipated effects, it may be that the features differ from one another in their impact upon perceptions of speaker power. For example, perhaps hedges are more clearly associated with powerlessness than are polite forms. Hedging may account for more of the variance in judgements of power than does politeness in most situations. Also, there is evidence that length of verbal response is *directly* related to perceptions of speaker influence (Jaffe and Lucas 1969), whereas the Lind and O'Barr descriptive data would argue for an inverse relationship.

There is a need for an experiment which compares the independent effects of the covariants of power upon several perceptual dimensions. A study by Newcombe and Arnkoff (1979) made such a comparison in terms of Lakoff's 'female register' hypothesis (1975), which is relevant to this discussion of power. Briefly, these researchers found that the use of tag questions ('This is a good paper, isn't it?'), hedges, or compound requests ('Won't you bring me some coffee?') produced judgements of relatively low speaker assertiveness (see Kramarae, this volume: ch. 5; Cacioppo and Petty, this volume: ch. 12). So, we can be reasonably sure that hedges are inversely related to perceptions of speaker power, but the independent effects of the other five covariants of the 'powerful/powerless' construct remain unknown.

Finally, there is a need to become more analytical in our thinking about the concept 'power' as it relates to language. Is power most usefully conceptualized as an objectively determinable role attribute? Or might researchers more fruitfully approach power as a situationally bound self-perception? An implication of the latter position would be that a judge may feel powerful in her courtroom but impotent when chastised by her doctor for smoking excessively (see Brown and Fraser 1979, pp. 53–5). This subjective difference might well be the crucial determinant of differences in speech style.

Verbal immediacy

As with the power variable, verbal immediacy could be discussed under lexical choice as well as under lexical patterning. The essential notion is that speakers approach or avoid the topics or referents of their messages through the positioning and choice of words (Wiener and Mehrabian 1967). One's liking for an object is reflected linguistically – the greater the liking, the more immediate the language. In a sense, speakers leak their feelings through language. Differences in levels of immediacy result from variations in adjectives (the *vs* that), verb tense (present *vs* past), order of occurrence of references in a sequence (earlier *vs* later), implied voluntarism (want *vs* must), mutuality (you and I eat cheese *vs* I eat cheese with you) and probability (you and I will *vs* you and I may). There is evidence that increased immediacy in a speaker's utterance is directly associated with untutored hearers' judgements of the speaker's liking for the referents of his or her message (Wiener and Mehrabian 1967). On the other hand, a receiver's liking for a communicator may be inversely related to the communicator's immediacy level in the case of a message which argues a position contrary to the receiver's. Other dimensions of the perception of speakers have been associated with immediacy also, e.g. perceived trustworthiness and competence have been shown to vary directly with speaker immediacy in a formal public communication context (Conville 1975).

Lexical diversity

Redundancy is a basic property of all communication systems (Watzlawick, Beavin and Jackson 1967). Repetition and recursion are essential to pattern formation and creativity (Hofstadter 1979). A digital system such as language entails the generation of novel structures from a small number of elements and rules for combination. These elements, e.g. phonemes, are necessarily repeated as structures are produced.

Words, the essential carriers of meaning, are commonly repeated within sentences and across sentences in discourse: 'The boy hit the dog'; 'The dog ran away'. Lexical diversity refers to the *degree* of repetition in a sample of language. This can be specified precisely. For example, the first sentence above has five words or 'tokens' and four 'types' since the word 'the' occurs twice. Thus, its type/token ratio is .80. The two sentences which comprise an utterance or discourse unit contain nine tokens and six types; so the type/token ratio is .67 in this case. This illustrates a property of natural language: the larger the linguistic unit, the greater the absolute redundancy value will tend to be.

Most of the studies of lexical diversity and related variables have focused on determinants of variation. For example, Sankoff and Lessard (1975) construed Bernstein (1971) as arguing that speakers from lower-class ghettoes exhibit a restricted vocabulary range as a result of relatively homogeneous social experience, i.e., communciation with a narrow range of persons. Their results failed to show a statistical relationship between social class and diversity level, revealing instead a direct relationship between diversity and both speaker age and years of formal schooling. Other researchers have demonstrated a relationship between neurological pathology and diversity level (Wachal and Spreen 1973), while still others have shown that a speaker's diversity level is inversely related to cognitive stress (Höweler 1972).

More to the point, Bradac and his colleagues have shown that large differences in diversity are recognized by normal listeners and are used to make judgements of a speaker's personality and abilities (Bradac, Davies, Courtright, Desmond and Murdock 1977). Generally, lower diversity results in receiver judgements of lower communicator competence, lower socioeconomic status, and higher anxiety. One study suggested that listeners are more likely to distinguish high redundancy than low redundancy from an average level (Bradac, Desmond and Murdock 1977).

Disfluency

This variable relates to diversity in that immediately repeated words or phrases are often taken as disfluent behaviour ('I . . . I . . . I won't'). But there are other components of disfluency in addition to the stutter, e.g. intruding incoherent sounds, false starts, and incomplete sentences (Kasl and Mahl 1965). In a general sense disfluency represents disrupted verbal performance. At some point disfluency is perceived by untutored listeners and used to make personality attributions, e.g. judgements of the extent to which a communicator is competent and trustworthy (Sereno and Hawkins 1967). But this 'point' is difficult to specify. It seems likely to vary as a complex function of the disfluency/fluency ratio, communicator attributes (e.g. age), and other situational variables. In many situations disfluencies in spontaneous speech go by unnoticed.

Observations about the lexical patterning variables

The concept of lexical patterning invites statistical analysis of messages in a way that consideration of individual lexical choices in terms of goodness, etc. does not. Perhaps this is most clearly seen in the case of diversity, which is *essentially* a statistical variable. Even syntax is amenable to mathematical approaches (Hays 1967). Another way of saying this is that one can investigate the *intrinsic structure* of messages from the standpoint of an external theory of numbers or logical system without recourse to the judgements of native speakers. This may be conducive to precision, objectivity, and replicability which are, of course, desirable. However, the statistical analysis of message structure is not *necessarily* desirable, a point which will be developed below.

The notion of linguistic universality should be mentioned in the context of patterning. The capacity to arrange lexical items in hierarchical structures appears to be biologically determined. Humans and possibly one other species (Rumbaugh 1977) are neurologically equipped to produce structured utterances. To this extent lexical patterning is pan-cultural or universal. However, the *particular* patterns, the *particular* rules which permit some combinations and prohibit others, are almost certainly learned. Thus, stylistic and syntactic rules vary between speech communities. Even within communities there is a degree of idiosyncratic variation among speakers (Bradac, Martin, Elliott and Tardy, 1980; J. R. Ross 1979).

The relationship between biology and culture ('nature' and 'nurture') is also interesting to think about in terms of the lexical power variable. Some ideological spectres are raised, including feminism and sexism (see Kramarae, this volume: ch. 5). It seems likely that most of the linguistic cues which indicate degree of speaker power are learned and therefore culturally idiosyncratic. For example, the connection between feminine forms of expression and perceived powerlessness

(Newcombe and Arnkoff 1979) should exist only in societies where femaleness is associated stereotypically with low power. Although certain phonetic forms *may* universally indicate strength or weakness via their association with size (a 'zug' is bigger than a 'zig'; see Brown 1958, pp. 110–54), it is difficult to imagine lexical patterns which are universally indicative of power or powerlessness. However, there may be a biologically based need for organisms to signal mutual recognition of power differences in *some* manner (Argyle 1969). Humans apparently have lin-guistic (as well as non-verbal) options for signalling such recognition.

Antecedents and consequences of lexical choice and patterning

The questions here are: What variables determine the choice and patterning of lexical items? And, once chosen and patterned, what are their consequences for communicators? The second question is, of course, especially important from the standpoint of this volume. But the question of determination is important also because listeners' reactions to a particular lexical pattern, e.g. low diversity, may differ as a function of their *perceptions* of the determinants of that pattern (see Bradac, Courtright, Schmidt and Davies 1976). For example, listeners may react differently to praise which they perceive to be situationally coerced on the one hand and genuinely intended by the speaker on the other (Bradac, Schneider, Hemphill and Tardy 1980). A detailed examination of antecedents and con-sequences of lexical variation has been offered previously by Bradac, Bowers and Courtright (1980), so the topic will be approached only generally here. The major conclusion made by Bradac *et al.* is contained in a summarizing causal model (p. 221) which indicates that a communicator's (source's) cognitive state affects his or her verbal style. Style variations interact with message valence, communicator characteristics, and receiver characteristics to affect receiver judgements of the communicator. Such judgements affect receivers' attitudes toward the message's proposition and their subsequent communicative behaviours *vis-à-vis* the source.

At a more general level, researchers have focused on two sources of variation: sociological and psychological. This distinction reflects the traditions in which researchers are socialized and the kinds of variables they are trained to examine. It is not a useful one for theory construction. Nonetheless, from the sociological per-spective, lexical variation occurs as a function of two major factors: group membership and situational context. Context will be discussed in some detail below. Social group differences which are examined reflect theoretical distinctions such as 'primary' and 'secondary' groups and social class (Bernstein 1971).

Psychological research on lexical variation has paid much attention to motiva-tional variables, e.g. arousal or drive (Bradac, Konsky and Elliott 1976). Research questions have typically taken the form: As a speaker's state changes from A to B, what are the consequences for verbal performance? The state of the speaker has been viewed as a variable under the control of external stimuli, both aversive and positive. Thus, certain stimuli, (e.g. a hostile interviewer) will increase arousal which in turn will decrease level of diversity (Höweler 1972). Less attention has been paid to trait variables, although some studies have related personality to lexical variation (Scherer 1979a) while others have examined consequences of neurological pathology (Wachal and Spreen 1973). In any case, psychological researchers of lexical variation have accepted overwhelmingly a deterministic model of behaviour: connections between stimuli and verbal behaviour are learned and modifiable by agencies external to the organism. Future research of a psychological sort may well profit by taking a cognitive as opposed to behaviouristic view, by focusing on the organization of thought and the relationship of this to lexical decisions (see Giles, Hewstone and St Clair in press) This sort of orientation would examine communicator choices instead of external forces which coerce behaviour. Relationships among speaker intentions, beliefs about hearer, and verbal patterns should be explored increasingly. Berger (1979), for example, discusses strategies which communicators use to gain knowledge about others under various circumstances. It should be very useful to examine in detail the lexical choices and patterns typically associated with such knowledge-gaining strategies (see Bradac, Hosman and Tardy 1978).

As for the consequences of lexical variation, sociologists have explored this problem infrequently; but when they have, an analytic or ethnographic method has typically been used (Goffman 1978). Psychologists have been much more interested in the problem of consequences, typically using experimental procedures (Giles and Powesland 1975). (Again, this sociologist-psychologist distinction refers to paradigms or traditions rather than to flesh-and-blood researchers.) Psychological research on consequences has been almost totally concerned with listeners' attitudes toward speakers who exhibit one or another variety of verbal performance. The following attitudinal dimensions have been examined, among others: speaker competence (Bradac, Konsky and Davies 1976), trustworthiness (Conville 1975), sociability (Giles, Wilson and Conway 1981), attractiveness (Bradac, Courtright and Bowers 1980), and persuasiveness (Burgoon, Jones and Stewart 1975). Many of the attitudinal variables reflect the more general constructs of ability and cohesion (Ryan 1979). That is, two broad classes of judgements have been shown to vary with speakers' lexical variation: the speaker is capable or not; the speaker is similar to me or not (see Simons, Moyer and Berkowitz 1970). In terms of the lexical variables discussed above, no simple generalizations can be offered about these two classes of judgement. Much depends upon the context in which lexical variation occurs (see Bradac, Bowers and Courtright 1980).

The focus on attitudes and the use of paper-and-pencil measures invites problems that are now familiar (Webb, Campbell, Schwartz and Sechrest 1966). The essential concern is the extent to which listeners' judgements made in a laboratory situation will generalize to their behaviours in other contexts. The use of behaviour measures in non-laboratory contexts should constitute a partial remedy (Cantor 1979). Perhaps the primary value of laboratory experimentation is that it can provide precise knowledge about perceptual thresholds – about lexical distinctions which are or are not perceived and about levels at which distinctions are or are not made. A non-linguistic analogue of this sort of endeavour is laboratory research on psychophysical judgements. In future work on consequences it should prove useful to broaden our conception of outcomes examining, for example, effects of lexical variation upon hearers' retention of information (Bradac, Desmond and Murdock 1977) and upon behavioural responses other than compliance with speaker requests (Bourhis, Giles, Leyens and Tajfel 1979; Cantor 1979).

An issue in the study of lexical variation

As suggested in the preceding section, verbal behaviour is contextualized. An utterance is influenced by situational antecedents and it has consequences which are situationally constrained. Traditionally, situational context has been viewed as a nominal variable which exists in the objective or 'real' world quite apart from the perceptions of naive interactants. Gumperz (1971) summarizes this view nicely:

> Most scholars visualize the relationship of linguistic to social categories as a match between closely connected but nevertheless conceptually independent systems. . . . Social categories are seen as part of the outside world, along with physical surroundings, artifacts, beliefs, etc. Just as concrete objects are identifiable through physical properties like shape, colour, texture, and weight, which are subject to independent measurements, so social facts are conceived as measurable by social indices independent of the communication process (pp. 222–3).

This sort of model assumes that members of a cultural group share a knowledge of objectively discoverable components of context and of appropriate forms of language (see Ervin-Tripp 1964; Hymes 1972). This assumption is compatible with the assumption of both structural and transformational-generative linguistics that members of a speech community share completely a knowledge of the elements of language, such as phonemes. This shared knowledge makes verbal communication possible. While entirely reasonable at one level, it should be noted that the assumption of consensual knowledge does not allow researchers or theorists to focus on interesting questions of idiosyncratic variation resulting from the unique perceptions of individual speakers. Moreover, an extreme version of this model probably incorrectly views situational context as having virtual hegemony over behaviour, with communicators being little more than rule-obeying 'sociolinguistic automatons' (Giles 1977).

Some recent views of context invite scrutiny of individual variation. These views might be characterized as social psychological in that their starting point is the individual's perception of social data. The key question is: How do individuals construe social encounters? An important assumption is that individuals employ systems of 'personal constructs' to assign meanings to social data (Delia 1977; Kelly 1955). These constructs may be highly idiosyncratic or widely shared by many individuals. For example, Bradac, Sandell and Wenner (1979) found that some persons paid primary attention to the attributes 'trustworthiness' and 'first-hand experience' when thinking about useful human information sources in a hypothetical decision-making situation, whereas others attended primarily to 'professional training' and 'expertise'. Thus, *Experiential Trusters* differed from *Competence-Oriented Information Seekers*, although *within* each type persons tended to agree on those attributes of information sources which were salient. It seems likely that the verbal styles of these two very dissimilar types of communicators will differ although this has not been investigated.

Another important assumption of this 'phenomenological' perspective is that the categories employed by social theorists may not be the same as those employed by naive persons in their construal of the social world. Forgas (1976), for example, found nothing resembling an informal/formal distinction in housewives' and students' perception of social episodes, although this distinction exists in various speculative taxonomies of the social world. The housewives used two primary dimensions to distinguish social episodes in their lives, perceived intimacy and subjective self-confidence, whereas the students used three dimensions, intimacy, self-confidence and evaluation. A cohesive group of faculty, staff and research students differentiated group-relevant social episodes along four dimensions: anxiety, involvement, evaluation, and socio-emotional versus task orientation (Forgas 1978). Giles, Hewstone and St Clair (in press) discuss some implications of Forgas's work for language behaviour.

The 'phenomenological' perspective and supportive empirical studies suggest that language choices will vary according to speakers' perceptions of the situations they are in. Some situations will be perceived similarly by many speakers as a result of shared cultural training, but others will be perceived dissimilarly which may produce disagreements. Disagreements can be of two general sorts: two interactants may understand that situation types 'A' and 'B' exist, but one may label *this* situation 'A' whereas the other thinks that it is 'B'; or one or both of the persons may construe the situation in a unique way, employing a label not even understood by the other. It should be rather difficult to resolve the latter sort of disagreement. In the absence of programmatic research, it is not clear how unique construals of situation will affect verbal communication. But perhaps where speakers construe situations idiosyncratically, mutual uncertainty will be high, i.e. each person will feel that the other is behaviourally and cognitively unpredictable (Berger and Calabrese 1975). This may lower the immediacy of each speaker's language if each attempts to withdraw (Wiener and Mehrabian 1967). If uncertainty is associated with subjective stress or anxiety, both language intensity and lexical diversity may be relatively low (Bradac, Bowers and Courtright 1980). Disfluency, on the other hand, should be high (Kasl and Mahl 1965). Special verbal strategies for expressing uncertainty may be used (Scotton 1976). Unfamiliar terms may be exchanged if the interactants discuss their idiosyncratic situational construals. If self-awareness is increased as a result of the recognition of one's own idiosyncracy, the use of 'I' and other self-oriented words may increase which may be associated with the decrease in immediacy ('you' and 'I' instead of 'we'). The almost certainly complex attitudinal consequences of these simultaneous variations remain to be investigated. But low diversity and high disfluency may well produce (or intensify) mutual dislike and mutual judgements of dissimilarity and incompetence (Bradac, Bowers and Courtright 1980).

The search for unique modes of situational construal and the consequences for language may lead to a closer examination of the kinds of attributes communicators assign to each other. Although we might expect persons to assign role-based attributes in initial encounters (therapist, therefore friendly), as relationships develop attributions should become increasingly psychological (Miller and Steinberg 1975), focusing on internal states and unique characteristics, which should result in increasingly 'person-centred speech' (Applegate and Delia 1980). An aspect of this move away from role-based attributions is the mutual assessment of intentions: Why is X doing/saying this at this point? (see Cacioppo and Petty, this volume: ch. 12; Street and Hopper, this volume: ch. 11). Some linguistic consequences of the mutual assessment of intentions have been examined in interesting recent research. For example, the convergence or divergence of speech styles has been shown to depend partially upon speakers' mutual assessments of the other's reason for using one style instead of another (Giles and Smith 1979).

If the idiosyncratic or person-centred construal of social situations can reasonably be discussed, might it be useful to extend this notion to the processing of linguistic stimuli? All of the studies described in the preceding sections have used categorical distinctions reflecting one or another theory of language or style. That is, researchers have assumed, very reasonably it seems, that words are psychologically relevant 'chunks' of reality and that sentences are equally relevant higher-order 'chunks'; therefore they have exposed subjects to messages exhibiting systematic variations in word choice and sentence structure (see Giles and Ryan, this volume, ch. 13).

The positive results of the research cited throughout this chapter show that this assumption is tenable – the judgements of many subjects have been affected in predicted ways by lexical variations controlled by the researchers. Of course, there is error variance in the results of all of these studies, in some cases a lot of it, so subjects' judgements have not been affected exactly as expected. Perhaps some of the 'deviant' subjects are organizing verbal input differently than the standard constructs of word, sentence, diversity ratio, etc. would suggest.

The traditional linguistic units are so deeply ingrained in both popular and technical treatments of language that it is difficult to imagine linguistic categories which are of a qualitatively different order. But it may be useful to explore the possibility empirically, perhaps using multivariate analytic techniques. For example, the author, Michael Hemphill, Robert Hertzog and Bryan Crow recently had undergraduates from two Iowa schools judge each of 48 sentences which exhibited various kinds of lexical repetition. All subjects judged each sentence along a nine-interval scale, the poles of which were 'effective' and 'ineffective'. Some repetitions were adjacent, others were separated by one or more words; some occurred within clauses, others between clauses; some were in an initial position in the sentence, others were in a final position; some were 'substantive' (nouns, verbs, adjectives), others were 'functional' (prepositions, articles, copulas), etc. Responses are being subjected to a Q-analysis (along with other analyses) which potentially will yield a picture of types of persons with regard to judgements of the effectiveness of repetitions. Purely speculatively, one type of person might use the dimension of repetition adjacency exclusively when rendering effectiveness judgements; another type might discriminate along a functional–substantive dimension; a third type might attend to position of the repetition in the sentence and to its functional –substantive nature. Of special interest here would be the emergence of a type (or types) which, on the basis of its constituents' judgements, would force the researchers to abandon their *a priori* distinctions among repetitions and to construct new ones. Equally interesting would be the emergence of a type which, compared to other types, consistently fails to discriminate among the various repetitions. This would indicate that lexical repetitions are not noticed by or perhaps are not meaningful to a significant sub-class of persons. The question then would become: what linguistic variations, if any, *are* noticed by and *are* meaningful to these individuals?

This kind of phenomenological approach to language processing is a radical one. But at least one theorist approaching the issue from a different viewpoint believes a radical conceptual revision is necessary. Specifically, Hudson (1980) argues that the very notion of 'variety of language' in its traditional sense is incorrect. He rejects concepts such as 'dialect', 'register', and 'pidgin', substituting for them the single concept 'linguistic item'. Although this concept is somewhat vague, he means by this 'not only lexical items but also syntactic constructions and morphological and phonological patterns of any type . . . simply a pattern which may be identified, at any level of abstraction, in the structure of the sentence (p. 189).' Hudson is calling our attention to 'bundles' of linguistic phenomena, the contents and boundaries of which vary with speakers and occasions. Thus, a given person or group of similar persons may attend to a particular concatenation of lexical and syntactic features in one kind of circumstance and another concatenation elsewhere.

In a similar vein, several workers in a recent collection of essays distinguish between 'etic' and 'emic' speech markers (Scherer and Giles 1979). For example, Giles, Scherer and Taylor (1979) indicate that:

Speech markers are defined as those extralinguistic, paralinguistic, and linguistic cues which differentiate between various biological, social and psychological categories or characteristics of speakers which are important – actually or potentially – for social organization and social interaction. . . . Emic speech markers are those which have social meaningfulness, while etic markers refer to those which may be highly correlated with, for instance, a social category or psychological state yet are not used in any sense by listeners in terms of recognition, evaluation, or behavioural response (pp. 360, 371).

An implication of this position is that 'bundles' of linguistic phenomena which are meaningful to a particular social group may represent distinctions ignored by linguists, for example. On the other hand, naive processors of linguistic stimuli may ignore distinctions typically preserved by linguists. Finally, the immediate goal of a phenomenological approach to language variation is not to revel in an idiosyncratic *reductio ad absurdum* but rather to discover important subgroups which differ in their perceptions and evaluations of speech.

Conclusions

Nine important lexical variables have been discussed in terms of their consequences for communicators. Some problems have been indicated with the hope that investigators of the attitudinal consequences of lexical variation will attend to these in future work. Specifically, it was suggested that the conceptual foundations of some of the lexical variables must be examined more carefully than they have been thus far. For example, 'powerful' and 'powerless' speech styles have been conceptualized essentially as a role attribute when they may be more accurately and usefully conceptualized as the reflection of a particular psychological state. In this case an obvious direction for research involves the analysis of language produced by persons who perceive themselves to be powerful or powerless. The ways in which this language changes as a function of social situation should be investigated also, as should the attitudinal consequences of this language in various settings.

Another suggestion cuts across all of the variables: researchers must increasingly *contextualize* their investigations of the attitudinal consequences of lexical variation (see Giles and Ryan, this volume, ch. 13). It is clear that a listener's perception of situational factors can strongly affect his or her reactions to a communicator's language; a shift in context can drastically alter reactions to a particular linguistic form (Bradac, Courtright, Schmidt and Davies 1976; Burgoon *et al.* 1975). A cruical aspect of context is the hearer's perception of the speaker's intent or, in other cases, interactants' mutual perceptions of intent. Surprisingly, this variable has been explored infrequently in the research on language attitudes. The recent formulations of an 'accomodation model' should help to remedy this situation (Giles and Powesland 1975; Giles and Smith 1979).

Perhaps the most basic issue addressed has been that of 'objectivity versus subjectivity' (or 'noumenonalism versus phenomenonalism' or 'behaviourism versus constructivism'). From the standpoint of this chapter, these distinctions refer to the fact that lexical variation can be defined independently of respondents' perceptions on the one hand or exclusively with reference to these perceptions on the other. Thus an extreme 'objectivist' would argue that particular lexical variations can affect respondents' behaviours even though the respondents are completely unaware of these variations and, further, that these are precisely the variations which should be researched. The extreme 'subjectivist' might counter that only those lexical variations of which respondents are aware are worthy of study, because these are the distinctions that respondents can act upon in their attempts to manage their social lives. A complete theory of attitudinal consequences of lexical variation will probably transcend both perspectives. Actually the two perspectives are not all that discrete in that knowledge which is initially available only to the 'objectivist' researcher can be communicated to naive respondents with the effect of their becoming aware of lexical distinctions which they had not previously noticed (see Robinson 1979). And the naive respondent can inform the researcher as well, a fact which suggests this chapter's final point.

Although in a particular sense language attitudes research has always leaned toward the subjective pole – an attitude is a subjective construct – it may be useful for research on lexical variation to become increasingly subjective or phenomenological in another sense. This 'other sense' will influence the conduct of research at the levels of both dependent and independent variables. On the one hand, subjects will inform the researchers about the dimensions of judgement which are salient to them in the context of a particular domain of linguistic phenomena; thus a particular measure of attitudes, e.g. communicator credibility scales, will not be imposed upon subjects simply because this measure has been used in previous studies of other possibly unrelated linguistic phenomena (see Delia 1977). On the other hand, apart from dimensions of judgement, subjects will inform the researcher about the linguistic distinctions they make, the differences they perceive, given an array of linguistic objects; the researcher's knowledge of such distinctions will be used subsequently in experiments to create the stimulus messages which subjects judge (see Bradac, Sandell and Wenner 1979). Of course naive respondents are typically rather inarticulate when asked to talk about a particular domain of phenomena. Specifically they may have an extremely limited verbal repertoire for characterizing the linguistic distinctions they perceive. Thus the researcher who desires to be 'informed' by respondents will often use a procedure which makes minimal demands upon their verbal abilities. In many cases tasks demanding nonverbal responses will be appropriate. In fact for many purposes the 'subjectivist' researchers will be not at all interested in respondents' particular verbal characterizations but rather in the discriminations they make however they label them. It is the *researcher's* task to articulate respondents' perceptions by relating these to theoretically embedded concepts via logical rules of inference. This is not to say that respondents' verbal characterizations are irrelevant but instead that such characterizations constitute one type of data among several other types.

With this sort of subjective approach, both the researcher *and* the respondents have a degree of control over stimuli and responses. Potentially such an approach is more than fashionably egalitarian. It can be a *corrective* to the currently one-sided approach where, on the basis of tradition, researchers call all the shots. One-sidedness has its special dangers, as transformational–generative linguists are beginning to discover (Bradac, Martin, Elliott and Tardy, 1980; Ringen 1975; J. R. Ross 1979). More positively, this sort of phenomenological method may well reveal a subtlety and multidimensionality – in other words, a *richness* – in naive construals of lexical variation, and this may rescue us from the tedium (and inaccuracy) of a linear and unidimensional universe of drab linguistic objects.

7

Children's attitudes toward language[1]

Richard R. Day

Since the early 1960s, research in various regions of the world has demonstrated that people have definite attitudes about their own languages and about other languages and dialects (Giles and Powesland 1975; Ryan 1979). The purpose of this chapter is to examine research into children's attitudes toward the languages or dialects used in their speech communities. In the first section we examine the relationship between language attitudes and communicative competence and discuss the notion that language attitudes are part of the latter. We then focus our attention on the age àt which children first become aware of language differences. The issue which ·forms the major portion of this chapter concerns attitudes of children toward minority and majority languages or dialects. We review research which indicates that minority children first acquire positive attitudes toward their home language, but later display attitudes which reflect those of the dominant culture. We also see that majority children, from a very young age, acquire attitudes consistent with those held by their families. These results are then compared to the findings from studies dealing with the development of racial and ethnic attitudes by young children in general. The chapter concludes with suggestions for future research and a summary of the findings.

It is important to note that while there have been a number of significant studies about the process of the socialization of children, there has been relatively little research on children's language attitudes, much less the acquisition of such attitudes. Perhaps one reason may be the general feeling about this subject as explained by Labov (1966), who claimed that he had evidence indicating that it was not until 19 or 20 years of age that full sensitivity to socially significant dialect features is acquired. Labov (1965) also claimed that children do not become aware of the social significance of their dialect characteristics until early adolescence. However, as we discover in this chapter, children from an early age are able to *discriminate linguistically*. In addition, we find evidence that children as young as 3:6 are able to make language attitudinal judgements which reflect adult beliefs prevalent in their speech community.

Communicative competence and language attitudes

We believe that language attitudes are an integral part of communicative com-

[1] I would like to express my appreciation to Howard Giles and Ellen Bouchard Ryan for their insightful comments on an earlier version of this chapter. A note of thanks should also be extended to Richard Schmidt for his helpful suggestions.

petence, which is the knowledge required to use a language appropriately in a speech community (Hymes 1972, pp. 63–4).[2] It includes, in addition to grammatical knowledge, social knowledge which acts to define the communicative process and to shape the way messages are realized in social situations. That language attitudes are a part of communicative competence is implicit in Hymes's formulation of this concept. We refer specifically to what Hymes calls norms of interaction – the specific behaviours and proprieties that attach to speaking – and norms of interpretation. Both of these norms involve the social relationships and the belief system of a community, of which language attitudes play a crucial role.

If we view language attitudes as an important component of communicative competence, of interest is when children first display an awareness of certain aspects of communicative competence. Halliday (1975) found that Nigel, at 10 months, had a general instrumental request form and a number of forms which regulated repetition or immediacy in people's actions. Bates (1976) also found that children in their first year displayed an ability to direct other people's behaviour. Dore (1973), using videotapes of four children early in their second year, found they were able to use directives also. In a later study, Dore (1976) reported that children aged 2:10 through 3:3 had developed competence in question–answer routines. Ervin-Tripp (1977), in a review of the acquisition of directives by children, discusses research which indicates that by the third year, children show variation in their use of directives (1977). Keenan (1977) claims that children aged 2:9 are sensitive to the illocutionary force of prior utterances in discourse. Because of these and similar findings (Berko-Gleason and Perlmann in press; Harrison and Piette 1980), we conclude that at least by the end of their second year children have begun to acquire communicative competence in their first language.

This conclusion allows us to expect that children will acquire attitudes toward language at a very young age. As we see later in this chapter, this expectation is fulfilled. Before examining this research, it is necessary to discuss an issue which, developmentally, is prior, *viz* the age when children are able to distinguish their language or dialect from a second language or dialect.

Recognition of language differences

Aboud (1976) claims that the ability of young children to distinguish between two languages/dialects – their own and another – is crucial for it shows that children realize that the way they speak is not the only way to communicate and that they speak *a* language as distinct from the *only* language. She claims this awareness of language differences enables children to help distinguish between themselves – those who speak their language – and others – those who don't speak their language. Aboud (1976) reviews the research others have done in this area and also reports the results of three of her own Canadian investigations of the social categories children use in identifying themselves and others. She used picture books in one study with white kindergarten and first-grade children to see if they identified with Canadians who were white, Indian, Eskimo, Chinese or black. In another study, Jewish-Canadian kindergarteners were asked if they could be English,

[2] We accept Hymes's definition of a speech community. 'Tentatively a *speech community* is defined as a community sharing rules for the conduct and interpretation of speech, and rules for the interpretation of at least one linguistic variety' (1972, 54).

Canadian, Canadian Indian, black Canadian, Jewish Canadian, French Canadian, or Canadian Eskimo. The third study had the subjects – Jewish Canadian children in kindergarten and first grade – place 12 stimulus persons on a board relative to a stimulus person representing MYSELF. The 12 stimulus persons varied in five major characteristics: ethnicity, language, nationality, behaviour and evaluation (Good People). In all three studies, the children, ages five and six, used language to help distinguish between themselves and others. Aboud (1976, 34) concludes that 'language becomes an important social factor around the age of five or six, that it is at least initially used as a basis for perceptions of similarity rather than differences, and that it is the more concrete aspects of language that are first recognized.'

Other research, however, indicates that children become aware of language differences before the age of five. In particular, Mercer (1975) investigated the ability of monolingual English-Canadian children between the ages of 3:6 and 5:8 to discriminate between English and French, English and French-accented English, and French and Greek. In what may be considered a tiring task for the young subjects, Mercer asked them individually to listen to two voices (e.g. one speaking English; the other, French) and then listen to other voices, telling the investigator if they sounded like either of the two voice samples (e.g. Judy or Michele). The youngest of the subjects – those between 3:6 and 4:0 years of age – were able to discriminate between French and English. The subjects older than 4:6 could also discriminate between English and French-accented English. However, none could tell any difference between the two foreign languages, French and Greek.

We may conclude that perhaps by the age of 3:6 – and certainly by the age of 5:0 – children are aware of language differences and can distinguish between the language they speak and languages other people speak.

The acquisition of language attitudes by members of majority and minority groups

In this section, we review a representative sampling of investigations of children's attitudes towards the various languages or dialects used in their speech communities. The results of these studies provide evidence to support the claim that young children are not only aware of differences in language before elementary school, but that they are able to make judgements about such differences. We begin our discussion by first examining studies showing that from an early age both majority and minority children gradually acquire the attitudes of the majority speech. Next, we look at those studies which indicate that minority children acquire such attitudes at an older age; finally, we look at research which indicates that perhaps minority children do not acquire the majority's language attitudes at all.

Rosenthal (1974) investigated the development of attitudes in black and white children between the ages of 3:0 and 5:11 toward black English (BE) and standard English (SE). Her research design called for two identical cardboard boxes, spray-painted with ears, eyebrows and noses to appeal to her young subjects and avoid racial identity. Inside each box she placed cassette recorders with pre-recorded tapes of two 17-year-old male speakers, one using SE and the other, BE.

The subjects, white children from what Rosenthal called the upper class, and lower-class black children from a semi-rural area, had two tasks – to listen to both boxes 'talk' and to answer a series of questions about the two boxes. Then the subjects were asked either to take a present from or give a present to the box of

their choice. The questions they were asked were:
Taking
1. Which box has nicer presents?
2. Which box sounds nicer?
3. Which box talks better?
4. Which box do you like better?
5. Which box do you want to take your present from?

Giving
1. Which box wants it more?
2. Which box needs it more?
3. Which box sounds nicer?
4. Which box do you want to give it to? (Rosenthal 1974, 58–9)

There are two drawbacks to Rosenthal's study. First, it suffers from a serious lack of statistical treatment of the results. The data are presented in tables which show only percentages. We do not know, for example, if there are any significant differences between the two populations. Second, as noted above, she used two different speakers, rather than one person proficient in the two varieties. Using two speakers leaves some doubt about what the subjects were responding to. For example, some of the subjects could have picked up certain idiosyncratic voice qualities, which were afforded far more importance than any racial vocal attributes.

Nevertheless, results suggest that the subjects had already formed attitudes toward the two varieties of English. They associated higher socioeconomic status with SE (has better presents) and lower socioeconomic status with BE (needs the present more). Rosenthal also points out that the two groups agreed that the SE speaker talked better. However, while the subjects were in agreement as to status and quality, they differed on preference. The upper-class white children expressed more of a preference for the SE speakers than did the black children.

In a study which used a similar design but whose subjects were slightly older than Rosenthal's, Day (1980) investigated the attitudes and preferences of kindergarten and first-grade children to SE and Hawaiian Creole English (HCE). HCE is best considered a creole continuum in which decreolization is taking place (Bickerton and Odo 1976). Varieties of HCE are spoken at many socioeconomic levels in the Hawaiian Islands, with the more creolized forms spoken by members of the lower socioeconomic groups. HCE has little prestige and is often blamed for the poor academic achievements of its speakers (Carr 1972).

Day used the same technique as Rosenthal, as noted above, and the subjects were asked the same questions. But the speech samples for his study were produced by only one person – a 27-year-old female, fluent in both HCE and SE. The subjects, who were between the ages of five and seven, attended two different schools in Honolulu. One school, labelled School A, was located in an industrial area of the city; the other, School B, in a more residential neighbourhood. The parents of School A students were employed in less prestigious occupations, and many received some type of federal or state aid. While the two populations were similar in ethnic background (representing most if not all of the different cultural and ethnic groups in Hawaii), the children from School A are generally believed to be somewhat disadvantaged economically and academically compared to the children from School B. The former generally speak more creolized forms of HCE;

the latter, while fluent in the acrolect of HCE (referred to as standard Hawaiian English in Tsuzaki 1971) also have the ability to speak the more creolized forms of HCE.

Although Day's study, like Rosenthal's, suffers from a lack of rigorous statistical treatment of the data, it does show that his subjects had indeed developed particular attitudes toward and preferences for the two speech codes. For example, the first-graders from School B favoured the SE speaker 77.8 per cent of the time. This overwhelming preference for and positive attitude toward the SE speaker was also reflected in the children's judgements that she had nicer presents, sounded nicer, talked better, had better presents, and so on. The first-graders from School A also showed a definite preference for the SE speaker (63.9 per cent), but not quite to the degree that the first-graders in the other school did. These children also indicated an awareness of the socioeconomic status of HCE when they said that the HCE box needed the present more, but that the SE box had better presents.

The results of the kindergarten children's responses in Day's study contain an interesting phenomenon. The children from School B, the one located in the middle-class neighbourhood, favoured the SE speaker only 54.2 per cent of the time (compared to 77.8 per cent for their first-grade classmates). They actually favoured the HCE speaker in response to question 1 (Which box has nicer presents?; 60 per cent said the HCE speaker did) and question 9 (Which box do you want to give it to?; 56 per cent said they wanted to give it to the HCE speaker). The kindergarten children from the less-advantaged neighbourhood are even more different; they favoured the HCE speaker 62.3 per cent of the time. These data support an interpretation that the kindergarten children in a speech community which uses both minority and majority codes are less in favour of the majority code than children in first grade; and further, that the minority children are less in favour of the majority code than the majority children. Then, after both groups of children spend time in a school system in which the majority code is the language of instruction, both groups exhibit preferences for and favourable attitudes toward the majority language. However, longitudinal research is necessary for documenting any posited changes during the first years of school.

Additional evidence that children who speak a nonstandard or minority dialect gradually acquire the language attitudes of the standard or majority culture comes from a study by Cremona and Bates (1977) in an investigation of the development of attitudes toward standard Italian and a southern Italian dialect, Valmontonese. Their subjects were in grades one through six (ages 6:0–10:0), living in a small town in a rural area in which Valmontonese is used almost exclusively at home. Each child listened through a set of headphones to eight pairs of sentences, spoken once in Italian and once in Valmontonese by one person, a male fluent in both dialects. The child was then asked which one spoke better and why. The youngest children (the six-year-olds) exhibited equal preference for both dialects. However, the seven-year-olds displayed a preference for standard Italian, and the eight-year-olds preferred standard Italian almost 100 per cent. Although these subjects did not reflect the attitudes of the dominant culture at the same age as Day's subjects, the pattern is clear: children speaking a minority dialect, whether it is creolized or geographic, apparently enter school with a preference for or at least a neutral attitude towards their speech code, but as they grow older, tend to acquire the language attitudes of the dominant culture. They come to value more highly the dominant variety, and associate the socioeconomic stereotypes held by the dominant culture with their primary speech code.

This pattern is also apparent in children who speak a majority dialect. Giles, Harrison, Smith and Freeman (1981) in a study in Bristol, England, found that younger children (seven years old) evaluated Welsh-accented English more positively than British Received Pronunciation (RP), while the older children (nine and ten years of age) apparently switched – evaluating RP more positively than the Welsh-accented English. They used a matched – guise technique with a male speaker reading a neutral passage lasting 30 seconds. Two female speakers were used as filler voices – one using Bristolian-accented English and the other, RP. The subjects rated each speaker on six 5-point scales, three relating to prestige (clever, successful and lazy) and three to pleasantness (likeable, funny and nasty). Giles *et al.* found that the older subjects rated the Welsh-accented speaker as funnier than the RP speaker, with the reverse being true for the seven-year-olds. The ten-year-olds considered the RP speaker as more successful, the middle group indicated there was little difference between the two guises, and the youngest subjects believed the Welsh-accented speaker to be more successful than the RP speaker. The other four traits were not affected. Thus we see that by the age of ten, the subjects were socialized into the perceived socioeconomic correlates of RP speech.

These results are similar to those of Day and of Cremona and Bates in that the younger subjects evaluated the regional variety positively. However, there is a difference in that the children in the latter studies spoke the regional variant as their first language, while Giles's subjects did not speak the Welsh-accented variety.

We should also note that Giles and his colleagues investigated whether the social context of evaluating the speakers affected their subject's ratings. After listening to the speakers, the subjects evaluated them according to three experimental treatments. One was the regular method, in which the subjects were asked to rate the speaker as soon as he or she had finished talking. The second treatment, the group condition, had the subjects relate their impressions of the speakers to members of a four-person group. This lasted about 90 seconds, and then the subjects made their individual ratings. In the control condition, the third treatment, the subjects were requested to think about their impressions silently for 90 seconds before making their ratings. They found that the only interaction effects to emerge were those between condition and age for two scales, lazy and likeable. The older children rated the speakers more likeable and less lazy in the group discussion condition than in the other two conditions; however, the seven-year-old subjects found speakers less likeable and more lazy in the group discussion condition than in the other two. Giles *et al.* concluded that the social context of evaluation could affect their subjects' ratings, a point to which we return later in this chapter.

Bouchard-Ryan's (1969) study of white middle-class children in the United States and their attitudes toward SE, low-class white English, and BE also provides evidence that majority children by the age of 10 and 11 are aware of the social significance of language variation. Her subjects, in the fifth and sixth grades, listened to a tape recording containing excerpts of conversations by six different speakers using the three varieties. Using a semantic differential scale, the subjects rated the speakers on 15 traits (e.g. wise, tall, religious, trustworthy, goodlooking, kind) and in terms of occupation (janitor, gas station attendant, fireman, teacher, and doctor). The children rated the SE speakers significantly higher than the other two speakers, and the lower-class white speakers significantly higher than the speakers of BE. In addition, the subjects assigned the speakers to occupations consistent with the fifteen traits. For example, the SE speakers were ranked signi-ficantly more often as teachers or doctors than were the other dialect speakers. Thus in the studies by Giles *et al.* and Bouchard-Ryan, we see that majority children by the ages of 10 and 11 apparently have learned the attitudes of the majority toward both the majority language variety and the minority variety.

Since research indicates acceptance of the language attitudes of the majority by both majority and minority children, of interest are the attitudes of bilinguals towards their languages. Lewis (1975) investigated the attitudes of both mono-linguals and bilinguals toward Welsh and English in Wales. His data were based on an extensive survey conducted between 1967 and 1971 among children in junior and secondary schools. Unfortunately, Lewis gives little information about the research design, except that Thurstone type tests were used to measure attitudes from the students; a semantic differential scale was administered to the secondary school students only. Lewis found that the 'attitude to Welsh becomes increasingly less favourable in all areas and types of schools as the students grow older, and increasingly favourable to English' (1975, p. 109).

The next three studies have somewhat different results. They indicate that their subjects, children whose first language was not the majority code, did not display total acceptance of the language attitudes of the majority. These findings should not be considered unusual or unexpected, for like the language attitudes displayed by the subjects in the studies discussed above, they reflect the subjects' involve-ment in their speech communities. To the extent that minority children accept the values of the majority speech community, they will display similar language atti-tudes as part of their overall communicative competence.

Ramirez, Arce-Torres, and Politzer (1978) investigated attitudes of Spanish-speaking fourth and fifth graders (nine and ten-year-olds) and their teachers in a number of California schools where English was the medium of instruction. A matched-guise design was used to measure their subjects' attitudes towards SE, his-panized English, standard Spanish, and a style of speech which was characterized by code-switching between SE and Spanish. The guises were produced by four adult speakers (two men and two women). Their subjects were asked to rate each guise on three dimensions: correctness, appropriateness, and likelihood-of-achievement. As we might expect, the children and their teachers displayed similar attitudes toward English and Spanish, rating SE more highly than Spanish. However, in evaluating what Ramirez *et al.* called the children's primary speech style, Spanish-English code-switching, the children disagreed with their teachers. They evaluated the code-switching style more favourably than hispanized English; their teachers, on the other hand, viewed hispanized English more favourably than the code-switching style. In addition, pupil achievement scores were positively related to the degree to which the children downgraded the code-switching style compared to SE (i.e. the degree to which they displayed attitudes congruent with their teachers). It is important to note that there was agreement on what may be viewed as the most visible and legitimate of the languages (SE and Spanish) but dis-agreement on the relative merits of the mixing of these two languages. This could indicate that while the teachers and their students shared the beliefs and attitudes of a broad speech community, they each belonged to a more restricted group or immediate speech community, those individuals with whom a person has daily and intimate contact. This narrower group to which the teachers belonged might not have included the language mixing found in the students' immediate speech community. For the latter, code-switching plays a major role in intra-group communication and is valued (see Carranza, this volume: ch. 3).

In a study in which teachers and students apparently belong to the same immediate speech community, Anisfeld and Lambert (1964) found that their monolingual French-Canadian 10-year-olds, in a matched-guise study, rated the personalities of the speakers who used French higher than the English guises. Anisfeld and Lambert speculate that at 10 years of age, perhaps these monolingual students were not yet cognizant of the attitudes of the majority toward the two languages. By way of contrast, in the same study, bilingual French-Canadians of the same age rated the guises as similar. We speculate that these language attitudes probably developed as a result of their bilingual school environment.

A study by Schneiderman (1976) with French-Canadian children in an English-dominant area also provides evidence that not all minority children exhibit favourable attitudes toward the majority language as they grow older. Even though this study again suffers from a lack of statistical analysis, the results show that her subjects, who ranged in age from five to eleven, expressed more favourable attitudes toward French than toward English, with the older subjects showing a higher degree of favourable attitudes toward French. The subjects, in grades kindergarten through sixth, attended public schools in which French was the medium of instruction. However, Schneiderman believed that, by age 10, they used English exclusively in peer group interactions away from the classroom. Given this use of English in situations which did not apparently require it, Schneiderman hypothesized that the older subjects would have more favourable attitudes towards English than the younger children.

Schneiderman used a video-taped puppet show to measure her subjects' language attitudes. The script for the show was recorded by four bilingual ten-year-olds, two boys and two girls, from the speech community. They also helped to write it. There were eight versions of the show, four in each language, lasting about five minutes.

Her subjects, aged five to eleven years, viewed a version of the show and were asked individually ten questions in what their teachers had determined to be the child's stronger language. Five of the questions treated issues or events which took place (e.g. Which puppet threw the ball better?), but some of these questions were designed to require inferences concerning what took place (e.g. Which puppet cheated?). For example, the puppets accuse each other of cheating, although neither one actually does cheat. Schneiderman claims that this procedure means 'the subject's attitude towards the two puppets, rather than his perceptual skills or memory, is considered to be reflected in his response to the question' (1976, p. 63). Four of the remaining questions required the subjects to rate four character traits: stupidity, kindness, nastiness and destructiveness; the final question measured social distance (Which puppet would you invite to your birthday party?) (1976, p. 63).

The results fail to provide support for Schneiderman's hypothesis that the older children would exhibit more favourable attitudes toward English than the younger children. All of her subjects, except the kindergarteners (five-year-olds), exhibited more favourable attitudes toward the French puppet than toward the English puppet. The kindergarten children exhibited a slight preference for the English puppet. With the exception of the second-graders (seven-year-olds), who were the most favourable to the French puppet, the older children expressed stronger French preference than the younger.

Discussion

The general findings of the research into children's attitudes toward language show how children, both minority and majority, reflect the attitudes toward language variation which are consistent with those of members of their immediate speech community. Up to the age of three, a child's immediate speech community generally is composed of parents and other caregivers, siblings and relatives. However, it broadens as the child gets older, exposing him or her to a wider range of attitudes. Minority children with exposure to the majority culture tend to display attitudes which reflect their exposure.

It is important to point out that we do not mean to imply that a speech community is monolithic and homogeneous, or that the language attitudes of the majority are always acquired by all members of a given speech community. The last three studies presented in the preceding section should serve to illustrate these two points. For example, in the Anisfeld and Lambert study, the monolingual French-Canadian subjects exhibited favourable attitudes toward the French guises probably because of relatively little exposure to the broader speech community which includes both French and English speakers. The bilingual French-Canadian subjects did have different language attitudes (i.e. they rated the guises as similar), perhaps because of their exposure to English speakers in their school environment.

Schneiderman's results do not seem to fit the general pattern, however. Her subjects apparently learned English, although they went to a school in which French was the medium of instruction. Their learning English means that they must have had contact with English speakers which would broaden their exposure to the majority culture. Despite these experiences, presumably increasing with age, the findings showed a developmental pattern in favour of French. In attempting to account for this discrepancy, we should mention that her particular (puppet) technique might have enabled her to tap her subjects' attitudes more accurately than other techniques. This could be an important variable in some of the research but not in the Rosenthal and Day investigations, which used talking boxes. Moreover, eliciting interpretations of ambiguous intergroup interactions may be an especially sensitive procedure. Whether Schneiderman's results are unique or can be generalized to other minority children must be determined by future research.

It is also important to note that while the studies presented in the preceding section provide valuable insights concerning the status which the majority language comes to occupy in the lives of both minority and majority children, we know relatively little about minority children's subsequent attitudes toward their first language or dialect. The forced-choice design of all of the investigations provides information about which code the subjects prefer, but it does not provide us with information about the subjects' attitudes toward the code not chosen. Attaching good or positive qualities toward one group – the majority – does not necessarily reflect bad or negative attitudes toward the other stimuli in the investigation. A child could feel positively towards English, for example, while still liking, or being neutral or even disliking his or her language. For example, in Cremona and Bates, the older children said Italian was better than Valmontonese. In Day, the older children said they liked the SE box better, that it sounded nicer, and that it talked better. None was asked if they disliked HCE or Valmontonese or if either dialect was no good.

A study by Light, Richard and Bell (1978) might help to clarify this point. They investigated the reactions of black and white children to two varieties of BE: standard and nonstandard (not SE *vs* BE). The subjects, ages eight and nine, were in the fourth grade in three different schools. Sixty children (all but two were white) came from middle and upper-middle-class suburban schools while 32 others (22 white, 10 black) attended school in a lower and working-class neighbourhood in a large city. The children listened to two recorded speech samples: an educated black woman and an uneducated black woman, both from the South, of the same age. They used a simplified version of the semantic differential scale (smart–dumb; pretty–ugly; nice–mean; rich–poor; white–black). The positive qualities were attributed more often to the standard BE speaker, with the negative qualities being attributed more often to the nonstandard BE speaker. Thus we see that positive values can be assigned to a minority dialect by both majority and minority children. The subjects did not refuse to respond by saying that no one who speaks BE, either standard or nonstandard, can be smart or pretty or nice.

Given these results by Light and his colleagues and those of Schneiderman's study, we must be cautious in interpreting the attitude studies which involve minority versus majority speech codes. We cannot infer from such studies that minority children dislike or do not value their primary speech codes. Perhaps the best we can do is to assume that they have come to recognize the value of the majority language, at least under the circumstances of the data-gathering situation and the dimensions of the research designs; the former issue is discussed later in this chapter. We focus our attention at this point on the latter for, as Ryan (1979, p. 153) claims, the method used to gather the data is important since it can have a significant effect on the results (see Ryan, Giles and Sebastian, this volume: ch. 1).

The Giles *et al.* study and one conducted by Price, Fluck and Giles (1983) provide support for Ryan's claim. The investigators in the latter project were interested in determining the way the language used when administering the matched-guise method (Welsh or English) affected their subjects' evaluations of three different language varieties (Welsh, RP, or West Welsh-accented English). The speaker read a prose passage on a neutral subject in the three guises. As in the study conducted by Giles *et al.*, a filler voice was used so it would not be obvious to the subjects that only one person was speaking. The subjects, ten and twelve-year-old Welsh bilinguals, were instructed in either Welsh or RP to listen to the speakers and to rate each one on nine 5-point rating scales. Whether the children received instructions in Welsh or English affected only two traits, selfishness and intelligence. Only the subjects receiving the instructions and questionnaire in Welsh differentiated evaluatively between the guises in terms of selfishness and not those receiving the English instructions and questionnaire. Only those in the English condition made a distinction between the speakers' perceived intelligence.

These findings by Price *et al.* are of considerable importance to future investigations of language attitudes, whether the subjects are children, adolescents or adults. Investigations which employ a matched-guise technique generally have been loaded in a school-achievement-standard direction. However, when this bias is changed, as in the study by Price and her colleagues, different emphases may result (see Bradac, this volume: ch. 6).

One additional point should be raised about the matched-guise technique and its possible influence on results. Although some of the investigators report that their young subjects seemed to have no difficulty handling the task, it could be that this method is inappropriate for accurately measuring language attitudes of minority children. Indeed, perhaps one of the reasons, aside from Labov's claim noted earlier, that little research has been conducted on children's attitudes toward language is the difficulty in finding appropriate measures. Would-be researchers might not want to tackle the difficult methodological problem of making sure that they have tapped what is inside the children's heads. The innovative research designs by Schneiderman and Rosenthal have provided considerable advances and should help future research.

Racial/ethnic attitudes and language attitudes

It is helpful to put the findings of the research on the development of children's attitudes toward language in perspective by comparing them with the research conducted on the development of racial and ethnic attitudes. In reviewing the literature, we discover that even very young children are aware of racial and ethnic differences (e.g. Goodman 1952; Lasker 1929; Milner 1975). Both Milner (1981) and Katz (1976a, 1976b) provide excellent surveys of the psychological literature on how children acquire racial attitudes and of attempts to change or reduce negative racial attitudes.

Tajfel *et al.* (1972), in research on the attitudes of children toward ethnic and national groups, found that they are very sensitive to the evaluations of their own ethnic and national groups held by the older members of their community. Their data were obtained by using 20 standardized photographs of young men which were presented to the subjects individually. Each child was asked to place each photograph in one of four boxes with labels, 'I like him very much', 'I like him a little', 'I dislike him a little', and 'I dislike him very much' (1972, pp. 235–6). A second part of the study called for the children to return two or three weeks later and place the photographs in one of two boxes labelled Scottish or English for the subjects from Glasgow and Oxford; British or not British for additional children from Glasgow; and Israeli or not Israeli for the children from Haifa, Israel. All of the subjects were aged from six to eleven. The photographs used in the Haifa study were of young Israeli men with half being those of European background and half of the physical type representative of Mediterranean Europe.

The results show their subjects to be 'highly sensitive to the socially prevailing evaluations of national and ethnic groups' (p. 243) and that minority children tended to absorb the negative attitudes from members of socially or economically superior classes. For example, both younger and older English children displayed significant preferences for photographs they classified as English compared to those classified as Scottish, but Scottish children did not display a preference for Scottish compared to English.

The significance of the findings of Tajfel and his colleagues on the social identity of young children may be seen by examining the work of Vaughan on interpersonal behaviour and socialization of children. For example, Vaughan (1978) reports the results of an investigation into the development of social categories. His subjects, aged seven and eleven, were asked to allocate pennies. It was found that the minimal group categorization used – children were arbitrarily assigned to a red or a blue category – was just as important in determining who got the money as was the categorization, your best friend at school *vs* your most disliked classmate.

Aboud and Skerry (1980) summarized and interpreted the development of children's thoughts, feelings and actions toward persons belonging to other ethnic groups. It is beyond the scope of this chapter to discuss fully their exciting review; we will, though, recognize their work as it touches specifically on issues which relate directly to language attitudes of children. In looking at the age when children first recognize what they term owngroup members and othergroup members, Aboud and Skerry concluded that research indicates that most children do so by the age of three or four.

They also examined research on children's perception of the similarities and dissimilarities of both owngroups and othergroup members. Aboud and Skerry found that perceived owngroup similarity develops early, around four or five years of age, and seems to improve with age. There is also evidence that it is at this same age when most children perceive themselves as dissimilar to other ethnic groups, and that this perceptual differentiation may increase for approximately five or six more years. In addition, Aboud and Skerry presented research to indicate that children acquire around the age of five the ability to categorize stimuli according to ethnicity and that this ability is fully developed by the age of seven. These findings are important for they are consistent with the findings of the development of children's language attitudes. Thus we could speculate that language attitudes are part of a larger group of feelings which children acquire and develop as they grow older and become socialized.

However, a major difference emerges when Aboud and Skerry discuss children's attitudes toward owngroup and othergroup members. Positive and negative othergroup attitudes appear around four years of age for black and white children and about one year later for such minority children as Amerindians, Chicanos, and Chinese. The initially positive owngroup and negative othergroup attitudes for white children exhibit change with age so that owngroup positive attitudes decrease and positive othergroup attitudes increase. With regard to minority children, the research Aboud and Skerry review is mixed. Yet, some research does indicate that minority groups such as the three mentioned earlier develop preferences for whites which are maintained as they grow older.

These findings are different from the language attitudes results in that majority (or, in Aboud and Skerry's term, white) children do not seem to develop a greater tolerance for minority dialects (e.g. Bouchard-Ryan 1969; Giles, Smith, Harrison and Freeman 1981). Indeed, what little research has been done in this area indicates that language attitudes of majority children tend to become more reflective of the speech community in that minority dialects or languages are associated with lower education, less prestigious occupations, and so on. We should note that Aboud and Skerry's findings for minority children developing preferences for the majority culture are consistent with the development of minority children's language attitudes.

Aboud and Skerry review the literature to try to account for the development of ethnic attitudes. In looking at social-demographic factors, they find that only ethnic status seems to be related; socioeconomic status, sex, and intelligence do not appear to be promising variables. Of three psychological factors – affective, perceptual and cognitive – only the first two seem important in the development of ethnic attitudes. Since our review of children's language attitudes indicates an almost complete lack of research into the cause of the development of such attitudes, Aboud and Skerry's work has important implications for future research in this area. There is an urgent need to examine ethnicity and affective and perceptual factors in relation to language attitude development.

Future research

Language is much more than a means of communicating verbal messages. It serves as a powerful symbol of cultural identity, of ethnic identity, of personal identity and can convey information about social class, education, and occupation (Scherer and Giles 1979). The very choice of one particular variety in certain circumstances can signal specific attitudes and feelings of the speaker to the listener. Yet with few exceptions, this complexity of language is not recognized in the research into language attitudes. The majority of research designs make use of the matched-guise technique and the semantic differential scale. The setting for the research is the school. Perhaps we turn to the schools for subjects because school children are readily available, packaged, and labelled. They are sitting in their rooms and all that is required is for the researcher to obtain permission and show up. It has been well established that different circumstances – including setting – call for different language varieties (e.g. Brown and Fraser 1979; Ros and Giles 1979), even in apparently monolingual speech communities. The school setting demands the use of a standard code. It is not unreasonable to assume that our subjects, after sufficient socialization, might parrot their teachers' language attitudes in the school setting. Yet this awareness has been only minimally reflected in language attitude studies of minority children[3] (see Giles and Ryan, this volume: ch. 13).

One welcome exception to this is a study by Carranza and Ryan (1975). In investigating the reactions to Spanish and English speakers of bilingual Anglo-and Mexican-American adolescents, they assumed that their subjects' reactions would be affected by the context of the speech sample (home *vs* school) and by the type of rating scale (status *vs* solidarity). They point out that 'if context were to be ignored, the results would have indicated only an overall preference for English . . . this research established that listeners also react to the appropriateness of the language variety used by the speaker for a particular situation' (1975, p. 99). The importance of context was similarly established in a subsequent study by Ryan and Carranza (1975) comparing reactions to standard and Spanish-accented English (see Carranza, this volume: ch. 3).

Not only is setting a crucial variable, but we should also be aware of the covert and overt feelings and attitudes of our subjects. Even if we do manage to assess children's attitudes away from the school setting, we must ensure that we discover, in addition to what they believe they are *supposed* to feel, what they *actually* believe. Trudgill (1975b) in an investigation of the speech of the working class of Norwich, England, found evidence that working-class nonstandard speech was covertly highly valued and prestigious:

> For example, many informants who initially stated they they did not speak properly, and would like to do so, admitted, if pressed, that they perhaps would not *really* like to, and

[3] In making this point we do not intend to disparage the work on children's attitudes toward language variation which has been conducted in the school setting. There is no question that these studies have yielded valuable insights and have demonstrated how extremely sensitive children are. That is, children were evaluated in the formal school contexts and generally displayed the formal attitudes appropriate for school contexts. It is our intent to point out that by restricting ourselves to the classroom we may be only obtaining information on attitudes appropriate to those settings.

that they would almost certainly be considered foolish, arrogant or disloyal by their friends and family if they did. (1975b, p. 93)

The importance of and the interaction between these two factors – setting and the distinction between covert and overt attitudes – may be seen in a study of attitudes of adult blacks toward standard BE and nonstandard BE by Hoover (1978). The 64 subjects were parents of children in either first or sixth grades in East Palo Alto, California. Their attitudes were measured by administering a questionnaire in the format of an interview. This enabled the interviewer to assess each subject's proficiency in BE and to follow up answers which needed clarification. The results showed that the parents did not hate nonstandard (vernacular) BE; that there are rules for the use of the two codes, *viz* nonstandard BE is considered appropriate for speaking and listening, but not for reading and writing, and for informal but not formal contexts; and that standard BE seemed to be acceptable for most occasions. Note the differences between Hoover's findings and those reported earlier by Light *et al.* The latter found that the subjects, black as well as white, attributed the positive qualities more often to the standard BE speaker than to the nonstandard BE speaker. Apparently Hoover's design enabled her to get beyond the overt attitudes and probe into her subjects' deeper attitudes. Future research studies into the language attitudes of minority children must take into account setting as well as covert attitudes.[4]

In addition to these two variables, we should take into account the typical techniques used in assessing attitudes forcing a choice. It could be argued that presenting a subject (young or old) with a choice between two languages or dialects forces him or her to choose one over the other, when the subject may not normally make such a distinction.

More research is needed on the attitudes toward language of two different groups of minority children: those speaking what may be termed as low-prestige dialects or creolized codes (e.g. BE, HCE) and those who speak languages which have only low status in a particular speech community but have higher status elsewhere (e.g. French). Further, we know little about how children who speak lower-status varieties acquire their attitudes toward their first language. The evidence presented in this chapter points to the family as being the primary source, but we need an examination of how children absorb these attitudes from their families.

Also needed are longitudinal studies. That our review of the literature did not uncover any such studies is an indication of the dearth of information about this important research. If such studies are undertaken, we should be aware of possible sex differences in attitude change. Do boys come to prize their vernacular, feeling it is more masculine? Are girls more likely to maintain their favourable attitudes toward the higher-status code? (See Kramarae, this volume: ch. 5). Some research has been done by Labov (1966) and Trudgill (1975b) on adolescents and adults which indicates that indeed speech with lower overt prestige is felt to be more masculine. We should also look at the period between childhood and adolescence to see what happens to the language attitudes of minority children. Do such children maintain the pattern of favourable attitudes toward the majority code or is there a switch in favour of the minority code? Schneidermann (1976) suggests there is, but she offers no evidence for her position.

---

[4] There is a danger, however, in this type of investigation. Probing might induce the subjects to produce the type of feelings or attitudes which they think the interviewer has or wants them to exhibit.

It might be insightful for future research in minority–majority speech communities to use Lambert's (1978) distinction between subtractive and additive bilingualism. If we think in terms of subtractive and additive bidialectalism, we could attempt to determine if minority children were acquiring new language attitudes while losing their original ones (subtractive) or were acquiring new and maintaining their old (additive). Gardner (this volume: ch. 8) discusses subtractive and additive bilingualism in detail.

Other areas which should be studied include the age at which children become aware of language. At what age do they become aware of the differences in their speech and their parents, their siblings, their friends? Ferguson (1959) believes that most speech communities value their first language. He notes that the positive attributes held by speakers may vary from speech community to speech community. This is a rich mine for researchers of language attitudes who could investigate such issues as: (1) the age when children first become aware of such positive features; (2) how children become aware of these features; and (3) differences within the speech community toward these features based on class, region, and so on.

Gleason and Weintraub (1978) review research on children's acquisition of communicative competence and the sources and types of linguistic input. They claim that the linguistic input apparently is directed at helping the child acquire linguistic competence before the more referential and social aspects of language are conveyed:

> Speech to the child, from whatever source, appears to follow a typical development pattern: speech to infants is affect-laden and may have as its primary purpose the establishment of a warm bond between infant and caretaker; speech to young children just learning language is characterized by the lexical and grammatical simplification we noted earlier and appears to be a language-teaching language, speech to school age children becomes grammatically complex and is no longer concerned with teaching the rules of language, but, instead, concentrates on the rules and beliefs of the culture (p. 206).

As we discussed earlier in this chapter, there is support for a claim that the acquisition of communicative competence begins sometime during a child's first year. If Gleason and Weintraub are correct in their assessment of the nature of the linguistic input, then we must investigate other possible sources of input to the child. Or, research might be done to substantiate their claim.

We also know relatively little about the attitudes which children have toward language in a monolingual speech community. Such studies are needed to serve as benchmarks in studies of language attitudes in multilingual speech communities. We should investigate the acquisition of language attitudes and the choice of appropriate registers and styles (e.g. baby talk, teacher talk, foreigner talk).

Conclusions

In this chapter we reviewed research into children's attitudes toward language. We made explicit a claim that language attitudes are a vital factor in communicative competence and that the acquisition of language attitudes is part of the general development of communicative competence in a child's speech community. We presented research which reveals that by the age of three, minority and majority group children are aware of language differences and that they hold attitudes about these differences. We also learned that as minority children grow up, their attitudes toward language tend to reflect sterotypes of the majority culture toward their speech and themselves. Whether we can interpret these attitudes and pre-ferences to mean that minority children reject their first language or hold it in an unfavourable light is open to question. We have also seen that in general, research concerning the development of language attitudes is consistent with research find-ings on the development of racial and ethnic attitudes. There is, however, a dif-ference – in the development of outgroup attitudes of majority children – which investigators should seek to resolve. Finally, we discovered that relatively little work has been done on the factors which either influence or cause the acquisition of language attitudes.

We believe that this review has shown that some excellent work has been done. However, a great deal more is needed. If additional progress and insights are to be accomplished, we must not limit ourselves to conducting similar studies using similar research designs and techniques. When we move in new directions, we should be able to answer some of the questions raised in this chapter.

8

Language attitudes and language learning

Robert C. Gardner

Although 'languages' are viewed by many as just another subject in the school curriculum, there are many reasons to believe that second (or foreign) language acquisition is different in that it implicates a series of social factors which are reflected in language attitudes. Research concerned with this topic has focused on providing answers to one of two questions. The first, and by far the most extensively investigated, concerns the effects of language attitudes on second-language acquisition. The second is concerned with the effects of second-language acquisition on attitudes, particularly the effects of special language programmes. We will discuss both aspects in this chapter before considering the theoretical rationale underlying the role of language attitudes in second language acquisition. This entire topic, however, involves the relationship between attitudes and behaviour so it is first necessary to discuss briefly the possible effect that attitudes can have on behaviour.

The potential role of attitudes in behaviour

Although there are many definitions of attitudes, Allport's (1954) conceptualization tends to encompass most of the agreed upon meaning. He states: 'An attitude is a mental and neural state of readiness, organized through experience, exerting a directive or dynamic influence upon the individual's response to all objects and situations with which it is related.' (Allport 1954, p. 45). The important aspect of this definition in the present context is that attitudes influence individuals' responses to attitude objects or situations, not that they determine them. This is an important distinction. Ever since Wicker's (1969) review article demonstrated that attitudes account for only about 10 per cent of the variability in behaviour, many individuals have questioned the utility of the attitude concept. If it is recognized, however, that attitudes influence behaviour and not determine it, we should not expect much of a higher relationship. To do so would be to deny the actual nature of the attitude concept.

An attitude is an inference that one makes from behaviour (often behaviour on 'attitude' scales), and the hypothesis is that once we know an individual's attitude toward some attitude object we have a better chance of understanding and predicting his/her behaviour toward that object. For example, we might infer that an acquaintance has a negative attitude towards fruit-cake based on his stated opinions about fruit-cake, his lack of willingness to eat it, and/or his responses on an 'Attitudes towards Fruit-Cake' scale if we were to administer one to him. To predict, however, that he would never eat fruit-cake, that he would not admire one, or that he would not purchase one, etc . . . would be wrong. The chances that he would frequently engage in such behaviour are very low, but on occasion, presumably because other factors also influence his behaviour, he might demonstrate such inconsistency between his attitude and his behaviour.

The point is that behaviour is influenced by a number of factors, and to expect high relationships between one of these factors and behaviour is to overemphasize the importance of any one 'determinant' of behaviour. Ajzen and Fishbein (1977) argue that in order for there to be a high correlation between attitudes and behaviour, there must be correspondence between the attitudes and behaviour, in terms of target, action, context, and time. That is, if the attitude and the behaviour both refer to the same action toward the same target in the same context at the same time, the correlation between the two will be high. Obviously! This is tantamount to saying that if the major determinant of behaviour is attitude, then there will be a strong correlation between the two. Ajzen and Fishbein's analysis adds considerably to those factors which a researcher might wish to consider in developing measures of attitudes if his/her prime consideration is the prediction of behaviour, but it does little to explicate the functional role played by attitudes in influencing behaviour. To do this requires a careful analysis of the context in which the attitude is presumed to operate, and a specification of the actual function(s) served. Research in the area of second language acquisition has adopted this approach by considering not only the empirical associations between attitudes and second language acquisition but also by striving to understand the functions served by the attitudes (see Giles and Ryan, this volume: ch. 13).

The relation of attitudes to second language learning

Many studies have investigated the relation between attitudes and achievement in a second language, others have studied the correlation between attitudes and perseverance in language study, while still others have considered the association between attitudes and classroom behaviour. It must be emphasized that in all of these investigations, however, all that has been demonstrated is that there is a relationship between attitudinal characteristics and the behaviour in question, and that such associations are open to many possible interpretations. Nonetheless, one parsimonious and meaningful interpretation is that the attitudes influence the behaviour. There are at least two reasons why this is the most meaningful interpretation, and these will be reviewed in a subsequent section discussing correlation and causation.

The relation of attitudes to second language achievement

By far the greatest amount of research conducted to date has focused on the correlation between measures of attitudes and achievement in the second language. In many, but not all cases, the attitude measures are obtained considerably earlier than the achievement measures so that the resulting correlations are in fact predictive validity coefficients.

Some studies investigating attitudinal correlates of second-language achievement employ only a few variables and focus on the correlations themselves. This is particularly true of the early research conducted in the United Kingdom which found positive relations between attitudes toward Welsh (Jones 1950a; 1950b), and French (Jordan 1941) and achievement in the language in question, as well as in a more recent longitudinal study of French achievement in England (Burstall, Jamieson, Cohen and Hargreaves 1974). Significant relations were also obtained between attitudes toward German and proficiency in German (Neidt and Hedlund 1967), attitudes toward French-speaking people and achievement in French (Mueller and Miller 1970), and Japanophilia and achievement in Japanese (Jacobsen and Imhoof 1974). Not all results have been predictable, however. Inconsistent findings were reported by Anisfeld and Lambert (1961) where significant negative relationships (as expected) were obtained between measures of anti-semitism and achievement in Hebrew in some samples, but not others, and by Lambert, Gardner, Barik and Tunstall (1963) who obtained a significant positive correlation between Francophilia and achievement in French for adults in an elementary level intensive language programme, but a significant negative correlation for students at the advanced level.

Other studies have employed batteries of attitude and aptitude measures and have used factor-analytic procedures to investigate the relationships among these measures as well as their relationships with achievement. The first of these (Gardner and Lambert 1959) obtained two independent factors which were both related to achievement in French among Canadian high-school students. One of the factors was defined as Language Aptitude because the major contributors were measures of language aptitude and verbal intelligence. The other was identified as an attitudinal–motivational dimension because it involved favourable attitudes toward French Canadians, an interest in learning French in order to become closer psychologically to the French Canadian community and a high level of motivation to learn French. Although identical factor structures have not been obtained in subsequent studies (possibly because of the different numbers and nature of the tests used), the structures have supported the generalization that both attitudes and aptitude are related to achievement in a second language. Such confirming results have been reported by Gardner and Lambert (1972) with elementary and secondary students of French in Maine, Louisiana, and Connecticut, by Smythe, Stennett and Feenstra (1972) with senior elementary-school students in either traditional or audiolingual French programmes, by Gardner and Santos (1970) with students in the Philippines learning English as a second language, and by Clément, Gardner, and Smythe (1977, 1980) with elementary and secondary-school Francophone students learning English. Cavanaugh (1977) did not include measures of aptitude in his investigation of high-school students learning French in California, but the relations of the attitude measures to achievement were comparable to those obtained in these studies.

Most of the research has made a contrast between integrative and instrumental orientations. An integrative orientation refers to an interest in learning a second language in order to facilitate interaction with the other language community. An instrumental orientation, on the other hand, focuses on the utilitarian aspects of learning the language. One example of an integrative orientation is learning the language 'in order to learn more about French Canadians and their way of life'. An instrumental orientation is reflected in such reasons as 'in order to get a good job'. Some research has made use of a scale, the Orientation Index, in which students must select from among exemplars of both orientations that which is most descriptive of themselves. The results suggest that students who indicate an integrative orientation are generally more motivated to learn the second language, have more favourable attitudes toward the other community and are more proficient in the second language than those who are instrumentally oriented (see, for example, Gardner and Lambert 1959, 1972; Gardner and Santos 1970; Smythe *et al*. 1972). Because of this association, the total configuration has been referred to as an integrative motive (Gardner 1979, 1981). Other investigations have had students rate the extent to which learning the second language was important to them for various integrative and instrumental reasons, and individual differences were indexed for both types of ratings. Investigations involving these measures have tended to show both orientations loading on a factor in common with other attitudinal and motivational measures (see, for example, Clément, Gardner and Smythe 1977, 1980; Gardner and Smythe 1975). Since the total configuration also tended to emphasize attitudes toward the other community and the language, it too has been interpreted as reflecting an integrative motive.

Other studies have used factor-analytic procedures applied primarily to the predictor variables, and then correlated factor scores with measures of achievement. Some results have confirmed those obtained above; some have not. Oller, Hudson and Liu (1977), for example, found a positive correlation between achievement in English for Chinese adults living in the USA and factor scores derived from a factor characterizing Americans as helpful, sincere, kind, etc . . . suggesting that proficiency in a second language is related to attitudes toward the language community. Such an interpretation is not, however, supported by other studies using this approach. For example, Chihara and Oller (1978) found that Japanese students who perceived English speakers as confident, modest, etc . . . performed poorly in English, Oller, Baca and Vigil (1978) obtained a negative relation between Mexican American women's ratings of Anglos as religious, sensitive, etc . . . and their achievement in English, while Teitelbaum, Edwards and Hudson (1975) reported a significant positive correlation between the 'Belief that Chicanos are not democratic' (p. 259) and proficiency in Spanish among American students. Such results might suggest that in some instances negative attitudes toward the other language community promote achievement in the language of that group, or as Oller (1979) suggests, that extraneous sources of variance account for reported relationships between affective variables and second-language achievement. Gardner (1980) has considered these studies in some detail, however, and indicated conceptual, contextual, and statistical reasons why such negative or null results should be interpreted cautiously. Paramount among these is the fact that the affective 'measures' used were not, in fact, carefully constructed measures with any assessed reliability and validity, but rather were *post hoc* indices derived from exploratory factor analyses of heterogeneous collections of rating scales gathered together for the specific investigation. This unorganized approach contrasts rather dramatically with that underlying most of the studies obtaining positive relations between attitudes and achievement which make use of measures with demonstrated high levels of reliability, and validity established with a number of different criteria (for reviews see Gardner 1979, 1980, 1981).

In general, therefore, there has been considerable research demonstrating that attitudinal and motivational variables are related to achievement in a second language, and that this association is independent of language aptitude. Although some possibly 'negative' results may have been reported, the overwhelming evidence indicates that attitudinal variables are related to, and possibly influence (as opposed to determine), proficiency in the second language. Other research indicates the possible role of attitudinal variables.

The relation of attitudes to perseverance

One potential reason why attitudes are related to achievement in a second language is that they influence how seriously the individual strives to acquire the language. Such an interpretation is supported by the relations already noted between attitudes and verbal report measures of how hard the individual works to acquire the language (e.g., the measure of motivational intensity). It is also supported by studies of the relation of attitudes to perseverance in language study. Bartley (1970) was the first to investigate the relationship between attitudes and the tendency to drop out of language programmes. In 1970, she obtained measures of attitudes toward the language among senior elementary-school students studying different languages, at both the beginning and the end of the academic terms. Students opting to drop out showed significantly lower attitudes at both testing sessions. Furthermore, these students also demonstrated an appreciable decrease in their attitudes from the first to the second testing, while those who had decided to stay in maintained their generally positive attitude. Bartley (1970) demonstrated that 'drop-outs' were lower than 'stay-ins' in both attitudes toward the language and language aptitude. Such findings demonstrate, therefore, that attitudes (and sometimes language aptitude) are related to verbal reports reflecting an interest in language learning.

Bartley classified students as 'drop-outs' and 'stay-ins' on the basis of their stated intention. Other researchers, however, have focused instead on the actual behaviour of registering in the language class in the subsequent year. Using this more objective index of perseverance, Burstall *et al.* (1974) found that boys with poor attitudes toward learning French dropped out when given the opportunity though similar results were not obtained with girls. Gardner and Smythe (1975) contrasted 'stay-ins' with 'drop-outs', initially in grades 9, 10, and 11, on a large battery of attitude, aptitude, and French-achievement measures, obtained while they were still registered in the French programme. Significant effects at each grade level were obtained on measures of attitudes and motivation directly associated with French (e.g., attitudes toward French Canadians, toward learning French, motivational intensity) and on measures of French achievement. Although in the predicted direction, and often (but not always) significant, the differences involving aspects of language aptitude, intelligence and also other attitudinal characteristics such as ethnocentrism were not so consistent. The implications of these studies then is that attitudinal variables are related to achievement in a second language because they help to maintain an individual's motivation to succeed in the language (see also Gardner 1979).

The relation of attitudes to classroom behaviour

Another indication of the role played by attitude variables in second-language acquisition is given by three studies which suggest that attitude variables influence how students approach the language-classroom situation. Although none of these studies included any measure of language aptitude, the independence of language aptitude and attitudes noted above suggests that the effects of attitudes cannot be attributed to differences in aptitude. Two of the investigations were conducted by

Gliksman (1976), who administered a battery of attitudinal/motivational measures to students at the beginning of the academic year, and made classroom observations at various times throughout the term. The first study, involving 90 grade 9 students of French, showed that students who were integratively motivated (based on a median split on six of the attitude/motivation tests) volunteered more frequently, gave more correct answers, and appeared to receive more reinforcements from the teacher during class sessions than students not classified as integratively motivated. The second investigation involved a total of 150 students in grades 9, 10, and 11, and showed that those classified as integratively motivated volunteered more frequently, gave more correct answers and were rated by the observers as being more interested in the class than those not so classified. The third study, conducted by Naiman, Fröhlich, Stern and Todesco (1978) correlated scores obtained on the attitude/motivation test battery (Gardner, Clément, Smythe and Smythe 1978) with observations made over a total of 250 minutes of class time on a sample of 24 students. They found significant correlations between volunteering (defined, as above, in terms of hand raising) and composite scores they referred to as integrative orientation, motivation and evaluations of the teaching methods, respectively. These measures were not, however, related to other types of classroom behaviour such as asking the teacher questions and indications of anxiety in speech. The consistent finding, involving volunteering, over the three studies, however, does suggest that one possible reason why attitudinal variables are implicated in second-language acquisition is simply that they serve to make the student enthused about learning the other language.

Correlation and causality

All of the findings relating attitudinal variables to second-language achievement, perseverance in language study and classroom behaviour are based on correlational data, and it is a truism that correlation does not mean causation. That is, simply because two variables are correlated does not mean that one variable causes the other. This is a difficulty inherent in research concerned with individual differences. Since the prime data are associations between two (or more) individual difference variables, the interpretation of a significant association is not unambiguous. The interpretation favoured by many researchers in this area, and the one proposed in the present chapter, is that the attitudinal/motivational variables facilitate or influence second-language acquisition.

This interpretation is favoured because of two considerations. First, it appears to be the most parsimonious. That is, it seems logically less complex to assume that individual differences in attitudinal/motivational characteristics influence second-language achievement, perseverance in language study and classroom behaviour than to search around for some hypothetical variable which might account for the associations. A second consideration has to do with the nature of data gathering in most studies. In the majority of investigations, the attitudinal/motivational indices are obtained at one time and the indices of achievement, or perseverance, or classroom behaviour are obtained at a later time. The resulting correlation coefficients are, as a consequence, predictive validity coeffcients. It must be emphasized, however, that alternative interpretations are always possible when dealing with a single correlation coefficient.

Techniques have been developed, however, to permit stronger causal inferences from correlatioṇal data. Cross-lagged panel analysis (see Kenny 1979) is one such technique. It requires that individuals be tested on both the 'predictor' and the 'criterion' on two different occasions, referred to as Time 1 and Time 2. If the predictor 'causes' the criterion, it would be expected that the correlation between the Time 1 predictor and the Time 2 criterion would be higher than the correlation between the Time 2 'predictor' and the Time 1 'criterion'. If, on the other hand, this second correlation were higher it would suggest that the 'criterion' in fact 'caused' the 'predictor'.

Table 1 presents results based on a sample of 194 students in Ontario who were tested while they were in grade 7 and again when they were in grade 8. Students completed the short form of the Modern Language Aptitude Test (Carroll and Sapon 1959) around October in both academic years, the Attitude/Motivation Test Battery (Gardner *et al.* 1978) and a measure of their Behavioural Intention to Continue French study in November of both years, and objective measures of French proficiency around April of each year. Grades in French were obtained from the academic records. Based on these data we developed two predictors, an Attitude/Motivation Index (AMI) based on a composite of nine attitude and motivation measures (see Gardner *et al.* 1978), and a Language Aptitude score based on the Modern Language Aptitude Test. We also constructed three criteria, Behavioural Intention to Continue French study (BI), an objective measure of French Achievement, and French grades.

Table 8.1   Correlations between attitude and aptitude predictors and criteria assessed at different times

Predictor	Criterion	Time 1 Predictor with Time 2 Criterion	Time 2 Predictor with Time 1 Criterion	Time 1 Predictor with Time 1 Criterion	Time 2 Predictor with Time 2 Criterion
AMI X	BI	$.53^{xxx}$	$.40^{xxx}$	$.57^{xxx}$	$.66^{xxx}$
APTITUDE X	BI	$.15^{x}$	$.27^{xxx}$	$.17^{x}$	$.35^{xxx}$
AMI X	GRADES	$.33^{xxx}$	$.38^{xxx}$	$.32^{xxx}$	$.42^{xxx}$
APTITUDE X	GRADES	$.25^{xxx}$	$.23^{xxx}$	$.24^{xxx}$	$.32^{xxx}$
AMI X	ACHIEVEMENT	$.45^{xxx}$	$.52^{xxx}$	$.51^{xxx}$	$.58^{xxx}$
APTITUDE X	ACHIEVEMENT	$.46^{xxx}$	$.42^{xxx}$	$.37^{xxx}$	$.51^{xxx}$

x $p < .05$
xxx $p < .001$
Correlations are based on N's varying from 157 to 194 cases.

Only the correlations between AMI and BI are directly relevant to cross-lagged panel analysis since only these two measures were obtained at the same time in both years. The correlation of AMI at Time 1 with BI at Time 2 ($r = .53$) is higher than that for AMI at Time 2 with BI at Time 1 ($r = .40$) supporting the 'causal' interpretation that attitudinal variables facilitate perseverance in language study.

None of the other correlations presented in Table 1 are applicable to cross-lagged panel analysis since the assessment times for any other predictor and criterion were not contemporaneous. They are nonetheless important, however, because they demonstrate the general stability of the validity coefficients over time. Note that the coefficients in column 1 which involve prediction of up to 18 months are generally comparable and sometimes greater than those in other columns which involve prediction over shorter time periods (five or six months in the same academic year as in columns 3 and 4), or post-diction (six or seven months involving two academic years as in Column 2). Note too that in 11 comparisons involving the same criterion with the same time lag, AMI evidences higher correlations than Aptitude.

The relation of second language training to attitudes

Some researchers have hypothesized that learning a second language influences attitudinal characteristics. For example, Lambert (1967) proposed that as individuals acquire second language, they begin to identify with the other language community and to experience feelings of alienation or anomie. A less basic form of attitude change is proposed by Burstall *et al.* (1974) who argue that success in learning the other language will promote favourable attitudes toward the language and all factors (such as the other language community) associated with it.

Although both hypotheses have intuitive appeal, it appears that the relevant research either has not been conducted, or is relatively ambiguous in its support. To begin with, no research appears to have been published which examines the effects of traditional second-language training on attitudinal characteristics. Data from research we have conducted with samples of students in grades 7 to 11 in various regions in Canada demonstrate little if any change which can be associated with degree of success in the programme. They do indicate a general deterioration in attitudes toward most aspects of second-language acquisition including the language and the other community, but the data are such that it cannot be determined whether this is due to age, education, experience with the attitude instruments, etc. .., or whether it is the result of the language learning experience itself.

Instead of investigating the effects of success or failure in language courses on attitudes, some researchers have been more concerned with the effects of simple participation in the course itself. Rather than involving regular programmes, however, this research has been conducted with special types of programmes, such as short-term summer language programmes or long-term immersion programmes.

Short-term language programmes

One of the first studies of attitudinal changes associated with intensive short-term language training was conducted by Lambert *et al.* (1963). They investigated changes in attitudes which took place during a six-week French Summer-school programme in Montreal for adult language learners. Students registered at the elementary French level demonstrated significant increases in authoritarianism and anomie from the beginning to the end of the programme, while advanced-level students increased significantly only in anomie. Neither group changed significantly in their attitudes toward French Canadians. One facet of this programme was that the students agreed beforehand not to speak English during the programme. Many of them reported subsequently that this was very difficult and that they had broken their pledge. Hence it is not possible to ascertain whether the attitude changes were due to the language learning experience, the pressures of trying to perform exclusively in a second language, or some other factor. Tucker and Lambert (1970) have in fact demonstrated that the direction of changes in anomie are influenced by the type of situation. They investigated three groups of adult language learners, one which participated in a Foreign Language Leadership and French language training programme in France, one which had only intensive language training in France, and one which was involved in a similar language training programme in the USA. The first group decreased in anomie, the second became more anomic, and the third did not change.

Clément (1979) has also demonstrated that attitudinal changes are influenced by the nature of the situation. He contrasted a short-term immersion programme in which students took part in extensive language training with an exchange programme where students simply visited partners in the other community. He found that both situations improved attitudes toward French Canadians and decreased French classroom anxiety, but that the exchange programme had a more pronounced effect on the attitudes while the immersion programme was more effective in reducing anxiety. Presumably, the exchange programme gave students an opportunity to meet with French Canadians in a warm social atmosphere thus promoting positive attitude change, while those in the extensive training programme had considerable opportunity to use French in the classroom environment thus reducing their anxiety in that context.

Gardner, Smythe and Brunet (1977) obtained results from a five-week intensive programme for high-school students, which appear to indicate two types of changes. On the one hand, students tended to become more ethnocentric, less interested in foreign languages and less integrative in their orientation to study French. On the other hand, they also exhibited less French classroom anxiety, a heightened motivation to learn French (i.e. higher scores on the Motivational Intensity scale), a feeling that French was easier than initially anticipated, and a tendency to make greater use of any opportunities to speak French. That is, the programme simultaneously had the negative effect of making students less tolerant of other groups and languages, and the positive effects of increasing their motivation to learn and use the language and decreasing their anxieties about it.

Long-term language programmes

The effects of long-term (or immersion) programmes on attitudes have rarely been studied, possibly because such effects are not that pronounced. The most extensive investigation was that conducted by Lambert and Tucker (1972), and even here the results were ambiguous. They found that grade 1 and 2 students (ages 6 and 7) in a French immersion programme had more favourable attitudes toward French speaking people than did an English control group, but these effects, obtained with objective tests, were not maintained in later years. Other ways of eliciting attitudes did show effects, however, thus making interpretation difficult. When these same students were in grade 5 they indicated in response to direct questioning that they liked French Canadians more than when they began their study of French and that they would be just as happy if they had been born French Canadian. Using different ways of assessing attitudes, Genesee, Tucker and Lambert (1978) also obtained inconclusive results.

Cziko, Lambert and Gutter (1979) have suggested that the inconsistency of such findings might be due to the way attitudes are typically assessed using objective measures. They compared early immersion students with late immersion students and two control groups on their multidimensional scaling profiles of a number of concepts involving linguistic and cultural identity (e.g. bilingual French Canadians, myself). The results indicated that early immersion students tended to see themselves as more similar to both bilingual French and English Canadians than did the other three groups suggesting possibly that continued intensive French study tends to reduce feelings of social distance toward both ethnic communities. These are not, however, necessarily attitudinal differences. Such perceptions of similarity might simply reflect an appreciation of their own increased bilinguality and hence similarity to other bilinguals, without any corresponding affective change.

One study has been conducted of American university students studying French for a semester in France, but the findings were negative. Reynolds, Flagg and Kennedy (1974) failed to obtain any significant changes in attitudinal-motivational characteristics on their students from the beginning to the end of the course even though measurement characteristics ruled out possible ceiling effects. Although it might be argued that the lack of change could be due to the mature age of the students involved, the generally inconsistent results of the various studies make it more reasonable to assume that whatever attitudinal changes might result from instruction in a second language could be quite subtle and largely dependent upon other variables operating in the situation at the time. This conclusion is also made, in another context, by Halpern, MacNab, Kirby, Tuong, Martin, Hendleman and Tourigny (1976). They did not investigate immersion programmes, but instead contrasted samples of students in regular programmes with those in extended French programmes, but they too obtained inconclusive results. No effects of increased time were obtained for samples of grade 1 and 2 students, though some effects were noted for students in grades 5 to 7. They conclude that any effects may be due not to the learning of a second language but to situational factors (e.g. parental attitudes, teacher interest) and the actual decision to enter the programme. It may be more meaningful to conclude that for language training in the school setting the effects on attitudes are minimal. This is not to say that the development of bilingual proficiency may not foster identification with the other community and in some instances promote feelings of anomie. Such changes could result because of the changed social environment in which individuals find themselves and not necessarily their changed linguistic competence.

A theoretical analysis of attitudes and language learning

The preceding sections have reviewed the literature relevant to the role of attitudes on second language acquisition and the effects of such acquisition on attitudes. The major impetus for much of this research was a theoretical model proposed by Lambert (1963) which implicated a broad range of attitudes in the language learning process. Although others have provided somewhat more elaborated models in recent years (see for example, Gardner 1979, 1981; Schumann 1975), the major components were contained in Lambert's (1963) formulation. He argued,

> that an individual successfully acquiring a second language gradually adopts various aspects of behaviour which characterize members of another linguistic-cultural group. The learner's ethnocentric tendencies and his attitudes toward the other group are believed to determine his success in learning the new language. His motivation to learn is thought to be determined by his attitudes and by his orientation toward learning a second language. (p. 114)

It is important to note that this formulation does not state that attitudes and motivation are the only determinants of proficiency in a second language. In fact, more recent formulations (see Gardner 1979, 1981) would argue that they are not even determinants, but rather that they facilitate language acquisition. One might well ask, however, just why this is the case.

The answer would seem to reside in the close association between language and ethnic identity. In attempting to explain why low-prestige language varieties persist, for example, Ryan (1979) states that 'the value of language as a chief symbol of group identity is one of the major forces for the preservation of non-standard speech styles or dialects' (p. 147). In a related vein, Lambert (1967) argues that individuals learning a second language tend to maintain some speech styles distinct from the other ethnic group in order to maintain their own identities. Simard (1981b) has demonstrated, furthermore, that at least French Canadians prefer to form friendships within their own ethnolinguistic community rather than with English Canadians even though they are proficient in English. Simard (1981a, 186) argues that speaking one's native language promotes cultural solidarity and that 'this reason might be particularly important for French Canadians who are surrounded by English speakers in the North American context'. This emphasis on the vitality of the native language and its effect on language acquisition and behaviour has recently been formally incorporated into an intergroup approach to second language acquisition by Giles and Byrne (1982), who make specific predictions about, the development of second language proficiency under varying conditions of linguistic vitality and ingroup identification.

There is, in fact, some evidence that feelings about ethnic identity play a role in second language acquisition. Taylor, Meynard and Rheault (1977) demonstrated that perceptions, among French speaking university students, that learning English posed a threat to ethnic identity were associated with poor self-ratings of English skill. Furthermore, such perceptions tended to be more prevalent in those regions of Quebec where personal contact with English speakers would be low (see Bourhis, this volume: ch. 3). A multiple regression analysis demonstrated moreover that personal contact and perceived threat to ethnic identity were the best two predictors (in that order) of achievement in English. A measure of Threat to Ethnic Identity was also included in a factor-analytic investigation of attitudes and motivation in second language acquisition. Clément *et al.* (1980) found that this measure contributed negatively to their Integrative Motive factor. These findings suggest, therefore, that such feelings of potential danger from language acquisition detract from a motivation to learn the language because of any positive affect for the other community.

It seems highly likely that the association between language and ethnic identity would materially influence an individual's reactions to the language learning situation in school depending upon the nature of the context. If the individual were to perceive second language acquisition as a positive achievement which broadened his or her horizons, the educational context and the language learning experience would be expected to be very reinforcing. If, on the other hand, second language acquisition were perceived as a negative experience, the educational context and the acquisition of the second language would be non-reinforcing or even aversive. This distinction, it should be emphasized, is directed toward the individual's perception of the context (see Carranza, this volume: ch. 4).

Lambert (1974) has made a very similar distinction between two different types of bilingualism. He describes additive bilingualism as an enriching experience, where, in learning the second language, the individual does not suffer any potential loss in his/her first language or its importance. Subtractive bilingualism, on the other hand, is seen to involve a weakening of the first language and a decrease in its importance. In describing these two types of bilingualism, Lambert (1974) associates them with communities rather than individuals. He links additive bilingualism with members of a majority or politically dominant group, and subtractive bilingualism with ethnic minority group members. That is, to the extent that English speaking Canadians are the majority group, developing proficiency in French for them would constitute additive bilingualism. To the extent that French Canadians are a minority group, bilinguality for them represents subtractive bilingualism (see Lambert 1978).

Although it is likely that instances of additive and subtractive bilingualism would covary with ethnicity as Lambert suggests, it is not necessary logically to link additive and subtractive bilingualism only to ethnic group membership. The dynamics would be equally appropriate to any individual regardless of his or her ethnicity. Some individuals may view the acquisition of another language as an enriching experience, others might consider it as a threat to their very identity, while still others might see it as being of no consequence one way or the other. The major variable would seem to be the individual's affective reaction to the acquisition of the language.

This emphasis on the individual rather than community interpretation of additive and subtractive bilingualism has recently been employed by Gardner (in press) to explain language loss and language maintenance. He suggests that rather than assume an association between ethnic group membership and type of bilingualism, it would seem more fruitful to assess the community's views of the implications of bilingualism. Such an assessment would involve determining the relative prestige of the two languages, and one way recommended to do this is by means of the matched-guise procedure in which individuals evaluate speakers in both languages (see, for example, Lambert, Hodgson, Gardner and Fillenbaum 1960; Ryan and Carranza 1977; Ryan 1979). Community reactions to both languages would be indexed by the extent to which speakers of either language are downgraded by samples of subjects. The extent to which any individual shares this assessment would be indicated by his or her relative downgrading. Gardner (in press) hypothesized that in those communities where both majority and minority groups tended to downgrade minority group speakers, this would signal a subtractive bilingualism context for minority group members, and it might be anticipated that in this context their language would evidence a decline. Even so, however, some individuals tend to retain their first language, and it was predicted that this would be true of those who did not completely share (or perhaps disagreed with) the group tendency to downgrade ethnic language speakers. Even in terms of second language acquisition, it is clear that a subtractive bilingualism context can be overcome. Lambert (1978), for example, refers to research conducted by Padilla and Long (1969) which demonstrated that Spanish-American children were more successful learning English if their Spanish heritage were continually reinforced from the time they were infants. Presumably, such children, even if they were in a potentially 'subtractive bilingualism' environment would not experience the same pressures operating on their ethnic identity.

Viewed in this light, all the research which has been conducted linking attitudes with second language acquisition is seen to be concerned with only one factor, *viz*, the individual's perception of the motivational properties of the language learning process. This perspective does not underplay the importance attributed to positive attitudes toward the other community, the teacher, or the classroom environment. Instead, it emphasizes only that such attitudinal variables will more often than not be positively associated with the perception that language acquisition is an enriching experience. The attitudes are important, however, only to the extent that they influence the individual's level of motivation to study and use the language. Thus arguments about whether an instrumental or integrative orientation is more important to language acquisition or whether this attitude or that attitude is dominant become relatively meaningless. The more important question is which is more related to the individual's level of motivation because it will be this orientation which will relate more consistently with the individual's success in learning the language.

These considerations have been incorporated in a social-educational model of second-language acquisition which considers such acquisition to be a function of two major classes of variables, motivation and language aptitude (see Gardner 1979; 1981). These variables are viewed as operating within the individual's sociocultural environment but are nonetheless seen as the major determinants of second language acquisition regardless of the individual's ethnic group membership. A variant of that model is presented in Figure 8.1. It suggests that the cultural milieu, reflected in beliefs held in the community about second language learning and bilingualism, will influence individuals' attitudes and beliefs about a number of factors associated with second language learning. These factors could include the implications of bilingualism to the individual (i.e. additive or subtractive), or any other factor involved with language acquisition; hence, the model is completely general to all contexts. In the figure, these attitudes are indicated as reflecting two major constructs, Integrativeness and Attitudes toward the Learning Situation, but it should be emphasized that others might be implicated. These have been highlighted because they are the ones which have been investigated most thoroughly (see for example, Gardner 1981; Gardner *et al.* 1978).

It is always possible, however, that Integrativeness and Attitudes toward the Learning Situation, in the general case, reflect the major attitudinal constructs involved in second language acquisition. Integrativeness refers to attitudinal reactions toward the other ethnic community and ethnic groups in general which might influence the extent to which individuals are willing to take on behavioural patterns of another ethnolinguistic community. Some relevant measures, applicable to learning French are indicated in Figure 8.1, but others such as Threat to Ethnic Identity and Ethnocentrism could also be postulated. Attitudes toward the Learning Situation involve affective reactions to the classroom setting. Again, some relevant measures are indicated in Figure 8.1, but others could be postulated. Although other general attitudinal constructs are not indicated in the figure, it is clear as suggested above that many others might be considered. The important point is that their function is to provide the foundation for the motivation to learn the language, and this is indicated by the arrows connecting each of the classes of attitude constructs and motivation.

As indicated in Figure 8.1, Motivation itself is seen to be a complex of three aspects, effort (Motivational Intensity), desire, and affect (Attitudes toward Learning French). Effort refers to the drive displayed by the student to learn the language, desire refers to how much the student wants to learn the language, and affect involves the student's emotional reactions toward the experience of learning

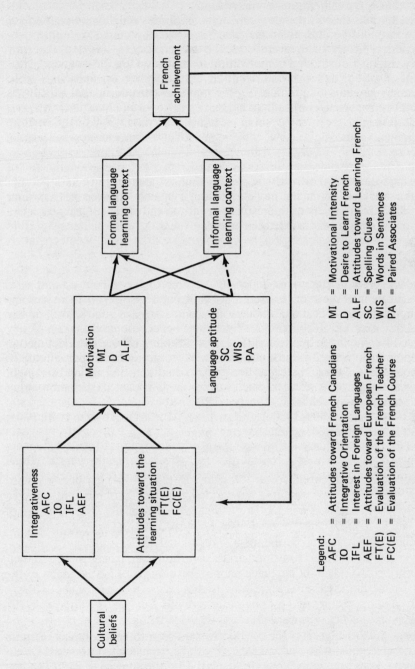

Fig. 8.1 Schematic representation of the role of attitudes, motivation, and language aptitude in the acquisition of French as a second language.

Legend:
AFC = Attitudes toward French Canadians
IO = Integrative Orientation
IFL = Interest in Foreign Languages
AEF = Attitudes toward European French
FT(E) = Evaluation of the French Teacher
FC(E) = Evaluation of the French Course

MI = Motivational Intensity
D = Desire to Learn French
ALF = Attitudes toward Learning French
SC = Spelling Clues
WIS = Words in Sentences
PA = Paired Associates

the language. Such a tripartite conceptualization seems necessary to describe adequately what is typically meant by motivation.

Figure 8.1 also shows another component, aptitude, which is separated from both the attitudinal and motivational clusters. This characterization reflects the relative independence of aptitude from the other factors as well as the commonality among the attitude and motivational variables. Figure 8.1 also indicates, by means of solid arrows, that both aptitude and motivation are implicated in the formal language acquisition context (e.g. the language classroom), but that motivation (with the solid arrow) more than aptitude (with broken arrow) is involved in informal contexts (e.g. any choice situation which permits language practice). Both contexts aid in promoting language achievement. These associations are supported by previous research, and discussed above. Attitudinal/motivational variables and, to some extent, aptitude are related to perseverance in language study. In the figure, achievement is shown having a reciprocal influence on attitudes. Perhaps this is the weakest link in the model. Although it seems reasonable and some support exists for it, many of the results relevant to the effects of learning a language on attitudes, as discussed above, are equivocal.

Directions for future research

This model serves to summarize much of the preceding research, as well as to indicate future directions for research. Five problem areas, in particular, are suggested by the social-educational model of second language acquisition and the material discussed in this chapter.

A first, and very basic question is the generalizability of relations described in this chapter and proposed in the model. Much of the research has been conducted in Canada, and it is a legitimate question to ask whether attitudes, motivation, or language aptitude would relate to aspects of second language acquisition in other cultural settings. Some studies (e.g. Bartley 1970; Burstall *et al.* 1974; Jacobsen and Imhoof 1974; Jones 1950a, 1950b; Jordan 1941; Mueller and Miller 1970; Neidt and Hedlund 1967) would suggest that they might, but others (e.g. Oller, Baca and Vigil 1978; Teitelbaum *et al.* 1975) would suggest they might not. One important prerequisite for such investigations in any cultural context is that experimenters direct considerable attention toward developing tests with high demonstrated levels of reliability and validity, before investigating the relations of attitudinal/motivational measures and language aptitude measures with measures of second language proficiency, or other aspects of second language acquisition.

A second issue suggested by the social-educational model is the causal association between attitudes and motivation and second language achievement and their links with the two classes of language acquisition contexts. One approach to the causality issue discussed in this chapter is that of cross-lagged panel analysis. Another presently being used by this writer is Path Analysis (see Kenny 1979), which permits direct testing of specific causal models through the use of regression techniques. Still other approaches exist. For example, very few laboratory studies have been conducted where actual control can be exercised over precisely what language material is presented and thus learned. Furthermore, analogues of formal and informal language acquisition contexts could be introduced to determine the role played by attitudinal/motivational characteristics and aptitude on the acquisition of material presented in the two different contexts.

A third issue involves uncovering other individual difference variables related to second language achievement. As indicated in this chapter it seems highly likely that if they are not cognitive ability variables such as language aptitude, they will probably relate to achievement only if they reflect motivational characteristics. Clément *et al.* (1977, 1980), for example identified a factor defined as Self-Confidence with English which was related significantly to English Proficiency. It involved an appreciable motivational component, however. Nonetheless, it seems important that we continue to search for individual difference variables which contribute to our understanding of the process of second language acquisition.

A fourth issue concerns the roles of attitudes and motivation, and language aptitude for that matter, on classroom behaviour. As indicated in this chapter some research has been conducted on the relation of the first two attributes to aspects of classroom behaviour, but it would be beneficial to replicate those studies and introduce the variable of aptitude. Since aptitude and attitudinal/motivational variables are relatively independent, it would be possible to study their independent effects on classroom behaviour. In this same vein, it would seem possible in a large school setting to attempt to set up some classes in which students are pre-selected on the basis of both language aptitude and attitudinal/motivational attributes. If classes were relatively homogeneous with respect to either or both attributes, it is very reasonable to expect that the atmosphere of the classroom, and the very interaction between teacher and pupils would be affected considerably. An in-depth examination of the classroom behaviour would undoubtedly aid in our understanding of the actual role played by these individual difference variables in the classroom.

The fifth issue concerns the effects of language learning on attitudinal/motivational characteristics of students. As indicated in this chapter, it seems logical that experiences in the language learning situation would influence students' attitudes and motivation, but the findings with respect to such an association are sparse and equivocal. Because of its importance, however, such an association should be thoroughly investigated. If it could be shown, for example, that some aspects of language acquisition promote favourable attitudes and increase motivation, it might be possible to work on these aspects and thus ultimately improve the level of second language proficiency.

These five issues undoubtedly do not cover all the research questions which can be directed to the second language acquisition situation. They all result, however, directly from the social-educational model and research described in this chapter, and their answers will help not only in testing the validity of the model, but also in improving the level of second language proficiency attained by students in the future. As such research in this area is important.

9

The social significance of speech in medical, legal and occupational settings[1]

Rudolf Kalin

In the applied settings of concern in the present chapter, speech is clearly of paramount importance. Doctors attempting a diagnosis engage in a dialogue with patients. Talk is ubiquitous in legal settings. Clients talk to lawyers to convey their problems. Prosecuting and defence attorneys examine and cross-examine witnesses through questions and answers. Speech figures prominently in the presentation of evidence, in judges' instructions to juries and in jury deliberations. Answers given by job applicants in employment interviews can determine success or failure in obtaining a job. In all these settings, the explicit premise for talk is objectivity and the pursuit of truth. To that end, the verbal content of speech is the main *acknowledged* focus for the participants in these settings. Readers of this book will undoubtedly realize, however, that non-content characteristics of speech, such as speech style (Giles and Powesland 1975) or vocal qualities have profound effects on the perception of and reaction to speakers.

Precisely because accurate communication is important in medical, legal and occupational settings, nonverbal aspects of speech may be particularly significant. Many nonverbal aspects of speech are relatively difficult to change and manipulate for the purpose of impression management. They are not like clothing, or attitudes and opinions, or even facial expressions (Ekman and Friesen 1974) which are presented or changed for reasons of expediency to create particular impressions. Nonverbal aspects of speech are less under voluntary control than explicit content. They are, therefore, more 'leaky' (Ekman and Friesen 1969), in that they provide cues to the emotional state of the speaker. Accents may be more or less immutable but are inevitably the source of many inferences regarding the speaker.

The last two decades have seen a tremendous burgeoning of research on the social significance of speech (Giles and Powesland 1975; Giles, Robinson and Smith 1980; Giles and St Clair 1979; Scherer and Giles 1979; St Clair and Giles 1980). Previous chapters in this book have provided organized summaries of much of this work and provide a useful background for an understanding of the social significance of speech in applied settings.

The following sections review studies of cognitive and behavioural reactions to nonverbal aspects of speech in medical, legal and employment settings. The review is limited to investigations where speech is the independent variable. However, for a full appreciation of the present topic area the whole context of speech

[1] The invaluable assistance given by Ellen Bouchard Ryan and Howard Giles in the preparation of this chapter is gratefully acknowledged. I also profited greatly from discussions with my colleague J. W. Berry.

148

research, as outlined in chapter 1 of this volume, should be kept in mind. From this perspective, it will be readily apparent that the studies conducted in applied contexts have tapped only some of the factors examined in other areas. However, substantial progress has been made since 1975, when Giles and Powesland reviewed only one study of speech in the employment context and, after emphasizing the importance of speech in the medical and legal contexts, were unable to find any studies in these areas.

The medical context

The direct and explicit functions of speech in medical settings are obviously important. Accurate diagnosis requires questions posed by the physician that can be understood by the patient. The adequacy of patients' answers determines largely how fast an accurate diagnosis can be made. Treatment frequently consists of advice, directives or exhortations (get rest, take these pills, stop smoking, lose weight). Speech characteristics of the physician giving these treatments may well influence their effectiveness. In addition to physicians, several other groups are involved in the provision of health services (e.g. nurses, orderlies, psychologists, rehabilitation therapists) complicating the problem of communication among the various groups. A further complication derives from the existence of special languages of professionals which exist, in part, to differentiate themselves from non-professionals (Heath 1979). Heath has culled from the medical literature a number of 'rules' which guide doctor–patient discourse. Among these are: 'allow discussion of only certain topics', 'restrict the choice of conversational partners', 'use a detailed procedure for interviewing patients', 'avoid the truth' (pp. 106–7).

Barber (1979) has further examined the communication process between doctor and patient, particularly as it affects compliance. He points out that earlier studies of compliance have concentrated on patient culpability, and have neglected doctor characteristics, including speech. Studies by Davis (1967, 1968), were an exception, in that they focused on communication between doctor and patient and found that compliance was made more likely if physicians gave information and suggestions and was less likely if doctors only asked for information and provided no feedback. A broad discussion concerning language policy in medicine has been provided by Shuy (1979), highlighting the language issue in the areas of learning by disabled children, certification of foreign-trained physicians, geriatrics and doctor–patient communication.

There are not many investigations dealing specifically with reactions to *speech* characteristics of doctors and patients. In one, Milmoe *et al.* (1967) related differences in compliance to paralinguistic features of doctors' voices. They wanted to find out if emotion, conveyed unintentionally in the speech of doctors, was associated with the success these doctors had in referring alcoholic patients for further treatment. Milmoe *et al.* obtained tape recordings of the referring doctors talking about their experiences with alcoholics. The recordings were passed through a filter making speech content unintelligible but retaining variations in pitch and volume. Unfiltered and filtered voices were then presented to judges to be rated on such dimensions as anger and sympathy. Results showed that the more 'angry' the content-filtered speech had been rated, the less successful the doctors were in referring alcoholics. It is not far-fetched to assume that the anger conveyed in the doctors' voices was a reflection of their negative attitudes towards alcoholics, and that this negative attitude was accurately perceived by the alcoholics, making them less likely to comply with the doctors' requests. One could generalize a bit further and assume that physicians' attitudes toward different diagnostic entities vary, and that these attitudes can sometimes be conveyed vocally by doctors to their patients.

The process of diagnosis itself was investigated by Fielding and Evered (1980) who tested the hypothesis that patients whose accents reveal them as being lower class are more likely to be diagnosed in physical terms, while on the other hand, patients with a middle-class accent are more likely to be given a diagnosis implying a psychiatric classification. This hypothesis was based on a number of studies showing that middle as compared with lower-class patients are more likely to present their symptoms in sociopsychological terms and that doctors' responses to these presentations are influenced by the perceived social class of patients. Fielding and Evered employed the 'matched-guise' technique (Lambert, Hodgson, Gardner and Fillenbaum 1960) to create two versions of the same presenting symptoms (an ambiguous problem with physical, emotional and behavioural symptoms). In one, the patient adopted a RP (received pronunciation or high-status English) accent. In the other, the patient spoke with a rural regional accent characteristic of southwestern England (see Edwards, this volume: ch. 2). Each tape version was presented to a different group of British medical students who had to make a diagnostic judgement and give their perceptions of the patient's personality and language characteristics and social status.

The results of the study were in line with predictions. The RP-accented patient was perceived as being of higher status and as more likely to have symptoms of psychosomatic origin than the patient with the rural regional accent. This latter result was somewhat marginal in that it only reached the 5 per cent level of significance with a one-tailed test. An additional finding was that the difference in accent prompted the medical student listeners to perceive different grammar and vocabulary in the two patients, despite the fact that syntax and lexicon in the two interviews were identical.

.These studies of the social significance of speech in medical settings constitute only a small beginning in the investigation of problems and issues in this area. The significance of our present knowledge, as well as the limitations will be discussed at the end of this chapter. The review now turns to the area of language and the law.

The legal context

Opportunities for reactions to language variations are vast and of potentially great significance in the legal context. Consider the situation of the police apprehending a suspect who speaks in Spanish-accented English, or receiving a report of rape from a woman with a West Indian accent. The speech occurring in the interactions between clients and lawyers, attorneys and witnesses, judges and juries can have far-reaching consequences for all concerned. Particularly important issues within legal settings are communication accuracy and the credibility and social influence of speakers.

Communication accuracy is a problem in these settings in part because of the professional language of lawyers. It may be difficult at times, even for an intelligent and literate lay person to understand the complicated and somewhat archaic special language of legal documents, procedures and arguments. Charrow and

Charrow (1979) have conducted a linguistic analysis of instructions to juries and isolated a number of linguistic constructions that are largely responsible for incomprehensibility. Among the most problematic were nominalizations, difficult lexical items and 'as to' phrases.

Problems of communication in the courtroom are magnified when defendents are primarily or exclusively fluent in a non-official language. In the United States, this issue has been recognized in the Court Interpreters Act, which provides for the appointment of interpreters in criminal and civil cases initiated by the US Federal Government (Pousada 1979). The problem is far from being solved because the determination of the need for an interpreter is left to the court, and courts have considered the failure to request an interpreter by defendants who do not speak English as a waiver of their right. In addition, most statutory provisions at the state level provide interpreters for witnesses but not for defendants. The need for interpreters exists, of course, in all countries that have large numbers of speakers of non-official languages.

Participants in legal interactions must also be credible. Studies outside legal settings of how paralinguistic characteristics can influence the perception of credibility can provide suggestions for the legal context. Streeter, Krauss, Geller, Olson and Apple (1977) recorded the voices of speakers who lied and who told the truth. Deceptive speech tended to have a higher pitch than truthful speech and higher-pitched speech was also judged to be less truthful by listeners (see Street and Hopper, this volume: ch. 11).

Within the legal context the issue of speech and credibility has been discussed by Naylor (1979) in a case of two Filipino nurses in Michigan who were accused of poisoning patients. Naylor argued that their linguistic and cultural background caused them to answer questions in a way that made them appear to be lying and trying to mislead the jury. Naylor identified several linguistic differences between English and Tagalog (a language of the Philippines). There is, for example, a difference between English and Tagalog verbs on a dimension called 'punctual' *vs* 'durative'. As an illustration, the nurses were asked 'How did you feel when you *came* to the Veterans' Hospital and found out that the understaffing was worse?' One of the nurses replied, 'I didn't know that until I was in the V.A.' This reply appears strange and evasive, but in fact it is based on the difference in meaning of the verb 'to come' in English and Tagalog. In English *came* in that sentence has duration and means something like 'having arrived and been there for a while'. In Tagalog the verb is 'punctual' and can only mean the act of arriving. There were many instances like these where the nurses *appeared* to be evasive and non-responsive and as a consequence the jury may have believed them to be guilty.

The issue of social influences has received empirical attention in several careful investigations recently. Lind and O'Barr (1979) have studied what they call 'power' and 'powerless' speech. These investigators reinterpreted sex differences in American English, described by Lakoff (1975), to reflect differences in the 'power' of speakers. Lakoff had found that female as compared with male speech contained more frequent use of *intensifiers* ('so', as in 'it is so lovely'). *empty adjectives* ('divine'), *hypercorrect grammar, polite forms, hedges* ('you know'), *rising intonation* and a *wider range of intonational patterns*. Lind and O'Barr had observed low-status witnesses (whether female or male) to use these features and, therefore, termed the frequent use of these features the 'powerless' speech mode and their infrequent use the 'power' mode (see Bradac, this volume: ch. 5; Kramarae, this volume: ch. 6).

In order to test the effects of the two modes of speech on the perception of a witness using a particular mode, tape recordings of the testimony in two modes were prepared and presented to subjects for reactions. Witnesses using power speech were rated as more competent, attractive, trustworthy, dynamic and convincing than witnesses using the powerless mode. However, the actual *acceptance* of the testimony, although different in the predicted direction in the two modes, did not reach standard levels of significance. Lind and O'Barr argued, however, that the evaluative dimensions found to discriminate between the two speech modes were found in other investigations to influence the acceptance of a communication.

The possibility that perseverance *vs* acquiescence in simultaneous speech has power implications was also investigated by Lind and O'Barr. Four tapes of a male witness – male attorney interaction during testimony were recorded. In a control version, there were no instances of simultaneous speech; three other versions showed varying degrees of attorney perseverance in simultaneous speech. The major result of this experiment was that the attorney was perceived as having less control in comparison with the witness in the tape versions where there was simultaneous speech as compared with the control tape (with no simultaneous speech). Apparently, subjects felt that the occurrence of simultaneous speech during testimony indicated that the attorney had lost control over the interactions. Comparisons of the tapes with simultaneous speech where the attorney showed a lot *vs* little perseverance resulted in perceptions that the witness had less opportunity to present evidence, and that the attorney was less fair to the witness. These results suggest that attorneys should avoid simultaneous speech and acquiesce rather than persist once simultaneous speech occurs lest they be perceived in unfavourable terms.

The experiments by Lind and O'Barr are groundbreaking attempts to discover those non-content characteristics of speech that are associated with social influence during presentation of testimony. The voice of social influence during simulated jury deliberations has been studied by Scherer and his associates. Scherer (1979b) made audio- and video-recordings of simulated jury discussions involving adult males from Cambridge, Massachusetts and Cologne, Germany, therefore providing a cross-cultural dimension to the study of the social significance of speech. Information was available on the jurors' *personality*, through self-ratings and ratings by others. The perceived *social influence* of each juror was also assessed by having jury participants rank each other in terms of the influence on the final verdict. A number of *voice qualities* (e.g. pitch, loudness) were rated by phoneticians from content-filtered audio tapes. In addition, several *speech parameters* (e.g. productivity, uncertainty–certainty) were measured from transcriptions.

The importance of the cross-cultural dimension was apparent for the relationship between voice quality and perceived influence. In the American (but not the German) group of jurors, higher pitch range (i.e. having a more expressive voice) and loudness were related to perceived influence. Further analysis revealed that among American speakers high pitch range was associated with perceived task ability and loudness with perceived sociability, suggesting that the two voice qualities are associated with alternative forms of social influence. It appears therefore that at least among American speakers, the well-established two-dimensional nature of leadership (Gibb 1969) expresses itself in voice quality.

There is support for Scherer's results from a study of voice outside the legal context. Aronovitch (1976) had male and female university students read neutral passages aloud. Male voices with high pitch range were rated by listener–judges as being more self-confident, extraverted, bold and dominant. The fact that Scherer found significant relationships between voice quality and social influence in the American but not the German sample, and the fact that Aronovitch found different perceived personality correlates of male and female speakers, should alert us to the fact that reactions to voice quality may be dependent on the type of speaker involved.

Of speech characteristics assessed from transcriptions in Scherer's study, only participation rate (productivity) was a consistent predictor of perceived social influence for both German and American jurors. Participation rate, of course, is not usually considered an aspect of speech *style*. Scherer has emphasized the cultural context and has characterized the influential American jurors as having 'a determined, confident and somewhat aggressive style' and German jurors with influence 'to be characterized mostly by verbal fluency and rather a lack of dramatic style' (p. 118). These conclusions are intriguing and suggestive, but they must be treated with considerable caution because the sample of speakers studied from the two cultures was very small.

The social influence of various speech patterns in the courtroom has also been studied by comparing the speech of successful and unsuccessful attorneys. Parkinson (1979) investigated criminal cases in which the defendant was acquitted (success for defence attorney) and compared them with similar cases where the defendant was convicted (success for prosecuting attorney). He found that successful as compared with unsuccessful prosecutors were verbally assertive and they spoke longer. Successful as compared with unsuccessful defence attorneys used more abstract or ambiguous language and more legal jargon. The variables studied by Parkinson referred primarily to content, rather than speech style.

These studies from the legal context dealing with communication accuracy, credibility and social influence will be reviewed again in a broader context at the end of this chapter, after an examination of the social significance of speech in the employment setting.

The employment interview

The occupational setting is multifaceted. Speech plays a potentially significant role in a variety of circumstances. However, research dealing with speech in occupational settings has been limited to the employment interview, and even there it is of relatively recent origin. The review by Arvey (1979) on unfair discrimination in the employment interview mentioned no study dealing with speech. Most of the studies reviewed by Arvey concerned themselves with the sex of the job applicant, and a handful (only three in fact) dealt with race. Despite a dearth of empirical studies, Arvey convincingly documents the potential significance of unfair discrimination in job interviews. He states that the personnel interview is the most widely used method of selecting employees, despite research showng that it is of limited reliability and validity. This issue is important not only from a scientific and social, but also from a legal point of view. In 1964, the Congress of the United States passed the Civil Rights Act and Title VII of this Act makes it illegal to discriminate in employment on the basis of race, national origin, religion or sex. According to Arvey (1979), the Equal Employment Opportunity Commission (EEOC), the agency that interprets and enforces the Act, has issued guidelines concerning the fairness of 'employment tests'. Employment interviews are explicitly included under such tests. Some of these employment tests (general intelligence, mechanical aptitude) have already been ruled illegal. In addition, the Supreme Court of the United States has advocated a *'shifting-burden-of-proof'* principle. This principle means that once adverse effects due to a selection device have been documented (e.g. when more minority than majority members are refused a job on the basis of a 'test'), the burden of proof is *shifted on the employer* to demonstrate the validity of the device.

In Canada there is also legislation prohibiting discrimination in employment on the basis of race, sex and national origin. This legislation is embodied in Federal and Provincial Human Rights Codes and there are Human Rights Commissions charged with enforcing them. Challenges of selection devices appear not to have been made yet in Canada, but the legislation and the procedures already in force would allow the possibility of such challenges. It is, therefore, not difficult to imagine that a considerable amount of litigation may ensue in the United States, as well as in Canada at a later time, should there be evidence that job interviews discriminate against members of minorities. The question of whether minority status revealed through speech results in unfair evaluation is, therefore, of considerable legal, as well as social and psychological significance.

The earliest study of speech in the employment interview context was conducted by Baird (1969). He analysed listener reactions to certain variations in pronunciation used by lower-class Negro women in the context of a job interview. Among the variations were alternation of the morphemic ending -ing with -in. Listeners, who were white first-year psychology students, did not show differential reactions to these linguistic variations.

In another of the early investigations, Shuy (1973) studied reactions to tape-recorded segments of the speech of 16 male adults, representing a wide range of socioeconomic status in Washington, DC. Listener–judges were persons who were engaged in actual hiring for various employers. The judged employability of the speakers varied with their socioeconomic status. However, when asked directly about the importance of speech in their evaluations, most listeners denied such influence.

Hopper and Williams (1973) conducted the first comprehensive study of the social significance of speech in the job interview. The investigation was carried out in two phases. In the first phase, 23 employers rated four 90-second recordings of male job applicants in an employment interview. The four speakers were representative of standard American English, Black English, Spanish-influenced English and Southern White English. Ratings of the speakers were made on 40 semantic differential scales; and listeners were also asked to indicate the probability that they would hire the speakers for each of seven job categories, from executive to manual labourer. A factor analysis of the semantic differential scales yielded the dimensions (1) Intelligence/Competence, (2) Agreeableness, (3) Self-assurance, and (4) Anglo-like/non-Anglo-like. These four dimensions were than related to hiring decisions. Results showed that the dimension Intelligence/Competence was the best predictor, and became particularly important for jobs that involved executive or leadership skills. These results do not necessarily implicate speech in the hiring decisions. It is possible that the same rating dimensions based on a different stimulus presentation would have been similarly related to hiring decisions. An additional and somewhat surprising result was that judged ethnicity (Anglo-like/non-Anglo-like) was unrelated to the employment decisions.

In the second phase of the study, a black speaker was substituted for the Spanish accented one. Two white and two black speakers were therefore present and Hopper and Williams were able to investigate directly the effects of race of speaker. The four taped speech samples were presented to 40 employment interviewers for ratings on 15 adjectives and judgements of employability for five jobs. A factor analysis of the speech ratings revealed the dimensions of (1) Competence, (2) Agreeableness and (3) Self-assurance. The dimension of competence was the best predictor of employment decisions regarding the executive supervisory positions. The predictive power of all dimensions decreased as job status decreased. As in phase one, race of speaker was only minimally implicated in the employment decisions. Differences due to race were investigated through discriminant analyses and were only apparent for the executive position where the standard American English speaker was rated most employable.

In a subsequent study, Hopper (1977) investigated the effects of three independent variables: (1) race of speaker (black *vs* white, indicated to the rater by a notation on the background information sheet), (2) standard *vs* non-standard accent, and (3) qualifications, on judgements of employability for jobs involving supervision, sales, and technical positions. Tapes were presented to 104 employment interviewers who had to give their impressions of the speakers on semantic differential scales and also rated the probability that the speaker would be hired for each of the three positions. A factor analysis of the semantic differential scales revealed two factors, *competence* to do a job and *likeability* of the interviewee. These two dimensions were significant predictors of the hiring decisions. Regarding the effects of race and standardness of accent, somewhat surprising results were obtained. Although both of these factors showed significant main effects, these were overshadowed by a very large interaction between the two. The reason for this interaction was the *very positive* evaluation given to the black speaker with the standard accent. In other words a form of reverse discrimination appeared in favour of the black speaker when he spoke with a standard accent. This favouritism for the black speaker with the standard accent was apparent for the salesman and supervisor, but not for the technician position. In explaining the absence of discrimination against blacks, Hopper entertained the possibility that his results reflect the increasing acceptance of blacks *or* the *suppression* of discrimination to the overt listing of the applicants' race on the information sheet. Neither of these two explanations accounts for the favouritism shown toward the standard accented black speaker. This favouritism seems best explained by accommodation theory (see Simard, Taylor and Giles 1976). Blacks who have converged to standard (White) speech elicit particularly favourable reactions from white listeners. Giles and Bourhis (1976a) applied accommodation theory to parallel results of favouritism toward black speakers in Britain. They found that speakers with a standard (RP) accent were rated more favourably than RP accented white speakers. Thus, it appears that perceived convergence towards the speech of a positive reference groups results in favourable evaluation (see Street and Hopper, this volume: ch. 11).

Absence of discrimination (or favouritism) on the basis of the ethnicity of speakers is unfortunately not always the case. In fact very definite discrimination was found by Rey (1977) who collected speech samples from four white Americans, four blacks and eleven Cuban nationals (sex of speaker not specified, but presumably males and females were used), who were categorized according to whether they had a minimal, medium or heavy Spanish accents. Speech samples were rated for status and employability for seven jobs of varying status by listener–judges who were actual employers in the South Florida area. Employers were defined as those in a position to hire or interview for the purpose of hiring. The listener–judge sample consisted of 20 white Americans, 11 black Americans and 12 Cubans. Results showed that white American speakers were consistently rated highest in status. Several other analyses pointed to the conclusion that listeners tended to group the speakers into three categories, (1) white, (2) black and speakers with minimal and medium Spanish accents and (3) the heavily Spanish accented speakers. Unfortunately, no overall analysis of variance was carried out for the occupational suitability judgements by only multiple t-tests, apparently without corrections, making reliable statistical inferences difficult. An inspection of the table of means reveals the following trends. White speakers were most favourably evaluated for all jobs except manual labourer. Black speakers were generally deemed more suitable for most jobs than Cubans, especially if these had a heavy accent. Quite surprisingly, there was a relatively strong consensus among listener–judges from the three ethnic group about the job suitability of the various speakers. For example, black and Cuban judges agreed with whites that white speakers are considerably more suitable than either blacks or Cubans for the job of executive. A consensus concerning the relative status of various groups, shared even by groups low in the status hierarchy, is surprising, though not entirely unexpected. In attitude studies similar consensual hierarchies have been found in Canada (Berry and Kalin 1979).

The results of Rey's study are, therefore, quite different from the earlier investigations of Hopper and Williams (1973) and Hopper (1977) who found minimal discrimination on the basis of speakers' ethnicity. As possible reasons for the difference, Rey proposed the topics used in the two sets of studies (talk about pets in Rey's study and employment interview talk in the studies by Hopper), or the possibility that the Federal civil rights legislation may not yet have made an impact in the South Florida, as opposed to the Washington, DC area.

Further evidence for discrimination against Spanish accented speakers comes from a study by de la Zerda and Hopper (1979) who measured attitudes towards Mexican American speech from responses to attitude statements as well as reactions to taped speech samples of Mexican Americans, judged as accented or standard in a pilot study. The listener–judges were employers from San Antonio, Texas. In addition to rating the speakers on several personality dimensions, the listener–judges were also asked to 'predict the likelihood of a speaker being hired for each of three positions (supervisor, skilled technician and semi-skilled worker)' (p. 128). Reactions to speech samples were the best predictors of hiring decisions for all positions. The importance of these reactions as predictors decreased with decreasing status of the job. A direct comparison of accented and standard speakers revealed that standard speakers were favoured for supervisor while accented speakers were more likely to be hired for the semi-skilled position. No accent differences were discovered for the position of skilled technician. It is of interest to note that 'professed language attitudes' (i.e. responses to opinion statements) predicted hiring decisions only minimally or not at all. This absence of a relationship may well have been due to the fact that an attitude measure with unknown validity was used and that items with apparently opposite valence were added. The most interesting result from this study, nevertheless, is the double discrimination shown, that is, deeming standard speakers as appropriate for high and inappropriate for low-status jobs and deeming accented speakers as appropriate for low and inappropriate for high status positions (see Carranza, this volume: ch. 3; Street and Hopper, this volume: ch. 11). The following two studies from the Canadian context have also shown this double discrimination.

Kalin and Rayko (1980) asked university students to act the role of personnel consultants of a large manufacturing enterprise. They had to predict how well each of ten job applicants would do in each of four jobs varying in status (foreman, industrial mechanic, production assembler and plant cleaner). Information on applicants was provided through brief biographical dossiers and 30-second recordings of their speech, purportedly from a job interview. Five candiates spoke with an English Canadian accent and five of the speakers were foreign born and spoke fluent English but with a foreign accent (Italian, Greek, Portuguese, West African, Slovac). Listeners rated each speaker's suitability for each of the four jobs. Definite discrimination appeared in these judgements in favour of English Canadian and against foreign accented speakers. Foreign accented applicants, as compared with English Canadian speakers, were rated less suitable for the higher-status jobs, but more suitable for the lower-status jobs. Measures of ethnocentrism and authoritarianism were also obtained from the listener–judges. Ethnocentrism showed low but significant correlations with discrimination against foreign accented speakers, defined as the difference in the evaluation of foreign *vs* English Canadian speakers. Authoritarianism showed similar but even lower correlations. These results suggest that general ethnic tolerance influences reactions to accented speech, a conclusion supported in studies by Giles (1971a, 1972).

The foreign accented speakers in the study by Kalin and Rayko were treated as one group because a pilot study had revealed no significant differences in the reactions to them. This finding is somewhat surprising in view of studies showing a consistent hierarchy of Canadians' evaluations of various ethnic groups (e.g. Berry, Kalin and Taylor 1977). Several features in the study by Kalin and Rayko may have obscured real differential preferences for various ethnic accents: the perceived social status range of the ethnic accents may have been too limited; a contrast effect between 'foreign' and standard English Canadian speakers may have overshadowed perceived differences among the foreign accents; or the number of listener–judges may have been too small to detect actual differences. In order to eliminate these possibly obscuring factors, Kalin, Rayko and Love (1980) conducted a subsequent study. To guarantee a wider range of perceived status, accents were selected from ethnic groups at different levels of the evaluative hierarchy. A group rated very high (English) in the survey by Berry, Kalin and Taylor (1977), one rated very low (South Asian), one slightly above average (German) and one below average (West Indian) were chosen. To remove contrast effects, English Canadian speakers were not included. A preliminary study was also conducted to ascertain whether correct ethnic labels would be assigned to the speech samples presented. In this preliminary study, subjects listened to 16 speakers representing the four accents, rated them for comprehensibility and tried to identify them. Correct identifications ranged from 20 to 94 per cent, but were all better than chance. Misidentifications tended to be with ethnic groups adjacent in the evaluative hierarchy. Regarding comprehensibility, English (from England) accented speakers were rated most comprehensible; German accented speakers were found to be more comprehensible than South Asians and West Indians.

In the main experiment, the procedure used by Kalin and Rayko was basically repeated. Subjects acting as personnel consultants rated the suitability of the same 16 speakers for four jobs, varying in status. For the highest-status job (foreman), English accented candidates were rated the most suitable, then German, South Asian and finally, West Indian. But for the job of least status (industrial plant cleaner), the order of suitability was exactly reversed. Double discrimination was again evident as in earlier studies because English accented speakers were judged to be *more* suitable for higher, but *less* suitable for lower status jobs. The exact opposite pattern prevailed for South Asian and West Indian speakers.

To examine whether the patterns of job suitability ratings obtained in North America would also apply to standard *vs* non-standard accented speakers in Great Britain, Giles, Wilson and Conway (1981) carried out a similar study. A second aim of their study was to determine whether lexical diversity would also influence reactions to speakers (see Bradac, this volume: ch. 6). Following the matched-guise technique, a bidialectic speaker used either a standard RP or non-standard South Welsh accent and showed either high or low lexical diversity. Following a procedure similar to Kalin and Rayko (1980), English undergraduates, acting as personnel consultants, rated the personality of the speakers and made several judgements of job performance for each of four job categories, varying in status. The speech samples were purportedly excerpts from job interviews. The standard speaker was perceived as having more competence but less integrity and social attractiveness as compared with the non-standard Welsh speaker (see Edwards, this volume: ch. 2). Contrary to previous work in the United States (e.g. Bradac, Courtright and Bowers 1980), *low* rather than *high* diversity speakers were perceived as more agreeable and good-natured. Evaluations regarding job performance also favoured low rather than high diversity speakers.

In line with North American results, Giles *et al.* found that low-status jobs were seen as more suitable for the individual with the non-standard accent. However, the standard accented speaker was not seen as significantly more suitable for the highest status job (foreman) under consideration in the study. In a follow-up study, Giles *et al.* (1981) found that standard as compared with non-standard speakers *were* rated more suitable when judgements pertained to positions of higher status (clerical, executive, professional).

In the previous three studies, university students acted as listener–judges and made employment decisions from simulated employment interviews. A legitimate question can be raised about the validity of such a procedure. Would similar results emerge if actual employment interviewers were used? In addressing this issue Kalin and Rayko (1980) argued that because of their intelligence, education and social status student subjects should be less likely than the average employment interviewer to show discrimination, and that many students are future employers who would soon be making real hiring decisions. In addition to these somewhat indirect arguments, there is direct empirical support. Bernstein, Hakel and Harlan (1975) reviewed a number of studies that compared the responses of students to those of employment interviewers and concluded that the decisions made by the two groups were very similar. The only consistent difference to emerge was the fact that student judges, as compared with actual interviewers, were somewhat more lenient. The use of student subjects appears therefore to be appropriate in the study of the employment interview.

The various investigations of language variation and occupational suitability are not entirely consistent with regard to the question of whether the social and ethnic background of speakers influence judgements of job suitability. Hopper and Williams (1973) and Hopper (1977) found little discrimination on the basis of the ethnic background of speakers. However, discrimination against accented speakers was found in several other studies (de la Zerda and Hopper 1979; Giles *et al.* 1981; Kalin and Rayko 1980; Kalin *et al.* 1980; Rey 1977; Shuy 1973).

Various explanations are possible for the difference in the two sets of studies. Likely ones involve the salience of race and the sensitivity to charges of discrimination against blacks among the US public and especially among American employment interviewers used as subjects by Hopper and Williams (1973) and Hopper (1977). The salience of race and sensitivity to possible discrimination against blacks may *suppress* such discrimination or even trigger favouritism. There may be less public consciousness and sensitivity regarding discrimination against Hispanics in the US. Listeners in Canada or England may be less sensitized than Americans to possible charges of discrimination and may therefore be less likely to suppress judgements based on attitudes and stereotypes.

In several of the studies reviewed a type of double discriminaton was observed (de la Zerda and Hopper 1979; Giles *et al.* 1981; Kalin and Rayko 1980; Kalin *et al.* 1980). That is, speakers with a standard or high-status accent were judged to be particularly suited for high-status and unsuited for low-status jobs. The reverse was the case for speakers with nonstandard (ethnic or regional) accents. It appears therefore that the perception of an accent triggers a judgement regarding the social status of the group represented by the speaker (see Sebastian, Ryan and Corso, in press). The speaker is then judged to be suitable for an occupation corresponding to the status of the accent category. In other words, there is a consensual status hierarchy of accents as well as occupations and speakers with a particular accent are deemed appropriate for a given job level. We might call this a status-matching process. Particular speakers can be found unsuitable for given jobs, because the status indicated by their accents is higher *or* lower than the status of the job for which they are considered.

This status-matching hypothesis has certain important implications for the relationship between speech characteristics and judged employability. It would question the conclusion reached by Hopper and associates (de la Zerda and Hopper 1979; Hopper 1977; Hopper and Williams 1973) that the importance of speech characteristics decreases as the status of the job decreases. The empirical results obtained by Hopper are undoubtedly correct, however they may be limited to certain status ranges. For jobs of very low status speech characteristics may again become very important, in that speakers with high-status accents are deemed inappropriate and speakers with low-status accents appropriate.

The status-matching hypothesis also challenges an alternative hypothesis of linguistic deficiency as the basis for discrimination. Following the deficiency hypothesis one would argue that people with non-standard accents are deemed unsuitable for high-status jobs because the non-standard accent would be a hindrance in communicating with others, particularly those of high status. Without dismissing such an argument entirely, it definitely has limitations. Among other things it could not explain why speakers with standard accents are considered unsuitable for the low-status jobs. It is difficult to see how a standard accent could be an objective hindrance in the performance of any job, in the sense of causing problems of communication. From the listener–judges point of view, however, having a standard (or high prestige) accent may well *appear* to be a hindrance, in the sense that such a person may be considered out of place in a low-status job. It is possible that the apparent mismatch between the status of the job applicant and the job may cause listener–judges to anticipate interpersonal friction and lack of cooperation leading to lower productivity and disharmony in a particular work setting. Whatever the precise reason, judgements that standard (or high-status) accented speakers are considered relatively inappropriate for low-status jobs has important implications in an economic climate where high unemployment affects various status levels. Unemployed persons with standard accents who might be willing to take any job, may find it difficult to find employment in lower-status jobs because their accents reveal them to be 'above' and therefore unsuitable for such jobs.

The limitations of the status-matching hypothesis must of course be acknowledged. It may be useful to explain judgements of job suitability, but it does not explain all reactions to non-standard speech. Among the explanations for these reactions that must be entertained are the belief similarity and the discomfort hypothesis. Sebastain, Ryan and Corso (in press) showed that accentedness was associated with perceived belief dissimilarity (see also Ryan and Sebastian 1980). Sebastian, Ryan, Keogh and Schmidt (1980) have argued that negative reactions to accented speech are mediated by negative affect arousal stemming from the difficulty listeners have in understanding non-standard speakers. Reasons for negative reactions to non-standard speech have been discussed more extensively by Sebastian and Ryan (in press).

In comparison with the medical and legal context, the employment interview has received relatively more research attention regarding the domain of language attitudes. Much remains to be explored, however. Before pointing out some specific avenues for future research, an integrated look at the social significance of speech in the various applied settings is provided.

Perspectives and prospects

As problems relating to speech in applied settings are varied and multifaceted, there has been quite a variation in the methods employed in the study of these problems. Particular methods employed have co-varied to some extent with the host disciplines. Researchers from speech and communications departments have been prone to use correlational designs (factor analyses, multiple regressions) while those from psychology, experimental designs. While it is sometimes possible to translate problems and inferences from one type of design into the other, that is not always the case. It would therefore seem most appropriate to use experimental designs (and consequent analyses of variance) for problems of cause and effect and correlational approaches for problems dealing with covariation.

In future studies of reactions to speech several other methodological issues also require attention. It does not seem appropriate to draw firm conclusions about reactions to a speech community (e.g. black speech) on the basis of studying responses to only one or two exemplars of that community. Using several representatives of a language group is advisable in order to reduce the idiosyncratic effects of single speakers. Using several speakers, however, calls for hierarchical (nested) designs, where speaker becomes a random factor (see Kalin, Rayko and Love 1980, for an application of this advice and Meyers 1972, for treatment of the statistical issues involved). In addition to a concern with details of design, other methodological issues deserve attention. This is not the place to discuss the relative merits of laboratory and analogue *vs* field studies, but it seems reasonable to advocate that both should be used in a complementary manner. For the sake of greater generality it is also most appropriate to use actual behaviours as dependent measures in addition to the ubiquitous rating scales. The compliance research in the medical setting might serve as an example here.

The research on reactions to speech reviewed in this chapter has revealed themes common to evaluative reactions to speech in a broader context. In summarizing that research in 1975, Giles and Powesland found two general dimensions, competence and social attractiveness, to be particularly important. The same or very similar dimensions have also emerged in the studies currently under review, or were found to be useful when included as *a priori* measures. Perceived competence (or closely related clusters) was important in the studies by Fielding and Evered (1980), Lind and O'Barr (1979), Hopper (1977) and Giles *et al.* (1981), Scherer (1979b) and Hopper and Williams (1973). Social attractiveness was important in Lind and O'Barr (1979) and Giles *et al.* (1981). Related concepts figured prominently in other studies (likeability/benevolence in Scherer 1979b; agreeableness in Hopper and Williams 1973; and likeability in Hopper 1977). Common dimensions such as competence and likeability seem therefore to characterize a large variety of reactions to speech variation (see Giles and Ryan, this volume: ch. 13).

Turning to an assessment of the state of knowledge in the medical, legal and employment contexts, a significant improvement since the review by Giles and Powesland (1975) has to be acknowledged, but a modest recognition that only the surface has been scratched is also in order. In the medical context the study by Milmoe *et al.* (1967) has shown that physicians' attitudes toward alcoholics are revealed unintentionally in speech with the effect of lowering the compliance rate in seeking treatment. A number of questions arise and should provide the stimulus for future research. What are the affective reactions revealed through speech toward various diagnostic categories (medical, psychiatric)? Are other forms of compliance (taking prescription drugs; exercise) affected by physicians' attitudes conveyed by speech? Do physcians' attitudes vary according to the gender or social and ethnic origin of patients and do physicians then express these attitudes in their speech?

The study by Fielding and Evered (1980) showing that doctors attribute symptoms to psychosomatic rather than physical origins in patients with middle-class accents opens another line of research. How do voice cues revealing gender or ethnic origin affect diagnosis and how are other diagnostic categories or treatment alternatives (pharmacological, psychological or lifestyle changes) affected by the speech style of patients? Other questions, not touched by the studies reviewed suggest themselves. How are interactions between nurses and patients, or nurses and doctors, affected by their respective speech styles? The issue of between language differences must also be raised by way of an example. An Arabic-only speaking patient was recently treated as a psychiatric patient in Toronto. Her compliants about severe pain (conveyed in part through an interpreter) were ignored and attributed to her mental condition. She died within a short time from physical causes.

The language difference between patient and staff was most likely involved in the misdiagnosis resulting in the tragic death of the patient.

While the significance of speech in the medical setting cannot be under-estimated, its importance probably does vary to some extent according to the medical specialty involved. Speech is likely to be most crucial in the area of family medicine and psychiatry where reliance on communication between physician and patient is very great. It is probably less important in traumatic medicine and other areas where the nature of the medical problem and the treatment are quite evident and physical.

As was the case with the medical setting, we have just seen the beginning of research into the social significance of speech in the legal context. These begin-nings, however, have pointed to crucial areas of concern. *Communication accuracy* can be impeded when participants are not entirely familiar with each others' language (Charrow and Charrow, 1979; Pousada 1979). *Credibility* is influ-enced by tone of voice (Scherer 1979b; Streeter *et al.* 1977) and cultural appro-priateness of speech (Naylor 1979). *Social influence* has received the most empirical attention in this context. Social influence is enhanced by the use of 'power' as opposed to 'powerless' speech (Lind and O'Barr 1979), by voice expres-siveness (Scherer 1979b) and by high participation rate (Parkinson 1979; Scherer 1979b). Not only is research in this area in its infancy, but already certain con-flicting results have appeared. According to both Scherer (1979b) and Aronovitch (1976) 'high pitch range' leads to positive judgements (perceived influence and self-confidence). According to Lind and O'Barr, however, 'higher range of intonational patterns is associated with powerless speech'. Although it is not clear that the speech characteristics described by these phrases are identical, it is nevertheless evident that this issue requires definitional and empirical attention.

While important beginnings have been made in exploring the significance of speech in legal settings, these investigations have been limited to speech in the courtroom. Many other settings remain for enquiry. There is the area of police relations with the public in general and suspects in particular. Does a suspect having non-standard speech provide a police constable with the opportunity to translate a statement in a biased way that suits the purposes of the police? Does a defendant with a lower-class dialect appear intransigent and therefore unapol-ogetic? These and many more questions can be raised and should be the subject of study. The social significance of speech in a variety of other legal settings also deserves investigation. In these endeavours the search for knowledge should be extended to help the plight of the powerless, in addition to enhancing the power of the already powerful (i.e. attorneys).

Within the legal settings the social significance of speech is likely to be more crucial in some areas than others. Or particular importance are those situations that consist of initial encounters and brief acquaintance, situations in other words, where speech can contribute to first and lasting impressions (see Giles and Ryan, this volume: ch. 13). Encounters with police and courtroom settings are prime examples. Also crucial are interactions where the opportunity for miscommunica-tion exists, as when participants speak different codes (dialects, languages, tech-nical *vs* ordinary language). The social significance of speech probably decreases with long-term acquaintance, as might happen between judge and attorney, or prisoner and guard.

Research into the social significance of speech in the occupational setting has thus far been restricted to the employment interview. Within this area several issues have emerged which require further attention. One concerns the question of when discrimination on the basis of ethnic or social origin of speaker will be evident in judgements of occupational suitability. Is such discrimination absent because of civil rights legislation, as argued by Hopper and Williams (1973)? Is it due to the particular salience of black speakers (i.e. racial cues) which leads to an active suppression of discrimination? What role does perceived accommodation play in the manifestation of positive or negative discrimination? These and other questions require studies of speakers with various ethnic backgrounds conducted in different societal contexts, but employing similar methods.

The status-matching hypothesis, explaining how judgements of occupational suitability are based on a comparison of the status of speakers with the status of jobs, also deserves further investigation. The perceived status of jobs and groups of speakers must be independently assessed, and it should be confirmed that status matching occurs over all ranges of the status hierarchy.

The employment interview itself is of course only a small part of the complete occupational setting. Speech is important and deserves investigation in other areas as well. Consider the work place and the role speech plays in relations between subordinates and superiors. Do variations in speech (due to ethnic, social class and regional origin) exacerbate and highlight industrial conflict by emphasizing group differences and group distinctiveness of workers *vs* management or one group of workers *vs* another? Are speech characteristics a factor in promotion and occupational advancement? It is not unreasonable to predict that convergence to standard speech facilitates and divergence impedes promotion. These and many other questions await research.

It has been stated repeatedly throughout this chapter that the study of the social significance of speech in applied settings is complex. This complexity derives from the fact that it can be, and has been approached from several disciplines (social psychology, sociolinguistics, anthropology, speech and communication studies, etc.). It also relies on basic as well as applied issues, concepts and methods. Finally, the cross-cultural dimension can never be ignored. The complexity of the problem, however, combined with the fact that most of the territory to be explored is still uncharted, makes the prospects of exploration both exciting and challenging.

10

From social history to language attitudes

Robert N. St Clair

To understand fully how language attitudes develop, it may be necessary to reach back into the past and investigate the social and political forces operating within the history of a nation. These patterns of development may have once surfaced in the form of social movements and, even when these events are now a part of the written record, their forces still remain. They are evident in the subtle metaphors of everyday speech; and they can be found implicitly stated in standardized tests, teacher training courses, federal legislation, and administrator's handbooks. When linguists were concentrating on how language operates as a formal system (Chomsky 1965b); their research took them away from the social contexts of language. More recently, however, with the advent of sociolinguistics, there has been a greater awareness of the varieties of linguistic expression and how these are intrinsically related to the social contexts in which they are characteristically found. As a consequence, sociolinguists have been concerned with documenting patterns of language variation (Labov 1972). These descriptive studies have been enhanced by interdisciplinary theoretical models which attempt to provide some insight into the social psychology of language attitudes (Giles and Powesland 1975; Giles and St Clair 1979). One area of sociolinguistic research not fully covered in the literature, however, is the role that such historical forces play in the creation of language attitudes. Hence the focus of this chapter.

If the study of social history is to be instructive in understanding how such forces can influence language attitudes, these investigations must go beyond a chronological review of the factual knowledge of past events. These facts must be related to a systematic framework of theoretical claims. Aspects of such a model can be found within the sociology of deviance (Becker 1973). This framework is of particular relevance to the study of language attitudes because it relates social history and political movements to how people feel about the forms of language they associate with members of different social and economic groups. However, prior to discussing this model and its implications, it is necessary to first consider the rationale which has been developed for the use of standard language within society.

The rationale for standard language

What is commonly referred to as a 'language' is no more than one of many 'dialects' spoken within a nation. What makes it different from these other forms of social and regional expression is that it is considered to be the only 'officially recognized' form of speech. It is the only language variety that is legitimated[1] by the government of a nation for use in the school system, the public media, literature and government. It is the dialect which one finds in the dictionary, and as a consequence it performs the role of an idealized form of speech. There is no consistent way in which these languages appear. In Spain, for example, the official dialect is known as Castellano, and it is the dialect that was spoken under the political hegemony of Castile at the time when this group defeated the other provinces of Spain and imposed its regional dialect on them (see Carranza, this volume: ch. 4). Another pattern of legitimation can be found in Italy where the language of the country comes from the local aristocracy of Florence. The most interesting case can be found in Germany where a common lingua franca emerged from the various dialects in the highlands. It is this form of 'hoch Deutsch' which was officially accepted as the language of Germany in comparison to the various forms of language variation among the lowlands (platte Deutsch) which still remain as regional and social forms of expression. Although an understanding of linguistic variety can be informative, it does not explain fully how some dialects come to be legitimated at the expense of others. For this insight, one must turn to some of the structural parallels between language and culture; for it is through the process of political socialization that one can begin to see how social movements relate to historical attitudes toward language.

Each nation has an obligation to imbue its citizenry with a respect for its civic culture (Dawson, Prewitt and Dawson 1977; Karabel and Halsey 1977; Katz 1975). This use of political socialization channels social behaviour in line with the mainstream values of a nation. It teaches the populace to work within the system provided by the government, to respect its laws and to abide by its dictates. What is interesting about this phenomenon is that language standardization is one of the more dominant instruments for inducing common social expectations among its citizenry (O'Neil 1972; Sledd 1972). This sociopolitical process need not be thought of as sinister. However, the more conservative a nation becomes, the more it uses language as a constraint against social, political, religious and ethnic minorities in order to deny them full access to the mainstream culture. This process has been documented in language planning studies dealing with linguistic purification (Polenz 1972), and it relates to the needs and concerns of the power elite of a nation. Hence, the following structural parallels between the similar processes of legitimating both language and culture can be informative.[2]

What these structural parallels demonstrate is that language and culture play a similar function in the process of political socialization. They both define one variety of language and culture as the officially recognized pattern of expression and utilize public policy to legitimate this point of view. Just as history is rewritten

---

[1] This is a technical term within the political sociology of language and consequently differs from 'legitimize' which is a common term in ordinary language.

[2] Linguistic purification can take many forms. In the work of Polenz (1972) he noted how the German language was gradually cleansed of foreign words. This movement began before the turn of the century and intensified with the rise of the Third Reich. In the United States, there is another form of language purification going on. The focus here is not on borrowed lexical items and their Anglo-Saxon etymologies, but on the standardized use of syntax. The 'Back to Basics' movement and the 'Competency-Based' movement both attempt to guarantee the success of those children whose home language coincides with the legitimated dialect of the school system. All other forms of non-standard language such as Black English, Chicano English, Indian English, and so on, are penalized.

Table 10.1: Structural parallels

	Language	Culture
Power	Power defines the offical dialect of a nation	Power defines the official social reality of a nation
History	The legitimacy of diachrony is defined from the view of the establishment	When a new group achieves political control, it rewrites its national history to reflect its own heritage and to enhance its own self-image
Instrument	Language is an instrument of the power structure and is used in controlling the access of social mobility through literacy tests	Culture is used as a reference marker for social behaviour and control. It reflects the political needs of the power structure
Deviancy	Non-standard dialects are deemed deviant and those who adhere to these forms of speech are stigmatized	Sub-cultures are labelled as deviant and its advocates are chastized
Change	The focus of linguistic control is against change brought about by contact with other social and political influences	Culture is the focus of social change. Those who resist it are purists or conservatives. Those who want change really want their own system of values to be legitimated nationally
Accommodation	Language standardization is a form of accommodation by all dialect speakers in favour of the official language of power	The official culture provides the basis for public policy in which minority cultures are required to assimilate or mainstream

to reflect the mainstream value system so is linguistic diachrony viewed from the point of view of the standard language. This is implicit in the use of the standardized forms of language evident in language tests, dictionaries, the language of government and the mass media, and other forms of sociolinguistic accommodation. What these structural parallels demonstrate, in effect, is that the legitimation process is related to the concept of power.

Language, power and social distance

In order to understand how power relates to language attitudes as well as to describe more fully the pattern indicated in Table 10.1, it is necessary to consider in some detail the literature on the sociology of deviance and to draw from these studies those implications which have relevance for the social genesis of language attitudes (St Clair, in press). Although there are many interesting models of deviance which relate to language loyalty, the most insightful one relating to the interaction of language, power and social distance comes from the labelling theory of Becker (1973). His approach to deviance is based on the root metaphor of social stigma in which the mere act of defining a group as deviant by isolating its members from the remainder of society and punishing them as rule breakers creates and perpetuates a community of outsiders (Douglas 1970). Those who do the labelling usually belong to a well organized pressure group or professional organization whose views are found to be acceptable to the power structure. Hence, they share ideological frameworks. These beliefs are developed into public policy through legislation or some other form of agenda setting. Once these laws are passed and the attitudes implicit within them are legitimated, they are subsequently enforced by various institutions within the public domain. Those who do the enforcing of these policies are best characterized as public servants whose occupations require them to be social enforcers of the status quo. Although they may not openly support the ideology of the moral entrepreneurs who created the legislation, they will do so tacitly through their actions. From their point of view, they are merely good public servants who are just trying to do their job. Consequently, they feel obligated to demonstrate to their superiors that the 'new problem' as defined by the recent policies does indeed exist and they go out of their way to demonstrate that they are on the verge of controlling it. Such enforcement, however, is not always applied equally to all law breakers. Their ability to perceive deviant behaviour depends on who is allegedly breaking the rule. This form of labelling through political socialization involves three groups. There are the *moral entrepreneurs* who create the problem; next, there are the *social enforcers* who follow the new policies as public-minded civil servants; and finally, there are the victims to whom the social system is addressed. They are the powerless ones who are kept at great social distance from the mainstream culture. They are the ones whose values have not been legitimated and whose attempts to gain access to the system have been blocked. They are the ones against whom the social enforcers of the system want to label. These social enforcers, it should be noted, are to be found among the policemen, the school teachers, the psychometrists, the programme administrators, and other common forms of public service.

Becker (1973) has characterized four kinds of social behaviour (see Table 10.2). He considers the *pure deviant* to be one who breaks a rule and who is also perceived as deviant by everyone. These outsiders to the mainstream of society have been defined by the social times in which they live. Before the turn of the century, for example, a divorced woman was clearly deviant in the eyes of everyone. Now, it appears that if one is not divorced, it is not in keeping with the norm. At the other end of the spectrum defined by Becker (1973), there is the *conformist* who always obeys the law and is never perceived as deviant. Such people are considered to be good citizens in that their behaviour is in keeping with the dictates of the ruling civic culture. An interesting category is the *secret deviant*. This person is a member of the privileged classes and as a consequence when he or she breaks a rule, such behaviour is almost never perceived as deviant. Such actions are usually classified as eccentricities or the chic experiences of the jet set. They are conveniently excused by the public servants of the law who respect them as holders of power within the system. The final category of deviancy is the *falsely accused*. This individual is an obedient citizen who obeys the laws of society, but who is frequently perceived as deviant by the police, educators and other public servants. The reason why this category is of special interest is because the falsely accused can be found among the political, social, religious, and ethnic minorities within the system. They lack the power to challenge the status quo and consequently remain its victims. An interesting account of blaming the victim is portrayed by W. Ryan (1972). He speaks of the stigma that is acquired by certain ethnic minorities as a result of a system which views them in terms of deprivation and neglect. These victims are classified in the lower economic class because they fail to possess and control any wealth that would provide them with a respectable ranking on the economic ladder. They are without status in a society which has defined them in economic terms. They are without power because they possess no viable resources of economic interest by means of which to entice others to support their interests. Hence, they are placed at a great social distance from the political elite of the nation, and their language and culture have been pejoratively defined. (See also the related social psychological research on victim derogation: Berkowitz and Walster 1976; Lerner 1977; Tajfel, in press.)

Table 10.2: Power and social deviance

	Obedient behaviour	Rule breaking behaviour
Perceived as deviant	Falsely accused	Pure deviant
Not perceived as deviant	Conforming	Secret deviant

What is significant about this research into the sociology of deviance is that it provides great insight into how language attitudes reflect power and social status between groups within a political framework. Power is used to legitimate the language and the culture of the ingroup and to separate them from those whom they define as their outsiders (Blakar 1979). This is accomplished verbally by means of oppressive language (Bosmajian 1974) in which pejorative and demeaning labels are used to create social distance between groups (Eiser 1980; Khleif 1979; Lukens 1979; LeVine and Campbell 1972; Peabody 1970). It can also be accomplished quite naturally in conversations through the use of pronouns in that they reflect both power and solidarity (Brown and Gilman 1960), or the use of social distance can be found in the Manichaean dichotomies of speech in which the positive qualities of a culture are allocated to the ingroup and the pejorative ones are attributed to the members of the outgroup (St Clair 1979). Evidently, different attitudes towards language will be held towards those who are part of the power structure and those who are defined as part of the outgroup. Only those with power find their speech patterns emulated by the masses. Their sociolinguistic patterns are deemed prestigious. Consider, as a case in point, the non-prestigious pronunciation in the Southern United States of 'hep' for 'help'. The loss of the liquid resonant 'l' is a natural linguistic phenomenon and can be found in many other languages. It is evident in the change from Latin *alter* 'other' to *autre* in French and *otro* in Spanish. The 'l' sound was modified to a bilabial semivowel 'w' and eventually the combination of 'a + w' produced a new sound 'o' in Spanish. What is important about this change is that it is a natural part of language. However, this change is not considered to be worth emulating and is usually treated with derision by those outside the South. By way of contrast, consider the rule in the prestigious Massachusetts dialect where the medial resonant 'r' is lost before a consonant (e.g. 'four children') and retained before a vowel (e.g. 'four animals'). There is a hypercorrection of this rule and a restructuring of the lexicon for such words as 'Asia and Cuba' which President Kennedy pronounced as 'Asiar and Cubar'. Obviously, this form of hypercorrection could have been easily characterized as a speech problem in need of correction by a clinical pathologist, but because of the status and the power attributed to its speaker, it was considered to be a prestigious form of speech. President Kennedy, it appears, was not stigmatized for his deviations from the 'norm', but those in the South who continue to naturally pronounce 'hep' for 'help' remain falsely accused. The common attitude toward their language remains one of disdain. Hence, there are certain social forces within society which favour the speech of certain groups over others for sociopolitical reasons. What is interesting is that the social forces which may lead to a contemporary language attitude may have developed many generations ago. This point can be exemplified by an overview of the social history around the turn of the century.

In his study of the development of language policies and attitudes among Francophones, Bourhis (this volume: ch. 3) has aptly demonstrated through his research into social history how the dialect of Paris was promoted by scholars, politicians and other representatives of the establishment into official status as the only language of France. It was in Paris where the intellectual, social, commercial and political forces were to be found and consequently it was in Paris where prestige of the dialect was to gain recognition among the populace. What is unique to the French situation, however, is that the dialect of the 'Ile de France' was not merely another form of speech, but it was considered to be the very vehicle of French civilization just as Latin was once the language of the intellectual world. In the forms and expressions of Parisian French there was a rationality which gave it the special virtues of clarity and purity of thought. But the standardization of the French language did more than please French intellectuals; it was a common force in the rise of nationalism at the time. When a decree was signed banning the use of Latin, Breton, Basque and Occitan in the sixteenth century, this legislation did much to promote a unilingual nation state. The loyalty of the populace was shifted away from their own regionalisms and toward the unifying force of the new lingua franca. By the nineteenth century, the teaching of the national dialect was mandatory at the primary level of education. Those who did not speak Parisian French were held in contempt. They were punished for speaking their 'home language' at school. Such regionalisms were considered to be deficient and incorrect. There was a growing movement among academics, educators, policy makers, and other specialists to 'stamp out' all non-standard forms of French.

Another informative discussion of how language is legitimated can be found in the work of Kramarae (this volume: ch. 5). She demonstrates how pejorative attitudes towards the speech of women have emerged in many European and American proverbs, advice books such as Emily Post's *Etiquette*, and in the popular stereotypes of the language. Male speakers, for example, are supposed to be demanding, dominating, authoritarian, use swear words, show anger, have a sense of humour, be aggressive, and so on. Female speakers, by contrast, are said to be able to enunciate clearly, have high pitch, use more hand and facial expressions, gossip, be gentle, dwell on trivial topics, talk a lot and use gibberish. These characteristics remain as stereotypes and clearly reflect the social and historical forces of a male-dominated society. In face-to-face interaction, for example, it is the female who asks more questions and the male who makes most of the interruptions. What this means, in essence, is that people in power are not interested in the views of others, and so they feel free to interrupt and curtail the expressions of others. Those who are not in power, on the other hand, always feel obliged to buffer their speech and can only express themselves indirectly by the non-threatening use of questions. Hence, not only are dialects legitimated when they are associated with regional power (e.g. the standardization of Parisian French), but they are also legitimated when they are associated with social and political power (e.g. the use of dominant speech by males and the concomitant passive speech of females).

Social forces and linguistic prescriptivism

Drake (1977) has documented the growing concern for 'correctness' as a recurring theme in the social history of American linguistics. Although there is an abundance of evidence from the descriptive study of language that there are no innately superior linguistic systems, this concept continues to survive among the guardians of language such as journalists, editors, composition teachers and other social enforcers of prescriptivism. Given the theoretical model of the sociology of deviance, it is only natural to ask how this form of linguistic labelling came into being. Who are the moral entrepreneurs of this linguistic ideal? Who are its enforcers? And who are its victims? The answer to these questions can be explained in the rise of the movement of social Darwinism in Europe and in the United States during the late nineteenth century (Hofstadter, 1955).

In 1882, Herbert Spencer, a noted sociologist, visited the United States at the request of numerous academic intellectuals and enterprising captains of industry who were interested in learning more about his views on the natural evolution of industrialized societies (Boller 1970). He espoused an extension of Charles Darwin's metaphor and included human societies in the evolutionary chain. He located all human groups on an evolutionary scale of survival, and at the top of the ladder of progress he located the industrialized societies in which *laissez-faire* capitalism was the dominant ideology. In the 'struggle for existence' he argued, they represent the 'survival for the fittest'. Hence, they are models for other nations to emulate. Evidently, Spencer was very popular in the United States. He was openly praised by such industrialists as Andrew Carnegie and John D. Rockefeller because he epitomized and legitimated their self-images of captains of industry within a *laissez-faire* capitalism. What he said was a reaffirmation of the Protestant ethic and a verification of their belief that the growth of big business reflects the survival of the fittest. Those who did not attain success, they argued, lost because of their inferior abilities. They were not endowed with the innate abilities that these more successful giants of industry had for organization and control. They did not have business minds. What is interesting about this equation of the survival for the fittest and the success of the robber barons who demolished their competitors is that this ideology became the implicit business ethic of the times.

The social values of capitalism and the industrial mentality of this earlier period of social history is still to be found in the many expressions in everyday use. This is particularly true in the case of metaphor. These figures of speech are important because they not only provide a perspective on how social interaction is to be defined, but they also have a cognitive status (Brown 1978). Metaphors are, after all, pervasive in everyday life. They are no longer viewed as mere devices of poetic imagination or rhetorical flourishes. They govern the attitudes and the beliefs that people hold. An interesting case in point can be found in the metaphor which equates time with money (Lakoff and Johnson 1980). The following examples demonstrate how endemic this view is in the language of everyday interaction:

METAPHOR: TIME IS MONEY

You are wasting my time.
This task is time consuming.
I don't have the time to give you.
It cost me an hour of my time.
I am running out of time.
This is not worth my while.
Don't lose any time.
Thank you for your time.

In addition to these common expressions, it should be noted that there are other uses of time and how it relates to money. There is the budgeting of time, the scheduling of time, the work for hourly wages, the rent of a room on time, the buying of computer time, the rental of time through parking meters, the rental of money on time (interest), etc. All these figures of speech demonstrate how the influences of capitalism have become an intrinsic part of the English language. Evidently, social Darwinism continues to be an historical force in the language.

The idea of natural selection within Spencer's framework was translated into more than a struggle among societies for progress through evolution. It also meant that there was a struggle between classes within a society and between different nations and even between different races. Just as there were supposed to be superior men belonging to the power elite, it was also assumed that these very men belonged to the upper class and were of a superior race and that the nation in which they resided was also above others in the world market (Berkhoffer 1979; Feldstein 1972; Jordan 1973). In addition to this ideology of supremacy, it was a time when the old immigrants in the United States were beginning to demonstrate their achievement of power within the system and were consequently severely threatened by the large masses of new immigrants from Eastern Europe and the Mediterranean countries (Gossett 1977; Jones 1974; Novotny 1974; Ramirez and Castaneda 1974). It was this social movement of Herbert Spencer's that naturally led to other expressions of moral entrepreneurism in America. About the turn of the century, for example, there was a movement among the Protestant churches known as the Social Gospel movement. According to the newly emerging framework of social Darwinism, it was considered wrong to help the poor and the helpless. But according to Christian thought, it is both proper and just to provide assistance to those who are less fortunate than one's self. As a consequence of this contrast in beliefs, there emerged a religious controversy over science and social justice. This led also to the question of racial discrimination because it was inherent in the model espoused by Spencer while at the same time contrary to the religious dictates of the time (Gossett 1977). It is interesting to follow the ways in which religious content was restructured in order to accommodate the ethnocentrism of the power structure. Josiah Strong, one of the most influential clergymen of the Social Gospel Movement, addressed the race issue. He lamented the gradual disappearance of the American Indian and other indigenous minorities and reasoned that this extinction was inevitable as it was the will of God that the new land be prepared for a better race, the Anglo-Saxons. It was this same Josiah Strong who argued that the Anglo Saxon was a superior race designed by God to conquer and populate the world. This idea is reminiscent of the Manifest

Destiny (Goetzman 1978) and was shared by other notable clergymen of the time, viz, Theodore Munger, Washington Gladden, Lyman Abbott, Walter Rauschenbush, and George T. Herron (Gossett 1977). Hence, social Darwinism was used as an excuse to legitimate the quest for further power among the old immigrants. They used it to create an ideology for their ingroup and labelled others who threatened their position as outsiders. The Social Gospel Movement was merely an extension of this rationale for power and control.

Another movement related to social Darwinism around the turn of the century was the Eugenics Movement. Francis Galton, a cousin of Charles Darwin, laid the foundations for this line of thinking; and it was he who coined the term (Hofstadter 1955) and dedicated his career to promulgating the concept. What this movement advocated was a programme of government intervention to regulate and control patterns of human breeding. It led to the eventual adoption of sterilization laws in 31 states, and it also led to the passage of miscegenation laws in the Southern United States. It is interesting to note just who were the moral entrepreneurs behind this movement. They included such noted psychologists as Lewis Terman, Henry Goddard, and Robert Yerkes. These men were all instrumental in the psychometrics movement also and were active in the creation of IQ tests (Luigman 1977). Even Edward L. Thorndike, the country's leading educational psychologist of the time, was a member of the Galton school and shared in these concepts of racial superiority (Houts 1977). Mrs E. G. Harriman, the wife of the railroad magnate, provided the Eugenics Record Office with substantial financial assistance; and President Theodore Roosevelt gave it his political support (Lawler 1978). What is important about the intrinsic relationship between psychometrics and the Eugenics Movement is the charge that these moral entrepreneurs legitimated their belief systems within testing instruments which were standardized during the first quarter of this century (Houts 1977; Lawler 1978). This built-in bias has been openly questioned recently (Blum 1978); and the general consensus among historically oriented psychologists is that these instruments measure a sensitivity to the mainstream values of the power structure rather than intelligence. However, the reason why the Eugenics Movement and the standardization of intelligence tests are mentioned in this essay is because they provide further evidence of the social and political climate of the United States about the turn of the century. As a consequence, they demonstrate how the language attitude of prescriptivism was merely one aspect of a whole ideological pattern which discriminated against those who were both powerless and different. It did not recognize those social or regional dialects outside of the standardized language of the school system, the mass media and government. It did not accept cognitive styles and cultural patterns which ran contrary to the established framework of the educational system. And, it looked down upon those whose racial origins were not concomitant with the ideological claims of the old immigrants and their growing power structure.

Conclusions

The main point of this essay is that one has to look into the social history of the United States in order to understand how many of the common language attitudes of this country have actually come about. This is particularly true of that period about the turn of the century in which the dictates of social Darwinism were embraced by the power structure and legitimated within the religious circles in the

form of the Social Gospel Movement, and also officially accepted by academic professionals as evidenced by the development of psychometrics in psychology and
the Eugenics Movement in medicine and genetics. These leaders of industry and
science were the moral entrepreneurs of their time. It was through their efforts that
socioeconomic class, religion, race and other issues relating to a threat to their
power elite became social issues requiring control and repression through formal
legislation. It was because of them that the social enforcers for the system
embraced these new policies and strenuously imposed them on social, political and
ethnic minorities while condescendingly excusing the power elite for infractions of
these very same rules. It was through these beliefs and the actions of their social
enforcers that many minorities became the victims within the system. These
powerless persons found themselves attacked for having different social and/or
regional dialects. They became the falsely accused. It was against them that many
of the negative attitudes towards language were directed. In comparison, those
who were a part of the power structure were not falsely accused and their speech
was held up for others to emulate.

Although social history can be informative, it can *also bring into focus* the
phenomenon of accommodation (see Table 10.1). People want to identify with the
power elite. They want to emulate those whom they perceive as being above their
station. This concern for prestige dialects is readily accounted for by recent
research in accommodation theory (Giles and Smith 1979). If the mainstream of
society has been socialized through the educational system and through the mass
media to accept a certain belief system, they will attempt to please and impress one
another in their speech behaviour and in the contents of their attitudes. It is this
reinforcing pattern of behaviour that accounts for the category of well-behaved
citizens which Becker (1973) calls the 'conforming' group. What is interesting
about the work of Giles and Smith (1979) is that it also provides a rationale for conforming behaviour among those groups Becker (1973) has labelled 'career
deviants'. Because these members of the subculture share a belief system, it is only
natural that they should readily accommodate to each other's values. The languages of the pickpocket, the forger, the con man, and other members of these political and social minorities are held together by the same kind of social bond or
Gemeinschaft that unites the mainstream society. In addition, accommodation
theory accounts for the development of social attitudes historically because once
the social forces operating within a society are known, it is just a matter of documenting why these forces were so appealing to the populace and consequently successful models for accommodation of beliefs. Sennett (1978) describes some of
these forces in his study of the rise of narcissism as a language attitude; and Ewen
(1976) provides similar evidence from social history in his study of the rise of the
consumer mentality in the United States. The impact of accommodation theory in
explicating the forces of social history merits further discussion,[3] but suffice it to

[3] Social history is important because it provides the background from which issues are foregrounded for
discussion and evaluation. The forces of social history continue to play a role in outlining the parameters of scientific investigation. It helps to define the context of the *Zeitgeist* in which theoretical
issues are addressed and empirical studies are carried out. Most of the current research in linguistics, for
example, is in direct response to some of the assumptions made by the positivists in Paris during the last
century. They promulgated the belief that physics represented the acme of scientific accomplishment
and that all other fields of investigation should try to emulate this approach to science. Language
scientists were quick to adopt this model; and, to this day, linguists continue to openly admonish each

say that the patterns of convergence and divergence of language attitudes in relation to social history is readily apparent in this survey.

Many of the concepts presented in this chapter are merely outlined for clarity of presentation. When the final chapters of linguistic historiography are written, they will require a more voluminous documentation in which the findings of social psychologists are related directly to research within the tradition of social history. The work of Bourhis (this volume: ch. 3) provides a strong beginning in this direction. He discusses the political forces within France over the last three centuries that dictated the rise of the Parisian dialect as the language of French civilization. In his survey of the various French colonies, he demonstrates how in each case the language policies were merely a continuation of the ideology of the metropole. In another empirically based study, he presented another informative account of the social forces which led to the divergence of languages in Belgium (Bourhis, Giles, Leyens and Tajfel 1979). More studies of this nature need to be done.

Finally, there is also the issue of a theoretical model of language which can adequately integrate all of these factors across a wide range of separate disciplines. The *framework* provided by Becker (1973) provides an interesting organization for the body of literature on language and the sociology of the deviance as does his account of some of the political forces which influence labelling through language. It does not take into consideration, however, the dynamics of social interaction or the renegotiation of social reality and emergency (St Clair, in press) which are already incorporated in the social psychological perspective of Giles and his associates.

Although the data for this study were limited to some of the major movements of social history in the United States, such an investigation provides a model that can be readily followed with data from other sociohistorical traditions.

other for not being as good at science as physicists are. Another example which illustrates how the forces of social history determine the parameters of contemporary research can be found in the area of psychological testing. Psychometrics grew out of the climate of social Darwinism and at the height of the Eugenics movement. Those who were active in developing intelligence tests were also active in social movements to curtail the growth of ethnic minorities. The tests that they developed reflected these attitudes; and, to this day, their design favours the ethnicity of the early immigrants into the United States and stigmatizes those who are among the new immigrants or among the indigenous groups in the nation. With all of its apparent neutrality, these tests remain as products of social history. They cannot be separated from the *Zeitgeist* in which they emerged.

11

A model of speech style evaluation

Richard L. Street, Jr and Robert Hopper

The complaint resounds throughout human history: 'It's not *what* you said, but how you said it!' Sometimes this statement is used with less than complete truthfulness, but evaluative judgements of speech that are independent of message content are of considerable importance. Such evaluative judgements play a role in some of the most significant, yet least understood communication events that humans experience – racial and ethnic stereotyping, corrections of other's grammar usage, expressing deep emotions at the mere sound of another's voice. In each of these situations, and many others that could be listed, listeners appear to react in a primarily evaluative–affective way to speech patterns, irrespective of message content.

The present chapter reviews research that has considered speech style evaluation and proposes a holistic model of this process. Such a model has not been feasible until recently. Bradac, Giles, Lambert, Williams and other researchers have attempted integrations of numerous studies in ways that foster theoretical and conceptual development. It is our goal that our model of speech style evaluation will continue in these directions and be a useful theoretical supplement to the preceding chapters in this volume.

Speech style is an important dimension on which interactants appear to base evaluative judgements and encoding choices. These cognitive and behavioural processes appear influenced by three categories of variables: perceptual constructs and biases (e.g. stereotypes, information processing, role and normative expectations, personality variables), message characteristics (e.g. accent, dialect, and paralanguage or vocal behaviours such as rate, pauses, intensity, quality, and pitch), and communicator goals and motivations. Based on the above considerations, we have formulated a model of the speech style evaluation process.

In the pages that follow, we (1) sketch a model of the speech evaluation process, (2) examine previous research in light of the proposed model, and (3) provide a series of theoretical generalizations, with suggestions for future research. We proceed first with a description of the speech evaluation model.

The model

A schematic of this model is presented in Figure 11.1. The speech style evaluation process begins at the upper left of the figure in the component labelled 'message'. This component depicts the actual, physical representation of the message – including dialect, paralinguistics and the like. Only the message parts of our model have physical–behavioural characteristics. The other aspects of the model

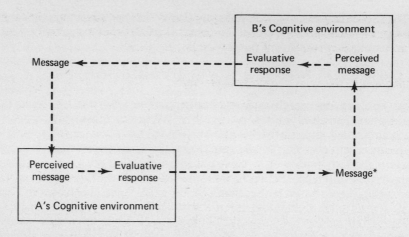

*Components of message display accommodation: convergence and divergence on matters of speech style.

Fig 11.1 A model of speech style evaluation.

are mediational in the sense that they represent hypothetical versions of cognitive processes.

The first such process is the listener's transformation of a message into a *perceived message*. These perceptions are the main triggers for both the listener's evaluative response and the type of accommodation exhibited in the subsequent message. A number of variables have been mentioned in the literature and preceding chapters as being important to this transformation. We review these variables below under the headings of *perceptual biases and listener goals*.

The second process featured in our model is the link (within the cognitive environment) between the perceived message and the individual's evaluative response to the message. This link is reviewed below under the main variables isolated as important in that research: *perceived similarity*, *language attitude* (including influences of *race/ethnicity* and *status*), *sex*, *age*, and *judgements of paralanguage behaviours*.

Finally, our model features the connection between these evaluative responses and the accommodative aspects in the responding-speech of the original listener. Speech accommodation theory posits that speakers have motivational reasons for making their speech more similar (e.g. approval seeking, social integration) or dissimilar (e.g. show disfavour, social distinctiveness) to the speech of their listeners (see Giles and Powesland 1975; Giles 1977; and Thakerar, Giles and Cheshire, 1982, for reviews). As such, accommodative responses are products of speakers' evaluative responses to listeners, goals, and perceptions of listeners' message characteristics. Of course, there are other aspects of the message represented here that may not involve accommodative processes. We consider these outside the scope of the present chapter. In sum, our discussion of accommodation research as viewed through our model pictures accommodation as following from evaluative responses.

The succeeding sections of this chapter deal with these three major links: actual message characteristics to perceived message characteristics to evaluative response to accommodative aspects of the responding message.

Transforming message to perceived message

Most research on speech style evaluation and accommodation treats actual message and perceived message as the same; that is, overt message characteristics are manipulated experimentally and are treated as the message features communicators act upon. Our model emphasizes the message/perceived message distinction and the primacy of perceived messages. Certain perceived attitudinal or demographic differences between communicators may create perceptions of more speech differences or similarities than actually exist. Perceptual biases and listener goals appear to be cognitive elements instrumental in this process.

Perceptual biases. Hamilton (1979) and Tajfel (1981) state that stereotypic schemes influence processing of information about a person in several ways: by focusing perceivers' attention on aspects of a person's behaviour salient to the stereotype (e.g. dress, sex, and language); by leading a perceiver to interpret behaviours in a biased manner; and by allowing for selective retention of information about the person. Such stereotypic conceptions often result in the perceiver 'seeing' things not actually in the stimulus field. For example, if strongly associating 'being black' with 'lazy', a perceiver may fill in the gaps to confirm these relationships (Hamilton, 1976). Phenomena of this sort have been reported regarding speech style. Williams, Whitehead and Miller (1972) showed that, when white subjects viewed videotapes showing black children but using the voices of white children, the children's speech was rated more nonstandard and less confident than the same speech from a white mouth. On the other hand, black teachers, probably as a function of more experience with such speech, tend to make more distinctions in perceiving black speech (Robinson 1979; Williams 1976). Lowery, Snyder, and Denney (1976) reported that women were judged more aggressive when uttering a threatening remark to a woman than when the same message was delivered to a man. Also, stereotypes may be elicited and message perception biased if a receiver has very positive or very negative initial reactions to a source. Nisbett and Wilson (1977b) noted that a European speaker was judged as having a heavier accent when he had a cold, distant style as opposed to a warm friendly one.

Similar to the notion of stereotypes is the person perception prototype, an amalgamation of characteristics typically associated with certain types of people such as waitresses, librarians, and extroverts (Cantor and Mischel 1979). If a person is classified under one of these categories, actual features of this behaviour also may be perceptually distorted. Scherer (1979a) noted that listeners tend to perceive 'dominant' speakers as typically louder than actuality. Finally, context appears to play an important role in the perception of messages. Thakerar and Giles (1981) observed that listeners believing a speaker possessed a high-status position perceived his speech rate to be significantly faster and pronunciation significantly more standard than did listeners believing the same speaker had low-status characteristics.

Listener goals. Some of the differences between messages and perceived messages are due to listeners' biases resulting from goals, motivation or needs. Examples of these goals are desire for social rewards, maintenance of self-esteem, and positive group identity (Giles, Scherer and Taylor 1979). Bourhis, Giles, Leyens and Tajfel (1979) found that when a Francophone interlocuter threatened the identity of Flemish listeners, the listeners rated the speaker as sounding more Francophone and themselves as more Flemish than did subjects in the lower-threat conditions. Larsen, Martin and Giles (1977) reported that subjects perceived the speech of a speaker with a lisp as more similar to their own when the speaker was given high as opposed to low social cost characteristics. Biased scanning can distort perceptions of others' and one's own speech. Some receivers perceive non-standard forms in the speech of Blacks and Mexican Americans where none in fact exist (Williams *et al.* 1972; Williams 1976). Labov (1966) claimed that many people say they use more standard phonological variants than were objectively measured whereas Trudgill (1975b) observed the reverse in England with certain informants who often over-reported nonstandard variants to gain greater covert prestige (see Edwards, this volume: ch. 2).

In short, elements of listeners' cognitive environments, such as stereotypes and goals of social rewards and self-esteem maintenance, influence the perception of messages (see Ryan and Giles, this volume: ch. 13) For example, Street's (1980, 1982) research on interviewees' accommodation to interviewers demonstrates the evaluative importance of perceived as opposed to actual message characteristics. In that study (discussed more fully later), subjects were apparently aware of some speech adjustments (e.g. divergence, or moves toward dissimilarity) more than others (e.g. partial convergence, or partial moves toward similarity). In turn, listener evaluations were more a function of *perceived* as opposed to actual accommodation levels. In addition, Thakerar *et al.* (1982) stated that dyadic partners often diverged on some speech behaviours while believing they were converging. Thus, perceived message characteristics seem an important concept regarding both the evaluation of and accommodation to another's speech. The degree to which actual and perceived message features overlap may be a function of speaker goals, level of involvement, perceptions of the situation, and prior experiences with the listener(s). Such issues hold much promise for future research.

Perceived message to evaluative response

Below we review research that describes the process of evaluative responses to the perceived message within the cognitive environment.

Perceived similarity. Perceptions of similarity appear strongly to influence formation of interpersonal impressions. One dimension on which similarity judgements lead to favourable evaluations (Byrne 1971) is the ingroup–outgroup distinction. Perceivers have a strong inclination to favour ingroups, even if the ingroup–outgroup differences are minimal. Additionally, there is a tendency to overestimate the similarity of ingroup members and overestimate the degree of dissimilarity of outgroup persons (Hamilton 1976; Tajfel 1981), a phenomenon bearing upon the message/perceived message distinction. Delia (1972) indicated that speech style, dialect in particular, is an important cue upon which ingroup–outgroup judgements are made. In his study, listeners' perceptions of accent similarity led to more favourable speaker evaluations and beliefs of attitude similarity than did perceptions of accent dissimilarity. Sebastian and Ryan (in press) have findings suggesting that accent similarity evokes perceived attitude–belief similarity.

Language attitudes. Listeners, teachers and employers tend to prefer certain speech forms to others. These attitudes toward speech style appear to fall into three overlapping categories: (1) a genearal attitude preferring one form to another and (2) attitudes toward speech style appropriateness in particular contexts and (3) speakers' speech adjustments relative to listeners' speech styles. Regarding the first, much research indicates dominant group listeners in Canada, England, United States and Peru respond favourably to speech and language patterns similar to their own; and less favourably to nonstandard varieties of subordinate groups (see, for example, Giles and Powesland 1975; Hopper 1977; Lambert 1967; Lambert, Frankel and Tucker 1966; Williams 1976; Wölck 1973). On the other hand, those subordinate group members having a large degree of ethnic pride, might more favourably evaluate their ethnic tongue over the dominant group's speech style. Flores and Hopper (1975) observed that Mexican-Americans calling themselves 'Chicanos', a label representing revitalized Hispanic pride, perceived Spanish-accented English more positively than Mexican Americans who did not consider themselves 'Chicanos'. Bourhis and Giles (1977) isolated two groups of speakers learning Welsh. The 'instrumental' group was interested in learning Welsh for personal reasons such as enhancing their promotional prospects. The 'integrative' learners were interested in Welsh for cultural affiliation reasons. Upon encountering culturally threatening messages from a Received-Pronunciation speaker (supposedly a higher prestige form), the integrative learners reacted more unfavourably toward the RP speaker in message content and by emphasizing Welsh markers in their speech than did the instrumental learners.

Secondly, research indicates listeners opt for certain speech forms for particular contexts. In formal settings, both dominant and subordinate group members choose standard speech variants whereas informal contexts such as homes, bars and street corners are characterized by ethnic and ingroup forms (Giles 1979a; Labov 1966; Ryan 1979). For example, Taylor and Clément (1974) found that independent judges reported that, although middle-class French Canadians would use a more standard French style in formal contexts than would lower-class speakers, both groups would use more nonstandard styles in informal settings. Not only do employers prefer standard over nonstandard speech (Hopper 1977), but these preferences are qualified by the job type (de la Zerda and Hopper 1979). In the latter study, standard English speech was chosen for supervisory positions whereas Spanish-accented speech was more highly rated for unskilled jobs (see Kalin, this volume: ch. 9).

Finally, listener evaluations of language/dialect/accent often depend on the manner in which a speaker adjusts his or her speech patterns within a given interaction: Bilingual listeners adopting the dominant language of their bilingual listeners are perceived more positively than those who do not (Giles, Taylor and Bourhis 1973; Simard, Taylor and Giles 1976). The evidence regarding accent adjustments, however, remains inconclusive (Doise, Sinclair and Bourhis 1976; Giles and Smith 1979).

Thus, negative evaluations of speakers in classrooms, speeches, and interviews are produced in the cognitive environment as a function of attitudes toward language in general and toward language inappropriateness. Certainly ethnic stereotyping is operating here.

Closely tied to the notion of language attitudes are *ethnic* and *racial stereotypes*. The process of stereotyping involves classifying a person into a particular cognitive category based on some salient cue (Hamilton 1976; 1979; Tajfel 1981), speech style being one such information source (Delia 1972; Miller 1975; Sebastian and Ryan 1982). Once assigned to a category and in the absence of other data, the individual assumes the evaluative content of that category. Thus, if the stereotype is negative, the person and his or her speech is frequently downgraded. Research to date supports the contention that race/ethnicity represent a cluster of speaker-related variables that affect speech evaluation. Sebastian and Ryan (in press) argue that degree of accent is a cue for stereotyping and categorizing such that the greater the accent the more negative the evaluation (Brennan 1977; Ryan, Carranza and Moffie 1977). Shuy (1970, cited in Robinson 1979) reported that subjects consistently placed the speech of black professionals in the category of manual and semi-skilled workers. Many white teachers with little exposure to black speech (Hewett 1971) or with racial biases (Naremore 1971) have stereotypical responses to black speech whereas black teachers show greater differentiation in evaluations (Robinson 1979; Williams 1976). Hopper (1977) was unable to separate the evaluative impact of race and dialect in employment hiring decisions. Even though majority group member's speaker judgements seemed derived from racist stereotypes, many teachers and employers believe their decisions are based on language, a finding emphasizing the influence of perceived messages on evaluative responses (see Giles and Ryan, this volume: ch. 13).

Stereotypes vary in strength and seem alterable by new information, both positive and negative (Delia 1972). Aboud, Clément, and Taylor (1974) posited that persons with characteristics more socially desirable than expected (e.g. standard speech form) may enhance an initially negative impression derived from a negative cue (e.g. race). Likewise, additional information more undesirable than expected serves to especially downgrade an initially favourable impression. Delia (1972) demonstrated that the relatively positive evaluations of General American dialect speakers (as opposed to Southern and New England dialects) were attenuated with the advent of even neutral information. On the other hand, in a job interview setting, blacks speaking standard English may receive more favourable ratings than white standard speakers (Hopper 1977). This latter finding seems inconsistent with Williams *et al.*'s (1972) finding of white listeners perceiving black children's talk as non-standard and hesitant even when this was not the case. The 'strength' and cultural value of the stereotype may be one of the variables operating in these studies. For example, one might argue that racial prejudice was greater in 1972, at least more obvious and culturally less desirable than in Hopper's 1977 research. Certainly the notion of stereotype strength, and the ways subsequent information alters the stereotype warrant additional research.

Perceptions of *status* also affect speech evaluation and are closely tied to ethnic and language attitudes (Robinson 1979). Research in several countries has indicated that speech differences between lower-class and middle-class students are somewhat more subtle than is generally believed (Edwards 1979b; Robinson 1979). Williams (1976) stated that teachers judged lower-status children as less confident and eager than middle-status children, especially if the lower-status child was a black child. Ryan and Sebastian (1980) have shown that Spanish-accented speakers are evaluated more favourably if they are perceived as middle-status than as lower-status. Thus, negative impressions based on speech style may be modified by perceptions of social status. However, low status paired with nonstandard speech tends to elicit the most negatively stereotyped reactions: 'double jeopardy'

(Dowd and Bengston 1978; Sebastian and Ryan, in press).

Sex. The influence of sex on perceptions of speech and speakers has been reviewed by Kramarae earlier in this book (ch. 5). With regard to our model, two points are emphasized. First, female speech with stereotypical linguistic features characterized by Lakoff (1975) and with higher and variable intonation patterns is judged more feminine, gentle, enthusiastic, tolerant, emotional, and less competent and independent (Berryman and Wilcox 1980; Kramer 1978a). Recent research (see Haas 1979 and Smith 1979, for reviews) de-emphasizes the importance of actual speech characteristics in this process, and highlights the influence of sex-linked stereotyping. Second, similar variations in the same speech behaviour can lead to more negative attributions for women than men. This has been found regarding speech rate (Addington 1968), vocal pitch (Kramer 1975b; Mannes 1969; Scherer 1979a), and language intensity (Bradac, Bowers and Courtright 1979). These results seem to indicate that sex-role attitudes are closely linked to the perceptions of male and female speech, and that such perceptions may work against the social standing of women much like stereotypes about race and status work against ethnic minorities.

Age. In general, negative attitudes exist toward old people, especially in western cultures (Bennett and Ekman 1973). Listeners are relatively accurate in identifying speakers' ages based on speech cues alone (Helfrich 1979; Sebastian and Ryan, in press). Thus, one would assume that young and middle-aged adults would respond unfavourably to speech of the aged. Ryan and Capadano (1978) observed that the speech of old women was viewed significantly more reserved, out-of-it, inflexible and passive than younger women. The speech of older men elicited perceptions of inflexibility. Sebastian, Ryan and Abbott (1981) have offered findings indicating college undergraduates perceive older speakers as less physically healthy and active, less intelligent, less independent, less ambitious, and less similar in attitudes than younger speakers. Thus, attitudes toward the aged are also tied to speech evaluation such that the negative reactions to old people can be produced from speech samples alone.

Paralanguage behaviours. Perceptions of paralanguage behaviours such as speech rate, pauses, vocalizations, vocal pitch, intensity and quality have significant evaluative consequences. Regarding *speech rate*, Brown, Rencher and Strong (1974) have found that subjects are relatively consistent in predicting a speaker's personality based on speech rate alone. However, research on the relationship between speech rate and reactions to it reveals somewhat inconsistent findings. Scherer (1979a) concludes that speech rate is linearly related to competence attributions; that is, increases and decreases in rate are associated with corresponding increases and decreases in competence judgements (see, for example, MacLachlan 1979; Scherer 1974; Scherer and Oshinsky 1977; Smith, Brown, Strong and Rencher 1975). Yet, for 'benevolence' ratings, an inverted-U relationship has been noted with speech rate (Brown, Strong and Rencher 1975; Smith et al. 1975). Effects of speech rate on persuasiveness is inconclusive. Miller, Maruyama, Beaber and Valone (1976) reported that faster speech rates enhance persuasion whereas Apple, Streeter and Krauss (1979) observed an inverted-U relationship between rate and persuasiveness.

The above studies on the effects of speech rate have primarily used as stimuli monologue speech by an individual speaker. Street (1980, 1982) has suggested that evaluation of speech rate may be a function of the rates of the other interactants and of the manner in which a speaker adjusts his or her rate within an inter-action. In his research, subjects evaluated a relatively faster-talking interviewee who either maintained his original speech rate or made it more similar or dissimilar to a relatively slower-talking interviewer whose rate remained stable. There was no difference between evaluations of the interviewee maintaining his original rate or making it more similar to the interviewer's. However, both of these conditions were evaluated as significantly more favourable than when rate was made more *dissimilar*. Street suggested that listeners accept initial differences and also move toward similar speech rates; but divergent moves toward dissimilarity are nega-tively received. Moreover, in an intercultural context, Giles and Smith (1979) noted that speech rate maintenance was viewed significantly less favourably than convergence.

Several studies indicate that number of silent hesitation *pauses* is inversely related to favourableness of evaluation; that is, the lower the frequency of hesita-tion pauses the more likely a speaker will be perceived competent, extroverted and likeable (Lay and Burron 1968; Scherer 1979a; Scherer, London and Wolf 1973). Though the length of pauses *within* speaking turns are not significantly dis-criminated in listener evaluations (Scherer 1979), response latencies, or pauses *between* speaking turns, appear to be. Baskett and Freedle (1974) reported that moderate latencies (1 to 3 seconds) were perceived more trustworthy than either shorter or longer latencies. Street (1980, 1982) observed similar results. With response latencies initially 2 and 3 seconds for the interviewer and interviewee res-pectively, Street discovered linear relationships between degree to which the interviewee later matched the interviewer's latency and listener responses. The interviewee was judged most positively when he adopted the interviewer's response latency and least favourably when he created greater dissimilarity.

A *turn* is defined as beginning the instant one interactant begins vocalizing alone and ends when another interactant starts vocalizing alone (Feldstein and Welkowitz 1978). Number of turns and amount of talk has been shown to cor-relate significantly with perceptions of dominance, likeability, extroversion and emotional stability (Scherer 1979a). Regarding turn length, positive associations have been found for ratings of emotional stability and conscientiousness (Scherer 1979a), 'zestfulness' (Cope 1969), and competence (Hayes and Meltzer 1972). However, medium-length turns tend to elicit higher likeability ratings (Stang 1973). Street (1980, 1982), in comparing impressions of interactants mutually adjusting their utterance durations, found that maintaining original talk duration performance or moving them in corresponding directions was perceived more positively than moves in opposite directions.

Impressions of *vocal pitch* levels are somewhat inconsistent. Scherer (1978, 1979a) noted that higher vocal pitch elicited judgements of relatively positive traits such as competence, dominance and assertiveness. Apple *et al.* (1979), however, reported negative attributions of nervousness, deceit and lower potency with increases in a speaker's pitch. Scherer (1979a) suggests these results may be an artifact of the experimentation (Scherer's studies used voices naturally varying in fundamental frequency whereas Apple *et al.* used synthetic adjustments), or that the relationship between pitch and competence and assertiveness ratings is cur-vilinear such that beyond a certain pitch level these judgements become increas-ingly negative. On the other hand, findings regarding pitch variability are con-sistent. Greater variability is associated with dynamism, potency, extroversion and benevolence (see Scherer 1979a, for a review).

To a certain point, increases in *vocal intensity* or loudness are perceived favourably, linked to impressions of extroversion, sociability and emotional stability (Scherer 1979a). However, excess loudness may downgrade evaluations in public communication contexts (Pearce and Brommel 1971). Addington (1968) has conducted one of the most thorough investigations of personality judgements derived from *vocal quality* behaviours. In particular, listeners readily provide attributions from speech qualities as breathiness (high strung, youthful), flatness (sluggish, immature, withdrawn), nasality (unattractive, neurotic, unemotional) and orotundity (vigorous, aggressive).

Researchers have also examined listener ratings of several paralanguage behaviours manipulated simultaneously. Speakers using a 'conversational' style, consisting of lower pitch, less volume, less use of pause and less pitch variety than a 'dynamic' style, were judged more credible, honest, trustworthy, and person-oriented (Pearce and Brommel 1971). These results are interesting since lower pitch and less vocal variety were relatively downgraded in other studies (see Aronovitch 1976; Scherer 1979a). This suggests that the influence of any one paralanguage behaviour may depend on its interaction with other vocal behaviours.

Summary. The listener's cognitive environment is of evaluative significance to the processing of perceived messages into evaluative responses. In this processing, where stereotypes and perceptual biases abound, language attitudes serve as major research predictors of evaluative responses to social groups stigmatized by markers of ethnicity, sex, status and age. In addition, paralanguage behaviours are salient cues for listeners' judgements of speakers.

Listeners' message responses

Listeners' affective reactions to speakers and their speech style may also be manifested in return messages to the original speaker (Giles and Powesland 1975; Sebastian and Ryan, in press). Speech accommodation theory explains such processes by accounting for the manner in which speakers alter messages in reference to another's speech characteristics. As such, accommodation is presumably generated cognitively by processing that begins with the listener's evaluative response. Speech convergence ordinarily counts as a move toward social integration. For example, receivers responding favourably to a source's characteristics (linguistic or otherwise) often make their speech more similar to the source's. In bilingual Canada, when listeners attributed a speaker's language accommodation to a desire to be cooperative and break down communication barriers, the listeners often returned the accommodation, i.e. spoke the dominant language of their conversational partner (Giles, Taylor and Bourhis, 1973; Simard *et al.* 1976). Communicators wishing to establish mutually open and intimate interaction environments often reciprocate self-disclosures (Drakeford 1969). Giles and Bourhis (1975) suggest that West Indians in England have adopted English pronunciation partly as a desire to become socially integrated into that culture. Natale (1975a, b) observed that interactants with a tendency to seek the approval of others converge more to their partners' vocal intensity and pause length than do those less predisposed to gain others' approval.

On the other hand, listeners reacting negatively to speakers often seek to distinguish themselves linguistically, a process labelled divergence. In bilingual settings, Welsh and Flemish listeners encountering culturally threatening remarks adopt their native speech patterns, diverging their speech language and accents from their antagonists' message features (Bourhis 1979; Bourhis and Giles 1977). In addition, language and accent divergence may be used as a strategy when a conversational partner is perceived as uncooperative (Simard *et al.* 1976) or when communicators wish to be culturally distinctive from other speakers around them (Bourhis 1979; Segalowitz and Gatbonton 1977). Likewise, interactants perceiving them attitudinally dissimilar converge less on pause length and vocal intensity than those perceiving similarity (Welkowitz and Feldstein 1969, 1970).

Presumably because the cognitive environment affects both evaluative responses and speech accommodation, the variables discussed above in relation to the perceived message-evaluative response processes (e.g. listener goals, race status and sex) have received attention from accommodation researchers. For instance, Giles, Bourhis and Taylor (1977) explain speech style accommodation of diverse ethnic groups in terms of a theory of intergroup relations. In intergroup encounters, two kinds of language or dialect convergence occur. First, in formal contexts involving members of a dominant or high-prestige group and a subordinate, less prestigious group, convergence is generally toward the dominant group (Giles 1979a). For example, blacks often produce more formal pronunciation patterns in interview situations with a white interviewer (Labov 1966). Second, individuals wishing to assimilate into an outgroup will often adopt that group's linguistic style. This has been demonstrated among certain blacks in England (Giles 1979a), Mexican Americans in the United States (Ryan and Carranza 1977), and Welsh speakers interacting with R-P accented Englishmen (Bourhis and Giles 1977).

On the other hand, dialect divergence and maintenance characterize intergroup situations where members of one group seek to distinguish themselves from another group. Support for this claim has been found among the Welsh (Bourhis and Giles 1977) and Flemish (Bourhis *et al.* 1979).

The relative *status* of interactants affects the nature of speech adjustments. In general, since the low-status party presumably has more to gain from the high-status party than vice-versa, Giles and Powesland (1975) claim that convergent speech will most likely come from the low-status person. Assuming the therapist is the high-status interactant, support for this claim can be found in Matarazzo's studies (see Matarazzo and Wiens 1972, for review) in which patients converged to therapist modifications in utterance duration and response latency. Webb (1970) has noted consistent findings that interviewees will converge toward the speech rate of an interviewer. Client speech influences therapist speech also, but to a lesser extent (Lauver, Kelly and Froehle 1971). Similarly, Giles (1973a) observed that, in the presence of a high-status standard-speaking interlocuter, lower-status speakers tend to standardize their accents. However, Thakerar *et al.* (1982) emphasize the importance of speech perception and accommodation in this process. In some cases, speakers who actually diverged in their behaviour believed that they were converging.

In male–female interactions, communicators often choose behaviours consistent with traditional sex–gender roles. Again, those who do not conspicuously exhibit such behaviours are often perceived to have done so. Thus, the more variables one mixes into the system, the more complex prediction becomes; and the more the cognitive systems of the interactants massage language data to fit motives, expectations or goals.

A number of other personality and perceptual elements in the cognitive environment appear to be involved in accommodative decisions. High *self-monitors* seem most likely to use others' behaviours as guidelines for their own (Ickes and Barnes 1977; Snyder 1979). Therefore, one might expect high self-monitors more capable of converging to another's speech style than lows (Berger 1980; Giles 1973a). In addition, Berger and Calabrese (1975) proposed that high levels of uncertainty produce high levels of reciprocity, and that similarity decreases uncertainty. Thus, one might expect the first part of an interaction to be characterized by more convergence than later in the encounter, a claim supported by Jaffe and Feldstein (1970). Furthermore, perception of *attitudinal similarity* has been shown to lead to convergence of vocal intensity and response latency (Welkowitz and Feldstein 1969, 1970).

Integrations across model components

Understanding of the speech evaluation process can be augmented through research integrating components of this model. One such endeavour was attempted by Street (1980, 1982). Street examined evaluative consequences of accommodating three non-content speech behaviours: speech rate, response latency and utterance duration. He treated accommodation as continuous, identifying four levels of message change: full convergence, partial convergence, no change and divergence. Following a $4 \times 4 \times 4$ design (all combinations of three behaviours accommodated at four levels), Street constructed scripted information-gathering interviews, and had matched-guise informants encode the interviews using varying utterance durations, speech rates, and response latencies. Street tested hypotheses about accommodation by having listeners evaluate interviewees' recorded speech patterns.

Factor analyses revealed two evaluative dimensions – positive/negative affect and confidence. All main effects were significant except one, speech rate accommodation on the confident measure. In general, these effects suggest that moves toward similar speech are evaluated more favourably than moves toward dissimilar speech. In addition, the interaction between speech rate and utterance duration was significant for both evaluative dimensions.

This research emphasizes the importance of the interface among the message, cognitive environment, perceived message and evaluative response components of the model. First, Street manipulated *actual message characteristics*. That is, using objective indices such as number of words and time units, the various accommodation levels were formulated. However, a post-test awareness measure indicated listeners did not always recognize specific accommodative adjustments. For example, subjects were rarely able to distinguish convergence from partial convergence though most noticed divergence. Thus, the *perceived message characteristics* were sometimes different from actual message features.

Second, the perceived levels were in large part the determinants of the *evaluative responses*. Subjects were highly aware of response latency accommodation. Correspondingly, the predicted linear relationship between degree of convergence and positive evaluation was confirmed. On the other hand, listeners only rarely discriminated evaluatively among speech rate convergence, partial convergence and maintenance. Yet, speech rate divergence was readily recognized and rated negatively.

Third, Street's procedure showed the importance of simultaneously examining several speech variables (see also Giles and Smith 1979). Few interactions were found among combinations of variables. Rather, it seems listeners reacted to each recording as primarily representative of one behaviour being accommodated. Future researchers, however, may predict a greater number of interactions, perhaps as a function of communication context among other factors (see Bradac, this volume: ch. 6). This appears to account for Street's speech rate by utterance duration interactions. Possibly due to the nature of the interview, two patterns of of interviewee accommodative adjustments were favourably received. One consisted of the interviewee maintaining relatively faster rates and longer talk durations than the interviewer. The listeners may have thought this pattern represented appropriate sociolinguistic distance (Thakerar *et al.* 1982) between interactants differing in role and status. Thus, the interviewee was evaluated positively for adhering to situational constraints and expectations. Another speech move highly regarded was when the interviewee became similar to the interviewer on both speech rate and floor time. Given the informality of this fact-finding interview, the participants could opt to discard role requirements in favour of similarity.

In short, Street's research stresses the importance of taking into account various components of the model. Future research can enhance theoretic development of speech evaluation processes by improving upon Street's efforts: directly testing the interrelationships among parts of the model, employing less complex research designs, and acquiring participant and observer responses to various speech styles.

The taken-for-granted. Most speech style evaluation research has employed empirical, often quasi-experimental, procedures. These approaches provide empirical data, but sometimes sacrifice descriptive richness. Hopper (1981) argues for the concept of the taken-for-granted to be integrated into a model of speech evaluation. Schutz (1967) coined this term to refer to uncoded propositions that are processed by speaker–listeners much as if they had been spoken. Examples for taken-for-granteds include underlying values communicated implicitly, missing premises of arguments, social stereotypes and the like.

Some taken-for-granteds discussed by recent scholars include pragmatic implications (Harris and Monaco 1978), indirect speech acts (Searle 1975) and implicature (Grice 1975). Additionally, the taken-for-granted perspective emphasizes alignment talk (Hopper, 1981; Stokes and Hewitt 1976) which denotes conversational tactics used in problem situations to achieve coordination about what is taken for granted. Excuses are one kind of alignment talk. If I say, 'Sorry I was late, I was with a client', you know some background information on the basis of which I was operating.

The ways in which such tactics are used in natural talk settings have not yet been adequately described. Future researchers may examine effects of various taken-for-granteds and alignment talk upon speech style evaluation. Perhaps future theorists will have to account not only for how utterances are said, but also for some aspects of the unsaid.

Conclusions

Our intent in this chapter has been to provide an integrated theoretical model of the speech evaluation process. The model proposed appears quite general, and the research reviewed seems to support it. We list here a few generalizations we believe are substantiated in the investigations reviewed:

1. Speech characteristics salient to the processes of interpersonal evaluation and message choice include linguistic choices, speech rate, pauses, turn-taking and vocal characteristics.

2. Perceived message characteristics appear to outweigh physical message characteristics in importance to both speech style evaluation and accommodation.

3. The relationship between actual message characteristics and perceived message characteristics is a function of the strength of the listener's goals and motivations, and of the strength of message expectations associated with particular perceptual biases.

4. Evaluative responses to speech communication are products of the cognitive environment's interaction with perceived message characteristics.

5. Speech accommodation emerges from the cognitive environment's interaction with perceived message characteristics and evaluative responses.

6. Elements of the cognitive environment influential in speech evaluation and accommodation processes include goals, language attitudes, stereotypes, perceptions of status and person perception prototypes.

The above generalizations apply to components of the speech evaluation model. Individual studies should seek to expand and clarify these statements by examining relationships between specific variables in various contexts. This undertaking appears to fall within the competence and capabilities of present researchers. We have isolated three basic transformation processes: actual message characteristics to perceived message characteristics, perceived message characteristics to evaluative responses, and evaluative responses to accommodative aspects of the next message. Each of these can be considered in terms of a finite list of variables that are familiar to social scientists.

Direction for future research

Multiple-variable approaches to speech evaluation research can be theoretical as well as empirical, as Bradac, Bowers and Courtright (1979) and Street (1980, 1982) demonstrate. Bradac *et al.* presented three variables: lexical diversity, language intensity and immediacy (see Bradac, this volume: ch. 6), and reviewed research to glean propositions concerning the effects of each of these variables alone as well as in combination with each other. In all, 26 generalizations were derived from three variables. Street's design was very complex, using 64 independent groups to examine all combinations of accommodation levels for three behaviours. Though a multiple-variable approach is called for, it would seem that neither theoretical nor quasi-experimental procedures are easily capable of combining more than three variables at a time.

Our recommendation is, for the moment, to proceed with these variables in sets of three until virtually all combinations of sets have been exhausted. Given that we have listed numerous potential variables in this chapter, these efforts could keep researchers profitably occupied for the foreseeable future.

In addition to the experimental research strategies described here, the complexity and richness of the proposed model suggest the usefulness of naturalistic, holistic studies of the speech evaluation process. We have reported research findings concerning many individual components of the model; yet very little empirical research to date has simultaneously considered communicator attitudes, actual message characteristics and accommodation behaviours. To do all this at once would be a massive undertaking, but even modest combinations of the above could yield interesting data. Further, our model appears to provide paths for programmatic research of theoretical import.

For example, consider a research paradigm in which two communicators (e.g. a job applicant and an employer, two strangers, or a teacher and a student) are introduced to each other after completing a battery of attitudinal and linguistic testing. Presumably the researchers could develop a fairly extensive measure of each interactant's state regarding major cognitive variables such as language attitudes, ethnic attitudes, normative and role expectations, prior experience with the partner or social groups to which the partner belongs, perceptions of status as well as personality variables such as self-monitoring tendencies, need for social approval, authoritarianism, cognitive complexity, cognitive uncertainty and machiavellianism. Several speech samples could be taken before the encounter to assess baseline speech performances of rate, pause length, language diversity and intensity, vocal intensity, accent and vocal pitch. When the two communicators come together and talk, actual accommodative behaviours could be noted by means of audio- or video-recording of the interaction. After the interaction was completed, the communicators could be asked (using scales or open-ended items) to provide their impressions of the other, the situation, their relative status, their own and the other's communicative behaviour, the effectiveness of the interaction, the attractiveness of the other, the legitimacy of the situation, the cooperativeness of the other and so on. Additionally, other outcome variables could be assessed: whether a job was offered or accepted, amount of attitude change, whether a grade was changed, whether a mutual goal was reached, and the evaluation of performance.

In sum, a unifiable theoretical programme seems to be emerging from studies of speech evaluation. Roots for the perspective come from language attitude research, speech accommodation theory and a number of other traditions. A holistic model of the evaluation-accommodation process has been presented. Major categories of variables in the model include message characteristics, perceived message characteristics and listeners' evaluative responses to perceived messages. We hope that this model provides a new level of integration in speech style evaluation research.

12

Language variables, attitudes, and persuasion[1]

John T. Cacioppo and Richard E. Petty

There is a consensus among experimental social psychologists that attitudes are general and enduring positive or negative feelings about an object, person or issue (e.g. Cacioppo, Harkins and Petty 1981; Insko and Schopler 1972). For example, a French-Canadian may like (i.e. hold a positive attitude toward) the proposition that Quebec should exercise its independence. An instance in which an active attempt is made to change this person's attitude would be termed persuasion.

Attitudes and persuasion are important aspects of social interactions for several reasons. First, an attitude serves as a convenient summary of the evaluative nature of a person's beliefs. The French-Canadian in our example above, for instance, may believe that Quebec is a self-sufficient province, that its culture and traditions are worthy of preserving, and that the governmental policies in Canada are sub-jugating Quebec's unique culture and traditions. Eliciting and scaling the valuations and probabilities of a person's beliefs about an object or issue could be done, but assessing the general attitude toward the object or issue is simpler and yields a useful summary of that information (Fishbein and Ajzen 1975). Second, knowing a person's attitudes renders the social interaction with that person more predictable since attitudes, in a general sense, influence behaviours (Ajzen and Fishbein 1980; Fishbein 1980). Finally, various aspects of a person's personality may be reflected in the attitudes the person holds and in the means found to be most effective in changing these attitudes (see Smith, Bruner and White 1956). Katz (1960), for example, proposed that attitudes can serve a variety of functions that are beneficial to an individual's personality. Katz listed four functions that he felt were most important: (1) *The utilitarian or instrumental function* – these attitudes are held because they help the individual to gain rewards and avoid punishments. A minority member may possess positive attitudes toward character-istics of the majority because these attitudes (i.e. their verbal and behavioural expressions) maximize the likelihood of obtaining social rewards and advance-ments. (2) *The ego-defensive function* – these attitudes are held because they help people protect themselves from embarassing or unflattering facts about themselves or about others who are important to them. By holding negative attitudes towards minority groups, for instance, a minority member might be able to enhance his or her own feelings of distinctiveness and self-worth. (3) *The value-expressive function* – this function occurs when a person holds an attitude because of the

[1] We thank Ellen Ryan, Howard Giles, Gertrude Nath, and Barbara Andersen for helpful comments on an earlier draft of this paper. Preparation of this chapter was supported by University Faculty Scholar Award No. A240.

satisfaction derived from expressing a position congruent with personal values and self-concept. For example, minority members who value personal freedom may be somewhat resistant to the majority influence to assimilate a particular style of speech because their attitudes toward their unique ethnic accent is serving as a means of expressing their independence. (4) *The knowledge function* – attitudes that serve this function help people to understand the people and events around them. If minority members dislike the majority leader in a province or country because it helps them to understand how the leader can be so insensitive to their unique needs and traditions, then this attitude would be said to serve the knowledge function. Katz went on to argue that an attitude is more susceptible to change when a persuasive attempt accurately targets the underlying function that the attitude serves (see Giles and Ryan, this volume: ch. 13).

The phenomena of attitudes and persuasion have been the focus of over 40 years of experimental research in social psychology. In the following sections, we survey the major approaches to attitudes and persuasion that characterize this research, we examine how these theoretical approaches might be used to account for the research on language variables and attitudes, and we suggest possible routes for future research.

Several of our emphases in this chapter are worth noting at the outset. First, we focus on the psychological *mechanisms* that underlie attitudes and persuasion, since accurately predicting attitude change and behaviour in unique settings is difficult unless the idiosyncratic reasons people have for holding a particular attitude are known. Second, we examine the effects of attitudes not only on self-report ratings, but also on comprehension of relevant material, elaboration of attitude-relevant material, and behaviour (e.g. assimilation of accentedness). As we shall show, different people may report the same attitude, but differ in the reasons for and the consequences of holding it. Finally, we explain how factors, such as the similarity or expertise of the communicator, have heterogeneous effects that are explicable only by viewing them from the perspective of the context in which they emerge.

Approaches to the study of attitudes and persuasion

In a recent text on attitude change, we have grouped the various theories that have emerged from experiments of attitudes and persuasion in social psychology into the following seven approaches (see Petty and Cacioppo 1981a): (1) conditioning and modelling, (2) message learning, (3) judgement, (4) motivation, (5) attribution, (6) combination approaches, and (7) self-persuasion. Each of these approaches postulates a unique process that is responsible for attitude change, and all continue to retain and gain adherents.

Conditioning and modelling

The first approach emphasizes some of the basic principles of learning that have been found in studies of classical and operant conditioning in animals, and in studies of modelling in humans. The focus of this approach is on the effects of the direct administration of rewards and punishments to the target of influence for expressing verbally or behaviourally certain attitudes, or on the effects of the target *observing* others being rewarded or punished for expressing certain attitudes. According to this view, attitudes toward stimuli become more favourable if they are associated with pleasant contexts (classical conditioning) or lead to positive outcomes (operant conditioning). Studies of modelling suggest that the classical and operant conditioning of attitudes can occur *vicariously* as well, with particularly intriguing implications for attitude development. For example, research by Ryan and her colleagues (see Ryan 1979; Ryan and Carranza 1977) suggests the possibility that the children of bilingual parents, after observing repeatedly the more positive contexts (i.e. vicarious classical conditioning) or outcomes (i.e. vicarious operant conditioning, or 'observational learning') that accompany their using their second language, may develop more favourable attitudes toward learning the second (majority) language than toward learning their ethnic language; moreover, they may develop stronger preferences to employ the second than ethnic language, and more favourable sets of beliefs and stereotypes about speakers of the second than ethnic language (see Day, this volume: ch. 7).

The research on vicarious classical conditioning is interesting in that it suggests that an initially neutral stimulus can become capable of eliciting a strong positive or negative attitude from people simply because they repeatedly observe others responding positively or negatively to it. Though this possibility has received little empirical attention, it suggests how people might acquire positive or negative attitudes (e.g. toward a minority group) even though they know very little about or have never been directly exposed to the attitude object (e.g. the minority group).

Similarly, accents or speech styles may elicit general positive or negative attitudinal responses from people because of their past (vicarious) learning history. Interestingly, these people initially should not be able to give any logical reasons for responding positively or negatively to the speaker, but rather they should be forced to generate rationalizations for their response. Future research using this approach to study stereotyped responses to language variations might be informative regarding the psychological processes underlying these stereotypes.

Message learning

The second major approach outlined by Petty and Cacioppo (1981a) considers the learning of the arguments contained in a persuasive message as the prerequisite for attitude change and evolved from the work by Carl Hovland and his associates (Hovland, Janis and Kelley 1953; Hovland, Lumsdaine and Sheffield 1949; Hovland, Mandell, Campbell, Brock, Luchins, Cohen, McGuire, Janis, Feierabend and Anderson 1957). In this approach, the focus is on how source (e.g. similarity, accentedness), message (e.g. exposure frequency, affectivity of vocabulary), recipient (e.g. self-esteem, speech style of recipient), and channel factors (e.g. print, audio–visual) affect attention to, comprehension of, and retention of the information contained in the message. Experiments were designed initially to assess the simple (i.e. main) effects of these factors on recall and attitude change, but a disarray of results across experiments led to the use of more complex designs and the discovery of interactive effects of source, message, recipient, and channel factors on attitude change (see reviews by McGuire 1966, 1969, 1978). Moreover, efforts to map inductively the role of message learning in the persuasion process have led to a serious questioning of its position as the pre-eminent mediator of attitude change (e.g. Cacioppo and Petty 1979b; Greenwald 1968; Insko, Turnbull and Yandell 1974; Petty 1977). Insko *et al.* (1974) have found the relationship between message comprehension and attitude change to be fairly flat, which means that sizeable differences in message comprehension are necessary before differences in attitude change emerge.

Nevertheless, Hovland and his colleagues' classification of independent variables as source, message, recipient, and channel factors and dependent variables as measures of attention, comprehension, retention, and yielding, and their rigorous experimental approach have had a significant impact on the study of persuasion. Studies of language variables and attitudes, for example, can be categorized into the cells of an independent x dependent variable matrix of persuasion studies (McGuire 1969). When this is done, you find that most studies of language variables and attitudes deal with perception of the source (see other chapters, this volume; Bradac, Bowers and Courtright 1980; Giles and Powesland 1975; Shuy and Fasold 1973). Among the findings is that faster speech rates enhance the perception of the source's competence whereas both increased and decreased speech rates lead to lowered evaluations of benevolence compared to normal rates (Brown, Strong and Rencher 1973; Brown, Strong, Rencher and Smith 1974; Smith, Brown, Strong and Rencher 1975; Street and Hopper, this volume: ch. 11). Moreover, the use of rhetoricals, or 'tag' questions, makes the speaker appear less confident and, perhaps, less competent since the source gives the impression of equivocating (see Kramarae, this volume: ch. 5; Newcombe and Arnkoff 1979), although the use of rhetoricals may also make the source appear more polite since the listener is given the opportunity to disagree (Bates 1976). The language, dialect and accent used by a speaker are also important determinants of source perceptions, with certain speech styles (e.g. standard accents) elevating the valuation of the source across a wide range of dimensions (e.g. competence, dynamics, dominance – Giles 1973b; Giles and Powesland 1975; Lambert 1967; Palmer 1973).

Source perceptions and attitude change in this area of research have occasionally been found to vary similarly. For instance, the simplest source effects that have emerged from the work of Hovland and his associates are that the level of source credibility (expertise and/or trustworthiness) and of similarity are directly related to attitude change. Hovland and his co-workers reasoned this was the case for credibility because highly credible sources are likely to be correct and, hence, offer the strongest incentives for message learning and yielding (Hovland *et al.* 1953), whereas this was the case for similarity because social approval from similar others is particularly rewarding. Consistent with this reasoning, Miller, Maruyama, Beaber and Valone (1976) found that increased relative to normal speech rates produced higher ratings of source credibility *and* more attitude change.

A number of exceptions to this simple effect have been indentified, however (e.g. see Cooper, Darley and Henderson 1974; Giles and Powesland 1975). In a field study using a political appeal, Cooper *et al.* (1974) illustrated how people who chose freely to listen to an unconventional rather than conventional (and more likeable) source actually changed their attitudes more to justify their choosing to listen to the unconventional-appearing source. Hence, caution should be exercised when generalizing the results of studies on language variation and impression formation to the recipients' susceptibility to the source's persuasive appeal.

In addition, one variable can affect more than one inference about a source. What happens, for example, if divergent inferences are made about a source's expertise and similarity as sometimes results in studies of language variables (see

Scherer 1979b)? Brock (1965) conducted an interesting study that bears upon this question. Brock trained two part-time salesmen to deliver a standard persuasive communication to customers who had decided to purchase house paint. A salesman would approach the customers as they headed toward the check-out counter and suggest to them that they purchase another brand of paint. To buttress his recommendation, the salesman would tell the customer either that he personally had tried both types of paint in the same quantities as the customer had chosen and that the alternative brand was much better (i.e. high similarity condition), or that he recently bought 20 times the amount of each type of paint and found the alternative brand to be much better (i.e. high expertise condition). Brock found that more customers bought the advocated brand of paint when the salesman presented himself as similar rather than dissimilar to (but more expert than) the customer.

There are important implications for the study of language variables and attitudes of this finding, since language variables may establish the speaker as being similar to the recipients, *or*, in some instances, as being more prestigious or competent than the recipients. Consider a study by Giles (1973b), who exposed 250 subjects in Great Britain who spoke with regional accents to a message arguing against capital punishment. Five groups of subjects were formed, each of which received the same basic information in a message but that differed in the style in which the message was delivered. One group read a typescript of the message, whereas the remaining groups each heard a recording of the message delivered by a male evincing either a Received Pronunciation (RP), South Welsh, Somerset or Birmingham accent (see Edwards, this volume: ch. 2). Giles (1970, 1971b) had previously documented that speakers exhibiting an RP accent were perceived as the most prestigious, a South Welsh accent the next most prestigious and so forth. On the other hand, the regional accented speakers were perceived as being more *similar* to the recipients than the RP speaker. Giles (1973b) found that the RP speaker and typescript produced no attitude change, while the use of regional accents led to more attitude change than these two conditions. These data are consistent with Brock's (1965) finding that similarity can be a more powerful determinant of persuasion than other source characteristics such as expertise, or prestige in this case, since the speaker using a regional accent similar to the recipients' accent was more persuasive than when using the more prestigious but less similar RP accent. Other interpretations of these data are also possible, of course, and we shall outline an alternative account in a subsequent section on the various approaches to attitudes and persuasion.

Another important finding in research on source factors and persuasion involves the difference in the effects of issue-relevant and issue-irrelevant source characteristics. Mills and Harvey (1972), for instance, asked subjects to read a message arguing in favour of broader education for college students. The message was attributed to either an expert or an attractive source. In addition, some subjects learned the identity of the source at the outset of the message, whereas others were told the identity of the source at the end of the message. Mills and Harvey found that subjects were more persuaded when the expert was identified at the outset compared to the end of the message, but that subjects were equally persuaded whether the attractive source was identified at the beginning or end of the message. Husek (1965) and Norman (1976) have obtained conceptually similar results. The implication of this finding is that issue-irrelevant source characteristics, such as the physical attractiveness of a communicator, may have temporary effects on persuasion that can be distinguished from the effects of the message arguments per se. Presumably, this occurs because these factors did not alter the subjects' interpretation of the information provided in the message. Issue-relevant source characteristics, on the other hand, may actually alter the meaning of the information provided in the message (see Asch 1948), which means that the effects on persuasion of source and message characteristics should be much less likely to manifest separately, either immediately or over time (e.g. in delayed-action attitude changes). Since language variables sometimes affect the (issue-relevant) source perceptions of competence and dominance in one way, and the (issue-irrelevant) source perceptions of benevolence and likeability in a contrary manner (see Scherer 1979b; Street and Hopper, this volume: ch. 11), the preceding distinction may prove useful in research on language variables and enduring attitude changes.

Of course, the effects of language variables are contingent upon encoding and decoding processes. Encoding refers to the speaker's selection and utilization of particular forms of delivering the message, whereas decoding refers to the judgemental aspects of the recipients processing the communication (e.g., comprehending/yielding; see Giles and St Clair 1979). A *recipient factor* that has received little attention but that is pertinent to the study of language variables (e.g. convergence/divergence possibilities) is the person's ability to encode or decode language variables (e.g. speech style, tone of voice). For instance, Hall (1980) asked subjects to deliver over the telephone a persuasive message dealing with the recipient's willingness to participate in psychological research. Half of the callers were told to use 'your vocal cues only' to influence the person to indicate *more* hours, and half of the callers were told to use their vocal cues only to influence the person to indicate *fewer* hours. In addition, Hall collected measures of the callers' and recipients' ability to encode and decode nonverbal signals in a separate experimental session. Hall found that there was a strong effect of recipients' decoding skill on persuasion in that good decoders agreed more to the caller's nonverbal request to participate in many or few hours of psychological research than poor decoders. The effect of encoding skill was less pronounced, but the greatest agreement occurred when skilled encoders were speaking to skilled decoders. In Hovland's framework, this combination would be expected to enhance comprehension and increase pressures to yield.

Perceptual judgements

The third approach encompasses the perceptual–judgemental theories of persuasion. These theories have in common their focus on factors that alter a person's perception of the position being recommended in a persuasive message, and how attitude judgements are made in the context of a person's past experiences (e.g. Eiser and Stroebe 1972; Ostrom and Upshaw 1968; Sherif and Hovland 1961). For instance, just as placing your hand in lukewarm water feels differently when you bring your hand from very hot or very cold water, an expression of attitude is perceived differently when coming from a very positive or very negative context.

In social judgement theory (Sherif and Hovland 1961; Sherif and Sherif 1967; Sherif, Sherif and Nebergall 1965), judgements about social as well as physical stimuli are postulated to be susceptible to two judgemental distortions: assimilation and contrast. Assimilation refers to a shift in judgement *toward* an anchor, such as the person's initial attitude. Contrast, on the other hand, refers to a shift in judgement *away* from an anchor. According to social judgement theory, assimilation occurs when a stimulus (e.g. the position recommended in a persuasive message) falls within a range of positions that the recipient finds acceptable, a range called the latitude of acceptance. The effect on an attitudinal statement that falls within the latitude of acceptance, then, is that the statement appears more similar to the recipient's own initial attitude than it is in fact, and is more likely to be endorsed. Conversely, contrast is thought to occur when a stimulus falls within a range of positions that the recipient finds unacceptable, a range called the latitude of rejection. The effect on an attitudinal statement that falls within the latitude of rejection is that the statement appears more distant from the recipient's own initial attitude than it is, and is, in most instances, more likely to be rejected.

Social judgement theory could be used to examine how speaker's attitudes toward ethnic memberships, as inferred from speech style for example, affect recipients' views of the speaker's positions on issues. For instance, Granberg and Brent (1974) analysed data from the 1968 presidential election in the United States. Specifically, they examined how voter's attitudes toward the Vietnam war affected their perceptions of the major presidential candidates' positions on the war. Granberg and Brent found the pro-Humphrey voters who favoured the war displaced Humphrey's position on the war toward their own (i.e. assimilation), whereas they displaced Wallace's position away from their own (i.e. contrast). Similar effects may occur if, by the intensity of the language they select to describe a (common) position, different speakers connote that they hold positions that fall differentially within the recipients' latitudes of acceptance or rejection (see Burgoon and Bettinghaus 1980; Burgoon and Miller 1971).

The concept of latitudes has been useful in other regards as well. Eagly and Telaak (1972), for example, exposed pro-birth control subjects who had either narrow, medium or wide latitudes of acceptance on the issue to an anti-birth control message that was either mildly, moderately, or strongly discrepant from their own position. For all three levels of communication discrepancy (i.e. the distance from the subjects' initial attitude and the advocated position), subjects with wide latitudes of acceptance showed greater attitude change than did subjects with either narrow or medium latitudes of acceptance. Contrary to social judgement theory, subjects with a narrow latitude of acceptance showed a slight negative reaction to the mildly discrepant message even though it fell within their latitude of acceptance, whereas subjects with a wide latitude of acceptance showed a positive reaction to the strongly discrepant message even though it fell within their latitude of rejection. Eagly (1981) suggests that the size of the latitude of acceptance on an issue may be a better predictor of *general susceptibility* to persuasion on an issue than susceptibility to messages of a specified level of discrepancy. This means that the width of people's latitudes of acceptance may serve as a useful means of identifying individual differences in their susceptibility to influence in studies of language variables and attitude change on an issue. For example, although Miller *et al.* (1976) demonstrated that a source's speaking rate influenced recipients' attitudes, it might be possible to account for additional variance by identifying those recipients who hold wide versus narrow latitudes of acceptance around their attitudes toward the issue (e.g. growing vegetables hydroponically).

Williams and his associates (Williams, Hewett, Hopper, Miller, Naremore and Whitehead 1976) provide a good example of how measures of these latitudes might be used in studies of language attitudes. Williams *et al.* (1976) asked 65 subjects to rate particular stereotypes and stimulus videotapes on scales designed to tap two factors: confidence–eagerness and ethnicity–nonstandardness. Measures included not only the category on each scale that *best* described the stimulus person (the 'best estimate'), but also the latitudes of acceptance, noncommitment, and rejection on each scale. Subjects rated their stereotype of an Anglo, Black, and Mexican American child, and videotapes of a lower-class and a middle-class child in each of the Anglo, Black, and Mexican American ethnic groups. Although their results were not subjected to statistical tests to determine the significance of the differences that they observed, Williams *et al.* (1976) reported that (a) the measures of best estimate and latitudes were reliable and valid; (b) the best estimate position and the midpoint of the latitude of acceptance were nearly identical, suggesting that this latitude is arranged symmetrically around the best estimate; and (c) the latitudes of acceptance and rejection are inversely though not strongly correlated ($r = -.55$), suggesting that as one varies the change can be derived from or imparted to the latitude of noncommitment rather than necessarily each other.

Finally, Eiser and Stroebe (1972) have proposed a judgemental theory that addresses how lexical intensity affects the perceptions of a speaker's position. Their theory, termed *accentuation theory*, identifies conditions in which an attitude *rating* changes, but the attitude content (i.e. the actual attitude) does not change. According to accentuation theory, an attitude rating is a function of a person's true attitude *and* evaluative connotations of the particular words that are used to label the extremes of the response scale. If you wanted to use a scale to measure what someone feels toward an ethnic group, you could anchor the response scale with the words 'like' and 'dislike', or you could anchor the scale with the words 'love' and 'hate'. If you get different ratings with these scales, you could not assume that you had tapped different underlying attitudes. The second set of words covers a broader content range than the former set of anchors. Eiser and his colleagues have demonstrated that the lexical intensity of the anchors can affect predictably how polarized subjects' attitude ratings are (see Giles and Ryan, this volume, ch. 13).

Eiser and Osmon (1978) have argued that anchors with positive connotations imply more moderate positions than do anchors with negative connotations. The implication of their argument is that subjects' attitude ratings will be more polarized (i.e. *appear* more extreme) on the positive than on the negative scale, since the scale anchored by positive or more moderately intense words corresponds to a smaller stimulus range than does the scale anchored by negative or lexically intense words.

One interesting implication of this work for research on language variables is that people from different regions or ethnic backgrounds may exhibit different attitude *ratings*, even though their true attitudes are similar, because the groups differ in their evaluative reactions to the scale-anchors. To date, this source of variance has been ignored in cross-cultural and inter-ethnic research.

Motivation

The fourth approach focuses on the different human motives as they relate to attitudes and persuasion. The most researched motive, the need to maintain cognitive consistency – consistency between beliefs, between attitudes and behaviours, and so forth – has important implications for attitude change. We survey the best known cognitive consistency theories in this section.

There are several characteristics that cognitive consistency theories of attitudes have in common. First, each describes the conditions for equilibrium and disequilibrium among units of information, called cognitive elements. Second, each asserts that disequilibrium motivates the person to restore consistency among the elements, usually in order to remove the feeling of unpleasant tension. Third, each describes the means by which equilibrium might be accomplished. The three major theories of cognitive consistency and attitudes are balance theory (Heider 1946), congruity theory (Osgood and Tannenbaum 1955), and cognitive dissonance theory (Festinger 1957).

Heider (1946) emphasized the person's own point of view about elements of information and their interconnections. Balance, Heider argued, was a harmonious, quiescent motivational state in which all of the elements appeared *to the individual* to be internally consistent. Balance was described by Heider as occurring when recipients agree with speakers they like or disagree with speakers they dislike. These situations were said to be the most pleasant, desirable, stable and expected state of relationships among any set of elements to which a person heeded (see Cacioppo and Petty 1981c).

One of the major complaints against balance theory is that there are no provisions for degrees of liking or belongingness between elements. A positive relation between two people is scored as $+1$, whether the couple is mildly friendly or madly in love. Congruity theory (Osgood and Tannenbaum 1955) overcomes this objection by quantifying gradations of liking between elements. Nonetheless, congruity theory can be considered to be a special case of balance theory. Congruity theory focuses on two elements, the source and a concept, and on a relation, the assertion made by the source about the concept. Hence, it is more limited in its range of application than balance theory even though it does make very specific, quantitative predictions about the effects of imbalance (incongruity) that fall within its domain.

Cognitive dissonance theory, first proposed by Festinger (1957), is unique among consistency theories in several important regards. First, most consistency theories can consider the interrelationships among a number of elements simultaneously to determine whether or not the structure of elements is balanced. Dissonance theory considers only pairs of elements at a time. The magnitude of the dissonance within a set of many elements is determined by (a) the proportion of relevant elements that are dissonance, and (b) the importance of the elements to the person. For example, let's say that you have to choose between two dialects. Using one dialect identifies you with friends of yours, but it also identifies you as being from an unprestigious background. The other dialect signifies 'good-breeding', but places you among a group in which you have no friends. There is a dissonant consequence of selecting either alternative (i.e. identifying with strangers rather than friends, or labelling yourself as belonging to a high or low socioeconomic group). If there were a third dialect that you could choose where you would have both friends and prestige, then there would be much less dissonance created by choosing the third over the former two alternatives. It would be less because the third alternative has all of the positive and none of the negative attributes that characterize the other decisional alternatives. Hence, the proportion of dissonant elements is low. (Indeed, in this example, the proportion is zero, and no dissonance would be aroused by choosing the third over the former two alternatives.)

Second, Festinger used dissonance theory to make a number of non-obvious predictions regarding attitude change. The non-intuitiveness of these predictions, coupled with the creative though sometimes questionable methods used to confirm these predictions (e.g. see Chapanis and Chapanis 1964), did much to stimulate research in this area.

The operation of cognitive consistency (specifically, balance and congruity theory) and attitude change can be illustrated with the Giles (1973b) study. The subjects were people who possessed regional accents and who had regional allegiances. The speaker varied his accent so that he appeared to have similar or dissimilar allegiances. When the speaker and recipients seemed *by their speech styles* to have similar allegiances, then a positive *unit* relation can be said to exist between these elements. When dissimilar, the unit relation is negative. The speaker argued against capital punishment, which constitutes a negative link between the speaker and the concept, capital punishment. These conditions can be viewed as constituting two sets of triads of elements with two relations specified in each triad (see Figure 12.1). According to both balance and congruity theories, the triad in which there is a positive speaker–recipient unit relation (i.e. the speaker appears similar to the recipients – see left panel of Figure 12.1) is in a state of equilibrium if the recipient moves toward agreement with the speaker about capital punishment (e.g. they both are against it). The triad in which there is a negative speaker–recipient unit relation (i.e. the speaker appears dissimilar to the recipients – see right panel of Figure 12.1), however, attains a state of equilibrium if the recipient moves toward disagreement with the speaker regarding capital punishment. The net effect of these pressures is that similarity between the speaker and recipient should lead to more attitude change than dissimilarity, which is what was observed by Giles (1973b).

Figure 12.1: When a speaker advocates a particular position on some issue to a recipient or audience, the social influence attempt can be viewed in terms of cognitive consistency (see text for an explanation.)

The same theories can be used to explain the pattern of data observed by Bourhis and Giles (1977). Bourhis and Giles identified Welshmen who valued their national identity and those who did not. The Welshmen were engaged individually in a conversation in English with an English interlocutor. Bourhis and Giles found that Welshmen who valued their national identity emphasized their (less prestigious) Welsh accents (i.e. diverged) when their interlocutor derrogated Wales, whereas Welshmen who did not value their national identity responded to the interlocutor's attacks by attenuating their Welsh accents (i.e. converged). In each instance, the Welshmen's change in speech style (i.e. divergence *vs* convergence) served to reinstate cognitive consistency among themselves, the English interlocutor, and their Welsh identity.

Cognitive dissonance theory typically applies to a different set of situations. According to dissonance theory, two elements are inconsistent (i.e. dissonant) when knowing one suggests the opposite of the other to the person. Festinger (1957) described cognitive dissonance as a motivational state that energizes and directs behaviour to remove dissonance. Dissonance can be reduced by: (a) changing one of the elements to make the pair more consonant, (b) adding consonant elements, or (c) changing the importance of the elements.

Let's return for a moment to individuals who must choose between a dialect that identifies them with family and friends but that also labels them as being from a lower-status social group and a dialect that indicates they are part of a prestigious social group. There are dissonant consequences regardless of their choice. According to cognitive dissonance theory, these individuals experience dissonance *following* a decision to the extent that the decision (a) is important to the person, (b) means giving up relatively attractive features of the unchosen alternative and/or accepting unattractive features of the chosen alternative, and (c) concerns alternatives that are dissimilar in their attributes but similar in their desirability. Festinger (1957) suggests four specific methods of reducing the dissonance aroused by making a decision: revoking the decision, increasing the attractiveness of the chosen alternative and/or decreasing the attractiveness of the unchosen alternative or viewing the consequences of the alternatives as similar. In the example we have described, the individuals ultimately must make a decision among alternatives with dissimilar attributes, which leaves them with the possibility of increasing the attractiveness of the chosen alternative and/or decreasing the attractiveness of the unchosen alternative to reduce dissonance. In fact, people typically use both these strategies, which results in a *post-decisional spreading* of the alternatives. The chosen alternative becomes more highly valued, whereas the unchosen alternative becomes less highly valued following a decision. Thus, a person who abandons his or her ethnic dialect for the majority dialect would, according to dissonance theory, tend to undervalue their ethnic background and overvalue the social rewards they acquire by their speech style.

Dissonance theory may offer an explanation for Baker's observations that 'frequently a judgement is made of an individual (with a similar speech style) on other grounds and then comments about speech are made to rationalize that judgement' (cited by Giles and Powesland 1975, 104). First, assume that employers expect to hire people similar to themselves in speech and appearance. When an employer decides *not* to hire an applicant with a similar speech style, dissonance may be aroused (see Kalin, this volume: ch. 9). To reduce this dissonance, the employer could: (a) change one of the elements to make the pair more consonant, such as altering his judgement regarding the applicant's speech style; (b) add consonant elements, such as finding fault with other aspects of the applicant's record; or (c) change the importance of the elements, such as deciding that speech style is not a relevant criterion upon which to select employees. Hence, although an employer's decision may be based upon other grounds, changes in views about the applicant's speech style (along with other characteristics) provides a simple means of reducing the cognitive dissonance aroused by the employer's decision not to hire the applicant.

Attribution

The fifth approach involves attitude-inference, or attributional, processes. The notion common to the theories that fall under this heading is that a person's inferences about the cause of a behaviour is the proximal mediator of the resulting attitude. These attitude-inferences might concern the communicator's behaviour ('why is he or she saying that?') or they might concern the person's own behaviour ('why did I do that?') (see Bem 1972). Bem has emphasized the importance of whether another or one's own behaviour is manded (determined by powerful situational forces) or tacted (voluntarily determined). When a behaviour is manded, one tends to attribute the behaviour to the situation. When a behaviour is tacted, however, one tends to attribute the behaviour to something about the person, such as his or her attitude.

Giles and his colleagues (Giles and Powesland 1975; Giles and Smith 1979; Simard, Taylor and Giles 1976) have employed attributional principles in their analysis of the antecedents and consequences of accomodation (i.e. convergence of speech style). They reasoned that an attempt by someone to speak in a more understandable fashion to an audience foreign to the speaker (i.e. convergence) will cause the audience to seek causes for the speaker's behaviour. For example, Simard *et al.* (1976) conducted a study in which they measured the evaluations that a French-Canadian audience made of an English-Canadian speaker who either converged (i.e. communicated in French) or did not converge (i.e. communicated in English). In half of the conditions, the English Canadian was *forced* to speak in a specific language (i.e. French or English; manded behaviour) and in half the conditions the English Canadian *chose* to speak in either French or English (i.e. tacted behaviour). The results were in accord with the attributional analysis: The French-Canadian audience rated the speaker most positively when he *chose* to speak in French and least positively when he *chose* to speak in English. When situational pressures forced the English Canadian to speak in either French or English, the evaluations of the speaker by the audience (and the dispositional attributions) were moderated.

There are two general attributional principles, proposed by Kelley (1972, 1973), that have guided much of the attribution research in the area of attitudes and persuasion. The first is the *discounting principle*, which states that to the extent that a response (or effect) has a number of plausible causes, the viability of any single cause is discounted or weakened. The second is the *augmentation principle*, which states that a response that is unexpected (i.e. unique) given the contextual cues is especially likely to be attributed to something unique about the actor. Eagly, Wood and Chaiken (1978) have used these principles to explain why communicators who argue *against* their own vested interests are more persuasive than communicators who argue *for* their own vested interests.

Eagly *et al.* (1978) reasoned that message recipients generally expect speakers to argue for their own vested interests. When speakers do indeed advocate a position that benefits themselves, the speakers confirm the recipients' *premessage* expectation. The recipients can attribute the speakers' supportive arguments to their veridical view of the world, to their biased (unrepresentative) body of information on the topic (referred to as a knowledge bias), or to their concealing issue-relevant information that is nonsupportive of the recommendation in order to secure personal gains (referred to as a reporting bias). If recipients draw the first attribution, they will be susceptible to influence; but since there are a number of alternative explanations for the speaker's appeal (e.g. knowledge and reporting biases), the recipients tend to discount the possibility that the message arguments reflect the true state of the world. This discounting makes the recipients more resistant to speakers' persuasive appeals.

If, however, speakers disconfirm the recipients' premessage expectations by advocating positions that are contrary to their own best interests, then Eagly argues that argumentation occurs. Eagly suggests that recipients have few, if any, explanations for the speakers' behaviour in these instances except that external reality is as they describe. Moreover, Eagly reasons, the unexpected nature of the speakers' behaviours enhances the likelihood that the recipients shall attribute the recommendation to something unique about the speakers, such as their unique understanding of the issues involved. One consequence of these attributions is that the recipients are rendered particularly susceptible to the speakers' persuasive appeals.

Eagly and her colleagues have provided substantial support for their attributional analysis of persuasion following the violation of pre-message expectancies (see Eagly and Chaiken 1975; Eagly *et al.* 1978). Eagly *et al.* (1978) established knowledge-bias expectancies by portraying a speaker as being committed to values represented by a pro-business or pro-environment side of a business decision (halting production and making radical changes in waste disposal) and reporting-bias expectancies by portraying the audience as having a strong commitment to one or the other side (i.e. continuing or halting production). In all conditions of the Eagly *et al.* study, the speaker advocated that the business halt production immediately and make the necessary changes in its waste disposal to protect the environment. Thus, discounting becomes likely in the context of a pro-environment speaker and/or audience, whereas augmenting becomes more likely on the part of the message recipients when they understand the speaker to be pro-business and/or to be addressing a pro-business audience. Eagly *et al.* (1978) found that, regardless of the type of bias that subjects expected (knowledge, reporting or both), they were more persuaded and perceived the speaker as being less biased when their pre-message expectations regarding the bias(es) were disconfirmed (i.e. when augmenting was most likely).

This attributional analysis can also be extended to account for the results of some studies on speech style and persuasion (see Giles 1973b; Powesland and Giles 1975). For instance, Giles and Powesland (1975, 95-100) indicated that arguing against capital punishment could be taken as an expression of liberal-mindedness by regional subjects in Great Britain. Moreover, Giles and Powesland (1975) suggested that the RP accent may elicit a stereotyped expectation that the speaker is a liberal, whereas the regional accents may elicit an expectation that the speaker is a conservative. When the RP speaker argues against capital punishment, the recipients' expectations are confirmed, and discounting can occur. When the speaker emits a regional accent against capital punishment, however, he violates the recipients expectations of his position on capital punishment, and augmentation beomes likely. Of course, formally, the speaker did not violate a pre-message expectation, but he did violate an expectation that developed early in the message as a result of his style of speech. The attributional consequences outlined by Eagly and her colleagues for violations of pre-message expectations should hold for these situations as well. The results of the above study were in accord with these predictions.

Finally, Scherer (1979b) has suggested that vocal qualities in some instances can be more important in social influence processes than content and visual cues. The attributional framework may be particularly useful in detailing the complex inferential processes that are initiated by variations in a speaker's voice quality. For instance, a beautiful voice might stimulate a halo effect that would cause one to infer that the speaker was honest, knowledgeable, and so forth, and these inferences may render the speaker particularly persuasive.

Combination

The sixth, combinative approach to attitudes and persuasion represents the precise mathematical models that have been developed to account for how the external *information* that a person receives is evaluated and integrated to form an overall judgement or attitude about a person, object or issue. Fishbein and Ajzen's 'theory of reasoned action' (Ajzen and Fishbein 1980; Fishbein 1980; Fishbein and Ajzen 1975) makes especially interesting predictions regarding attitudes and behaviours and, therefore, is discussed briefly here.

According to the theory of reasoned action, the single best predictor of behaviour is the behavioural intention, which in turn is viewed as the consequence of two other factors: (a) the person's attitude toward the behaviour, and (b) the person's subjective norm. Attitudes are viewed as being a function of the beliefs held by the person about the outcomes of a behaviour, including the likelihood that the behaviour would lead to certain outcomes, and the person's evaluation of those consequences. The subjective norm, on the other hand, is determined by what the person perceives the opinion of significant others regarding the performance of the behaviour to be (e.g. the opinions of one's friends), and the person's motivation to comply with their judgements. Little research to date has been done on the effects of language variables on attitudes, subjective norms, and behaviour but Fishbein and Ajzen's theory of reasoned action would seem to provide a cogent framework for research on these issues.

Finally, functional theory (Katz 1960), as we outlined it in the introductory section of this chapter, has not generated much research in attitudes and persuasion. The formulation has heuristic value, but operationalizing the theory has been difficult. Recently, Lutz (in press) reconceptualized functional theory in expectancy-times-value (i.e. combinative) terms and proposed specific operationalizations for the theoretical constructs. The interested reader might wish to consult Lutz (in press) for more information.

Self-persuasion

The final general approach to attitudes and persuasion is termed self-persuasion because the attitude change that occurs is viewed not as the consequence of the externally provided information per se, but rather as the result of thoughts, ideas and arguments that the recipients themselves generate. This approach is similar to that of Hovland and his colleagues in recognizing the importance of attention to and comprehension of an external message, but it is unique in postulating an additional stage of cognitive elaboration of the message. In other words, this approach focuses on the notion that recipients have available to them and utilize vast stores of information beyond that contained in the persuasive message.

Greenwald (1968) suggested that a persuasive message elicits subject generated *cognitive responses* that could either support or attack the information provided in the message. If the recipient generated favourable cognitive responses to the recommendation, then persuasion would likely result. If the recipient generated unfavourable cognitive responses to the recommendation, however, then persuasion would likely not result.

Cognitive responses can be measured in a variety of ways, including electrophysiologically (Cacioppo and Petty 1979a, 1981a) and mechanically (Carter, Ruggels, Jackson and Heffner 1973). The most commonly used measure of cognitive response in persuasion, however, is the 'listed thoughts procedure', which involves subjects reporting retrospectively everything about which they thought during a specified time period (e.g. during a persuasive message). Although there are a number of issues involved in and decisions to be made when selecting a specific procedure to obtain thought listings (see Cacioppo, Harkins and Petty 1981; Cacioppo and Petty 1981b for reviews and descriptions of procedures), the following procedure for assessing people's cognitive responses is common in studies examining cognitive responses to a brief persuasive message. Subjects read the following:

> We are now interested in what you were thinking about during the last few minutes. . . . Simply write down the first idea that comes to mind in the first box, the second idea in the second box, etc. Please put only one idea or thought in a box. You should try to record only those ideas that you were thinking during the last few minutes. You will have 2½ minutes to write your thoughts. . . . Please be completely honest and list all of the thoughts you had (Petty and Cacioppo, 1977, p. 648).

Twelve 8-inch (20.32 cm) horizontal lines each about 1 inch (2.54 cm) from the one above create the boxes in which subjects write their ideas.

When the 2.5 minutes for writing thoughts elapses, *subjects* are instructed to go back and rate their thoughts in the following manner. Ideas are rated as either + (in favour of the advocated position), − (opposed to the advocated position), or 0 (neutral toward or irrelevant to the advocated position). Each idea that a subject lists can also be submitted to two *judges* for independent scoring as either an unfavourable (opposed to the advocated position), favourable (in favour), or neutral (unrelated to the topic) thought. Inter-rater reliabilities are typically quite high, and the ratings of subjects and judges are also typically very similar (e.g. *r*s range .70 to .95). The simple sums of favourable, unfavourable, and neutral thoughts are used in the analyses, as these measures have proven to be as reliable and valid as more complex, combinations or weightings of cognitive responses (see Cacioppo and Petty 1981b).

Recent work in attitude change has demonstrated the rich utility of considering the idiosyncratic cognitive responses that recipients exhibit when they process the information in persuasive messages and settings. Investigators have studied how such variables as message repetition (Cacioppo and Petty 1979b, 1980a), source credibility (Cook 1969; Gillig and Greenwald 1974), distraction (Petty, Wells and Brock 1976), forewarning of persuasive intent (Petty and Cacioppo 1979a) and of topic and position (Petty and Cacioppo 1977), number of arguments employed

(Calder, Insko and Yandell 1974), issue involvement (Petty and Cacioppo 1979b, 1981b), heart rate (Cacioppo 1979), group discussion (Burnstein and Vinokur 1977), and so forth affect the profile of cognitions (e.g. unfavourable, favourable and neutral thoughts) and attitude change. As we have noted, the theoretical interest in the influence on persuasion of a person's idiosyncratic cognitive responses to an advocacy is not new (see Hovland *et al.* 1949), but the present level of research activity in the area marks a shift in emphasis toward this approach (see reviews by Cialdini, Petty and Cacioppo 1981; Perloff and Brock 1980; Petty and Cacioppo 1981a; Petty, Ostrom and Brock 1981).

One particularly interesting application of the cognitive response approach is Burnstein, Vinokur, and Trope's (1973) explanation for conformity, which refers to the tendency for people to go along with the opinions or judgements of other people in the absence of any supporting arguments. Various researchers have been interested in conformity effects. For example, Festinger's (1954) social comparison theory contends that people shift toward the majority viewpoint (i.e. conform) out of a desire to hold a veridical opinion. Moscovici's (1976) 'genetic' model of social influence contends that a resistant minority may shift toward a majority viewpoint while pulling this viewpoint toward their original position – a conflictive process that can yield innovation and societal change. Burnstein *et al.* (1973) account for these effects by proposing that when people are presented with the conflicting opinions of others, they are motivated to think of the arguments that might have led to these others to hold their discrepant views. 'That is to say, knowing others have chosen differently stimulates the person to generate arguments which could explain their choices' (Burnstein *et al.* 1973, 244). Thus, what appears on the surface to be conformity might actually be a biased scanning of arguments and self-persuasion.

Recently, we have extended this approach to the study of language variables and persuasion. For instance, Petty, Cacioppo and Heesacker (1981) conducted a cognitive response analysis of the use of rhetorical questions in persuasion. Recall that rhetoricals in contrast to declarative statements may cause the source to appear more polite (Bates 1976) and/or less confident and assertive (Newcombe and Arnkoff 1979). A major distinction between a cognitive response analysis of rhetoricals and analyses based upon source perceptions is that the former proposes that message style may affect how the information contained in the message is processed and, hence, how susceptible or resistant the recipient is to persuasion. That is, the use of rhetoricals is one language variable in which *the way something is said may affect the elaboration and integration of what is said.* According to source perception analyses, of course, the actual content of the message is less important, as style dominates over substance.

If rhetoricals affect persuasion by their direct effects on source perceptions, then the effect of rhetoricals should be the same for both strong, cogent messages and weak, specious messages. If, however, rhetoricals enhance the likelihood of message elaboration, then the use of rhetoricals should increase the persuasiveness of the strong message, but reduce the persuasiveness of the weak message. Furthermore, rhetoricals should be most effective in enhancing message elaboration when recipients are not naturally devoting much effort to processing the message. If the message was naturally eliciting a great deal of thought, then it would be unlikely that the use of rhetoricals could enhance elaboration further. Indeed, if recipients were already doing a great deal of thinking on their own about the message, then the use of rhetoricals might actually interfere with the lines of thought that recipients were pursuing on their own and, therefore, reduce the overall level of message processing. This latter notion developed from pilot work in which subjects heard a message on a highly involving topic. Rhetoricals were found to decrease rather than increase message elaboration, and subjects reported that they were trying hard to think about the message (since it proposed changes that were personally important to them) but that the questions asked by the speaker were distracting.

To test these hypotheses, students were exposed to a taped message advocating that seniors be required to pass a comprehensive exam in their major area of study before graduating. Half of the students believed that the recommendation might be adopted by their university the following year (high issue involvement), whereas half believed that it might be adopted by a distant university in ten years (low issue involvement). Previous research has reported that people do considerably more thinking on their own about issues of high than low issue involvement (Cialdini, Levy, Herman, Kozlowski and Petty 1976; Petty and Cacioppo 1979a, 1979b, 1981b). The message that subjects heard contained either strong arguments that were logical, defensible, compelling, and elicited predominantly favourable thoughts; or weak arguments that were open to refutation, skepticism, and elicited primarily unfavourable thoughts. Finally, subjects heard the message worded either in declarative form or such that six of the eight arguments were worded as rhetorical questions.

The results, which are illustrated in Figure 12.2, supported the cognitive response analysis of rhetoricals in persuasion. Analyses suggested that for the *low-*

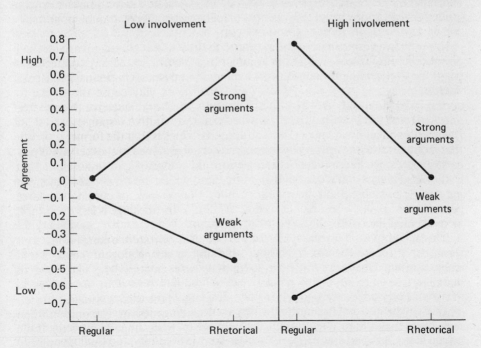

Figure 12.2: Mean level of agreement in relation to argument quality and use of rhetoricals for high and low involvement messages.

involvement versions of the messages, when subjects were not naturally motivated to engage in much thought about the recommendation, the use of rhetoricals enhanced message elaboration. Specifically, subjects hearing the rhetorical versions of the low-involvement messages in contrast to the regular statement versions best realized the virtues of the strong arguments and fallacies of the weak arguments contained in the messages. For the *high-involvement versions* of the messages, when subjects were already highly motivated to think about the recommendation and implications of the message arguments, the use of rhetoricals attenuated message elaboration by disrupting the recipients' natural flow of thoughts. Subjects hearing the regular rather than rhetorical versions of the high-involvement messages were more discriminating in their cognitive responses and attitudes in response to the strong and weak message arguments, and subjects exposed to the rhetorical version rated that they were more distracted from thinking about the message than did subjects exposed to the regular version. These distraction ratings, the cognitive response data and the complex three-way interaction pattern for attitudes displayed in Figure 12.2 make sense from the cognitive response perspective. These data, of course, cannot be explained parsimoniously by a source perception formulation.

Conclusions: two routes to attitude change

Seven approaches to attitudes and persuasion have been surveyed and some of their implications for language variables and attitudes have been noted. We have indicated that although these seven approaches postulate different mechanisms as underlying attitude change, they generally focus on one of two processes: (a) one in which the recipients respond to various non-content cues in the situation, making the message arguments virtually irrelevant to attitude change; and (b) one in which the recipients actively process the arguments presented in the message, often in ways that reflect the influence of source, style, message, channel and recipient factors.

We have proposed elsewhere that these two processes constitute two distinct *routes* to persuasion with different antecedents and different consequences in our 'elaboration likelihood model' of attitude change (Petty and Cacioppo 1981a, ch. 9). Under the first, or *central route*, thinking about issue-relevant information is the most direct determinant of the direction and amount of persuasion produced. Attitude changes induced via this route tend to be relatively enduring and predictive of subsequent behaviour. Under the second, or *peripheral route*, attitude change is the result of non-content cues in the persuasion setting (e.g. like demand characteristics, the physical attractiveness of the source, vocabulary difficulty in audiovisual presentations, or the rate of speech) that allow a recipient to evaluate a recommendation without thinking much about the issue under consideration. Changes in attitude induced via this route tend to be relatively temporary and are not highly predictive of subsequent behaviour (see reviews by Cialdini, Petty and Cacioppo 1981; Petty and Cacioppo 1981a, ch. 9).

One important determinant of which route will be followed is the extent to which the message recipient is personally involved with the issue under consideration (e.g. Cacioppo and Petty 1980b; Chaiken 1980; Petty and Cacioppo 1979b, 1981b). Language variables may be determinants of which route will be followed, perhaps due to their direct effect on issue involvement or to their direct effects on people's motivation and/or ability to think about an issue. Language variables may have interactive effects on cognitive responses and attitudes, as illustrated in the study on rhetoricals and persuasion (Petty, Cacioppo and Heesacker 1981). Finally, they may have simple, more temporary 'cue' effects on attitudes and persuasion when issue involvement is low, as suggested by Miller *et al.*'s (1976) study on speech rate. Utilizing separate measures of cognitive response, attitudes, and behaviours in immediate and delayed post-tests would be particularly helpful in partitioning these various routes to persuasion.

In sum, the present review offers a potpourri of theoretical frameworks within which to view research on language variables and attitudes, extends social psychological theories of attitudes and persuasion to include work on language variables, and suggests possible avenues for future research. At present, data suggest that the central (e.g. argument quality) in contrast to the peripheral route (e.g. source similarity) will predominate when recipients are both able and motivated to think about and elaborate upon the present and impending implications of the recommendation for themselves and significant others.

13

Prolegomena for developing a social psychological theory of language attitudes[1]

Howard Giles and Ellen Bouchard Ryan

Since the pioneering work of Lambert in the late 1950s on language attitudes, we have come a long way in terms of accumulated descriptive data, applied research, methodological sophistication and theoretical ideas. It has been our aim that this volume should be a comprehensive, integrated testament to these advances. Without wishing to underestimate unduly the enormous complexity of the data, we can very briefly overview as follows. In some detail, we have seen how dominant groups in society determine, by a variety of direct and indirect means (chapter 5), that their characteristic speech varieties are *the* norms for speaking properly to which we should all subscribe (chapter 10). This phenomenon appears almost universal across social groupings and linguistic features to the extent that it is accorded weight with respect to men's (as opposed to women's) verbal and vocal styles (chapters 5 and 6), languages and dialects of ethnic minorities as opposed to immigrant or indigenous minorities (chapters 3 and 4) as well as upper-class as opposed to working-class accents and codes (chapter 2). Hence, empirical research from numerous parts of the world has shown how speakers of 'powerless' speech styles are evaluated less favourably in terms of competence and traits related to socioeconomic status; and these impressions can have negative consequences for the types of decisions made in important applied settings (chapters 2 and 9). In other words, speech style is often believed to be socially 'diagnostic' (Kahneman and Tversky 1973), that is, it is judged to be usefully predictive of a whole range of outcomes, including speakers' psychological states, category memberships and behavioural capabilities. Moreover, the social meanings attached to these speech styles are fairly well developed for many children in early childhood (chapter 7). In other social contexts, however, the language varieties of many subordinate groups are accorded much pride by their own speakers (and sometimes conceded by others) on the more 'human' traits of solidarity (chapters 1 and 4), integrity and social attractiveness as well as in persuasive quality (chapters 2, 3 and 12). Such is the fundamental importance of speech characteristics for one's sense of group identity that many individuals have negative attitudes about acquiring the dominant group's prestige code and as a result may fail to become proficient in it (chapter 8). Not all of the chapters have been oriented in an intergroup direction of course, and many of them have explored the subtlety of social meanings for a variety of verbal and vocal parameters in interindividual encounters (e.g. chapters 6 and 11).

[1] We are most grateful to Miles Hewstone, Nick Pidgeon and Philip M. Smith for their extremely useful comments on an earlier draft of this chapter.

208

Prior to the preparation of the chapters for this volume, it would not be unfair to claim that the area of language attitudes had been characterized by theoretical sterility. Yet the two-dimensional model of the sociostructural factors affecting language attitudes espoused, and types of language attitude situations depicted, in chapter 1 should lay the foundation for making conceptual sense of the vast array of speech variables that can be manipulated in different cultural contexts. Previously, empirical confusion reigned in the sense that speakers of, say, a non-standard variety were upgraded on certain evaluative traits in some communities while downgraded on them in other communities. On the basis of the theoretical formulations presented in our Prologue, it is to be hoped that cross-national comparisons will become more viable and that cross-cultural collaborative efforts (see Bourhis, Giles and Lambert 1975) will consequently be fostered and considered essential for future developments. Indeed, one hallmark of the preceding contributions to this volume has been the vibrant concern for theory. This has been explicit not only in the models of chapter 1 but also in those of chapters 8, 10, 11 and 12 concerning language attitudes and the acquisition of a second tongue, political socialization, speech evaluation and persuasion respectively. It has also been implicit in the distinct concern in many other chapters for elucidating the cognitive processes (e.g. expectancies, attributions, consistency, social judgements, cognitive responses, situational construals) mediating listeners' perceptions of vocal and verbal characteristics and their subsequent responses to them under specified contextual conditions (see particularly, chapters 5, 6 and 12). It is to be hoped that such attention to mediating processes and theories of the middle range will be the stepping stone towards promoting the development of a theoretical framework for the study of language attitudes. Whether *a* grand theory of language attitudes is viable or even desirable is a contentious issue although recent linguistic, sociological and social psychological integrations within speech accommodation theory (e.g. Trudgill 1981 and chapters 10 and 11) suggest that this could be a feasible *interdisciplinary* goal.

In this chapter, we wish not only to collate a number of important suggestions for future research advocated in preceding chapters, but also to add some priorities of our own as a contribution to the evolving theory. In this latter regard, contemporary social psychological research with regard to social cognition (see for example, Hastie, Ostrom, Ebbesen, Wyer, Hamilton and Carlston 1980; Nisbett and Ross 1980; and Wyer and Carlston 1979), has alerted us to the value of promoting the exploration of certain of its phenomena and processes within the language attitudes paradigm; interestingly, this has been attempted recently across a range of communication science domains independently (see Roloff and Berger, in press). Needless to say, we do not see social psychology as a kind of panacea for any theoretical ills the language attitudes area possesses. As will be acknowledged, social psychology to date has few ready-made answers to the complexities of how we form and change our impressions of others, draw inferences about them during the course of a relationship, and act towards them in a variety of situations. Yet our social psychological background has sensitized us to the types of issues which, if researched programmatically enough, would provide a blueprint for some important avenues to follow as a complement to more sociological and linguistic directions. Indeed, it is even possible that language attitudes research, rarely cited within the social psychological fraternity, will in due course reciprocate by suggesting fruitful possibilities for the latter as well.

In the remainder of this chapter, we will structure our discussion around an attempt to alleviate what may be regarded as four of the major overriding deficiencies in traditional speaker evaluation studies. We shall devote ourselves exclusively to this type of investigation as it has been the methodological tack dominating the previous chapters in most cases. Although the four problem areas are separated conceptually in our analysis, it will become evident that they are highly interdependent. These four deficiencies are:

1. independent speech variables are concocted in a social, psychological and linguistic vacuum;
2. listener–judges feature almost as cognitive nonentities;
3. aspects of context are socially and subjectively sterile; and
4. dependent variables are devised without recourse to their situational, functional and behavioural implications.

A social psychological critique of speaker evaluation studies

The independent variables

In future, more attention should be directed towards the nature of the speech samples manipulated, not only in providing more detailed linguistic and acoustic descriptions of the stimulus voices as well as examining the relative evaluative salience of these particulars for different types of listeners (Batstone and Tuomi 1981), but also in avoiding a location of them in a verbal and paralinguistic vacuum (see Greenbaum 1976, 1977a). Many speaker-evaluation studies manipulate dialect or accent *only* while attempting to maintain paralinguistic constancy and keeping the amount of speech standard across the voices (see however, Giles, Brown and Thakerar 1981; Giles, Wilson and Conway 1981). However, the specific levels at which these controls are engineered can be judgementally crucial. For instance, it is entirely possible that so-called extraneous variables (e.g. speech rate, pitch and lexical diversity) in accent studies, for example, can alter what may have been erroneously regarded previously as the *fundamental* social meaning of accents. As work on the 'dilution effect' (Nisbett, Zukier and Lemley, 1981, p. 252) shows:

> The presence of individuating but nondiagnostic information about the target reduces the similarity between the target and those outcomes that are suggested by the diagnostic information. One of the major implications is that stereotypes and 'other social knowledge structures' may be applied to abstract, undifferentiated individuals and groups and may be largely set aside when judgements are made about concrete, individuated people.

In other words, the potentially debilitating effect on perceived competence of non-standard accent in some contexts may possibly be neutralized, or even reversed, when combined with high pitch variability, fast speech rate, high lexical diversity and an assertive, productive communication style (see Trower 1980).

Despite the values of the experimental method (Turner 1981a), speakers are too often presented as anonymous males without any regard for their social or psychological characteristics (see chapter 5). It is as if stimulus speakers have no socio-economic backgrounds, interests, occupations, values or ideological beliefs. Such a vacuum can be deleterious to the presumed influence of accented speech as pointed out by Ryan and Sebastian (1980) in the United States where they found that the negative consequences of nonstandard speech diminished when the speaker was known to derive from a middle-class background. Traditionally, speakers are presented as immobile and having no real opinions nor even allowed the privilege of not holding opinions or behaving badly (see however chapter 12 and Bishop 1979). Certainly, the whole literature on causal attributions (e.g. Harvey, Ickes and Kidd 1978; Major 1980) suggests that we do not often observe behaviour, linguistic (Hewstone, in press; Sillars, in press; Simard, Taylor and Giles 1976) or nonlinguistic, without making assumptions as to why it arose in the first place. Hewstone and Jaspars (1982) have proposed that attributions in a social context tend to be concerned less with explanations of the behaviour per se, and more with the outcomes of the behaviour or the social conditions which led to its inception. Thus, until we know how speech variables are assessed in accord with other cognitive functionings (see subsequent section below), we will not be able to assess the limitations of language attitudes; unless we know the boundaries of their operation we will never be able to comprehend their importance as dependent nor independent variables in social reality.

Finally, speakers are presented anonymously to the extent that they are unfamiliar to the listeners. It is quite likely that the importance of prestige speech as well as attributions made about it will be different at the initial stages of an encounter compared to when interactants are well acquainted, if not very intimate with each other (see Newman 1981; Riggs 1979). Berger's (1979) model of the acquaintanceship process wherein participants attempt to increase their knowledge about each other depends on their utilizing and searching for different cues (including linguistic ones) at different stages of their developing relationship in order to reduce cognitive uncertainty and to behave appropriately (see discussion of purpose of encounters below, and Berger and Roloff, in press; Duck and Gilmour 1981; Miller and Parks, in press). It is also well documented that observers of a situation may make quite different attributions about behaviour, or offer different kinds of explanation for it, from those who are actively engaged in the immediacy of the interaction (Buss 1978; Eisen 1979). In other words, how listener–judges respond to a stimulus speaker will undoubtedly be quite different from how they would react to him or her under more naturalistic and personally involving conditions (see chapters 2, 6, 7 and 12; also Anderson, Fine and Johnson's 1983 study evaluating voices on television).

Systematic research which manipulates speakers' SES, beliefs, actions and familiarity with the judges should also attend to disentangling the problem of when nonprestige speech colours the perceived content of a message (the cause) and when in contrast it is used as an 'excuse' for dismissal of the speaker owing to the nature of the content (see McArthur 1980 and notions of 'illusory causation and correlation' and chapter 12 on central *vs* peripheral routes). One could therefore introduce the seemingly simple-minded and yet rarely advanced proposition *that the causal influence of prestige–nonprestige speech on judges' evaluations will at least in part be a function of the amount of other positively valued cues (linguistic and nonlinguistic) perceived to be in the speaker's favour*. Hence, where these latter features are controlled out in speaker evaluation studies, voice characteristics *can* be expected to be important. However, when for example the speaker is an articulate, rational individual known to have expertise on many topics and thought to be a distant cousin of the listener–judge, the former's nonstandard dialect might have little evaluative impact but might instead introduce a unique social attractiveness all of its own (see Nisbett and Wilson 1977b who found different interpretations of a professor's accent depending on whether his personality was warm or cold; also notions of disconfirming expectations and language; Burgoon and Miller, in press; Lind and O'Barr 1979). Yet this particular dilution effect could occur by way of a different cognitive route. Had the non-linguistic information sufficient diagnostic value of its own, it could act so as to bias the perception of characteristics of the speech style (see chapter 11); this could occur whether this information was presented prior or even subsequent to listening to the voice (Thakerar and Giles 1981; Williams, Whitehead and Miller 1972). In other words, our aforementioned distant cousin's speech might have been heard by the judge as quite standard despite its objective characteristics (see also Beebe 1981; Thakerar, Giles and Cheshire 1982).

We need therefore to chart the ways in which the social consequences of dialect, other linguistic features and code- or style-shifting (Fitch and Hopper 1983; Gibbons 1983) can be quantitatively or qualitatively modified depending upon almost the entire matrix of (a) verbal/vocal possibilities, (b) social, psychological and behavioural characteristics, and (c) types of relationships reasonably possible. Obviously, there are other sources of variance and these will be considered in due course.

Cognitive processes

Robinson (1972), after Lambert (1967), introduced a two-stage model for cognitive processing in terms of categorization and inference whereby dialect (or other cues) enables judges to locate the speaker sociologically, with this categorization leading to stereotyped inferences from it (see Giles, Scherer and Taylor 1979 for a critique of this model). Indeed, Ryan and Cacioppo (1981) have levied a legitimate criticism at workers in this area for not taking into account current impression formation and inference models. In response to this challenge, a review of the relevant literature was undertaken which did indeed unearth some compelling research and ideas for incorporation into the language attitudes paradigm.

The cognitive processes which mediate between a judge's perception of the message and the inferences arising from them have received surprisingly little attention (for exceptions, see Delia 1972; Sebastian, Ryan, Keogh and Schmidt 1980). One important component of the mediating mechanisms is the judges' level of cognitive complexity. For instance, Delia (1974, 306) found that 'subjects high in cognitive complexity, in comparision to noncomplex subjects formed more differentiated, more abstract, more highly organized impressions after ten minutes of unstructured interaction with a stranger.' Delia (1972) showed that when subjects judge speakers on tape who sound similar to themselves, their levels of cognitive complexity are extremely important in discovering the underlying dispositional qualities of the speakers. Delia (1974) claims that cognitively complex perceivers have several advantages over the less complex by means of their greater use of abstract qualities: they have

greater permeability and hence, can summarize a wide range of specific behavioural acts. Second, the perceiver frees himself from the immediate situation through the use of abstract attributions. When behavioural acts are translated not into traces of the original behaviour but into interpersonal constructs which correspond to the underlying abilities and qualities that the perceiver presumes to be characteristic of the other person, a basis

is established for prediction and future action in the social setting. . . . A final advantage
. . . is that they permit the perceiver to recognize inconsistency in other people and to
account for it with some underlying set of processes. (p. 307)

Interestingly, Delia (1972) found that when judges heard a speaker with a dissimilar accent, cognitive differentiation diminished at the expense of stereotyping
irrespective of the judges' level of cognitive complexity (see Arthur, Bradford and
Farrar 1974).

Certainly, much can be gleaned from past and present work in terms of research
in social categorization (for reviews, see Cantor and Mischel 1979; Doise 1978), a
primary component of the aforementioned Robinson model. Tajfel and Wilkes
(1963) suggest that when people perceive representatives of different social
categories (which may of course be marked in speech, see Scherer and Giles 1979),
there is a tendency to accentuate the perceptual differences between them
especially when the categories are value-laden (see chapter 11). For example,
Belgian bilinguals hearing English spoken by Francophone and Flemish speakers
on tape would likely *hear* each of their accents as sounding more ethnic than if they
had heard them on different isolated occasions (see Helson's 1959 theory of
adaptation levels). The research on salience of the prior knowledge of base-rate
information as mediating judgements under some (but not other) conditions may
also be useful here (Manis 1977; Tversky and Kahneman 1980). Therefore, people
working upon the assumption that a speaker comes from a particular population
(social group) and that 80 per cent of the people within that group are working-class
would possibly categorize and make subsequent trait inferences about a nonstandard speaker on tape that would be different from someone who considered
the base rate to be 50 per cent. Categorization, of course, becomes more value-
laden depending upon the subjects' own identification with the social categories
concerned (Tajfel 1981). Unfortunately however, most studies in language
attitudes (see however Flores and Hopper 1975; Mercer, Mercer and Mears 1979)
do not check on whether listener–judges themselves subscribe to the social group
(e.g. racial, ethnic, class) into which they have been intuitively placed by the
investigators (Smith, Giles and Hewstone 1980). Given that we subscribe to the
importance of subjective, cognitive definitions of social group membership (see
Giles 1979; Turner 1982), it appears vital in future research to determine not only
with which social groups subjects identify at the time of testing, but also the
salience and value that they afford them (Giles and Johnson 1981). Without
question then, we need to elicit from subjects not only information in ways that do
not bias their evaluation of the language data to be judged, but also their cognitive
representations of relevant base-rate data. Furthermore, we need to investigate the
cognitive consequences of social categorization in greater depth as it can be a
fundamental precursor to the types of inferences that ensue from speaker perception (see Hamilton 1979).

Unfortunately we have available few models which can deal adequately enough
with the complexities involved in deriving inferences from social information. The
model which has gained in prominence over others is the weighted averaging
model (see Schneider, Hastorf and Ellsworth 1979 for a review). This model relates
to the fact that subjects usually average out their positive and negative evaluations
of a person while affording certain central traits heavier weightings than others in
order to come to an overall impression (e.g. likeability). Nevertheless, Delia (1976)
in a revision based on Peabody (1970) of the earlier 'change of meaning' hypothesis

has shown empirically that the weighted averaging model does not take into account (a) descriptive as opposed to evaluative elements of inference, (b) subjects going beyond the information provided them, and on the basis of their implicit personality theories (Grant and Holmes 1981) adding to the picture by inferring related traits, (c) the findings that people who are evaluated positively, but only on one descriptive dimension, are not evaluated in a positive manner in terms of likeability but are downgraded as rigid, narrow-minded and unidimensional, and (d) other dimensions having behavioural implications other than mere overall likeability. It should be noted that the methodology in trait inference research is quite different from that utilized in speaker evaluation studies in the sense that subjects in the former are presented with a list of traits considered typical of the supposed stimulus figure whereas subjects in the latter are asked actually to form an impression themselves, albeit on prescribed traits. For our purposes, Delia has usefully conceptualized the impression formation process as based on

1. the ordering of stimulus information according to the perceiver's conceptual dimensions,
2. the attribution by inference of other qualities based on related conceptual dimensions,
3. the establishment of unity and coherence in the impression through organization around central, motivational constructs,
4. an implicit evaluation of the total impression, and finally
5. a recoding of the impression into the subject's own verbal code if and when he is called upon to do so (p. 158).

Hence, future work in language attitudes could be concerned with (a) gleaning judges' prior evaluations and base rate estimations of a wide range of traits (see Anderson 1968), (b) determining judges' evaluations of the speaker on traits considered relevant to the judges themselves (Bourhis, Giles and Tajfel 1973) as well as the in-context favourability ratings of these traits, (c) obtaining judges' confidence ratings for the scales employed for overall evaluation (Edwards 1979a) and for specific evaluations of behavioural relevance (e.g. working with a colleague, see Aboud, Clément and Taylor 1974; also chapter 9). Data along these lines will be useful in determining more details concerning the inference process which may be of potential benefit in formulating general inference models effective for dealing with the complexities of more naturalistic conditions.

At the moment however, no adequate impression formation model is available which is immediately applicable to the language attitudes paradigm. Furthermore, recent critiques of social cognition research have pointed out that individuals often do not engage in elaborate and complex cognitive machinations at every opportunity. Indeed, more often than not they prefer to adopt a policy of 'cognitive economy' (Hansen 1980) from one encounter to another and not form impressions unless asked specifically to do so (see Bem 1972); in other words, being almost what has been described as 'mindless' (Langer and Newman 1979; Thorngate 1976). Thorngate (1979) has proposed what can be regarded as a kind of rapprochement between the two extremes: it may be reasonable to entertain the notion of a continuum from purely cognitive to purely habitual along which the thinking person moves from moment to moment. He suggests a 'Principle of Sagacious Allocation' which implies that 'whenever possible, the brain will favour cognitive processes which rely on perception and long-term memory to those which rely heavily on short-term memory and long intervals of undivided attention' (p. 290). Furthermore, when faced with a problem (e.g. evaluating a person speaking in a particular way), judges in the 'real world might adopt more parsimonious strategies than information processing, decision-making and high level cognitive activities that stretch attention span and short-term memory, and actually ask others for clarification, stall, copy others, publicize the dilemma, and seek advice, etc.' (pp. 309–10). Perhaps more often than not, speakers are evaluated by comparing them with previously stored schemata and prototypes (see Gilovich 1981) and more particularly those which are most easily accessible, recently activated, and processed extensively previously (Wyer 1980). Hence, involvement and prolonged experience with nonstandard speakers can probably affect one's base-rate information as well as evaluations about them in terms of the positivity –negativity of the events associated with them as stored in long-term memory.

One basic postulate of the many subtly different models of the acquisition and use of social knowledge is that the types of schema activated in memory for use in interpreting the present information depend on the purpose for which the information is being used. For instance, Hamilton, Katz and Leier's (1980) subjects recalled more behavioural descriptions of a stimulus person when provided with a prior directive requiring them to form an impression of that person than when asked simply to recall the items from the outset. Although intuitively perhaps a surprising result, the authors commented that 'the process of forming an impression inherently involves integrating the available information into an organized cognitive representation of the target person. Such organization of information would facilitate later retrieval of the individual descriptive items' (p. 1062). In a more recent study, Hoffman, Mischel and Mazze (1981) found that subjects who had been provided with recall as opposed to impression-formation instructions (or sets), organized a series of episodes primarily according to the character's goals rather than in terms of the latter's traits. Newtson and his colleagues in a series of investigations have also shown that the purpose of viewing an interaction can determine how one perceives its behavioural units (e.g. Massad, Hubbard and Newtson 1979). In this paradigm, subjects are typically asked to watch a video-recording and signal the beginning and end of each behavioural frame which is meaningful to them; that is, they are asked to 'chunk' the episodes (see chapter 6). Although there is a controversy concerning the theoretical status of such so-called 'unitizations', one interpretation is that during the 'breakpoints' between units those features necessary for the reconstruction of the behaviour enter long-term memory. In other words, the 'essentials', whether it be in a script or theme format, are coded for retrieval. Obviously, the finer grained the behavioural perceptions, that is the larger the number of breakpoints perceived over a set period of time, the more information that is potentially discriminable and codable. Newtson was able to obtain data suggesting that greater unitization was associated with greater confidence in impression formation and facilitated the internal attribution of behaviour and dispositional qualities. Our understanding of the processes of behavioural unitization is of course very far from complete (see Cohen and Ebbesen 1979), but nevertheless their seeming relationship to causal attributions and confidence ratings appears a promising avenue for language attitudes research. For example, it is possible that under some circumstances the perception of a nonstandard speech style and subsequent categorization into a negatively viewed group means that unitization as a reflector of cognitive attention decreases. Or is the mediating mechanism far more complex than this? Certainly, speaker evaluation studies fall into a very peculiar genre where the purpose of the task is blatantly obvious, viz, impression formation. Obviously, different modes of interpretation, unitization and schema activation will arise when subjects do not find themselves under conditions which are so explicitly predetermined in terms of purpose as, for example, in communication tasks where evaluation is incidental (Giles and Farrar 1979; Sebastian *et al.* 1980). In the same way as the vacuous nature of the independent variables in the previous section predisposed demand characteristics of their own kind, so too do the cognitive demands of the speaker evaluation paradigm create their own problems. Nevertheless, rich rewards in terms of theory-building will undoubtedly be reaped by studies which (a) manipulate cognitive complexity, cognitive responses (see Petty and Cacioppo 1977; also chapter 12), subjective definitions of social group membership and the perceived purpose of judgements, (b) measure unitizations, causal attributions and trait inferences, and also (c) explore the cognitive make-up of these judgements. Whilst social cognition may have its continuing debates and critiques (such as portraying people as generally 'too' thoughtful before action), the area has also been taken to task for reducing large-scale social processes to the level of cognitive individualism; an issue with which we shall jostle shortly.

The social context

Virtually every author in this volume argues the need to examine contextual constraints on language attitudes more thoroughly in the future (see also Romaine 1980; Smith and Bailey 1980). For instance, in chapter 1 we ourselves underlined the need, which is complemented by recent European revivals of psychological interest in social representations (e.g. Moscovici and Farr, in press), to consider the *macro*-contextual effects of sociostructural factors such as a language's institutional support on attitudes towards that variety (see Roberts and Williams 1980). In addition, chapters 2, 8 and 9 focused importantly upon the developments which have occurred recently in our understanding of how language variables influence the decision-making process in educational, occupational and medical arenas (see also chapter 6; Brennan and Brennan 1983; Seggie 1983; Seggie, Fulmizi and Stewart 1982). Moreover, chapter 6 in particular and in detail, points to the fact that we should be at least as concerned with *subjective* as objective characteristics of situation, the latter being characteristic of much traditional socio-linguistic research (see chapter 3 and Bourhis 1981b). Giles, Hewstone and St Clair (in press) illustrate the parameters of the problem as follows:

> objectively describing a social situation *as* a formal interview on a serious topic with a 90-year-old black woman will have little predictive value concerning her likely speech patterns if she herself defines the interview informally, considers the subject matter irrelevant and trivial and feels 'White' and 50 years of age. In other words, speech is far more likely to be dependent on how speakers cognitively represent their characteristics and subjectively define the scene than any objective classification imposed from without.

As mentioned previously with regard to perceived purpose of encounter, most of the speaker evaluation studies are contextually homogeneous (see Lee 1971; Giles and Bourhis 1976) but they are also homogeneous with respect to the manner in which listeners' judgements of speakers are elicited. For instance, people do not only form 'private' language attitudes when explicitly required by pencil and paper means in a laboratory situation while listening to a taperecording. Very often people publicly discuss and socially compare (see Feldman and Ruble. 1981; Festinger 1954) their views without recourse to prolonged individual meditation about them when listening to others in a whole variety of casual and formal contexts. Indeed the work on what was originally regarded as the 'risky-shift' phenomenon (Kogan and Wallach 1964) but recently regarded as the more general 'polarization' issue (Moscovici and Doise 1974; Myers and Lamm 1976) would predict that people will make more extreme judgements and attributions after group discussion than the average of their individual assessments beforehand (see Hewstone and Jaspars, 1982; and also Giles, Harrison, Smith and Freeman 1981, Taylor and Royer 1980, in the language attitudes domain). In other words, if they were initially favourable they will be even more positive, whereas if they were unfavourably disposed at the outset they will become more so. Obviously the nature, structure and purpose of the group discussion will also be influential factors (see Poole 1981 for a discussion of the various ways decisions develop in different small groups). Indeed, such notions underscore the malleability of language attitudes (see Williams 1974) within the framework of latitudes of acceptance and rejection (Sherif, Sherif and Nebergall 1965). In any case, the nature of evaluative settings and subjects' definitions of them are likely to affect judgemental decisions considerably as will respondents' perceptions of the judgemental language used on the rating scales (see Eiser 1980 and also chapter 12).

Recently, there has been a flurry of research activity into the social psychology of social situations (see Argyle, Furnham and Graham 1981 for a review). Although the specific demands of and changes in particular intimate interpersonal relationships do seriously affect people's cognitions of them (Forgas and Dobosz 1980; Kotler and Chetwynd 1980), the work of Wish (1978) demonstrates that people use more or less the same finite set of dimensions to construe quite a wide range of communicative settings. For instance, he has shown that people conceive of interactions (see also chapter 6) in terms of the five dimensions of cooperative–competitive, task-related–not task-related, equal–not equal, formal–informal, and relaxed–tense. Nevertheless, the dimensions used by different people (and subcultures also) may vary in complexity; and even when different individuals do use common dimensions, different weights may be placed upon them and the same communication episodes may actually be seen at opposite poles of the same dimension (Forgas 1980). Therefore, it can be hypothesized that greater weight would be placed on social attractiveness/solidarity than competence/status dimensions by listener–judges when rating a nonstandard dialect speaker who is believed to be in a casual, cooperative and relaxed situation but vice-versa if that same situation is construed by other listeners to be more tense, competitive and formal.

Obviously, other dimensions of situations (e.g. their perceived social difficulty, Bryant and Trower 1974) are also likely to have their evaluative consequences, but none probably more so than that highlighted by recent research into the dynamics of intergroup relations. In this regard, Tajfel and Turner (1979, 34) consider two types of interaction:

At one extreme is the interaction between two or more individuals which is *fully* determined by their interpersonal relationships and individual characteristics and not at all affected by various social groups or categories to which they respectively belong. The other extreme consists of interactions between two or more individuals (or groups of individuals) which are *fully* determined by their respective memberships of various social groups or categories, and are not at all affected by the inter-individual personal relationships between the people involved.

These two extremes are considered as anchoring a bipolar continuum (although Stephenson 1981 has perhaps rightly argued for their orthogonality) labelled inter-individual and group encounters (Brown and Turner 1981), and it has been argued that the more members of a group conceive of an encounter as being towards the group pole:

> the more uniformity will they show in their behaviour towards members of the relevant outgroups . . . and . . . the more they will tend to treat members of the outgroup as undifferentiated items in a unified social category rather than in terms of their individual characteristics (Tajfel and Turner 1979, 36).

Indeed, Turner (1981b, 1982) has suggested that as individuals conceive of a situation as moving towards this pole they will tend to be calling less upon processes of personal identity and moving more towards the forces of social identity. Moreover, Turner suggests that this will result in 'self-stereotyping' whereby individuals 'deindividuate' themselves and take on characteristic attributes, perceptions, and cognitions of their ingroup. In this sense, it has been argued that 'individualistic' social cognition studies are not sophisticated enough to take account of social identification and intergroup processes which characterize and are unique to intergroup behaviour even when it is in a one-to-one situation (Tajfel 1981; Turner and Giles 1981). Certainly, speaker evaluation studies with their apparent de-emphasis on individual characteristics of stimulus speakers may often be firmly planted in the intergroup arena for judges (see Delia 1972).

The question arises of course as to what factors promote individuals' perceiving the situation more in terms of their social than their personal identities (i.e. in group rather than inter-individual terms). While authors have pointed to such a factor as the relative numbers of in- and outgroup members present (e.g. McGuire, McGuire, Child and Fujioka 1978), it is undoubtedly true that the experimenter or interviewer can also be an important source of influence on the data gathered in psychological as well as linguistic investigations (see Innes and Fraser 1971, and Greenbaum 1977b respectively). For instance, a number of studies have now shown that the language in which bilinguals take a test will likely endear them towards expressing the values and attitudes associated with the language of the setting (Botha 1970; Ervin 1964; Feldman 1968), or at least affect the nature of the response in some other complex evaluative manner (Gardner, Kirby, Pablo and Castillo 1975; Gibbons 1983; Price, Fluck and Giles 1983). However, Yang and Bond (1980) found that when certain Chinese bilinguals were 'forced' to undergo a task in English they became more traditionally 'Chinese' rather than westernized in their values; a process they termed 'ethnic affirmation'. This research implies that under some conditions an investigator who is perceived by judges to be a member of a social outgroup and who has speech patterns (as well as outgroup-oriented items on the response questionnaire) bonding this impression can affect judgements made by the listeners in ways which could be mediated by the latter's sense of group belongingness. In other words, judges who perceive the experimental situation (including the experimenter) and the stimulus variables in an inter-individual fashion might be evaluatively most differentiating on person-oriented traits and with a bias favouring standard speakers. Those who construe the situation more in intergroup terms might be more discriminating on group-oriented traits (particularly group solidarity and loyalty ones; see next section) and with a bias which favours their own ingroup. The attitudinal content for the latter subjects might *function* (depending on the context) so as to justify their intergroup actions, or to explain their behaviours (towards members of the outgroup in the past and future), or to differentiate them positively from the outgroup (see Tajfel's 1981 functional analysis of social stereotyping).

Despite our concern to generate interest in the details of cognitive processes among language scientists, we ought not to lose sight of the fact that construal processes themselves remain intimately linked to objective parameters of situations. The significance of our consideration of the situation concept (see also Smith, Giles and Hewstone 1982) is not that it somehow frees the analyst from the task of empirical description but that it makes the callibration of situational parameters in formulae for linguistic and judgemental variations dependent on their psychological significance.

The dependent variables

As can be seen throughout this volume, members of speech communities do not have a single unitary attitude toward two contrasting language varieties. The extent to which language variety A is or is not preferred over language variety B depends upon the situation in which the assessment is made. In this vein, the conceptual distinction between the previous and present sections is almost impossible to draw successfully. The primary situational effects on language attitudes can be represented in terms of two dimensions as depicted in Figure 13.1 and discussed in our Prologue. First, the extent to which the situation is construed as status-stressing or solidarity-stressing at a particular time (Fishman 1971; see chapter 1) affects the relative weighting given to the status and solidarity values associated with the target varieties. Second, the extent to which the respondent defines the situation in terms of group membership rather than in terms of the personal characteristics of the people involved (see previous section) affects the symbolic values accorded the two varieties. An interpretation of the situation in terms of role relationships (see Brown and Fraser 1979; Brown and Levinson 1979) is intermediate between group- and person-oriented, and it is also more status-stressing than a person-oriented situation.

Within sociolinguistics, situations are viewed in terms of the setting, purpose and participants (e.g. Brown and Fraser 1979) and in terms of their overall formality or domain (Fishman 1971). These characteristics can be used – but with recourse to the 'subjective' proviso discussed previously – to predict the location of a particular language attitude situation within the two-dimensional model proposed here. For example, formal, public and intergroup situations tend to be more status-stressing than informal, private and ingroup situations. The school, government and work domains tend to be status-oriented whereas home, family and neighbourhood domains tend to be solidarity-oriented. Situations involving strangers are more likely to be status- and group-oriented than are situations involving friends. Also, two-person interactions are more likely to be person-centred with an audience absent than with one present. In addition, as Giles, Hewstone and St Clair (in press) argue, use of the standard or ingroup lan-

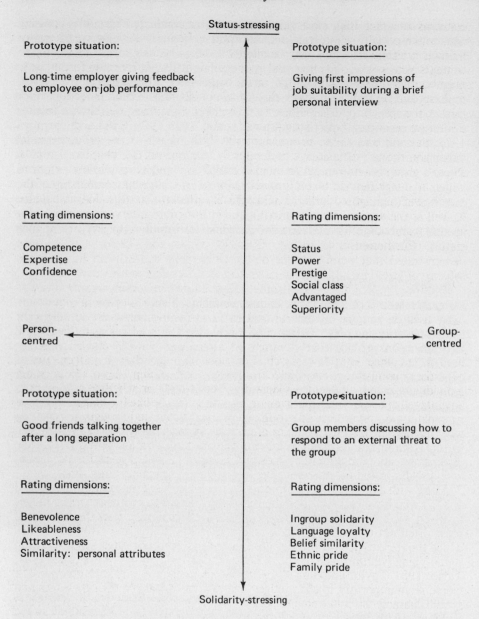

Figure 13.1: Perceived language attitude situations and evaluative ratings vary along two dimensions.

guage variety can cause a situation to be viewed as more or less status-stressing or group-oriented.

The value of this two-dimensional model can be illustrated with a number of important language attitudes issues. One of the major critiques of past research concerns the fact that most studies have been conducted in status-stressing situations especially schools (see chapters 4 and 7). Hence, the evaluative pattern of findings typically emerging may be altered if the assessments were conducted in contexts where group identity and group solidarity were more important (e.g. neighbourhood recreation centres, family situations). Also, whereas the typical topic spoken on tape in speaker evaluation studies has been either scholarly or formal, the speech topic (e.g. home *vs* school) has sometimes been shown to alter evaluative reactions importantly (Carranza and Ryan 1975; Ryan and Carranza 1975; Sassoon and Giles, in preparation). With regard to the group/personal dimension the use of language preference questionnaires (see chapters 1 and 4) forces a group-orientation while speaker evaluation studies vary in the extent to which an intergroup context is imposed. Moreover, the group membership of the interviewer (highlighted earlier) would probably affect the status/solidarity balance as well as the degree of group orientation (with ingroup interviewers enhancing solidarity and outgroup interviewers from a high status outgroup likely to enhance status). Furthermore, Christian, Gadfield, Giles and Taylor (1976) have demonstrated that manipulations of the assessment context can increase the salience of group membership in expressing attitudes and cognitions.

As Brown (1965) argued, the status and solidarity dimensions apply to inter-personal relations as well as to intergroup relations. The measurement scales typi-cally used in language attitudes studies can be grouped both in terms of status/solidarity and person/group centredness. Thus, as seen in Figure 13.1, these two dimensions provide a useful framework for organizing the diverse sets of scales used in language attitude research. For example, even though judgements of expertise or competence may derive from group membership, they are much more individualistic than judgements regarding social class or whether a speaker is advantaged or disadvantaged. Likewise, a speaker may be like the judge in terms of personal traits, regardless of group memberships; but judgements concerning whether his/her beliefs are similar are based primarily on group categorization. Future research could benefit greatly from a systematic development of evaluative dimensions, and the present framework provides an initial basis for predicting which scales would be more sensitive in particular assessment situations.

Along with a number of contributors to this volume (see for example chapters 8 and 12) who have focused upon the function of language attitudes for the judges involved, we believe that the *content* of these reflect in large part the functional roles, often not of unitary dimensionality (Gardner, Kirby and Arboleda 1971), which the stereotypes perform for group members. Recent analyses of intergroup stereotyping will undoubtedly be of considerable value in this vein (Tajfel 1981; Taylor 1981; Taylor and Simard 1979). Moreover, and in line with chapter 2, it would seem important to elicit judges' *beliefs* about speakers, their messages and speech characteristics (see chapter 1) as well as their evaluations (see Agheyisi and Fishman 1970; Sebastian and Ryan in press); for as Delia (1976, p. 153) has commented, 'beliefs conceived as substantive cognitions play a major role in linking attitudes to anticipated behaviour' (see Fishman 1969). Indeed, the controversy in social psychology as to whether attitudes cause behaviour or vice-versa has continued over two decades. Although not allowing us to specify precisely when language attitudes may predict overt behaviours toward a target speaker, this literature (see Ajzen and Fishbein 1980; Bentler and Speckart 1980) nevertheless does allow us some insights into when one might expect causal relationships to be diluted.

Bentler and Speckart (1980, 226) propose on the basis of previous findings that this will happen when there is a:

temporal instability of attitudes . . . lack of volitional control in behaviour . . . lack of direct experience on which to base attitudes . . . measures of attitudes and behaviour are not denoted according to identical action, target and context entities . . . the measurement of attitudes is subject to appreciable measurement error or when the behavioural criterion is too narrow and contains appreciable error variance as well.

Certainly, the issue of understanding how and when language attitudes cause particular behaviours in applied settings is likely to depend not only on future developments in structural equation analysis of the sort espoused by Bentler and Speckart (see also chapter 8), but also on further advances in our understanding of subjective situational norms and interactional rules (see Higgins 1980; McKirnan and Hamayan 1980; Planalp and Tracy 1980; Sigman 1980) as well as on various motivational strategies such as positive self/group presentation (Smith, Giles and Hewstone 1982). Attention ought also be directed towards devising more diverse and sophisticated measures of behavioural intention and actual behavioural responses towards linguistic variation (see chapters 2, 3, 9 and 11). A promising step in that direction, Rosenfeld's (1978) research has shown how listeners' subtle nonverbal reactions to their speakers can markedly affect, and sometimes even control the latters' speech actions (see in this regard the notion of 'behavioural confirmation', Snyder 1980). In any event, perceptions of episodic structure, normative demands of situation, inter-individual and intergroup construals need to be incorporated into a fine grain analysis of language beliefs, attributions, attitudes and behaviours.

Conclusions

For some, the foregoing may have appeared a potpourri of research areas in social psychology which have significance for language attitudes, without a concrete propositional bite. Language attitudes as an area of sociolinguistic inquiry has been criticized for amassing descriptive data *ad infinitum*. Nevertheless, we feel concrete propositions or a theory cannot be forthcoming until we have unearthed yet more descriptive data . . . *but of the type* espoused in this Epilogue. At the same time however, not only have we suggested a range of empirical hypotheses throughout this chapter together with an embryonic model of the relationship between evaluative context and rating scales, but we have also drawn attention to the types of independent variables, cognitive processes, contextual definitions and dependent variables that are amongst those most likely to yield fruitful avenues of research in the near future. In this regard, categorization effects, attributional principles, acquaintanceship processes, cognitive complexity, perceived base-rates and goal structures, inference principles, social identification, interactional definitions, and unitizations have been highlighted. This in addition to our speculative, comparative models for conceptualizing language attitudes in the Prologue, should allow for greater theoretical sophistication in the future. A good speaker evaluation study should now for instance comment on the socio-cultural and political context of the macro-situation in such a way as to make it comparable to other situations, consider the constraints on generality imposed by the use of the particular independent variables chosen, take care with the selection of the dependent variables (e.g. how they relate to status and solidarity or some alternative dimensions) and determine (if not even manipulate) their perceived relationship to anticipated behaviours and subjects' cognitive apparatus and subjective contextual definitions. Information along these lines, and perhaps especially in the types of applied settings discussed in chapter 9, then will allow us to know which variables are evaluatively important when, how and why. Indeed, while much of this has been aimed at stimulating speaker evaluation research into the cognitive domain, it is hoped that this will not happen at the expense of exploring the question of why people assess linguistic variations as they do; that is, a functional orientation is extremely important and should be complemented by methodological eclecticism (see chapters 1, 2, 3, 4 and 6). All this in the broader context of more cross-national and interdisciplinary activity will permit the development of a wide ranging theory of language attitudes which can more directly focus on social planning and policy issues.

Finally, we have no desire to undermine the recent and obviously significant empirical and theoretical advances in this area documented in the previous chapters. Such a challenging and exciting set of theoretical prospects as we have just entertained would have been unthinkable and perhaps even threatening a decade ago. However, we must not be complacent, and we hope that this volume will be an important step along the road to where social psychologists will understand more clearly how language variables can determine importantly the ways in which we form and change our attitudes; sociolinguists will appreciate more clearly the complexities and consequences of attitude, inference and identification processes which cognitively mediate speech; and language planners will realize (and especially after chapters 3 and 10 and also Stevens 1983) that language attitude research allows them a crucial source for formulating their policies (as well as monitoring their subsequent effects) which will of necessity aid in their implementation and ultimate success.

References

Aboud, F. E. 1976: Social developmental aspects of language. *Papers in Linguistics* **9**, 15–37.

Aboud, F. E., Clément, R. and Taylor, D. M. 1974: Evaluational reactions to discrepancies between social class and language. *Sociometry* **37**, 239–50.

Aboud, F. E. and Skerry, S. A. 1980: *Ethnic attitude development*. Paper presented at the Fifth Conference of the International Association of Cross-Cultural Psychology, India.

Addington, D. W. 1968: The relationship of selected vocal characteristics to personality perception. *Speech Monographs* **35**, 429–503.

Adorno, W. 1973: *The attitudes of selected Mexican and Mexican American parents in regards to bilingual/bicultural education*. Unpublished doctoral dissertation, United States International University.

Agheyisi, R. and Fishman, J. A. 1970: Language attitude studies: A brief survey of methodological approaches. *Anthropological Linguistics* **12**, 131–57.

Aguirre, A., Jr. 1978: Chicano sociolinguistics: A review and proposal. *The Bilingual Review/La Revista Bilingue* **5**, 91–8.

Ajzen, I. and Fishbein, M. 1977: Attitude-behaviour relations: A theoretical analysis and review of empirical research. *Psychological Bulletin* **84**, 888–913.

―――― 1980: *Understanding attitudes and predicting social behaviour*. Englewood Cliffs: Prentice-Hall.

Albo, X. 1970: Social constraints on Cochabamba Quechua. Dissertation Series 19, Latin American Studies Program, Cornell University, Ithaca.

Alleyne, M. C. 1975: Sociolinguistic research in Latin America. In Ohannessian, S., Ferguson, C. A. and Polome, E. C., editors, *Language surveys in developing nations* (Arlington: Center for Applied Linguistics) 179–89.

Allport, G. W. 1954: The historical background of modern social psychology. In Lindzey, G., editor, *Handbook of social psychology* (Cambridge, Mass.: Addison-Wesley) 3–56.

―――― 1966: Attitudes in the history of social psychology. In Jahoda, M and Warren, N., editors, *Attitudes: Selected readings* (Harmondsworth: Penguin Books) 15–21.

Amastae, J. and Elias-Olivares, L. 1978: Attitudes toward varieties of Spanish. In Paradis, M., editor, *The fourth Lacus forum* 1977 (Columbia: Hornbeam Press) 286–302.

Ammon, U. 1977: School problems of regional dialect speakers: ideology and reality. Results and methods of empirical investigations in Southern Germany. *Journal of Pragmatics* 1, 47–68.

_____ 1979: Regionaldialekte und Einheitssprache in der Bundesrepublik Deutschland (BRD). *International Journal of the Sociology of Language* 21.

Anderson, C., Fine, M. G. and Johnson, J. L. 1983: Black talk on television: a constructionist approach to viewers' perceptions of Black English Vernacular in Roots II. *Journal of Multilingual and Multicultural Development*.

Anderson, N. H. 1968: Likableness ratings of 555 personality-trait words. *Journal of Personality and Social Psychology* 9, 272–9.

d'Anglejan, A. 1979: French in Quebec. *Journal of Communication* 29, 54–63.

d'Anglejan, A. and Tucker, G. R. 1973: Sociolinguistic correlates of speech styles in Quebec. In Shuy, R. W. and Fasold, R. W., editors, *Language attitudes: Current trends and prospects* (Washington: Georgetown University Press) 1–27.

Anisfeld, M., Bogo, N. and Lambert, W. E. 1962: Evaluational reactions to accented speech. *Journal of Abnormal and Social Psychology* 65, 223–31.

Anisfeld, M. and Lambert, W. E. 1961: Social and psychological variables in learning Hebrew. *Journal of Abnormal and Social Psychology* 63, 524–9.

Anisfeld, E. and Lambert, W. E. 1964: Evaluational reactions of bilingual and monolingual children to spoken language. *Journal of Abnormal Social Psychology* 69, 89–97.

Apperson, G. L. 1929: *English proverbs and proverbial phrases*. London: J. M. Dent & Sons.

Apple, W., Streeter, L. A. and Krauss, R. M. 1979: Effects of pitch and speech rate on personal attributions. *Journal of Personality and Social Psychology* 37, 715–27.

Applegate, J. A. and Delia, J. G. 1980: Person-centred speech, psychological development, and the contexts of language usage. In St Clair, R. N. and Giles, H., editors, *The social and psychological contexts of language* (Hillsdale: Lawrence Erlbaum Associates) 245–82.

Aracil, L. V. 1966: A short history of Valencia. *Identity* 24, 5–15.

_____ 1973: Bilingualism as a myth. *Interamerican Review* 2 (4), 1–6.

Argyle, M. 1969: *Social interaction*. Chicago: Aldine Atherton.

Argyle, M., Furnham, A. and Graham, J. 1981: *Social situations*. Cambridge: Cambridge University Press.

Aristotle 1932: *The rhetoric*. Cooper, L., translator. New York: Appleton & Company.

Arnov, V. B. 1978: *Analysis of the effects of language on impression formation: Evaluation reactions of Miami-Dade Community College students to the voices of Cuban-Americans speaking in English and in Spanish*. Unpublished doctoral dissertation, Florida Atlantic University.

Aronovitch. C. D. 1976: The voice of personality: Stereotyped judgements and their relation to voice quality and sex of speaker. *Journal of Social Psychology* 99, 207–20.

Arthur, B., Farrar, D. and Bradford, G. 1974: Evaluation reactions of college students to dialect differences in the English of Mexican-Americans. *Language and Speech* 17, 255–70.

Arvey, R. D. 1979: Unfair discrimination in the employment interview: Legal and psychological aspects. *Psychological Bulletin* **86**, 736–65.

Asch, S. E. 1948: The doctrine of suggestion, prestige and imitation in social psychology. *Psychological Review* **55**, 250–76.

Attinasi, J. 1979: Language attitudes in a New York Puerto Rican community. In Padilla, R. V., editor, *Bilingual education and public policy in the United States* (Ypsilanti: Bilingual Programs, Eastern Michigan University) 408–60.

Badia I Margarit, A. M. 1962: Some aspects of bilingualism among cultured people of Catalonia. In Lunt, H. L., editor, *Proceedings of the Ninth International Congress of Linguists* (The Hague: Mouton) 366–73.

_____ 1969: *La llengua dels Barcelonins*, vol. I. Barcelona: Edicions 62.

_____ 1973: *La llengua Catalana ahir i avui*. Barcelona: Curial.

Baehr, H. 1980: Women and media. Oxford: Pergamon Press. Special Issue of *Women's Studies International Quarterly* **3** (1).

Baer, J. 1976: *How to be an assertive (not aggressive) woman in life, in love, and on the job: A total guide to self-assertiveness*. New York: New American Library.

Bailey, K. M. and Galvan, L. 1977: Accentedness in the classroom. *Aztlan* **8**, 83–97.

Baird, S. J. 1969: *Employment interview speech: A social dialect study in Austin, Texas*. Unpublished dissertation, University of Texas at Austin.

Baker, S. 1966: *The Australian language*. Sydney: Currawong.

Balibar, R. and Laporte, D. 1974: *Le Français national*. Paris: Hachette.

Ball, P. 1980: *Stereotypes of Anglo-Saxon and non-Anglo-Saxon accents: Some exploratory studies with the matched-guise technique*. Unpublished manuscript, University of Tasmania.

Barbeau, V. 1970: *Le français du Canada*. Quebec: Librairie Garneau.

Barber, B. 1979: Communication between doctor and patient: What compliance research shows. In Alatis, J. E. and Tucker, G. R., editors *Language in public life. GURT 79* (Washington: Georgetown University Press) 119–25.

Barker, G. C. 1947: Social functions of language in a Mexican American community. *Acta Americana* **4**, 189–92.

Bart, P. 1977: Biological determinism and sexism: Is it all in the ovaries? In the Ann Arbor Michigan Science for the People Editorial Collective, editor, *Biology as a social weapon* (Minneapolis: Burgess Publishing Company).

Bartley, D. E. 1970. The importance of the attitude factor in language dropout: A preliminary investigation of group and sex differences. *Foreign Language Annals* **3**, 383–93.

Baskett, G. D. and Freedle, R. O. 1974: Aspects of language and the social perception of lying. *Journal of Psycholinguistic Research* **3**, 117–30.

Bates, E. 1976: *Language and context: The acquisition of pragmatics*. New York: Academic Press.

Batstone, D. and Tuomi, S. K. 1981: Perceptual characteristics of female voices. *Language and Speech* **24**, 111–23.

Bavendam, J. 1980: *Predictions of effects of reduced message comprehension*. Unpublished manuscript, the University of Iowa.

Bazalgue, G. 1973: Les organizations occitanes. *Les Temps Modernes* **324–6**, 140–62.

Beardsmore, H. 1971: *Le français regional de Bruxelles*. Bruxelles: Presse Universitaire de Bruxelles.

Bec, P. 1973: *La langue Occitane*. Collection Que Sais-Je? Paris: Presse Universitaire de France.

Becker, H. S. 1973: *Outsiders: Study in the sociology of deviance*. New York: The Free Press.

Bede, V. 1962: On schemes and tropes. Tanenhause, G. H., translator. *Quarterly Journal of Speech* **48**, 237–53.

Beebe, L., 1981: Social and situational factors affecting the communicative strategy of dialect code-switching. *International Journal of the Sociology of Language* **30**, 139–46.

Bem, D. J. 1972: Self-perception theory. In Berkowitz, L., editor, *Advances in experimental social psychology* **6** (New York: Academic Press) 1–62.

Bennett, R. and Eckman, J. 1973: Attitudes toward aging: A critical examination of recent literature and implications for future research. In Eisdorfer, C. and Powell, M.P., editors, *The psychology of adult development and aging* (Washington, DC: American Psychological Association).

Bentahila, A. 1981: *Attitudinal Aspects of Arabic-French Bilingualism in Morocco*. Unpublished doctoral dissertation. University College of North Wales, Bangor.

Bentler, P. M. and Speckart, G., 1980: Attitudes 'cause' behaviours: A structural equation analysis. *Journal of Personality and Social Psychology* **40**, 226–38.

Berechree, P. and Ball, P. 1979: *A study of sex, accent-broadness and Australian sociolinguistic identity*. Paper presented at the Second Australian Conference on Language and Speech, Melbourne.

Berger, C. R. 1979: Beyond initial interaction: Uncertainty, understanding, and the development of interpersonal relationships. In Giles, H. and St Clair, R. N., editors, *Language and social psychology* (Oxford: Basil Blackwell and Baltimore: University Park Press) 122–44.

_____ 1980: Self-consciousness and the study of interpersonal interaction: Approaches and issues. In Giles, H., Robinson, P. W. and Smith, P. M., editors, *Language: Social psychological perspectives* (Oxford: Pergamon Press) 49–53.

Berger, C. R. and Calabrese, R. J. 1975: Some explorations in initial interaction and beyond: Toward a developmental theory of interpersonal communication. *Human Communication Research* **1**, 99–112.

Berger, C. R. and Roloff, M. E. In press: Thinking about friends and lovers: Social cognition and relational trajectories. In Roloff, M. E. and Berger, C. R., editors, *Social cognition and communication*. Beverly Hills: Sage.

Berk-Seligson, S. 1980: A sociolinguistic view of the Mexican-American speech community: A review of the literature. *Latin American Research Review* **15**, 65–110.

Berkhoffer, R. E., Jr 1979: *The white man's Indian: Images of the American Indian from Columbus to the present*. New York: Vintage.

Berko-Gleason, J. and Perlmann, R. In press: Language acquisition: Interactive and social psychological perspectives. In Giles, H. and St Clair, R., editors, *Recent advances in language, communication and social psychology* (Hillsdale: Lawrence Erlbaum Associates).

Berkowitz, L. and Walster, E. 1976: *Equity theory: Towards a general theory of social interaction.* New York: Academic Press.

Bernardo, D. and Rieu, B. 1973: Conflit linguistique et revendications culturelles en Catalogne-Nord. *Les Temps Modernes* **324-6**, 302-32.

Bernstein, B. 1971: *Class, codes and control, vol. 1: Theoretical studies towards a sociology of language.* London: Routledge & Kegan Paul.

Bernstein, V., Hakel, M. D. and Harlan, A. 1975: The college student as interviewer: A threat to generalizability? *Journal of Applied Psychology* **60**, 266-8.

Berry, J. W. and Kalin, R. 1979: Reciprocity of inter-ethnic attitudes in a multicultural society. *International Journal of Intercultural Relations* **3**, 99-112.

Berry, J. W., Kalin, R. and Taylor, D. M. 1977: *Multiculturalism and ethnic attitudes in Canada.* Ottawa: Minister of Supply and Services, Canada.

Berryman, C. and Wilcox, J. R. 1980: Attitudes toward male and female speech: Experiments on the effects of sex-typical language. *Western Journal of Speech Communication* **44**, 50-9.

Bickerton, D. and Odo, C. 1976: *Change and variation in Hawaiian English*, vol. 2. NSF Report GS-39748. Honolulu: Social Sciences and Linguistics Institute, University of Hawaii.

Bishop, G. D. 1979: Perceived similarity in interracial attitudes and behaviours: The effects of belief and dialect style. *Journal of Applied Social Psychology* **9**, 446-65.

Blakar, R. 1979: Language as a means of social power. In Rommetveit, R. and Blakar, R., editors, *Studies of language, thought and verbal communication* (London: Academic Press) 109-45.

Bliss, A. 1979: The emergence of modern English dialects in Ireland. In Ó Muirithe, D., editor, *The English language in Ireland* (Dublin: Mercier).

Blom, J. P. and Gumperz, J. J. 1972: Social meaning in linguistic structures: Code-switching in Norway. In Gumperz, J. J. and Hymes, D., editors, *Directions in sociolinguistics – Ethnicity of communication* (New York: Holt, Rinehart & Winston) 407-34.

Blum, J. M. 1978: *Pseudoscience and mental ability: The origins and fallacies of the IQ controversy.* New York: Monthly Review Press.

Boller, P. F., Jr 1970: *American thought in transition: The impact of evolutionary naturalism, 1865-1900.* Chicago: Rand McNally & Co.

Bornstein, D. 1978: As meek as a maid: An historical perspective on language for women in courtesy books from the Middle Ages to *Seventeen* Magazine. In Butturff, D. and Epstein, E., editors, *Women's language and style* (Akron: Published with the assistance of the Department of English) 132-8.

Bosmajian, H. 1974: *The language of oppression.* Washington: Public Affairs Press.

Botha, E. 1970: The effect of language on values expressed by bilinguals. *Journal of Social Psychology* **80**, 143-5.

Bouchard-Ryan, E. 1969: Psycholinguistic attitude study. *Studies on language and language behaviour* **viii**, 437-50.

Boudreau-Nelson, L. 1976: Le maintien du français dans les Amériques: Utilité et motivation: Canada et Etats-Unis. In Runte, H. R. and Valdman, A., editors, *Identité culturelle et francophonie dans les Amériques*, vol. 2 (Bloomington: Indiana University) 43–50.

Boulanger, J. O. 1980: *Les français régionaux: Observations sur les recherches actuelles*. Montreal: Office de la Langue Française, Editeur Officiel du Québec.

Bourdieu, P. 1977: L'économie des échanges linguistiques. *Langue Française* **34**, 17–34.

Bourhis, R. Y. 1979: Language in ethnic interaction: A social psychological approach. In Giles, H. and St Jacques, B., editors, *Language and ethnic relations* (Oxford: Pergamon Press) 117–42.

——— 1981a: Cross-cultural communication in Montreal: Some survey and field data after Bill 101. *Paper presented at the 42nd Annual Convention of the Canadian Psychological Association, Toronto*.

Bourhis, R. Y. 1981b: Attitudes towards language usage and subjective vitality perceptions. *Paper presented at the 42nd Annual Conference of the Canadian Psychological Association, Toronto*.

Bourhis, R. Y. and Genesee, F. 1980: Evaluative reactions to code-switching strategies in Montreal. In Giles, H., Robinson, W. P. and Smith, P., editors, *Language: Social psychological perspectives* (Oxford: Pergamon Press) 335–43.

Bourhis, R. Y. and Giles, H. 1976: The language of cooperation in Wales: A field study. *Language Sciences* **42**, 13–16.

——— 1977: The language of intergroup distinctiveness. In Giles, H., editor, *Language, ethnicity, and intergroup relations* (London: Academic Press) 119–36.

Bourhis, R. Y., Giles, H. and Lambert, W. E. 1975: Social consequences of accommodating one's style of speech: A cross-national investigation. *International Journal of the Sociology of Language* **6**, 55–72.

Bourhis, R. Y., Giles, H., Leyens, J. P. and Tajfel, H. 1979: Psycholinguistic distinctiveness: Language divergence in Belgium. In Giles, H. and St Clair, R. N., editors, *Language and Social Psychology* (Oxford: Basil Blackwell and Baltimore: University Park Press) 158–85.

Bourhis, R. Y., Giles, H. and Rosenthal, D. 1981: Notes on the construction of a 'subjective vitality questionnaire' for ethnolinguistic groups. *Journal of Multilingual and Multicultural Development* **2**, 145–55.

Bourhis, R. Y., Giles, H. and Tajfel, H. 1973: Language as a determinant of Welsh identity. *European Journal of Social Psychology* **3**, 447–60.

Bowers, J. W. 1963: Language intensity, social introversion, and attitude change. *Speech Monographs* **30**, 345–52.

Bradac, J. J., Bowers, J. W. and Courtright, J. A. 1979: Three language variables in communication research: Intensity, immediacy, and diversity. *Human Communication Research* **5**, 257–69.

——— 1980: Lexical variations in intensity, immediacy, and diversity: An axiomatic theory and causal model. In St Clair, R. N. and Giles, H., editors, *The social and psychological contexts of language* (Hillsdale: Lawrence Erlbaum Associates) 193–223.

Bradac, J. J., Courtright, J. A. and Bowers, J. W. 1980: Effects of intensity, immediacy, and diversity upon receiver attitudes toward a belief-discrepant message and its source. In Giles, H., Robinson, W. P. and Smith, P., editors,

Language: Social psychological perspectives (Oxford and New York: Pergamon Press) 217–21. ·

Bradac, J. J., Courtright, J. A., Schmidt, G. and Davies, R. A. 1976: The effects of perceived status and linguistic diversity upon judgements of speaker attributes and message effectiveness. *Journal of Psychology* 93, 213–20.

Bradac, J. J., Davies, R. A., Courtright, J. A., Desmond, R. J. and Murdock, J. I. 1977: Richness of vocabulary: An attributional analysis. *Psychological reports* 41, 1131–4.

Bradac, J. J., Desmond, R. J. and Murdock, J. I. 1977: Diversity and density: Lexically determined evaluative and informational consequences of linguistic complexity. *Communication Monographs* 44, 273–83.

Bradac, J. J., Hemphill, M. R. and Tardy, C. H. 1981: Language style on trial: Effects of 'powerful' and 'powerless' speech upon judgements of victims and villains. *Western Journal of Speech Communication* 45, 327–41.

Bradac, J. J., Hosman, L. A. and Tardy, C. H. 1978: Reciprocal disclosures and language intensity: Attributional consequences. *Communication monographs* 45, 1–17.

Bradac, J. J., Konsky, C. W. and Davies, R. A. 1976: Two studies of the effects of linguistic diversity upon judgements of communicator attributes and message effectiveness. *Communication Monographs* 43, 70–9.

Bradac, J. J., Konsky, C. W., and Elliott, N. D. 1976: Verbal behaviour of interviewees: The effects of several situational variables on productivity, disfluency, and lexical diversity. *Journal of Communication Disorders* 9, 211–25.

Bradac, J. J., Martin, L. W., Elliott, N. D. and Tardy, C. H. 1980: On the neglected side of linguistic science: Multivariate studies of sentence judgement. *Linguistics, An Inter-disciplinary Journal of the Language Sciences.*

Bradac, J. J., Sandell, K. I. and Wenner, L. A. 1979: The phenomenology of evidence: Information-source utility in decision making. *Communication Quarterly* 27, 35–46.

Bradac, J. J., Schneider, M. J., Hemphill, M. R. and Tardy, C. H. 1980: Consequences of language intensity and compliance-gaining strategies in an initial heterosexual encounter. In Giles, H., Robinson, W. P. and Smith, P., editors, *Language: Social psychological perspectives* (Oxford: Pergamon Press) 71–5.

Bradley, R. 1976: Bilingual education and language maintenance in Acadian Louisiana. In Snyder, E. and Valdman, A., editors, *Identité culturelle et francophonie dans les Amériques*, vol. 2 (Québec: Les Presses de l'Université Laval) 62–80.

Brainard, C. H. 1977: *A comparison of the attitudes toward bilingual education of Cuban, Mexican American, Puerto Rican and Anglo parents in Palm Beach County, Florida.* Unpublished doctoral dissertation, Florida State University.

Braunstein, W., Köberl, J. and Stuckler, J. 1979: Vorurteile gegenüber Dialektsprechern. *Klagenfurter Beiträge zur Sprachwissenschaft* 5, 1–9.

Brekke, A. M. 1973: *Evaluational reactions of adolescent and pre-adolescent Mexican-American and Anglo-American students to selected samples of spoken English.* Unpublished doctoral dissertation, University of Minnesota.

Brennan, E. M. and Brennan, J. S. 1981a: Accent scaling and language attitudes: Reactions to Mexican-American English speech. *Language and Speech* **24**, 207–21.

_____ 1981b: Measurements of accent and attitude toward Mexican-American speech. *Journal of Psycholinguistic Research* **10**, 487–501.

_____ 1983: Language attitudes and service delivery judgements of social workers toward Spanish-accented speakers. *Journal of Multilingual and Multicultural Development*, in press.

Brennan, E. M., Carranza, M. A. and Ryan, E. B. 1980: Language attitudes of Mexican-American adolescents in two midwestern cities. In Schach, P., editor, *Languages in conflict: Linguistic acculturation on the Great Plains*. (Lincoln: University of Nebraska Press) 148–56.

Brennan, E. M., Ryan, E. B. and Dawson, W. E. 1975: Scaling of apparent accentedness by magnitude estimation and sensory modality matching. *Journal of Psycholinguistic Research* **4**, 27–36.

Brock, T. D. 1965: Communicator-recipient similarity and decision change. *Journal of Personality and Social Psychology* **1**, 650–4.

Brouwer, D., Gerritsen, M. and De Haan, D. 1979. Speech differences between women and men: On the wrong track? *Language in Society* **8**, 33–50.

Brown, B. L., Strong, W. J. and Rencher, A. C. 1973: Perception of accoustical parameters. *Journal of the Acoustical Society of America* **54**, 29–35.

_____ 1975: Acoustic determinants of the perceptions of personality from speech. *International Journal of the Sociology of Language* **6**, 11–32.

Brown, B. L., Strong, W. L., Rencher, A. C. and Smith, B. L. 1974: Fifty-four voices from two: The effects of simultaneous manipulations of rate, mean fundamental frequency, and variance of fundamental frequency on ratings of personality from speech. *Journal of the Acoustical Society of America* **55**, 313–18.

Brown, P. and Fraser, C. 1979: Speech as a marker of situation. In Scherer, K. R. and Giles, H., editors, *Social markers in speech* (Cambridge: Cambridge University Press) 33–62.

Brown, P. and Levinson, S. 1978: Universals in language usage: Politeness phenomena. In Goody, E. N., editor, *Questions and politeness: Strategies in social interaction* (Cambridge: Cambridge University Press) 56–89.

_____ 1979: Social structure, groups and interaction. In Scherer, K. R. and Giles, H., editors, *Social markers in speech* (Cambridge: Cambridge University Press) 291–342.

Brown, R. 1958: *Words and things*. New York: The Free Press.

_____ 1965: *Social psychology*. London: Collier Macmillan.

Brown, R. and Gilman, A. 1960: Pronouns of power and solidarity. In Sebeok, T., editor, *Style in language* (Cambridge, Mass.: MIT Press and New York: Wiley) 253–76.

Brown, R. H. 1978: *A poetic for sociology: Toward a logic of discovery for the human sciences*. Cambridge: Cambridge University Press.

Brown, R. J. and Turner, J. C. 1981: Interpersonal and intergroup behaviour. In Turner, J. C. and Giles, H., editors, *Intergroup behaviour* (Oxford: Blackwell) 33–65.

Bruner, J. S. 1975: From communication to language – a psychological perspective. *Cognition* **3**, 255–87.

Bryant, B. M. and Trower, P. 1974: Social difficulty in a student sample. *British Journal of Educational Psychology* **44**, 13–21.

Burgoon, M. and Bettinghaus, E. P. 1980: Persuasive message strategies. In Roloff, M. E. and Miller, G. R., editors, *Persuasion: New directions in theory and research* (Beverly Hills: Sage).

Burgoon, M., Jones, S. B. and Stewart, D. 1975: Toward a message-centered theory of persuasion: Three empirical investigations of language intensity. *Human Communication Research* **1**, 240–56.

Burgoon, M. and Miller, G. R. 1971: Prior attitude and language intensity as predictors of message style and attitude change following counter-attitudinal advocacy. *Journal of Personality and Social Psychology* **20**, 246–53.

_____ In press: An expectancy interpretation of language and persuasion. In Giles, H. and St Clair, R., editors, *Recent advances in language, communication and social psychology* (Hillsdale: Lawrence Erlbaum Associates).

Burke, K. 1950: *A rhetoric of motives.* New York: Prentice-Hall, Inc.

Burnstein, E. and Vinokur, A. 1977: Persuasive argumentation and social comparison as determinants of attitude polarization. *Journal of Experimental Social Psychology* **13**, 315–32.

Burnstein, E., Vinokur, A. and Trope, Y. 1973: Interpersonal comparison versus persuasive argumentation: A more direct test of alternative explanations for group induced shifts in individual choice. *Journal of Experimental Social Psychology* **9**, 236–45.

Burstall, C., Jamieson, M., Cohen, S. and Hargreaves, M. 1974: Primary French in the Balance. Windsor: NFER Publishing.

Buss, A. R. 1978: Causes and reasons in attribution theory: A conceptual critique. *Journal of Personality and Social Psychology* **36**, 1311–21.

Butler, M. and Paisley, W. 1980: *Women and the mass media.* New York: Human Sciences Press.

Byrne, D. 1971: *The attraction paradigm.* New York: Academic Press.

Cacioppo, J. T. 1979: The effects of exogenous changes in heart rate on the facilitation of thought and resistance to persuasion. *Journal of Personality and Social Psychology* **37**, 487–96.

Cacioppo, J. T., Harkins, S. G. and Petty, R. E. 1981: The nature of attitudes and cognitive responses and their relationships to behaviour. In Petty, R. E., Ostrom, T. M. and Brock, T. C., editors, *Cognitive responses in persuasion.* (Hillsdale: Lawrence Erlbaum Associates).

Cacioppo, J. T. and Petty, R. E. 1979a: Attitudes and cognitive response: An electrophysiological approach. *Journal of Personality and Social Psychology* **37**, 2181–99.

_____ 1979b: Effects of message repetition and position on cognitive responses, recall, and persuasion. *Journal of Personality and Social Psychology* **37**, 97–109.

_____ 1980a: Persuasiveness of commercials is affected by exposure frequency and communication cogency: A theoretical and empirical analysis. In Leigh, J. H. and Martin, C. R., editors, *Current issues and research in advertising* (Ann Arbor: University of Michigan).

_____ 1980b: Sex differences in influenceability: Toward specifying the underlying process. *Personality and Social Psychology Bulletin* **6**, 651–6.

_____ 1981a: Electromyograms as measures of extent and affectivity of information processing. *American Psychologist* **36**, 441–6.

_____ 1981b: Social psychological procedures for cognitive response assessment: The thought-listing technique. In Merluzzi, T. V., Glass, C. R. and Genest, M., editors, *Cognitive assessment* (New York: Guilford press).

_____ 1981c: Effects of extent of thought on the pleasantness ratings of p-o-x triads: Evidence for three judgemental tendencies in evaluating social situations. *Journal of Personality and Social Psychology* **40**, 1000–9.

Calder, B. J., Insko, C. A. and Yandell, B. 1974: The relation of cognitive and memorial processes to persuasion in a simulated jury trial. *Journal of Applied Social Psychology* **4**, 62–93.

Calvet, L. J. 1974: *Linguistique et colonialisme*. Paris: Petite Bibliothèque Payot.

Cantor, J. R. 1979: Grammatical variations in persuasion: Effectiveness of four forms of request in door-to-door solicitations for funds. *Communication Monographs* **46**, 296–305.

Cantor, N. and Mischel, W. 1979: Prototypes in person perception. In Berkowitz, L., editor, *Advances in experimental social psychology* **12** (New York: Academic Press) 1–52.

Caput, J. P. 1972: Naissance et évolution de la notion de norme en français. *Langue Française* **16**, 63–73.

Cardenas, G. 1977: Chicanos in the Midwest. *Aztlan* **7** (summer), special issue.

Carr, E. B. 1972: *Da Kine talk: From pidgin to standard English in Hawaii*. Honolulu: The University Press of Hawaii.

Carranza, M. A. and Ryan, E. B. 1975: Evaluative reactions of bilingual Anglo and Mexican American adolescents toward speakers of English and Spanish. *International Journal of the Sociology of Language* **6**, 83–104.

_____ In press: Language attitudes and other cultural attitudes of Mexican American adults: Some sociolinguistic implications. *International Journal of the Sociology of Language*.

Carroll, J. B. 1978: International comparisons of foreign language learning in the IEA project. In Alatis, J., editor, *Georgetown University Round Table on Languages and Linguistics 1978* (Washington: Georgetown University Press) 576–81.

Carroll, J. B. and Sapon, S. M. 1959: *Modern Language Aptitude Test, Form A*. New York: The Psychological Corporation.

Carter, R. F., Ruggels, W. L., Jackson, K. M. and Heffner, M. 1973: Application of signaled stopping technique to communication research. In Clarke, P., editor, *New models for mass communication research* (Beverly Hills: Sage) 15–44.

Casanova, J. D. 1975: *Une Amérique française*. Paris: La Documentation Française; and Québec: l'Editeur Officiel du Quebec.

Castonguay, C. and Marion, J. 1975: L'anglicisation du Canada. *La Monda Lingvo-Problemo* **5**, 145–56 (now: *Language Problems and Language Planning*).

Cavanaugh, N. F. 1977: The roles of atittude and motivation in second-language acquisition. *Dissertation Abstracts International* **38**, 674-A.

Centro de Estudios Puertorriqueños 1978: Language Policy and the Puerto

Rican community. *The Bilingual Review/La Revista Bilingue* **5**, 1–39.

Chaiken, S. 1980: Heuristic versus systematic information processing and the use of source versus message cues in persuasion. *Journal of Personality and Social Psychology* **39**, 752–66.

Chantefort, P. 1970: Diglossie au Québec: Limites et tendances actuelles. B-29, Québec: International Center for Research on Bilingualism.

Chapanis, N. and Chapanis, A. 1964: Cognitive dissonance: Five years later. *Psychological Bulletin* **61**, 1–22.

Charron, V. R. and Charron, R. P. 1979: Characteristics of the language of jury instructions. In Alatis, J. E. and Tucker, G. R., editors, *Georgetown University Round Table on Languages and Linguistics 1979* (Washington: Georgetown University Press) 163–85.

Chase, S. 1938: *The tyranny of words*. New York: Harcourt, Brace & Co.

Cheyne, W. 1970: Stereotyped reactions to speakers with Scottish and English regional accents. *British Journal of Social and Clinical Psychology* **9**, 77–9.

Chihara, R. and Oller, J. W. 1978: Attitudes and attained proficiency in EFL: A sociolinguistic study of adult Japanese speakers. *Language Learning* **28**, 55–68.

Chomsky, N. 1957: *Syntactic structures*. The Hague: Mouton.

———— 1965a: *Aspects of the theory of syntax*. Cambridge, Mass.: MIT Press.

———— 1965b: *Current issues in linguistic theory*. The Hague: Mouton.

Choy, S. and Dodd, D. 1976: Standard-English-speaking and non-standard Hawaiian-English-speaking children: Comprehension of both dialects and teachers' evaluations. *Journal of Educational Psychology* **68**, 184–93.

Christian, J. and Christian, C. C., Jr. 1966: Spanish language and culture in the southwest. In Fishman, J. A., editor, *Language Loyalty in the United States* (The Hague: Mouton) 280–317.

Christian, J., Gadfield, N., Giles, H. and Taylor, D. M. 1976: The multidimensional and dynamic nature of ethnic identity. *International Journal of Psychology* **11**, 281–91.

Cialdini, R. B., Levy, A., Herman, P., Kozlowski, L. and Petty, R. E. 1976: Elastic shifts of opinion: Determinants of direction and durability. *Journal of Personality and Social Psychology* **34**, 663–72.

Cialdini, R. B., Petty, R. E. and Cacioppo, J. T. 1981: Attitudes and attitude changes. In Rosenzweig, M. R. and Porter, L. W., editors, *Annual Review of Psychology* **32**, 357–404.

Clarke, S. 1981: *Speech stereotypes in Newfoundland: An initial investigation*. Unpublished manuscript, Memorial University of Newfoundland.

Clément, R. 1979: Immersion and residence programs: Their effects on attitude and anxiety. *Interchange* **9** (4), 52–8.

Clément, R., Gardner, R. C. and Smythe, P. C. 1977: Motivational variables in second-language acquisition: A study of francophones learning English. *Canadian Journal of Behavioural Science* **9**, 123–33.

———— 1980: Social and individual factors in second language acquisition. *Canadian Journal of Behavioural Science* **12**, 292–302.

Cohen, A. D. 1974: Mexican American evaluational judgements about language varieties. *International Journal of the Sociology of Language* **3**, 33–51.

Cohen, C. E. and Ebbesen, E. B. 1979: Observational goals and schema activation: A theoretical framework for behaviour perception. *Journal of Experimental Social Psychology* **15**, 305–29.

Cole, R. L. 1975: Divergent and convergent attitudes toward the Alsatian dialect. *Anthropological Linguistics* **17**, 293–303.

Coltharp, L. H. 1964: *The tongue of the Tirilones*. University: University of Alabama Press.

_____ 1975: Pachuco, Tirilon, and Chicano. *American Speech* **50**, 25–9.

Conville, R. 1975: Linguistic non-immediacy and self-presentation. *Journal of Psychology* **90**, 219–27.

Cook, T. D. 1969: Competence, counterarguing, and attitude change. *Journal of Personality* **37**, 342–58.

Cooper, J., Darley, J. M. and Henderson, J. E. 1974: On the effectiveness of deviant and conventional-appearing communicators: A field experiment. *Journal of Personality and Social Psychology* **29**, 752–7.

Cooper, R. L. 1974: Language attitudes I. *International Journal of the Sociology of Language* **3**.

_____ 1975a: Introduction to language attitudes II. *International Journal of the Sociology of Language* **6**, 5–9.

_____ 1975b: Language attitudes II. *International Journal of the Sociology of Language* **6**.

Cooper, R. L. and Fishman, J. A. 1974: The study of language attitudes. *International Journal of the Sociology of Language* **3**, 5–19.

_____ 1977: A study of language attitudes. In Fishman, J. A., Cooper, R. L. and Conrad, A. W., editors, *The spread of English* (Rowley: Newbury House) 239–75.

Cope, C. S. 1969: Linguistic structure and personality development. *Journal of Counseling Psychology* **16**, 1–19.

Corbeil, J. C. 1980: Aspects sociolinguistiques de la langue française au Québec. *The French Review* **53**, 834–8.

Cremona, C. and Bates, E. 1977: The development of attitudes toward dialect in Italian children. *Journal of Psycholinguistic Research* **6**, 223–32.

Crowll, T. and Nurss, J. 1976: Ethnic and regional influences on teachers' evaluations of oral answers. *Contemporary Educational Psychology* **1**, 236–40.

Cruz, J. S. 1977: *Study of Puerto Rican, Mexican and Cuban parents' views on bilingual/bicultural education*. Unpublished doctoral dissertation, Northwestern University.

Cučeloglu, D. and Slobin, D. I. 1976: Effects of the Turkish language reform on person perception. *Working Papers of the Language Research Laboratory*, University of California, Berkeley, No. 47.

Cziko, G. A., Lambert, W. E. and Gutter, J. 1979: French immersion programs and students' social attitudes: A multidimensional investigation. *Working Papers on Bilingualism* **19**, 13–28.

Daigle, J. 1980: *Les Acadiens des Maritimes*. Moncton: Centre d'Etudes Acadiennes.

Daoust, D. 1980: *La qualité de la langue et la norme au Québec dans le cadre de la planification linguistique: Evolution et perspective d'avenir*. Montreal: Office de la Langue Française.

_____ 1982: Corpus and status language planning in Quebec. In Cobrarrubias, J., editor, *Progress in language planning: International perspective* (The Hague: Mouton).

Davant, J. L. 1973: Lutte nationale et lutte des classes dans le mouvement basque. *Les Temps Modernes* **324-6**, 238-301.

Davis, M. S. 1967: Predicting non-compliant behaviour. *Journal of Health and Social Behaviour* **8**, 265-71.

_____ 1968: Physiological, psychological and demographic factors in patient compliance with doctors' orders. *Medical Care* **11**, 115-22.

Dawson, R. G., Prewitt, K. and Dawson, K. S. 1977: *Political socialization: An analytical study.* Boston: Little, Brown & Co.

Day, R. 1980: The development of linguistic attitudes and preferences. *TESOL Quarterly* **14**, 27-37.

Deaux, K. and Emswiller, T. 1974: Explanations of successful performance on sex-linked tasks: What is skill for the male is luck for the female. *Journal of Personality and Social Psychology* **29**, 80-5.

de la Zerda, N. and Hopper, R. 1979: Employment interviewers' reactions to Mexican American speech. *Communication Monographs* **46**, 126-34.

Delia, J. G. 1972: Dialects and the effects of stereotypes on interpersonal attraction and cognitive processes in impression formation. *Quarterly Journal of Speech* **58**, 285-97.

_____ 1974: Cognitive complexity and impression formation in informal social interaction. *Speech Monographs* **41**, 299-308.

_____ 1976: Change of meaning processes in impression formation. *Communication Monographs* **13**, 142-57.

_____ 1977: Constructivism and the study of human communication. *Quarterly Journal of Speech* **63**, 66-83.

Deprez, K. and De Schutter, G. 1980: Honderd Antwerpenaars en honderd Rotterdammers over dertien Nederlandse taalavrieteiten. Een attitude-onderzoek. *Leuvense Bijdragen* **69**, 166-256.

Deutsch, K. W. 1953: *Nationalism and social communication.* Cambridge, Mass.: MIT Press.

Dillard, J. L. 1973: *Black English: Its history and usage in the United States.* New York: Random House.

Doise, W. 1978: *Groups and individuals: Explanations in social psychology.* Cambridge: Cambridge University Press.

Doise, W., Sinclair, A. and Bourhis, R. Y. 1976: Evaluation of accent convergence and divergence in cooperative and competitive inter-group situations. *British Journal of Social and Clinical Psychology* **15**, 247-52.

Dore, J. 1973: *The development of speech acts.* Unpublished doctoral dissertation. City University of New York.

_____ 1976: Children's illocutionary acts. In Freedle, R., editor, *Discourse: Comprehension and production* (Hillsdale: Lawrence Erlbaum Associates) 227-44.

Dorian, N. C. 1980: Language shift in community and individual: The phenomenon of the laggard semi-speaker. *International Journal of the Sociology of Language* **25**, 85-94.

Douaud, P. 1979: Canada and France: Main trends in the sociolinguistics of French. *Anthropological Linguistics* 21, 163-81.

Douglas, J. 1970: *Deviance and respectability: The social construction of moral meaning.* New York: Basic Books.

Dowd, J. J. and Bengston, V. L. 1978: Aging in minority populations: An examination of the double jeopardy hypothesis. *Journal of Gerontology* 33, 427-36.

Drake, G. F. 1977: *The role of prescriptivism in American linguistics, 1820-1970.* Amsterdam: John Benjamins, B. V.

_____ 1980: The social role of slang. In Giles, H., Robinson, W. P. and Smith, P., editors, *Language: Social psychological perspectives* (Oxford: Pergamon Press) 63-70.

Drakeford, J. W. 1969: *Integrity Therapy.* Nashville: Broadman Press.

Duck, S. and Gilmour, R. 1981: *Developing personal relationships.* London: Academic Press.

Dugas, D. G. 1976: Franco-American language maintenance efforts in New England: Realities and issues. In Snyder, E. and Valdman, A., editors, *Identité culturelle et francophonie dans les Amériques*, vol. 1 (Québec: Les Presses de l'Université Laval) 44-57.

Duncan, H. D. 1962: *Communication and social order.* New York: The Bedminster Press.

Dupas, J. C. 1975: La langue régionale en Flandre, un cas particulier. *Langue Française* 25, 121-4.

Dusek, J. 1975: Do teachers bias children's learning? *Review of Educational Research* 45, 661-84.

Dworkin, A. G. 1965: Stereotypes and self-image held by native-born and foreign-born Mexican-Americans. *Sociology and Social Research* 49, 214-24.

_____ 1971: National origin and ghetto experience as variables in Mexican American stereotype. In Wagner, N. N. and Haug, M. J., editors, *Chicanos – Social and psychological perspectives* (St Louis: C. V. Mosby) 80-4.

Eagly, A. H. 1981: Recipient characteristics as determinants of response to persuasion. In Petty, R. E., Ostrom, T. M. and Brock, T. C., editors, *Cognitive responses in persuasion* (Hillsdale: Lawrence Erlbaum Associates).

Eagly, A. H. and Chaiken, S. 1975: An attribution analysis of the effect of communicator characteristics on opinion change: A field experiment. *Journal of Personality and Social Psychology* 32, 136-44.

Eagly, A. H. and Telaak, K. 1972: Width of the latitude of acceptance as a determinant of attitude change. *Journal of Personality and Social Psychology* 23, 388-97.

Eagly, A. H., Wood, W. and Chaiken, S. 1978: Causal inferences about communicators and their effect on opinion change. *Journal of Personality and Social Psychology* 36, 424-35.

Ebertowski, M. 1978: De relatie tussen taalatitudes en taalgedras – een sociaal-psychologische benadering. *Toegepaste taalwetenschap in artikelen* 4, 38-51.

Eble, C. 1976: Etiquette books as linguistic authority. In Reich, P. *Lacus Forum II 1975* (Columbia: Hornbeam Press) 468-73.

Edelsky, C. 1976: The acquisition of communicative competence: Recognition of linguistic correlates of sex roles. *Merrill-Palmer Quarterly of Behaviour and Development* **22**, 47–59.

Edwards, J. R. 1977a: Students' reactions to Irish regional accents. *Language and Speech* **20**, 280–6.

—— 1977b: The speech of disadvantaged Dublin children. *Language Problems and Language Planning* **1**, 65–72.

—— 1979a: Judgements and confidence in reactions to disadvantaged speech. In Giles, H. and St Clair, R., editors, *Language and social psychology* (Oxford: Basil Blackwell and Baltimore: University Park Press) 22–44.

—— 1979b: *Language and disadvantage.* London: Edward Arnold and New York: Elsevier-North Holland.

—— 1979c: Social class differences and the identification of sex in children's speech. *Child Language* **6**, 121–7.

—— 1980: Critics and criticisms of bilingual education. *Modern Language Journal* **64**, 409–15.

—— 1981: The context of bilingual education. *Journal of Multilingual and Multicultural Development* **2**, 25–44.

—— In press a: *The Irish language: An annotated bibliography of sociolinguistic publications, 1771–1977.* New York: Garland Publishers.

—— In press b: Psychological and linguistic aspects of minority education. *World Yearbook of Education* (1981).

Edwards, V. K. 1979: *The West Indian language issue in British schools.* London: Routledge & Kegan Paul.

Eisen, S. V. 1979: Actor-observer differences in information inference and causal attribution. *Journal of Personality and Social Psychology* **37**, 261–72.

Eiser, J. R. 1975: Attitudes and the use of evaluative language: A two-way process. *Journal for the Theory of Social Behaviour* **5**, 235–48.

—— 1980: *Cognitive social psychology.* New York: McGraw-Hill.

Eiser, J. R. and Osmon, B. E. 1978: Judgemental perspective and value connotations of response scale labels. *Journal of Personality and Social Psychology* **36**, 491–7.

Eiser, J. R. and Pancer, S. M. 1979: Attitudinal effects of the use of evaluatively biased language. *European Journal of Social Psychology* **9**, 39–48.

Eiser, J. R. and Stroebe, W. 1972: *Categorization and social judgement.* London: Academic Press.

Ekman, P. and Friesen, W. V. 1969: Nonverbal leakage and clues to deception. *Psychiatry* **32**, 88–105.

—— 1974: Detecting deception from the body or face. *Journal of Personality and Social Psychology* **29**, 288–98.

El-Dash, L. and Tucker, G. R. 1975: Subjective reactions to various speech styles in Egypt. *International Journal of the Sociology of Language* **6**, 33–54.

Elias-Olivares, L. 1976: Language use in a Chicano community: A sociolinguistic approach. *Working Papers in Sociolinguistics* Number 30 (Austin: Southwest Educational Development Laboratory).

Elizaincin, A. 1976: The emergence of bilingual dialects on the Brazilian-Uruguayan border. *Linguistics* **177**, 123–34.

Eltis, K. 1980: Pupils' speech-style and teacher reaction: Implications from some Australian data. *English in Australia* **51**, 27–35.

Elyan, O., Smith, P. M., Giles, H. and Bourhis, R. Y. 1978: RP-female accented speech: The voice of perceived androgyny? In Trudgill, P., editor, *Sociolinguistic patterns in British English* (London: Edward Arnold) 122–30.

Erasmus, D. 1963: *De utraque verborem ac rerum copia.* King, D. B. and Rix, H. D., translators. Milwaukee: Marquette University Press.

Erickson, B., Johnson, B. C., Lind, E. A. and O'Barr, W. 1978: Speech style and impression formation in a court setting: The effects of 'powerful' and 'powerless' speech. *Journal of Experimental Social Psychology* **14**, 266–79.

Ervin, S. M. 1964: Language and TAT content in bilinguals. *Journal of Abnormal and Social Psychology* **68**, 500–7.

Ervin-Tripp, S. 1964: An analysis of the interaction of language, topic, and listener. In Gumperz, J. J. and Hymes, D., editors, *The ethnography of communication*, American Anthropologist special publication (Menasha, Wisconsin: American Anthropological Association) 86–102.

———— 1977: Wait for me, roller skate! In Ervin-Tripp, S. and Mitchell-Kernan, C., editors, *Child discourse* (New York: Academic Press) 165–88.

Escobar, A. 1976: Bilingualism and dialectology in Peru. *Linguistics* **177**, 85–96.

Ettori, F. 1975: L'enseignement de la langue corse. *Langue Française* **25**, 104–11.

Ewen, S. 1976: *Captains of consciousness: Advertising and the social roots of the consumer culture.* New York: McGraw-Hill.

Feldman, N. S. and Ruble, D. N. 1981: Social comparison strategies: Dimension offered and options taken. *Personality and Social Psychology Bulletin* **7**, 5–10.

Feldman, R. H. L. 1968: The effect of administrator and language on traditional–modern attitudes among Gush students in Kenya. *Journal of Social Psychology* **96**, 141–2.

Feldstein, S. 1972: *The poisoned tongue: A documentary history of American racism and prejudice.* New York: William Morrow & Co.

Feldstein, S. and Welkowitz, J. 1978: A chronography of conversation: In defense of an objective approach. In Siegman, A. W. and Feldstein, S., editors, *Nonverbal Behaviour and Communication* (Hillsdale: Lawrence Erlbaum, Associates).

Ferguson, C. 1959: Diglossia. *Word* **15**, 325–40.

Festinger, L. 1954: A theory of social comparison processes. *Human Relations* **7**, 117–40.

———— 1957: *A theory of cognitive dissonance.* Stanford: Stanford University Press.

FFHQ. 1978: *The heirs of Lord Durham: Manifesto of a vanishing people.* Ottawa: Fédération des francophones hors Québec.

Fichtelius, A., Johansson, I. and Nordin, K. 1980: Three investigations of sex-associated speech variation in day school. *Women's Studies International Quarterly* **3** (2/3), 219–25. These issues also appear as: Kramarae, C., editor, *The voices and words of women and men* (Oxford: Pergamon Press).

Fielding, G. and Evered, C. 1980: The influence of patients' speech upon doctors: The diagnostic interview. In St Clair, R. N. and Giles, H., editors, *The social and psychological contexts of language* (Hillsdale: Lawrence Erlbaum Associates) 51–72.

Fishbein, M. 1980: A theory of reasoned action: Some applications and implications. *Nebraska Symposium on Motivation* **28**, 1–25.

Fishbein, M. and Ajzen, I. 1975: *Belief, attitude, intention, and behaviour.* Reading: Addison-Wesley.

Fishman, J. A. 1966: *Language loyalty in the United States: The maintenance and perpetuation of non-English mother tongues by American ethnic and religious groups.* The Hague: Mouton.

_____ 1967: Bilingualism and diglossia. *Journal of Social Issues* **23**, 29–37.

_____ 1969: Bilingual attitudes and behaviours. *Language Sciences* **5**, 5–11.

_____ 1971: *Sociolinguistics: A brief introduction.* Rowley: Newbury House Publishers.

_____ 1977: Language and ethnicity. In Giles, H., editor, *Language, ethnicity and intergroup relations* (London: Academic Press) 15–57.

Fishman, J.A. *et al* 1971: Attitudes and beliefs about Spanish and English among Puerto Ricans. *Viewpoints* **47**, 51–72.

Fishman, J. A., Cooper, R. L. and Conrad, A. W. 1977: *The spread of English.* Rowley: Newbury House.

Fishman, J. A., Cooper, R. L. and Rosenbaum, Y. 1977: English the world over – A factor in the creation of bilingualism today. In Hornby, P. A., editor, *Bilingualism: Psychological, social and educational implications* (New York: Academic Press) 103–40.

Fishman, J. A., Ferguson, C. A. and Das Gupta, J. 1968: *Language problems of developing nations.* New York: Wiley.

Fishman, J. A. and Hofman, J. E. 1966: Mother tongue and nativity in the American population. In Fishman, J. A., editor, *Language Loyalty in the United States* (The Hague: Mouton) 56–86.

Fishman, P. M. 1980: Conversational insecurity. In Giles, H., Robinson, W. P. and Smith, P. M., editors, *Language: Social Psychological Perspectives* (Oxford: Pergamon Press) 127–32.

Fitch, K. and Hopper, R. 1983: If you speak Spanish they'll think you're a German: Language attitudes and switching in multilingual environments. *Journal of Multilingual and Multicultural Development*, in press.

Flores, N. and Hopper, R. 1975: Mexican Americans' evaluations of spoken Spanish and English. *Speech Monographs* **42**, 91–8.

Ford, J. F. 1974: Language attitude studies: A review of selected research. *The Florida FL Reporter*, Spring/Fall, 53–5.

Forgas, J. P. 1976: The perception of social episodes: Categorical and dimensional representations in two different social milieus. *Journal of Personality and Social Psychology* **34**, 199–209.

_____ 1978: Social episodes and social structure in an academic setting: The social environment of an intact group. *Journal of Experimental Social Psychology* **14**, 434–48.

_____ 1980: *Social episodes: The study of interaction routines.* London: Academic Press.

Forgas, J., and Dobosz, B. 1980: Dimensions of romantic involvement: Towards a taxonomy of relationships. *Social Psychology Quarterly* **43**, 290–300.

Fraser, B. 1973: Some 'unexpected' reactions to various American-English dialects. In Shuy, R. and Fasold, R., editors, *Language attitudes: Current trends and prospects* (Washington: Georgetown University Press) 28–35.

Gal, S. 1978: *Language shift – Social determinants of linguistic change in bilingual Austria.* New York: Academic Press.

Galvan, J. L., Lodmer, E., Oschner, R., Plummer, D., Telatnik, M. and Walter, G. 1977: A comparison of the accented speech of seven Spanish-English bilingual speakers. *UCLA Workpapers in Teaching English as a Second Language.*

Galvan, J. L., Pierce, J. A. and Underwood, G. N. 1975: Relationships between teachers' attitudes and differences in the English of bilinguals. In Hoffer, B. and Ornstein, J., editors, *Swallow* V (San Diego: Institute for Cultural Pluralism) 15–25.

_____ 1976: The relevance of selected educational variables of teachers to their attitudes toward Mexican-American English. *Journal of LASSO* **2**, 13–27.

Gardner, R. C. 1979: Social psychological aspects of second language acquisition. In Giles, H. and St Clair, R. N., editors, *Language and social psychology* (Oxford: Basil Blackwell and Baltimore: University Park Press) 193–220.

_____ 1980: On the validity of affective variables in second language acquisition: Conceptual, contextual and statistical considerations. *Language Learning* **30**, 255–70.

_____ 1981: Second language learning. In Gardner, R. C. and Kalin, R., editors, *A Canadian social psychology of ethnic relations* (Toronto: Methuen).

_____ In press: Social factors in language retention. In Lambert, R. D. and Freed, B., editors, *The loss of language skills* (Rowley: Newbury House).

Gardner, R. C., Clément, R., Smythe, P. C. and Smythe, C. L. 1978: Attitudes and motivation test battery manual. *Research Bulletin* No. 468. Department of Psychology, University of Western Ontario.

Gardner, R. C., Kirby, D. M. and Arboleda, A. 1971: Ethnic stereotypes: A cross-cultural replication of their unitary dimensionality. *Journal of Social Psychology* **91**, 189–95.

Gardner, R. C., Kirby, D. M., Pablo, R. Y. and Castillo, E. S. 1975: Ethnic stereotypes: The role of language. *Journal of Social Psychology* **96**, 3–9.

Gardner, R. C. and Lambert, W. E. 1959: Motivational variables in second-language acquisition. *Canadian Journal of Psychology* **13**, 266–72.

_____ 1972: *Attitudes and motivation in second-language learning.* Rowley: Newbury House.

Gardner, R. C. and Santos, E. H. 1970: Motivational variables in second language acquisition: A Philippine investigation. *Research Bulletin* No. 149, Department of Psychology, University of Western Ontario.

Gardner, R. C. and Smythe, P. C. 1975: Second language acquisition: A social psychological approach. *Research Bulletin* No. 332, Department of Psychology, University of Western Ontario.

Gardner, R. C., Smythe, P. C. and Brunet, G. R. 1977: Intensive second-language study: Effects on attitudes, motivation and French achievement. *Language Learning* **27**, 243–61.

Garvin, P. L. 1964: The standard language problem – Concepts and methods. In Hymes, D., editor, *Language in culture and society* (New York: Harper) 521–6.

Gelfman, J. 1976: *Women in television news.* New York: Columbia University Press.

Gendron, J. D. 1972: *The position of the French language in Quebec*, Volumes 1, 2, 3. Québec: l'Editeur Officiel du Québec.

Genesee, F., Tucker, G. R. and Lambert, W. E. 1978: The development of ethnic identity and ethnic role taking skills in children from different school settings. *International Journal of Psychology* 13, 39–57.

Gibb, C. A. 1969: Leadership. In Lindzey, G. and Aronson, E., editors, *Handbook of social psychology*, vol. 4, 2nd edn. (Reading: Addison-Wesley).

Gibbons, J. 1983: Attitudes towards languages and code-switching in Hong Kong. *Journal of Multilingual and Multicultural Development*, in press.

Gilbert, G. G. 1981: French and German: a comparative study. In: Ferguson, C. A. and Heath, B., editors, *Language in the USA* (Cambridge: Cambridge University Press) 257–72.

Giles, H. 1970: Evaluative reactions to accents. *Educational Review* 22, 211–27.

_____ 1971a: Ethnocentrism and the evaluation of accented speech. *British Journal of Social and Clinical Psychology* 10, 187–8.

_____ 1971b: Patterns of evaluation in reactions to RP, South Welsh and Somerset accented speech. *British Journal of Social and Clinical Psychology* 10, 280–1.

_____ 1972: Evaluation of personality content from accented speech as a function of listeners' social attitudes. *Perceptual and Motor Skills* 34, 168–70.

_____ 1973a: Accent mobility: A model and some data. *Anthropological Linguistics* 15, 87–105.

_____ 1973b: Communicative effectiveness as a function of accented speech. *Speech Monographs* 40, 330–1.

_____ 1977: The social context of speech: A social psychological perspective. *ITL: A Review of Applied Linguistics* 35, 27–42.

_____ 1979a: Ethnicity markers in speech. In Scherer, K. R. and Giles, H., editors, *Social Markers in speech* (Cambridge: Cambridge University Press) 251–90.

_____ 1979b: Sociolinguistics and social psychology: An introductory essay. In Giles, H. and St Clair, R. N., editors, *Language and social psychology* (Oxford: Basil Blackwell and Baltimore: University Park Press) 1–20.

Giles, H., Baker, S. and Fielding, G. 1975: Communication length as a behavioural index of accent prejudice. *International Journal of the Sociology of Language* 6, 73–81.

Giles, H. and Bourhis, R. Y. 1973: Dialect perception revisited. *Quarterly Journal of Speech* 59, 337–42.

_____ 1975: Linguistic assimilation: West Indians in Cardiff. *Language Sciences* 38, 9–12.

_____ 1976a: Black speakers with white speech – a real problem? In Nickel, G., editor, *Proceedings of fourth AILA Conference*, vol. 1 (Stuttgart: HochschulVerlag) 575–84.

_____ 1976b: Methodological issues in dialect perception: Some social psychological perspectives. *Anthropological Linguistics* 18, 294–304.

Giles, H., Bourhis, R. Y. and Davies, A. 1979: Prestige speech styles: The imposed norm and inherent value hypotheses. In McCormack, W. and Wurm, S., editors, *Language in anthropology IV: Language in many ways* (The Hague: Mouton) 589–96.

Giles, H., Bourhis, R. Y. and Taylor, D. M. 1977: Towards a theory of language in ethnic group relations. In Giles, H., editor, *Language, ethnicity and intergroup relations* (London: Academic Press) 307–48.

Giles, H., Bourhis, R. Y., Trudgill, P. and Lewis, A. 1974: The imposed norm hypothesis: A validation. *Quarterly Journal of Speech* **60**, 405–10.

Giles, H. and Byrne, J. 1982: An intergroup approach to second language acquisition. *Journal of Multilingual and Multicultural Development*, in press.

Giles, H., Brown, B. and Thakerar, J. N. 1981: *The effects of accent, speech rate, and context on evaluative reactions to speakers.* Mimeo: Brigham Young University.

Giles, H. and Farrar, K. 1979: Some behavioural consequences of speech and dress styles. *British Journal of Social and Clinical Psychology* **18**, 209–10.

Giles, H., Harrison, C., Smith, P. M. and Freeman, N. 1981: *A developmental study of language attitudes: A British case.* Mimeo.: University of Bristol.

Giles, H., Hewstone, M. and St Clair, R. N. In press: Cognitive structures and a social psychology of communication: New integrative models and an introductory overview. In Giles, H. and St Clair, R. N., editors, *Recent advances in language, communication and social psychology* (Hillsdale: Lawrence Erlbaum Associates).

Giles, H. and Johnson, P. 1981: The role of language in ethnic group relations. In Turner, J. and Giles, H., editors, *Intergroup behaviour* (Oxford: Blackwell) 199–243.

Giles, H., Llado, N., McKirnan, D. J. and Taylor, D. M. 1979: Social identity in Puerto Rico. *International Journal of Psychology* **14**, 185–201.

Giles, H. and Marsh, P. 1979: Perceived masculinity and accented speech. *Language Sciences* **1**, 301–15.

Giles, H. and Powesland, P. F. 1975: *Speech style and social evaluation.* London: Academic Press.

Giles, H., Robinson, W. P. and Smith, P. 1980: *Language: Social psychological perspectives.* Oxford: Pergamon Press.

Giles, H. and St Clair, R. N. 1979: *Language and social psychology.* Oxford: Basil Blackwell and Baltimore: University Park Press.

Giles, H., Scherer, K. R. and Taylor, D. M. 1979: Speech markers in social interaction. In Scherer, K. R. and Giles, H., editors, *Social markers in speech* (Cambridge: Cambridge University Press) 343–81.

Giles, H. and Smith, P. M. 1979: Accommodation theory: Optimal levels of convergence. In Giles, H. and St Clair, R. N., editors, *Language and social psychology* (Oxford: Basil Blackwell and Baltimore: University Park Press) 45–65.

Giles, H., Smith, P. M., Browne, C., Whiteman, S. and Williams, J. A. 1980: Women's speech: The voice of feminism. In McConnel-Ginet, S., Borker, R. and Furman, N., editors, *Women and Language in Literature and Society* (New York: Praeger) 150–6.

Giles, H., Smith, P., Ford, B., Condor, S. and Thakerar, J. 1980: Speech styles and the fluctuating salience of sex. *Language Sciences* **2**, 260–82.

Giles, H., Taylor, D. M. and Bourhis, R. Y. 1973: Towards a theory of interpersonal accommodation through language: Some Canadian data. *Language in Society* **2**, 177–92.

_____ 1977: Dimensions of Welsh identity. *European Journal of Social Psychology* 7, 29–39.

Giles, H., Taylor, D. M., Lambert, W. E. and Albert, G. 1976: Dimensions of ethnic identity: An example from Northern Maine. *Journal of Social Psychology* 100, 11–19.

Giles, H., Wilson, P. and Conway, T. 1981: Accent and lexical diversity as determinants of impression formation and employment selection. *Language Sciences* 3, 92–103.

Gilliam, A. M. 1975: *Language attitudes, ethnicity and class in Sao Paulo and Salvador da Bahia (Brazil).* Unpublished doctoral dissertation, Union Graduate School.

Gillig, P. M. and Greenwald, A. G., 1974: Is it time to lay the sleeper effect to rest? *Journal of Personality and Social Psychology* 29, 132–9.

Gilman, C. P. 1911: *The man-made world; or, Our androcentric culture.* London: T. Fisher Unwin.

Gilovich, T. 1981: Seeing the past in the present: The effect of associations to familiar events on judgements and decisions. *Journal of Personality and Social Psychology* 40, 797–808.

Gleason, J. B. and Weintraub, S. 1978: Input language and the acquisition of communicative competence. In Nelson, K. E., editor, *Children's language* vol. 1 (New York: Gardner Press) 171–222.

Gliksman, L. 1976: *Second language acquisition: The effects of student attitudes on classroom behaviour.* Unpublished Master's Thesis, University of Western Ontario.

Goetzman, W. H. 1978: *Explorations and empire: The explorers and the scientists in the winning of the American west.* New York: W. W. Norton.

Goffman, E. 1971: *Relations in public.* New York: Harper & Row.

_____ 1977: The arrangement between the sexes. *Theory and Society* 4, 301–31.

_____ 1978: Response cries. *Language* 54, 787–815.

Goodman, M. E. 1952: *Race awareness in young children.* Cambridge, Mass. Addison-Wesley.

Goosse, A. 1970: La norme et les écarts régionaux. *Annales de la Faculté des Lettres et Sciences Humaines de Nice* 12, 91–105.

Gordon, D. C. 1978: *The French language and national identity.* The Hague: Mouton.

Goss, B. 1972: The effect of sentence context on associations to ambiguous, vague, and clear nouns. *Speech Monographs* 39, 286–9.

Gossett, T. F. 1977: *Race: The history of an idea in America.* New York: Schocken Books.

Granberg, D. and Brent, E. E. 1974: Dove–hawk placements in the 1968 election: Application of social judgement and balance theories. *Journal of Personality and Social Psychology* 29, 687–95.

Granger, R., Mathews, M., Quay, L. and Verner, R. 1977: Teacher judgements of the communication effectiveness of children using different speech patterns. *Journal of Educational Psychology* 69, 793–6.

Grant, P. R. and Holmes, J. G. 1981: The integration of implicit personality theory schemas and stereotype images. *Social Psychology Quarterly* 44, 107–15.

Grassi, C. 1977: Deculturization and social degradation of the linguistic minorities in Italy. *International Journal of the Sociology of Language* **12**, 45–54.

Grebler, L., Moore, J. W. and Guzman, R. 1970: *The Mexican American people: The nation's largest minority.* New York: The Free Press.

Greenbaum, S. 1976: Contextual influence on acceptability judgements. *International Journal of Psycholinguistics* **6**, 5–11.

——— 1977a: Judgements of syntactic acceptability and frequency. *Studia Linguistica* **31**, 83–105.

——— 1977b: The linguist as experimenter. In. Eckman, F. R., editor, *Current themes in linguistics* (New York: Hemisphere) 125–44.

Greenwald, A. G. 1968: Cognitive learning, cognitive response to persuasion and attitude change. In Greenwald, A. G., Brock, T. C. and Ostrom, T. M., editors, *Psychological foundations of attitudes* (New York: Academic Press).

Grice, H. P. 1975: Logic and conversation. In Cole, J. and Morgan, J. L., editors, *Syntax and Semantics, vol. III, Speech sets* (New York: Academic Press).

Griffiths, N. 1973: *The Acadians: Creation of a people.* Toronto: McGraw-Hill.

Guiraud, P. 1956 (7th edition, 1976): *L'Argot.* Collection Que Sais-Je? Paris: Presse Universitaire de France.

——— 1965 (4th edition, 1978): *Le Français Populaire.* Collection Que Sais-Je? Paris: Presse Universitaire de France.

——— 1968 (2nd edition, 1971): *Patois et dialectes français.* Collection Que Sais-Je? Paris: Presse Universitaire de France.

Gumperz, J. J. 1958: Dialect differences and social stratification in a North Indian village. *American Anthropologist* **60**, 668–80.

——— 1971: *Language in social groups*, introduced by A. S. Dil. Stanford: Stanford University Press.

——— 1978: The conversational analysis of interethnic communication. In Ross, E. L., editor, *Interethnic communication* (Athens: The University of Georgia Press) 13–31.

Gumperz, J. J. and Hernandez-Chavez, E. 1972: Bilingualism, bidialectalism, and classroom interaction. In Cazden, C., John, V. and Hymes, D., editors, *Functions of language in the classroom* (New York: Teachers College Press) 84–110.

Haas, A. 1979: Male and female spoken language differences: Stereotypes and evidence. *Psychological Bulletin* **86**, 616–26.

Hall, J. A. 1980: Voice tone and persuasion. *Journal of Personality and Social Psychology* **38**, 924–34.

Hall, J. A. and Braunwald, K. G. 1981: Gender cues in conversations. *Journal of Personality and Social Psychology* **40**, 99–110.

Halliday, M. A. K. 1975: *Learning how to mean: Explorations in the development of language.* London: Edward Arnold.

Halpern, G., MacNab, G. L., Kirby, D. M., Tuong, T. T., Martin, J. C., Hendleman, T. and Tourigny, R. 1976: *Alternative school programs for French language learning.* Toronto: Ontario Ministry of Education.

Hamilton, D. L. 1976: Cognitive biases in the perception of. social groups. In Carroll, J. S. and Payne, J. W., editors, *Cognition and social behaviour* (Hillsdale: Lawrence Erlbaum Associates) 81–94.

——— 1979: A cognitive-attributional analysis of stereotyping. In Berkowitz,

L., editor, *Advances in experimental social psychology*, vol. 12 (New York: Academic Press) 53–84.

Hamilton, D. L., Katz, L. B. and Leier, V. O. 1980: Organizational processes in impression formation. In Hastie, R., Ostrom, T. M., Ebbesen, E. B., Wyer, R., Hamilton, D. L. and Carlston, D. E., editors, *Person memory: The cognitive basis of social perception* (Hillsdale: Lawrence Erlbaum Associates) 121–53.

Hansen, C. 1980: Common sense attribution. *Journal of Personality and Social Psychology* **39**, 996–1009.

Harris, R. and Monaco, G. 1978: Psychology of pragmatic implication. *Journal of Experimental Psychology: General* **107**, 1–22.

Harrison, G. J. and Piette, A. B. 1980: Young bilingual children's language selection. *Journal of Multilingual and Multicultural Development* **1**, 217–30.

Harvey, J. H., Ickes, W. J. and Kidd, R. F. 1978: *New directions in attribution research*, vol. 2. Hillsdale: Lawrence Erlbaum Associates.

Hastie, R., Ostrom, T. M., Ebbesen, E. B., Wyer, R. S., Hamilton, D. L. and Carlston, D. E. 1980: *Person memory: The cognitive basis of social perception*. Hillsdale: Lawrence Erlbaum Associates.

Haugen, E. 1966: *Language conflict and language planning: The case of modern Norwegian*. Cambridge, Mass.: Harvard University Press.

Hayes, D. P. and Meltzer, L. 1972: Interpersonal factors based on talkativeness: Fact or artifact. *Sociometry* **35**, 538–61.

Hays, D. G. 1967: *Introduction to computational linguistics*. New York: American Elsevier Publishing Co.

Heath, S. B. 1979: The context of professional languages: An historical overview. In Alatis, J. E. and Tucker, G. R., editors, *Georgetown University Round Table on Languages and Linguistics 1979* (Washington: Georgetown University Press) 102–18.

Heider, F. 1946: Attitudes and cognitive organization. *Journal of Psychology* **21**, 107–12.

Helfrich, H. 1979: Age markers in speech. In Scherer, K. R. and Giles, H., editors, *Social markers in speech* (Cambridge: Cambridge University Press) 63–107.

Helson, H. 1959: Adaptation level theory. In Koch, S., editor, *Psychology: Study of science* (New York: McGraw-Hill) 565–621.

Henley, N. 1977: *Body politics: Power, sex and nonverbal communication*. Englewood Cliffs: Prentice-Hall.

Hermenet, A. M. B. 1971: *Ethnic identification of Puerto Rican seventh graders*. Unpublished doctoral dissertation, University of Massachusetts.

Heroux, M. 1978: *Les relations entre la langue anglaise et la langue française*. Québec: Office de la Langue Française, Editeur Officiel de Québec.

Hertz, B. 1950: *Where are your manners?* Chicago: Science Research Associates.

Hesbacher, P. and Fishman, J. A., 1965: Language loyalty: Its functions and concomitants in two bilingual communities. *Lingua* **13**, 146–65.

Hewett, N. 1971: Reactions of prospective English teachers toward speakers of a nonstandard dialect. *Language Learning* **21**, 205–12.

Hewstone, M. In press: The role of language in attribution processes. In Jaspars, J., Fincham, F. and Hewstone, M., editors, *Attribution theory: Essays and experiments* (London: Academic Press).

Hewstone, M. and Jaspars, J. 1982. Explanations for racial discrimination: The effect of group discussion on intergroup attributions. *European Journal of Social Psychology* **12**, 1–16.

Higgins, E. T. 1980: The 'communication game': Implications for social cognition and persuasion. In Higgins, E. T., Herman, C. P. and Zanna, M. P., editors, *Social cognition: The Ontario symposium* (Hillsdale: Lawrence Erlbaum Associates) 343–92.

Hoffman, C., Mischel, W. and Mazze, K. 1981: The role of purpose in the organization of information about behaviour: Trait-based versus goal-based categories in person cognition. *Journal of Personality and Social Psychology* **40**, 211–25.

Hofman, J. E. 1977: Language attitudes in Rhodesia. In Fishman, J. A., Cooper, R. L. and Conrad, A. W., editors, *The spread of English* (Rowley: Newbury House) 277–301.

Hofstadter, D. R. 1979: *Godel, Escher and Bach: An eternal golden braid*. New York: Basic Books.

Hofstadter, R. 1955: *Social Darwinism in American thought*. Boston: Beacon Press.

Holt, G. S. 1973: 'Inversion' in Black communication. In Kochman, T., editor, *'Rappin' and 'Stylin' Out; Communication in urban Black America* (Urbana-Champaign: University of Illinois Press) 152–9.

Hoover, M. 1978: Community attitudes toward Black English. *Language in Society* **7**, 65–87.

Hopper, R, 1977: Language attitudes in the job interview. *Communication Monographs* **44**, 346–51.

_____ 1981: The taken-for-granted. *Human Communication Research* **7**, 195–211.

Hopper, R. and Williams, F. 1973: Speech characteristics and employability. *Speech Monographs* **40**, 296–302.

Hosman, L. A. 1978: *Communicative competence: Adults' understanding of direct and indirect speech acts*. Unpublished doctoral dissertation, The University of Iowa.

Houts, P. L. 1977: *The myth of measurability*. New York: Hart Publishing.

Hovland, C. I., Janis, I. L. and Kelley, H. H. 1953: *Communication and persuasion*. New Haven: Yale University Press.

Hovland, C. I., Lumsdaine, A. A. and Sheffield, F. D. 1949: *Experiments on mass communication*. Princeton: Princeton University Press.

Hovland, C. I., Mandell, W., Cambell, E. H., Brock, T. C., Luchins, A. S., Cohen, A. R., McGuire, W. J., Janis, I. L., Feierabend, R. L. and Anderson, N. H. 1957: *Order of presentation in persuasion*. New Haven: Yale University Press.

Höweler, M. 1972: Diversity of word usage as a stress indicator in an interview situation. *Journal of Psycholinguistic Research* **1**, 243–8.

Hudson, R. A. 1980: *Sociolinguistics*. Cambridge: Cambridge University Press.

Husek, T. R. 1965: Persuasive impacts of early, late, or no mention of a negative source. *Journal of Personality and Social Psychology* **2**, 125–8.

Huygens, I. and Vaughan, G. 1983: Language attitudes, social class and ethnicity in New Zealand. *Journal of Multilingual and Multicultural Development*, in press.

Hymes, D. 1972: Models of the interaction of language and social setting. In Gumperz, J. J. and Hymes, D., editors, *Directions in sociolinguistics: The ethnography of communication* (New York: Holt, Rinehart & Winston) 35–71.

Ickes, W. and Barnes, R. D. 1977: The role of sex and self-monitoring in unstructured dyadic interactions. *Journal of Personality and Social Psychology* 35, 315–30.

Inglehart, R. F. and Woodward, M. 1967: Language conflicts and political community. *Comparative Studies in Society and History* 10, 27–40, 45.

Innes, J. M. and Fraser, C. 1971: Experimenter bias and other possible biases in psychological research. *European Journal of Social Psychology* 1, 297–310.

Insko, C. A. and Schopler, J. 1972: *Experimental social psychology*. New York: Academic Press.

Insko, C. A., Turnbull, W. and Yandell, B. 1974: Facilitative and inhibiting effects of distraction on attitude change. *Sociometry* 37, 508–28.

Instituto Caro y Cuervo 1965: *El simposio de Cartagena: Actas, communicaciones, informes*. Bogota: Instituto Caro y Cuervo.

Irwin, R. 1977: Judgements of vocal quality, speech fluency, and confidence of southern black and white speakers. *Language and Speech* 20, 261–6.

Isber, C. and Cantor, M. 1975: *Report of the task force on women in public broadcasting*. The Board of Directors, Corporation for Public Broadcasting.

Jacobsen, M. and Imhoof, M. 1974: Predicting success in learning a second language. *Modern Language Journal* 58, 329–36.

Jaffe, C. L. and Lucas, R. L. 1969: Effects of rates of talking and correctness of decisions on leader choice in small groups. *Journal of Social Psychology* 79, 247–54.

Jaffe, J. and Feldstein, S. 1970: *Rhythms of dialogue*. New York: Academic Press.

Jones, D. 1980: Gossip: Notes on women's oral culture. *Women's Studies International Quarterly* 3 (2/3), 193–8. These issues also appear as: Kramarae, C., editor, *The voices and words of women and men*. Oxford: Pergamon Press.

Jones, M. A. 1974: *American immigration*. Chicago: University of Chicago Press.

Jones, W. R. 1950a: Attitudes towards Welsh as a second language, a preliminary investigation. *British Journal of Educational Psychology* 19, 44–52.

_____ 1950b: Attitudes towards Welsh as a second language, a further investigation. *British Journal of Educational Psychology* 20, 117–32.

Jordan, D. 1941: The attitude of central school pupils to certain school subjects, and the correlation between attitude and attainment. *British Journal of Educational Psychology* 11, 28–44.

Jordan, W. D. 1973: *White over black: American attitudes toward the Negro, 1550–1812*. Baltimore: Penguin Books.

Joy, R. J. 1972: *Languages in conflict*. Toronto: McClelland & Stewart.

_____ 1978: *Les minorités des langues officielles au Canada*. Montreal: C. D. Howe Institute.

Kahneman, D. and Tversky, A. 1973: Subjective probability: A judgement of representativeness. *Psychological Review* 80, 237–51.

Kalin, R. and Rayko, D. 1980: The social significance of speech in the job interview. In St Clair, R. N. and Giles, H., editors, *The social and psychological
contexts of language* (Hillsdale: Lawrence Erlbaum Associates) 39–50.

Kalin, R., Rayko, D. S. and Love, N. 1980: The perception and evaluation of
job candidates with four different ethnic accents. In Giles, H., Robinson,
W. P. and Smith, P. M., editors, *Language: Social psychological perspectives*
(Oxford: Pergamon Press) 197–202.

Kanter, R. M. 1977: *Men and women of the corporation.* New York: Basic
Books.

Karabel, J. and Halsey, A. A. 1977: *Power and ideology in education.* New
York: Oxford University Press.

Kasl, W. V. and Mahl, G. F. 1965: The relationship of disturbances and hesita-
tions in spontaneous speech to anxiety. *Journal of Personality and Social Psychology* 1, 425–33.

Katz, D. 1960: The functional approach to the study of attitudes. *Public Opinion
Quarterly* 24, 163–204.

Katz, M. 1975: *Class, bureaucracy and schools: The illusions of educational
change in America.* New York: Praeger Publishers.

Katz, P. A. 1976a: The acquisition of racial attitudes in children. In Katz,
P. A., editor, *Towards the elimination of racism* (New York: Pergamon Press)
125–54.

――― 1976b: Attitude change in children: Can the twig be straightened? In
Katz, P. A., editor, *Towards the elimination of racism* (New York: Pergamon
Press) 213–41.

Keenan, E. O. 1977: Making it last: Repetition in children's discourse. In Ervin-
Tripp, S. and Mitchell-Kernan, C., editors, *Child discourse* (New York:
Academic Press) 125–38.

Kelley, H. H. 1972: Attribution in social interaction. In Jones, E. E., Kanouse,
D. E., Kelley, H. H., Nisbett, R. E., Valins, S. and Weiner, B., editors,
Attribution: Perceiving the causes of behaviour. Morristown: General
Learning Press.

――― 1973: The process of causal attribution. *American Psychologist* 28,
107–28.

Kelly, G. A. 1955: *The psychology of personal constructs*, vols. 1 and 2. New
York: Norton.

Kenny, D. A. 1979: *Correlation and causality.* New York: Wiley.

Kessler, S. and McKenna, W. 1978: *Gender: An ethnomethodological
approach.* New York: John Wiley & Sons.

Khleif, B. 1979: Insiders, outsiders and renegades: Toward a classification of
ethnolinguistic labels. In Giles, H. and Saint-Jacques, B., editors, *Language
and ethnic relations* (Oxford: Pergamon Press) 159–72.

Kimple, J., Cooper, R. and Fishman, J. 1969: Language switching and the
interpretation of conversation. *Lingua* 23, 127–34.

Kin, D. 1955: *Dictionary of American proverbs.* New York: Philosophical
Library.

King, J. and Scott, M. 1977: *Is this your life? Images of women in the media.*
London: Virago.

Kleiven, J. 1979: Social stereotypes elicited by linguistic differences. In
Rommetveit, R. and Blakar, R., editors, *Studies of language, thought and
verbal communication* (London: Academic Press) 401–7.

Kloss, H. 1971: *Les droits linguistiques des Franco-Américains aux Etats-Unis* Quebec: International Centre for Research on Bilingualism, Les Presses de l'Université Laval.

Kogan, N. and Wallach, M. A. 1964: *Risk taking: Study in cognition and personality*. New York: Holt, Rinehart & Winston.

Korzybski, A. 1933: *Science and sanity*. Lancaster: International Non-Aristotelian Library.

Kotey, P. F. A. and Der-Houssikian, H. 1977: *Language and linguistic problems in Africa*. Columbia: Hornbeam Press.

Kotler, T. and Chetwynd, J. 1980: Changes in family members during psychotherapy. *Human Relations* **33**, 101–10.

Kramarae, C. 1978: *Resistance to the public female voice*. Paper presented at the Ninth World Congress of Sociology, Uppsala, Sweden.

––––– 1981: *Women and Men speaking*. Rowley: Newbury House.

Kramer, C. 1974a: Folklinguistics. *Psychology Today*, June, 82–5.

––––– 1974b: Stereotypes of women's speech: The word from cartoons. *Journal of Popular Culture* **8**, 622–38.

––––– 1975a: *Excessive loquacity: Women's speech as presented in American etiquette books*. Paper presented at the meeting of the Speech Communication Association, Austin, Texas.

––––– 1975b: Women's Speech: Separate but unequal? In Thorne, B. and Henley, N., editors, *Language and sex: Difference and dominance* (Rowley: Newbury House) 43–56.

––––– 1977: Perceptions of female and male speech. *Language and Speech* **20**, 151–61.

––––– 1978: Women's and men's ratings of their own and ideal speech. *Communication Quarterly* **26**, 2–11.

Kramer, C., Thorne, B. and Henley, N. 1978: Review essay: Perspectives on language and communication. *Signs: Journal of Women in Culture and Society* **3**, 638–51.

Krear, S. 1969: The role of the mother tongue at home and at school in the development of bilingualism. *English Language Teaching* **24**, 2–4.

Krech, D. and Crutchfield, R. S. 1948: ·*Theory and problems of social psychology*. New York: McGraw-Hill.

Kwofie, E. N. 1977: *La langue française en afrique occidentale francophone*. B-69. Quebec: International Center for Research on Bilingualism.

Laberge, S. and Chiasson-Lavoie, M. 1971: Attitudes façe au français parlé à Montréal et degré de conscience des variables linguistiques. In Darnell, R., editor, *Language diversity in Canada* (Edmonton and Champaign: Linguistic Research) 89–128.

Labov, W. 1965: Stages in the acquisition of standard English. In *Social dialects and language learning* (Champaign: National Council of Teachers of English).

––––– 1966: *The social stratification of English in New York City*. Washington: Center for Applied Linguistics.

––––– 1969: The logic of non-standard English. *Monograph Series on Language and Linguistic* 22 (Washington: Georgetown University) 1–31.

_____ 1972: *Sociolinguistic patterns*. Philadelphia: University of Pennsylvania Press.

_____ 1973: The logic of nonstandard English. In N. Keddie, editor,` Tinker, tailor . . . The myth of cultural deprivation* (Harmondsworth: Penguin).

Laks, B. 1977: Contribution empirique a l'analyse socio-differentielle de la chute de /r/ dans les groupes consonantiques finals. *Langue Française* **34**, 109–25.

Lafont, R. 1973: Sur le probleme national en France: Aperçu historique. *Les Temps Modernes* **324–6**, 21–53.

Lakoff, G. and Johnson, M. 1980: *Metaphors we live by*. Chicago: University of Chicago Press.

Lakoff, R. 1973: Language and women's place. *Language in Society* **2**, 45–81.

_____ 1975: *Language and woman's place*. New York: Harper & Row.

Lambert, W. E. 1963: Psychological approaches to the study of language (Part II): On second language learning and bilingualism. *Modern Language Journal* **14**, 114–21.

_____ 1967: A social psychology of bilingualism. *Journal of Social Issues* **23**, 91–109.

_____ 1974: Culture and language as factors in learning and education. In Aboud, F. E. and Meade, R.D., editors, *Cultural factors in learning and education*, Fifth Western Washington Symposium on Learning. Bellingham: Western Washington University.

_____ 1978: Cognitive and socio-cultural consequences of bilingualism. *Canadian Modern Language Review* **34**, 537–47.

_____ 1979: Language as a factor in intergroup relations. In Giles, H. and St Clair, R. N., editors, *Language and Social Psychology* (Oxford: Basil Blackwell and Baltimore: University Park Press) 186–92.

Lambert, W. E., Frankel, H. and Tucker, G. R. 1966: Judging personality through speech: A French-Canadian example. *Journal of Communication* **16**, 305–21.

Lambert, W. E., Gardner, R. C., Barik, H. C. and Tunstall, K. 1963:` Attitudinal and cognitive aspects of intensive study of a second language. *Journal of Abnormal and Social Psychology* **66**, 358–68.

Lambert, W. E., Giles, H. and Albert, G. 1976: Language attitudes in a rural community in Northern Maine. *La Monda Lingvo-Problemo* **5**, 129–44, (now: *Language Problems and Language Planning*.)

Lambert, W. E., Giles, H. and Picard, O. 1975: Language attitudes in a French American community. *International Journal of the Sociology of Language* **4**, 127–52.

Lambert, W. E., Hodgson, R., Gardner, R. C. and Fillenbaum, S. 1960: Evaluational reactions to spoken languages. *Journal of Abnormal and Social Psychology* **60**, 44–51.

Lambert, W. E. and Tucker, G. R. 1972: *Bilingual education of children: The St Lambert experiment*. Rowley: Newbury House.

Langer, E. J. and Newman, H. 1979: The role of mindlessness in a typical social psychological experiment. *Personality and Social Psychology Bulletin* **5**, 295–8.

Language Policy Task Force 1980: Social dimensions of language use in East

Harlem. *Centro Working Papers* No. 7. (New York: Centro de Estudios Puertorriquenos).

Lanly, A. 1971: *Le Français d'Afrique du Nord*. Paris: Bordas.

Larimer, G. S. 1970: Indirect assessment of intercultural prejudices. *International Journal of Psychology* 5, 189–95.

Larsen, K. S., Martin, H. J. and Giles, H. 1977: Anticipated social cost and interpersonal accommodation. *Human Communication Research* 3, 303–8.

Lasker, B. 1929: *Race attitudes in children*. New York: Henry Holt & Co.

Lauver, P. J., Kelly, J. D. and Froehle, T. C. 1971: Client reaction time and counsellor verbal behavior in an interview setting. *Journal of Consulting Psychology* 18, 26–30.

Lawler, J. M. 1978: *IQ, heritability and racism*. New York: International Publishers.

Lay, C. H. and Burron, B. F. 1968: Perception of the personality of the hesitant speaker. *Perceptual and Motor Skills* 26, 951–6.

Leavitt, R. R. 1969: *A comparative study of sociocultural variables and stuttering among Puerto Rican elementary school children in San Juan, Puerto Rico, and New York, New York*. Unpublished doctoral dissertation, New York University.

Lee, R. 1971: Dialect perception: A critical review and reevaluation. *Quarterly Journal of Speech* 57, 410–17.

Lefebvre, C. 1974: Discreteness and the linguistic continuum in Martinique. *Anthropological Linguistics* 16, 47–75.

Lefebvre, G. R. 1976: Français regional et creole à Saint-Barthelemy, Guadeloupe. In Snyder, E. and Valdman, A., editors, *Identité culturelle et francophonie dans les Amérique*, vol. 1 (Quebec: Les Presses de l'Université Laval) 122–46.

Lefevre, J. 1978: Dialect and regional identification in Belgium: The case of Wallonia. *International Journal of the Sociology of Language* 15, 47–51.

_____ 1979: Nationalisme linguistique et identification linguistique: Le cas de Belgique. *International Journal of the Sociology of Language* 20, 37–58.

Leich, J. F. 1977: Minority languages in contemporary Louisiana. *La Monda Lingvo-Problemo* 6, 113–22. (now *Language Problems and Language Planning*).

Lennon, J. J. 1963: *A comparative study of the patterns of acculturation of selected Puerto Rican Protestant and Roman Catholic families in an urban metropolitan area (Chicago)*. Unpublished doctoral dissertation, University of Notre Dame.

Lentin, L. 1973: L'enseignement du français à l'école maternelle. *Le Français Aujourd' hui* 22, 55–60.

Léon, P. 1973: Reflexions idiomatologiques sur l'accent en tant que métaphore sociolinguistique. *The French Review* 46, 783–89.

_____ 1976: Attitudes et comportements linguistiques problèmes d'acculturation et d'identité. *Cahier de Linguistique* 6, 199–221.

Lerner, M. J. 1977: The justice motive: Some hypotheses as to its origins and forms. *Journal of Personality* 45, 1–52.

LeVine, R. A. and Campbell, D. T. 1972: *Ethnocentrism*. New York: Wiley.

Lewis, E. G. 1975: Attitude to language among bilingual children and adults in Wales. *International Journal of the Sociology of Language* 4, 103–21.

Lieberson, S. 1970: *Language and ethnic relations in Canada*. New York: Wiley.

Light, R. Y., Richard, D. P. and Bell, P. 1978: Development of children's attitudes toward speakers of standard and non-standard English. *Child Study Journal* **8**, 253–65.

Lind, E. A. and O'Barr, W. M. 1979: The social significance of speech in the courtroom. In Giles, H. and St Clair, R. N., editors, *Language and social psychology* (Oxford: Basil Blackwell and Baltimore: University Park Press) 66–87.

Lobelle, J. 1976: Le programme Codofil d'enseignment du français dans les écoles élémentaires en Louisianne. In Snyder, E. and Valdman, A., editors, *Identité culturelle et francophonie dans les Amériques*, vol. 1 (Quebec: Les Presses de l'Université Laval) 81–6.

Loeb, H., Jr. 1954: *He-Manners*. New York: Association Press.

_____ 1959: *She-Manners*. New York: Association Press.

Loman, B. 1976: Linguistic performance and social evaluation: A sociolinguistic attitude test. *International Journal of the Sociology of Language* **10**, 85–106.

Lorwin, V. R. 1972: Linguistic pluralism and political tension in modern Belgium. In Fishman, J. A., editor, *Advances in the sociology of language* (The Hague: Mouton) 386–412.

Lowery, C. R., Snyder, C. R. and Denney, N. W. 1976: Perceived aggression and predicted counteraggression as a function of sex of dyad participants: When males and females exchange verbal blows. *Sex Roles* **2**, 339–46.

Luigman, C. 1977: *What is IQ? – Intelligence, heredity, and environment*. London: Gordon Cremonisi.

Lukens, J. 1979: Interethnic conflict and communicative distances. In Giles, H. and Saint-Jacques, B., editors, *Language and ethnic relations* (New York: Pergamon Press) 143–58.

Lutz, R. J. 1981: A reconceptualization of the functional approach to attitudes. In Sheth, J. N. editor, *Research in marketing*, vol. 5 (Greenwich: JAI Press).

Lyczak, R., Fu, G. S. and Ho, A. 1976: Attitudes of Hong Kong bilinguals toward English and Chinese speakers. *Journal of Cross-Cultural Psychology* **7**, 425–38.

Macias, M. J. 1979: *The Galicians: Spain's forgotten minority*. Paper presented at the Third National Conference on the Third World, Omaha, Nebraska, October.

MacIntosh, R. and Ornstein, J. 1974: A brief sampling of West Texas teacher attitudes toward Southwest Spanish and English language varieties. *Hispania* **57**, 920–6.

MacKinnon, K. 1977: *Language, education and social processes in a Gaelic community*. London: Routledge & Kegan Paul.

Maclachlan, J. 1979: What people really think of fast talkers. *Psychology Today*, November, 113–16.

Macnamara, J. 1971: Successes and failures in the movement for the restoration of Irish. In Rubin, J. and Jernudd, B., editors, *Can language be planned?* (Honolulu: East-West Center Press) 65–94.

_____ 1973: Attitudes and learning a second language. In Shuy, R. and Fasold,

R., editors, *Language attitudes: Current trends and prospects* (Washington: Georgetown University Press) 36–40.

Major, B. 1980: Information acquisition and attribution processes. *Journal of Personality and Social Psychology* 39, 1010–23.

Manis, M. 1977: Cognitive social psychology. *Personality and Social Psychology Bulletin* 3, 550–66.

Mannes, M. 1969: Women are equal but — . In Bachelor, L., Henry, R. and Salisbury, R., editors, *Current thinking and writing* (New York: Appleton-Century-Crofts).

Marc, H. 1975: La situation en Alsace. *Langue Française* 25, 71–83.

Marcellesi, J. B. 1975: L'enseignement des langues régionales. *Langue Française* 25, 1–12.

_____ 1979: Quelques problèmes de l'hégémonie culturelle en France: Langue nationale et langues régionales. *International Journal of the Sociology of Language* 21, 63–80.

Marcos, L. R. 1979: Effects of interpreters on the evaluation of psycho-pathology in non-English-speaking patients. *American Journal of Psychiatry* 136, 171–4.

_____ 1980: The psychiatric evaluation and psychotherapy of the Hispanic bilingual patient. *Research Bulletin*, Hispanic Research Center 3, 1–7.

Marcos, L. R., Eisma, J. E. and Guimon, J. 1977: Bilingualism and sense of self. *American Journal of Psychoanalysis* 37, 285–90.

Marks, C. T. 1976: Policy and attitudes towards the teaching of standard dialect: Great Britain, France, West Germany. *Comparative Education* 12, 199–218.

Martin, L. W., Bradac, J. J. and Elliott, N. D. 1977: On the empirical basis of linguistics: A multivariate analysis of sentence judgements. In Beach, W. A., Fox, S. E. and Philosoph, S., editors, *Papers from the thirteenth regional meeting of the Chicago Linguistic Society* (Chicago: Chicago Linguistic Society) 357–71.

Martinet, A. 1969: *Le Français sans fard*. Paris: Presse Universitaire de France.

Martyna, W. 1980a: Beyond the 'he/man'approach. *Signs: Journal of Women in Culture and Society* 5, 482–93.

_____ 1980b: The psychology of the generic masculine. In McConnell–Ginet, S., Borker, R. and Furman, N., editors, *Women and language in literature and society* (New York: Praeger) 69–78.

Massad, M., Hubbard, M. and Newtson, D. 1979: Selective perception of events. *Journal of Experimental Social Psychology* 15, 513–32.

Matarazzo, J. D. and Wiens, A. W. 1972: *The interview: Research on its anatomy and structure*. Chicago: Aldine-Atherton.

Mayo, P. E. 1974: *The roots of identity*. London: Penguin Books.

McArthur, L. A. 1980: Illusory causation. *Personality and Social Psychology Bulletin* 6, 507–19.

McCauley, C., Stitt, C. L. and Segal, M. 1980: Stereotyping: From prejudice to prediction. *Psychological Bulletin* 87, 195–208.

McConnell-Ginet, S. 1978a: *Feminism in linguistics*. Paper given at Feminist Scholarship '78 conference Urbana, Illinois. A revised version will appear in Treichler, P., Kramarae, C. and Stafford, B., editors, For *Alma Mater* Urbana: University of Illinois Press, in press.

_____ 1978b. Intonation in a man's world. *Signs: Journal of Women in Culture and Society* 3, 541–59. A revised version will appear in Thorne, B., Kramarae, C. and Henley, N. editors, *Language and sex* II, (Rowley: Newbury House).

McGuire, W. J. 1966: Attitudes and opinion. *Annual Review of Psychology* 17, 475–514.

_____ 1969: The nature of attitudes and attitude change. In Lindzey, G. and Aronson, E., editors, *Handbook of social psychology*, vol. 3 (Reading: Addison-Wesley).

_____ 1978: The communication/persuasion matrix. In Lipstein, B. and McGuire, W. J., editors, *Evaluating advertising: A bibliography of the communication process*. New York: Advertising Research Foundation.

McGuire, W. J., McGuire, C. V., Child, P. and Fujioka, T. 1978: Salience of ethnicity in the spontaneous self-concept as a function of one's ethnic distinctiveness in the social environment. *Journal of Personality and Social Psychology* 36, 511–20.

McKirnan, D. J. and Hamayan, E. V. 1980: Language norms and perceptions of ethno-linguistic group diversity. In Giles, H., Robinson, W. P. and Smith, P. M., editors, *Language: Social psychological perspectives* (Oxford: Pergamon) 161–70.

McNeill, D. 1970: *The acquisition of language*. New York: Harper & Row.

Mercer, G. V: 1975: *The development of children's ability to discriminate between languages and varieties of the same language*. Unpublished M. A. thesis, McGill University, Montreal.

Mercer, N., Mercer, E. and Mears, R. 1979: Linguistic and cultural affiliation amongst young Asian people in Leicester. In Giles, H. and Saint-Jacques, B., editors, *Language and ethnic relations* (Oxford: Pegamon) 15–26.

Metcalf, A. A. 1974: The study of California Chicano English. *International Journal of the Sociology of Language* 2, 53–8.

Meyers, J. L. 1972: *Fundamentals of experimental design*, 2nd edn. Boston: Allyn & Bacon.

Miller, D. T. 1975: The effect of dialect and ethnicity on communicator effectiveness. *Speech Monographs* 42, 69–74.

Miller, G. R. and Parks, M. R. In press: Communication in dissolving relationships. In Duck, S. W., editor, *Personal Relationships 4: Dissolving Personal Relationships*. London and New York: Academic Press.

Miller, G. R. and Steinberg, M. 1975: *Between people: A new analysis of interpersonal communication*. Chicago: Science Research Associates.

Miller, N., Maruyama, G., Beaber, R. J. and Valone, K. 1976: Speed of speech and persuasion. *Journal of Personality and Social Psychology* 34, 615–24.

Mills, C. W., Senior, C. and Goldsen, R. K. 1950: *The Puerto Rican journey: New York's newest migrants*. New York: Harper Brothers.

Mills, J. and Harvey, J. 1972: Opinion change as a function of when information about the communicator is received and whether he is attractive or expert. *Journal of Personality and Social Psychology* 21, 52–5.

Milmoe, S., Rosenthal, R., Blane, H. T., Chafetz, M. E. and Wolf, I 1967: The doctor's voice: Postdictor of successful referral of alcoholic patients. *Journal of Abnormal Psychology* 72, 78–84.

Milner, D. 1975: *Children and race*. Harmondsworth: Penguin.

_____ 1981: Racial prejudice. In Turner, J. C. and Giles, H., editors, *Intergroup Behaviour (Oxford: Blackwell)* 102–43.

Milroy, L. and McClenaghan, P. 1977: Stereotyped reactions to four educated accents in Ulster. *Belfast Working Papers in Language and Linguistics* 2 (4).

Mioni, A. M. and Arnuzzo-Lansweert. A. M. 1979: Sociolinguistics in Italy. *International Journal of the Sociology of Language* 21.

Mitchell, A. and Delbridge, A. 1965: *The pronunciation of English in Australia.* Sydney: Angus & Robertson.

Moscovici, S. 1976: *Social influence and social change.* London: Academic Press.

Moscovici, S. and Doise, W. 1974: Decision-making in groups. In Nemeth, C., editor, *Social psychology: Classic contemporary integrations* (Chicago: Rand McNally) 250–88.

Moscovici, S. and Farr, R. In press: *Social representations.* Cambridge: Cambridge University Press.

Mougeon, R. 1979: *Compte-rendu périodique du programme de récherche sociolinguistique du centre d'études Franco-Ontarienne.* Toronto: Ontario Institute for Studies in Education.

Mougeon, R. and Canale, M. 1979: Maintenance of French in Ontario: Is education in French enough? *Interchange* 9, 30–9.

Mueller, T. H. and Miller, R. I. 1970: A study of student attitudes and motivation in a collegiate French course using programmed language instruction. *International Review of Applied Linguistics* 8, 297–320.

Mulac, A. 1976a: Assessment and application of the revised dialect attitudinal scale. *Communication Monographs* 43, 238–45.

_____ 1976b: Effects of obscene language upon three dimensions of listener attitude. *Communication Monographs* 43, 300–7.

Mulac, A. and Lundell, T. L. 1980: Differences in perceptions created by syntactic-semantic productions of male and female speakers. *Communication Monographs* 47, 111–18.

Myers, D. G. and Lamm, H. 1976: The group polarization phenomenon. *Psychological Bulletin* 83, 606–27.

Naiman, N., Fröhlich, M., Stern, H. H. and Todesco, A. 1978: The good language learner. *Research in Education Series* No. 7, Ontario Institute for Studies in Education, Toronto.

Naremore, R. C. 1971: Teachers' judgements of children's speech: A factor analytic study of attitudes. *Speech Monographs* 38, 17–27.

Natale, M. 1975a: Convergence of mean vocal intensity in dyadic communication as a function of social desirability. *Journal of Personality and Social Psychology* 32, 790–804.

_____ 1975b: Social desirability as related to convergence of temporal speech patterns. *Perceptual and Motor Skills* 40, 827–30.

Naylor, P. B. 1979: *Linguistic and cultural interference in testimony.* Paper presented at the first International Conference on Social Psychology and Language, University of Bristol.

Neidt, C. O. and Hedlund, D. E. 1967: The relationship between changes in attitudes toward a course and final achievement. *Journal of Educational Research* **61**, 56–8.

Newcombe, N. and Arnkoff, D. B. 1979: Effects of speech style and sex of speaker on person perception. *Journal of Personality and Social Psychology* **37**, 1293–303.

Newman, E. 1974: *Strictly speaking – Will America be the death of English?* New York: Warner Books.

Newman, H. 1981: Communication within ongoing intimate relationships: An attributional perspective. *Personality and Social Psychology Bulletin* **7**, 59–70.

Nichols, P. C. 1978: *Dynamic variation theory as a model for the study of language and sex.* Paper given at the Ninth World Congress of Sociology, Uppsala, Sweden. A revised version of this paper will appear in Thorne, B., Kramarae, C. and Henley, N. editors, *Language and sex* II (Rowley: Newbury House).

Nisbett, R. E. and Ross, L. 1980: *Human inference: Strategies and shortcomings of social judgement.* Englewood Cliffs: Prentice-Hall.

Nisbett, R. E. and Wilson, T. D., 1977a: Telling more than one can know: Verbal reports on mental processes. *Psychological Review* **84**, 231–59.

_____ 1977b: The halo effect: Evidence for unconscious alteration of judgement. *Journal of Personality and Social Psychology* **35**, 250–6.

Nisbett, R. E., Zukier, H. and Lemley, R. E. 1981: The dilution effect: Nondiagnostic information weakens the implications of diagnostic information. *Cognitive psychology* **73**, 248–77.

Nixon, R. M. and The Staff of the *Washington Post* 1974: *The presidential transcripts.* New York: Delacorte Press.

Norman, R. 1976: When what is said is important: A comparison of expert and attractive sources. *Journal of Experimental Social Psychology* **12**, 294–300.

Novotny, A. 1974: *Strangers at the door.* New York: Bantam Books.

O'Barr, W. M. and Atkins, B. K. 1980: 'Women's language' or 'powerless language'? In McConnell-Ginet, S., Borker, R. and Furman N., editors, *Women and language in literature and society.* (New York: Praeger) 93–110.

O'Connor, L. 1954: *Pioneer women orators: Rhetoric in the ante-bellum reform movement.* New York: Columbia University Press.

Ogden, C. K., authorized by the Orthological Institute and prepared by E. C. Graham, 1968: *Basic English.* New York: Harcourt, Brace & World.

O'Kane, D. 1977: Overt and covert prestige in Belfast vernacular speakers: The results of self-report tests. *Belfast Working Papers in Language and Linguistics* **2** (3).

Oller, J. W. 1979: *Language tests at school: A pragmatic approach.* London: Longman.

Oller, J. W., Baca, L. and Vigil, F. 1978: Attitudes and attained proficiency in ESL: A sociolinguistic study of Mexican Americans in the southwest. *TESOL Quarterly* **11**, 173–83.

Oller, J. W., Hudson, A. and Liu, P. 1977: Attitudes and attained proficiency in ESL: A sociolinguistic study of native speakers of Chinese in the United States. *Language Learning* **27**, 1–27.

O'Neil, W. 1972: The politics of bidialectalism. *College English* **33**, 439–56.

Orjala, P. R. 1970: *A dialect study of Haitian Creole.* Unpublished doctoral dissertation. Hardford: Hardford Seminary Foundation.

Ornstein, J. 1974: The sociolinguistic studies on southwest bilingualism: a status report. In Bills, G. D., editor, *Southwest Areal Linguistic* (San Diego: Institute for Cultural Pluralism) 11–34.

Ortego, P. 1969: Some cultural implications of a Mexican-American border dialect of American English. *Studies in Linguistics* 21, 77–84.

Orwell, G. 1949a: *1984.* New York: Harcourt Brace.

Orwell, G. 1949b: The principles of Newspeak. In G. Orwell, *1984* (New York: Harcourt Brace).

Osgood, C. H. May, W. H. and Miron, M. S. 1975: *Cross-cultural universals of affective meaning.* Urbana: University of Illinois Press.

Osgood, C. E. and Tannenbaum, P. H. 1955: The principle of congruity in the prediction of attitude change. *Psychological Review* 62, 42–55.

Osgood, C. H., G. J. Suci, and Tannenbaum, P. H. 1957: *The measurement of meaning.* Urbana: University of Illinois Press.

Oskamp, S. 1977: *Attitudes and opinions.* Englewood Cliffs: Prentice-Hall.

Ostrom, T. M. and Upshaw, H. S. 1968: Psychological perspective and attitude change. In Greenwald, A. G., Brock, T. C. and Ostrom, T. M., editors, *Psychological foundations of attitudes.* (New York: Academic Press).

Padilla, A. M. and Long, K. K. 1969: *An assessment of successful Spanish-American students at the University of New Mexico.* Paper presented at the annual meeting of AAAS, Rocky Mountain Division, Colorado Springs.

Padilla, E. 1958: *Up from Puerto Rico.* New York: Columbia University Press.

Paivio, A. 1971: *Imagery and verbal processes.* New York: Holt, Rinehart & Winston.

Palmer, L. A. 1973: A preliminary report on a study of the linguistic correlates of rates: Subjective judgements of non-native English speech. In Shuy, R. W. and Fasold, R., editors, *Language attitudes: Current trends and prospects.* (Washington: Georgetown University Press) 41–59.

Paris, R. 1976: Le maintien du français dans les Amériques: Utilité et motivation: Canada et Etats-Unis. In Runte, H. R. and Valdman, A., editors, *Identité culturelle et francophonie dans les Amériques*, vol. 2 (Bloomington: Indiana University Press) 42–50.

Parkinson, M. 1979: *Speech patterns and the outcome of trials.* Paper presented at the First International Conference on Social Psychology and Language, University of Bristol.

Parsons, E. C. 1913: *The old-fashioned woman: Primitive fancies about the sex.* New York: G. P. Putnams' Sons.

Peabody, D. 1970: Evaluative and descriptive aspects in personality perception: A reappraisal. *Journal of Personality and Social Psychology* 16, 639–46.

Pearce, W. B. and Brommel, B. J. 1971: Vocalic communication in persuasion. *Quarterly Journal of Speech* 58, 298–306.

Peñalosa, F. 1980: *Chicano sociolinguistics – A brief introduction.* Rowley: Newbury House.

Perez-Alonso, J. 1979: Catalan – an example of the current language struggle in Spain: Sociopolitical and pedagogical implications. *International Journal of the Sociology of Language* 21, 109–25.

Perloff, R. M. and Brock, T. C. 1980: '... And thinking makes it so': Cognitive responses to persuasion. In Roloff, M. E. and Miller, G. R., editors, *Persuasion: New directions in theory and research* (Beverly Hills: Sage).

Person, Y. 1973: Impérialisme linguistique et colonialisme. *Les Temps Modernes* **324–6**, 90–118.

Petty, R. E. 1977: *A cognitive response analysis of the temporal persistance of attitude changes induced by persuasive communications.* Unpublished doctoral dissertation, Ohio State University.

Petty, R. E. and Cacioppo, J. T. 1977: Forewarning, cognitive responding, and resistance to persuasion. *Journal of Personality and Social Psychology* **35**; 645–55.

_____ 1979a: Effects of forewarning of persuasive intent and involvement on cognitive responses and persuasion. *Personality and Social Psychology Bulletin* **5**, 173–6.

_____ 1979b: Issue involvement can increase or decrease persuasion by enhancing message-relevant cognitive responses. *Journal of Personality and Social Psychology* **37**, 1915–26.

_____ 1981a: *Attitudes and persuasion: Classic and contemporary approaches.* Dubuque: Wm. C. Brown.

_____ 1981b: Issue involvement as a moderator of the effects on attitude of advertising content and context. *Advances in Consumer Research* **9**, 20–4.

Petty, R. E., Cacioppo, J. T. and Heesacker, M. 1981: The use of rhetorical questions in persuasion: A cognitive response analysis. *Journal of Personality and Social Psychology* **40**, 432–40.

Petty, R. E., Ostrom, T. M. and Brock, T. C. 1981: *Cognitive responses in persuasion.* Hillsdale: Lawrence Erlbaum Associates.

Petty, R. E., Wells, G. L. and Brock, T. C. 1976: Distraction can enhance or reduce yielding to propaganda: Thought disruption versus effort justification. *Journal of Personality and Social Psychology* **34**, 874–84.

Phelps, S. and Austin, N. 1975: *The assertive woman.* San Luis Obispo: Impact Publishers.

Philips, S. 1980: Sex differences and language. *Annual Review of Anthropology* **9**, 523–44.

Piriou, Y. B. 1973: Usages spontané et littéraire. *Les Temps Modernes* **324–6**, 195–212.

Piron, M. 1970: Aperçu des études relatives au français de Belgique. *Annales de la Faculté des Lettres et Sciences Humaines de Nice* **12**, 31–48.

Planalp, S. and Tracy, K. 1980: Not to change the topic but ... A cognitive approach to the management of conversation. In Nimmo, D., editor, *Communication Yearbook* **4** (New Brunswick: Transaction Books) 237–58.

Polenz, P. von 1972: *Die Geschichte der deutschen Sprache.* Berlin: Walter de Gruyter.

Politzer, R. L. 1978: Errors of English speakers of German as perceived and evaluated by German natives. *The Modern Language Journal* **62**, 253–61.

Politzer, R. L. and Ramirez, A. G. 1973a: Judging personality from speech: A pilot study of the attitudes toward ethnic groups of students in monolingual schools. *R & D Memorandum* No. 107 (Stanford: Stanford Center for Research and Development in Teaching, Stanford University).

_____ 1973b: Judging personality from speech: A pilot study of the effects of bilingual education on attitudes toward ethnic groups. *R & D Memorandum* No. 106. (Stanford: Stanford Center for Research and Development in Teaching, Stanford University).

Pompilus, P. 1969: Le fait français en Haiti. Annales de la *Faculté des Lettres et Sciences Humaines de Nice* 7, 37–42.

Poole, M. S. 1981: Decision development in small groups 1: A comparison of 2 models. *Communication Monographs* 48, 1–24.

Poplack, S. 1978: Dialect acquisition among Puerto Rican bilinguals. *Language in Society* 7, 89–103.

Post, E. 1945: *Etiquette: The blue book of social usage*. New York: Funk & Wagnalls.

Pottier, B. 1968: La situation linguistique en France. In Martinet, A., editor, *Le Langage, Encyclopedie de la Pléiade* (Bruges: Editions Gallimard).

Pousada, A. 1979: Interpreting for language minorities in the courts. In Alatis, J. E. and Tucker, G. R., editors, *Language in public life. Georgetown University Round Table 1979* (Washington: Georgetown University Press) 186–208.

Powesland, P. and Giles, H. 1975: Persuasiveness and accent–message incompatibility. *Human Relations* 28, 85–93.

Price, S., Fluck, M. and Giles, H. 1983: The effects of language of testing on bilingual pre-adolescents' attitudes towards Welsh and varieties of English. *Journal of Multilingual and Multicultural Development*, in press.

Priestly, T. M. S. 1981: Attitudes to language among German/Slavic bilinguals in Southern Austria. In *Selected Proceedings from the Central and East European Studies Association of Canada Conference*, Edmonton, March 13–15, 1980. Edmonton: CEESAC.

Ramirez, A. G., Arce-Torres, E. and Politzer, R. L. 1978: Language attitudes and achievement of bilingual pupils in English language arts. *The Bilingual Review/La Revista Bilingue* 5, 169–206.

Ramirez, C. 1978: Lexical usage of, and attitudes toward, southwest Spanish in the Ysleta, Texas area. In Gilbert, G. and Ornstein, J., editors, *Problems in applied educational sociolinguistics* (The Hague: Mouton) 43–53.

Ramirez, K. G. 1974: Socio-cultural aspects of the Chicano dialect. In Bills, G. D., editor, *Southwest areal linguistics* (San Diego: Institute for Cultural Pluralism, San Diego State University) 79–84.

Ramirez, M. III and Castaneda, A. 1974: *Cultural democracy, bicognitive development, and education*. New York: Academic Press.

Report of the Committee on Irish Language Attitudes Research 1975: Dublin: Government Stationery Office.

Rey, A. 1977: Accent and employability: Language attitudes. *Language Sciences* 47, 7–12.

Rey, A. 1978: La normalisation linguistique dans la perspective des nouvelles dispositions legislatives. In Hudon, F., editor, *Les implications linguistiques de l'intervention juridique de l'état dans le domaine de la langue* (Québec: l'Office de la Langue Française, Editeur Officiel du Québec) 23–40.

Reynolds, A. G., Flagg, P. and Kennedy, W. 1974: *Language study abroad: Evaluation and prediction*. Paper presented at meetings of the Northeastern Educational Research Association, Ellenville, NY.

Rhodes, N. C. 1979: *Attitudes toward Guarani and Spanish: A pilot study in Paraguay.* Unpublished manuscript, Georgetown University.

_____ 1980: Attitudes towards Guarani and Spanish: A survey. *Linguistic Reporter* **22**, 4–5.

Riggs, C. J. 1979: Thee and they: A natural look at some effects of long-term interaction on individual perception and behaviour. *Journal of Applied Communication Research* **7**, 35–44.

Ringen, J. D. 1975: Linguistic facts: A study of the empirical scientific status of transformational generative grammars. In Cohen, D. and Wirth, J. R., editors, *Testing linguistic hypotheses* (Washington: Hemisphere Publishing Company) 1–41.

Rioux, M. 1974: *Les Québécois.* Paris: Editions du Seuil.

Ris, R. 1979: Dialekte und Einheitssprache in der deutschen Schweitz. *International Journal of the Sociology of Language* **21**.

Rist, R. 1970: Student social class and teacher expectations: The self-fulfilling prophecy in ghetto education. *Harvard Educational Review* **40**, 411–51.

Roberts, C. and Williams, G. 1980: Attitudes and ideological bases of support for Welsh as a minority language. In Giles, H., Robinson, W. P. and Smith, P. M., editors, *Language: Social ·psychological perspectives* (Oxford: Pergamon Press) 227–32.

Robinson, D. 1979: *Systems of modern psychology.* New York: Columbia University Press.

Robinson, J. 1976: Review of La llengua dels Baracelonins: resultats d'una enquesta sociologice-linguistica by Antoni M. Badia i Margarit. *Language in Society* **5**, 115–19.

Robinson, W. P. 1972: *Language and social behaviour.* Harmondsworth: Penguin.

_____ 1979: Speech markers and social class. In Scherer, K. R. and Giles, H., editors, *Social markers in speech* (Cambridge: Cambridge University Press) 211–49.

Rodriguez, R. 1975: On becoming a Chicano. *Saturday Review*, 8 February, 46–8.

Roloff, M. and Berger, C. R. In press. *Social cognition and communication.* Beverly Hills: Sage.

Romaine, S. 1980: Stylistic variation and evaluative reactions to speech: Problems in the investigation of linguistic attitudes in Scotland. *Language and Speech* **23**, 213–32.

Ros, M. and Giles, H. 1979: The Valencian language situation: An accommodation perspective. *ITL: Review of Applied Linguistics* **44**, 3–24.

Rosaldo, M. 1980: The use and abuse of anthropology: Reflections on feminism and cross-cultural understanding. *Signs: Journal of Women in Culture and Society* **5**, 389–417.

Rosenfeld, H. M. 1978: Conversational control functions of nonverbal behaviour. In Siegman, A. W. and Feldstein, S., editors, *Nonverbal behaviour and communication* (Hillsdale: Lawrence Erlbaum Associates).

Rosenthal, M. 1974: The magic boxes: Pre-school children's attitudes toward black and standard English. *The Florida FL Reporter* **12**, 55–62, 92–3.

Rosenthal, R. and Jacobson, L. 1968: *Pygmalion in the classroom.* New York: Holt, Rinehart & Winston.

Ross, J. 1979: Sampling, elicitation, and interpretation: Orleans and elsewhere. In McCormack, W. C. and Wurm, S. A., editors, *Language and Society* (The Hague: Mouton) 231–48.

Ross, J. A., 1979: Language and the mobilization of ethnic identity. In Giles, H. and Saint-Jacques, B. editors, *Language and ethnic relations* (Oxford: Pergamon Press) 1–13.

Ross, J. R. 1972: Doubl-ing. *Linguistic Inquiry* 3, 61–86.

_____ 1979: Where's English? In Fillmore, C. J., Kempler, D. and Wang, W. S-Y, editors, *Individual differences in language ability and language behaviour* (New York: Academic Press) 127–63.

Roudaut, R. 1973: Histoire du Mouvement Breton. *Les Temps Modernes* **324-6**, 170–94.

Royal Commission on Bilingualism and Biculturalism, Book 1–4, 1969: Ottawa: Queen's Printer.

Rubin, J. 1968: *National bilingualism in Paraguay.* The Hague: Mouton.

_____ 1978: Toward bilingual education for Paraguay. In Alatis, J. E., editor, *Georgetown University Round Table on Languages and Linguistics 1978*: International dimensions of bilingual education (Washington: Georgetown University Press) 189–201.

Rumbaugh, D. M. 1977: *Language learned by a chimpanzee: The Lana project.* New York: Academic Press.

Ryan, E. B. 1979: Why do low-prestige language varieties persist? In Giles, H. and St Clair; R.N., editors, *Language and social psychology.* (Oxford: Basil Blackwell and Baltimore: University Park Press) 145–57.

Ryan, E.B. and Cacioppo, J. T. 1981: Review of 'Social Markers in Speech'. edited by Scherer, K. R. and Giles, H. *Language in Society* **10**, 443–7.

Ryan, E. B. and Capadano, H. L. 1978: Age perceptions and evaluative reactions.toward adult speakers. *Journal of Gerontology* **33**, 98–102.

Ryan, E. B. and Carranza, M. 1975: Evaluative reactions of adolescents toward speakers of standard English and Mexican American accented English. *Journal of Personality and Social Psychology* **31**, 855–63.

_____ 1977: Ingroup and outgroup reactions toward Mexican American language varieties. In Giles H., editor, *Language, ethnicity and intergroup relations* (London: Academic Press) 59–82.

Ryan, E. B., Carranza, M. A. and Moffie, R. W. 1975: Mexican American reactions to accented English. In Berry, J. W. and Lonner, W. J., editors, *Applied Cross-Cultural Psychology* (Amsterdam: Swets & Zeitlinger B. V.) 174–8

_____ 1977: Reactions toward varying degrees of accentedness in the speech of Spanish-English bilinguals. *Language and Speech* **20**, 267–73.

Ryan, E. B. and Sebastian, R. 1980: The effects of speech style and social class background on social judgements of speakers. *British Journal of Social and Clinical Psychology* **19**, 229–33.

Ryan, W. 1972: *Blaming the victim.* New York: Vintage Books.

Sabourin, C. and Lamarche, R. 1979: *Le français québécois: Bibliographie analytique.* Montreal: Office de la Langue Française, Editeur officiel du Québec. (over 3300 titles).

Sabourin, C. and Petit, N. 1979: *Langues et Societés: Bibliographie analytique informatisée*. Montreal: Office de la Langue Française, Editeur Officiel du Québec (over 5000 titles).

Sachs, J. 1975: Cues to the identification of sex in children's speech. In Thorne, B. and Henley, N., editors, *Language and sex: Difference and dominance* (Rowley: Newbury House) 152–71.

St Clair, R. N. 1979: The politics of language. *Word* **29**, 40–64.

_____ In press: The social genesis of language attitudes. *Language Sciences*.

St Clair, R. N. and Giles, H. 1980: *The social and psychological contexts of language*. Hillsdale: Lawrence Erlbaum Associates.

Sanchez, R. 1977: Chicano bilingualism. *New Scholar* **6**, 209–25.

Sandell, R. 1977: *Linguistic style and persuasion*. London: Academic Press.

Sanders, R. E. and Martin, L. W. 1975: Grammatical rules and explanations of behavior. *Inquiry* **18**, 65–82.

Sankoff, D. and Lessard, R. 1975: Vocabulary richness: A sociolinguistic analysis. *Science* **190**, 689–90.

Sarnoff, I. 1970: Social attitudes and the resolution of motivational conflict. In Jahoda, M. and Warren, N., editors, *Attitudes* (Harmondsworth: Penguin) 279–84.

Sassoon, C. and Giles, H. In preparation: *The effects of British accent usage and SES background on impression formation*. Mimeo.: University of Bristol.

Sattel, J. 1976: The inexpressive male: Tragedy or sexual politics. *Social Problems* **23**, 469–77. A revised version of this paper will appear in Thorne, B., Kramarae, C. and Henley, N. editors, *Language and sex* II, (Rowley: Newbury House).

Schank, R. and Abelson, R. P. 1977: *Scripts, plans, goals and understanding: An inquiry into human knowledge structure*. Hillsdale: Lawrence Erlbaum Associates.

Scherer, K. R. 1974: Voice quality analysis of American and German speakers. *Journal of Psycholinguistic Research* **3**, 281–90.

_____ 1978: Personality inference from voice quality: The loud voice of extroversion. *European Journal of Social Psychology* **8**, 467–87.

_____ 1979a: Personality markers in speech. In Scherer, K. R. and Giles, H., editors, *Social markers in speech* (Cambridge: Cambridge University Press) 147–209.

_____ 1979b: Voice and speech correlates of perceived social influence in simulated juries. In Giles, H. and St Clair, R. N., editors. *Language and social psychology* (Oxford: Basil Blackwell and Baltimore: University Park Press) 88–120.

Scherer, K. R. and Giles, H. 1979: *Social markers in speech*. Cambridge: Cambridge University Press.

Scherer, K. R., London, H. and Wolf, J. J. 1973: The voice of confidence: Paralinguistic cues and audience evaluation. *Journal of Research in Personality* **7**, 31–44.

Scherer, K. R. and Oshinsky, J. 1977: Cue utilization in emotion attribution from auditory stimuli. *Motivation and Emotion* **1**, 331–46.

Schermerhorn, R. A. 1970: *Comparative ethnic relations*. New York: Random House.

Schlesinger, A. 1946: *Learning how to behave: A historical study of American etiquette books*. New York: The Macmillan Company.

Schlieben-Lange, B. 1977: The language situation in southern France. *International Journal of the Sociology of Language* 12, 101–8.

Schneider, D. J., Hastorf, D. J. and Ellsworth, P. C. 1979: *Person perception*. Reading: Addison-Wesley.

Schneiderman, E. 1976: An examination of the ethnic and linguistic attitudes of bilingual children. *ITL* 33, 59–72.

Schumann, J. H. 1975: Affective factors and the problem of age in second language acquisition. *Language Learning* 25, 209–35.

Scott, K. 1980: Perceptions of communication competence: What's good for the goose is not good for the gander. *Women's Studies International Quarterly* 3 (2/3), 199–208. These issues also appear as Kramarae, C., editor, *The voices and words of women and men* (Oxford: Pergamon Press).

Scotton, C. M. 1976: Strategies of neutrality: Language choice in uncertain situations. *Language* 52, 913–41.

Scotton, C. M. and Ury, W. 1977: Bilingual Strategies: The social functions of code-switching. *International Journal of the Sociology of Language* 13, 5–20.

Schutz, A. 1967: *The phenomenology of the social world*. Trans. G. Walsh and F. Legnert. Evanston: Northwestern University Press.

Searle, J. R. 1969: *Speech acts*. Cambridge: Cambridge University Press.

Searle, J. 1975: Indirect speech acts. In Cole, J. and Morgan, J. L., editors, *Syntax and semantics, vol. III, Speech acts* (New York: Academic Press) 59–82.

Sebastian, R. J. and Ryan, E. B. In press: Speech cues and social evaluation: Markers of ethnicity, social class and age. In Giles, H. and St Clair, R. N., editors, *Recent advances in language, communication, and social psychology* (Hillsdale: Lawrence Erlbaum Associates).

Sebastian, R. J., Ryan, E. B. and Abbott, A. R. 1981: *Evaluative reactions toward adult speakers of varying ages*. Paper presented at the annual meeting of the Midwestern Psychological Association, Detroit.

Sebastian, R. J., Ryan, E. B. and Corso, L. In press: Social judgements of speakers with differing degrees of accent. *Social Behavior and Personality*.

Sebastian, R. J., Ryan, E. B., Keogh, T. F. and Schmidt, A. C. 1980: The effects of negative affect arousal on reactions to speakers. In Giles, H., Robinson, W. P. and Smith, P. M., editors, *Language: Social psychological perspectives* (Oxford: Pergamon Press) 203–8.

Secord, P. and Backman, C. 1964: *Social psychology*. New York: McGraw-Hill.

Segalowitz, N. and Gatbonton, E. 1977: Studies of the non-fluent bilingual. In Hornby, P. A., editor, *Bilingualism: Psychological, social and educational implications* (New York: Academic Press) 77–90.

Seggie, I. 1983: Attributions of guilt as a function of accent and crime. *Journal of Multilingual and Multicultural Development*, in press.

Seggie, I., Fulmizi, C. and Stewart, J. 1982: Evaluations of personality traits and employment suitability based on various Australian accents. *Australian Journal of Psychology*, in press.

Seligman, C., Tucker, G. R. and Lambert, W. E. 1972: The effects of speech style and other attributes on teachers' attitudes toward pupils. *Language in Society* 1, 131–42.

Sennett, R. 1978: *The fall of public man: On the social psychology of capitalism*. New York: Vintage Books.

Serbin, L. A., O'Leary, K. D., Kent, R. N. and Tonick, I. J. 1973: Preacademic and problem behaviour of boys and girls. *Child Development* **44**, 796–804.

Sereno, K. K. and Hawkins, G. J. 1967: The effects of variations in speakers' nonfluency upon audience ratings of attitude toward the speech topic and speakers' credibility. *Speech Monographs* **34**, 58–64.

Shafer, R. and Shafer, S. 1975: Teacher attitudes towards children's language in West Germany and England. *Comparative Education* **11**, 43–61.

Sherif, C. W., Sherif, M. and Nebergall, R. E. 1965: *Attitude and attitude change: The social judgement–involvement approach*. Philadelphia: W. B. Saunders Company.

Sherif, M. and Hovland, C. 1961: *Social judgement: Assimilation and contrast effects in communication and attitude change*. New Haven: Yale University Press.

Sherif, M. and Sherif, C. W. 1967: Attitude as the individual's own categories: The social judgment-involvement approach to attitude and attitude change. In Sherif, C. W. and Sherif, M., editors, *Attitude, ego-involvement, and change* (New York: Wiley).

Sherry, R. 1961: *A treatise of schemes and tropes (1550)*. Introduction and index by H. H. Hildebrandt (Gainesville: Scholars' Facsimiles and Reprints).

Shuy, R. W. 1973: Language and success: Who are the judges? In Bailey, R. W. and Robinson, J., editors, *Varieties of present-day English* (New York: Macmillan).

_____ 1979: Language policy in medicine: Some emerging issues. In Alatis, J. E. and Tucker, G. R., editors, *Georgetown University Round Table on Language and Linguistics* (Washington: Georgetown University Press) 126–36.

Shuy, R. W. and Fasold, R. W. 1973: *Language attitudes: Current trends and prospects*. Washington: Georgetown University Press.

Shuy, R. and Williams, F. 1973: Stereotyped attitudes of selected English dialect communities. In Shuy, R. and Fasold, R., editors, *Language attitudes: Current trends and prospects* (Washington, Georgetown University Press) 85–96.

Siegler, D. M. and Siegler, R. 1976: Stereotypes of males' and females' speech. *Psychological Reports* **39**, 169–70.

Siegman, A. W. 1978: The telltale voice: Nonverbal messages of verbal communication. In Siegman, A. W. and Feldstein, S., editors, *Nonverbal behaviour and communication* (Hillsdale: Lawrence Erlbaum Associates).

Sigman, S. J. 1980: On communication rules from a social perspective. *Human Communication Research* **7**, 37–51.

Sillars, A. L. In press: Perspectives on attribution and communication: Are people 'naive scientists' or are they just 'naive'? In Roloff, M. E. and Berger, C. R., editors, *Social cognition and communication*. Beverly Hills: Sage.

Simard, L. 1981a: Intergroup communication. In Gardner, R. C. and Kalin, R., editors, *A Canadian social psychology of ethnic relations* (Toronto: Methuen).

_____ 1981b: Cross-cultural interaction: Potential invisible barriers. *Journal of Social Psychology* **113**, 171–92.

Simard, L., Taylor, D. M. and Giles, H. 1976: Attribution processes and inter-personal accommodation in a bilingual setting. *Language and Speech* **19**, 374–87.

Simons, H. W., Moyer, R. J. and Berkowitz, N. W. 1970: Similarity, credibility, and attitude change: A review and a theory. *Psychological Bulletin* **73**, 1–16.

Sledd, J. 1972: Doublespeak: Dialectology in service of big brother. *College English* **33**, 439–56.

Smith, B. L., Brown, B. L., Strong, W. J. and Rencher, A. C. 1975: Effects of speech rate on personality perception. *Language and Speech* **18**, 145–52.

Smith, M. B., Bruner, J. S. and White, R. W. 1956: *Opinions and personality*. New York: Wiley.

Smith, M. E. 1968: The Spanish-speaking population of Florida. In Helm, J., editor, *Spanish-speaking people in the United States* (Seattle: University of Washington Press) 120–33.

Smith, M. K. and Bailey, G. H. 1980: Attitude and activity: Contextual constraints on subjective judgements. In Giles, H., Robinson, W. P. and Smith, P. M., editors, *Language: Social psychological perspectives* (Oxford: Pergamon) 209–16.

Smith, P. M. 1979: Sex markers in speech. In Scherer, K. R. and Giles, H., editors, *Social markers in speech* (Cambridge: Cambridge University Press) 109–46.

Smith, P. M., Giles, H. and Hewstone, M. 1980: Sociolinguistics: A social psychological perspective. In St Clair, R. N. and Giles, H., editors, *The social and psychological contexts of language* (Hillsdale: Lawrence Erlbaum Associates) 283–98.

_____ 1982: New horizons in the study of speech and social situations. In Bain, B., editor, *The sociogenesis of language* (New York: Plenum).

Smith-Rosenberg, C. 1975: The female world of love and ritual: Relations between women in nineteenth-century America. *Signs: Journal of Women in Culture and Society* **1**, 1–29.

Smythe, P. C., Stennett, R. G. and Feenstra, H. J. 1972: Attitude, aptitude, and type of instructional program in second language acquisition. *Canadian Journal of Behavioural Science* **4**, 307–21.

Snyder, M. 1979: Self-monitoring processes. In Berkowitz, L., editor, *Advances in experimental social psychology* **12** (New York: Academic Press) 85–128.

_____ 1980: Seek, and ye shall find: Testing hypotheses about other people. In Higgins, E. T., Herman, C. P. and Zanna, M. P., editors, *Social cognition: The Ontario symposium* (Hillsdale: Lawrence Erlbaum Associates) 277–303

Sole, Y. 1977: Language attitudes toward Spanish among Mexican American college students. *Journal of LASSO* **2**, 37–46.

Spence, J. T. and Helmreich, R. 1972: The attitudes toward women scale. *JSAS Catalog of Selected Documents in Psychology* **2**, 66.

Spilka, I. V. 1970: *Force study of diglossia in French Canada*. Montreal: Mimeo Université de Montréal.

Spurgeon, C. F. E. 1970: *Leading motives in the imagery of Shakespeare's tragedies*. New York: Haskell House.

Staats, A. and Staats, C. 1958: Attitudes established by classical conditioning.

Journal of Abnormal and Social Psychology **57**, 37–40.

Stang, D. J. 1973: Effect of interaction rate on ratings of leadership and liking. *Journal of Personality and Social Psychology* **27**, 405–8.

Steinig, W. 1976: *Soziolekt und soziale Rolle*. Düsseldorf.

_____ 1978: Deutscher Gesprächsunterricht mit ausländischen Studenten. In Wierlacher, A. u. a., editor, *Jahrbuch. Deutsch als Fremdsprache* **4**. Heidelberg, 127–37.

Steinig, W. 1980: Zur sozialen Bewertung sprachlicher Variation. In Cherubim, D., editor, *Fehlerlinguistik: Beiträge zum Problem der sprachlichen Abweichung*. Tübingen: Max Neimeyer Verlag.

Stephenson, G. 1981: Intergroup bargaining and negotiation. In Turner, J. C. and Giles, H., editors, *Intergroup behaviour* (Oxford: Blackwell) 168–98.

Stevens, P. 1980: Modernism and authenticity as reflected in language attitudes: The case of Tunisia. *Civilizations* **30**, 37–59

Stevens, P. 1983: Ambivalence, modernization and language attitudes: French and Arabic in Tunisia. *Journal of Multilingual and Multicultural Development,* in press.

Stevenson, J. M. 1973: *Cuban-Americans: New urban class*. Unpublished doctoral dissertation, Wayne State University.

Stewart, W. A. 1968: A sociolinguistic typology for describing national multilingualism. In Fishman, J. A., editor, *Readings in the sociology of language* (The Hague: Mouton) 531–5.

Stokes, R. and Hewitt, J. P. 1976: Aligning actions. *American Sociological Review* **41**, 838–49.

Strainchamps, E. 1974: *Rooms with no view: A woman's guide to the man's world of the media*. New York: Harper & Row.

Street, R. L., Jr. 1980: *Evaluations of noncontent speech accommodation*. Unpublished doctoral dissertation, The University of Texas at Austin.

_____ 1982. Evaluation of noncontent speech accommodation. *Language and Communication* **2**, 13–31.

Streeter, L. A., Krauss, R. M., Geller, V., Olson, C. and Apple, W. 1977: Pitch changes during attempted deception. *Journal of Personality and Social Psychology* **35**, 345–50.

Strongman, K. and Woosley, J. 1967: Stereotyped reactions to regional accents. *British Journal of Social and Clinical Psychology* **6**, 164–7.

Suarez, Y. L. de 1978: Bilingualism in Mexico. In Alatis, J. E., editor, *Georgetown University Round Table on Languages and Linguistics 1978*: *International dimensions of bilingual education* (Washington: Georgetown University Press) 202–13.

Swift, J. 1898: A letter to a young clergyman. In Scott, T., editor, *The prose works of Jonathan Swift*, vol. 3 (London: George Bell & Sons) 199–217.

Tabouret-Keller, A. 1981: Introduction: Regional languages in France: Current research in rural situations. *International Journal of the Sociology of Language* **29**, 5–14.

Tajfel, H. 1974: Social identity and intergroup behaviour. *Social Science Information* **13**, 65–93.

_____ 1981: Social stereotypes and social groups. In Turner, J. C. and· Giles, H., editors, *Intergroup Behaviour* (Oxford: Basil Blackwell) 144–67.

_____ In press: Social justice in social psychology. In Fraisse, P., editor *La psychologie du futur* (Paris: Presses Universitaires de France).

Tajfel, H., Jahoda, G., Nemeth, C., Rim, Y. and Johnson, N. B. 1972: The devaluation of children of their own national and ethnic group: Two case studies. *British Journal of Social and Clinical psychology* **11**, 235–43.

Tajfel, H. and Turner, J. C. 1979: An integrative theory of intergroup conflict. In Austin, W. C. and Worchel, S., editors, *The social psychology of intergroup relations* (Monterey: Brooks Cole) 33–53.

Tajfel, H. and Wilkes, A. L. 1963: Classification and quantitative judgement. *British Journal of Psychology* **54**, 101–14.

Taylor, D. M. 1981: Stereotypes and intergroup relations. In Gardner, R. C. and Kalin, R., editors, *A Canadian social psychology of ethnic relations* (Toronto: Methuen).

Taylor, D. M. and Clément, R. 1974: Normative reactions to styles of Quebec French. *Anthropological Linguistics* **16**, 202–17.

Taylor, D. M., Meynard, R. and Rheault, E. 1977: Threat to ethnic identity and second language learning. In Giles, H., editor, *Language, intergroup relations, and ethnicity* (London: Academic Press) 99–118.

Taylor, D. M. and Royer, L. 1980: Group processes affecting anticipated language choice in intergroup relations. In Giles, H., Robinson, W. P. and Smith, P. M., editors, *Language: Social psychological perspectives* (Oxford: Pergamon) 185–92.

Taylor, D. M. and Simard, L. 1979: Ethnic identity and intergroup relations. In Lee, D. J., editor, *Emerging ethnic boundaries* (Ottawa: University of Ottawa Press).

Taylor, O. 1973: Teachers' attitudes toward Black and nonstandard English as measured by the Language Attitude Scale. In Shuy, R. and Fasold, R., editors, *Language attitudes: Current trends and prospects* (Washington: Georgetown University Press) 174–201.

Teitelbaum, H., Edwards, A. and Hudson, A. 1975: Ethnic attitudes and the acquisition of Spanish as a second language. *Language Learning* **25**, 255–66.

Thakerar, J. N. and Giles, H. 1981: They are – so they speak: Noncontent speech stereotypes. *Language and Communication* **1**, 251–6.

Thakerar, J. N., Giles, H. and Cheshire, J. 1982: Psychological and linguistic parameters of speech accommodation theory. In Fraser, C. and Scherer, K. R., editors, *Advances in the social psychology of language* (Cambridge: Cambridge University Press) 205–55.

Thompson, R. M. 1974: Mexican American language loyalty and the validity of the 1970 census. *International Journal of the Sociology of Language* **2**, 7–18.

——— 1975: Mexican-American English: Social correlates of regional pronunciation. *American Speech* **50**, 18–24.

Thomson, J. 1977: Social class labelling in the application of Bernstein's theory of the codes to the identification of linguistic advantage and disadvantage in five-year-old children. *Educational Review* **29**, 273–83.

Thorngate, W. 1976: Must we always think before we act? *Personality and Social Psychology Bulletin* **2**, 31–5.

——— 1979: Memory, cognition and social performance. In Strickland, L., editor, *Soviet and Western perspectives in social psychology* (New York: Pergamon) 289–316.

Tilley, M. P. 1950: *A dictionary of the proverbs in England in the sixteenth and seventeenth centuries*. Ann Arbor: University of Michigan Press.

Tovar, I. 1973: The changing attitude of La Raza toward the Chicano idiom. In Hoffer, B. and Ornstein, J., editors, *Sociolinguistics in the Southwest* (San Antonio: Trinity University) 63–74.

Triandis, H. C., Loh, W. D. and Levin, L. A. 1966: Race, status, quality of spoken English and opinions about civil rights as determinants of inter-personal attitudes. *Journal of Personality and Social Psychology* 3, 468–72.

Trower, P. 1980: Situation analysis of the components and processes of behav-iour of socially skilled and unskilled patients. *Journal of Consulting and Clinical Psychology* 48, 327–39.

Trudgill, P. 1974a: *Sociolinguistics*. Harmondsworth: Penguin.

_____ 1974b: *The social differentiation of English in Norwich*. London: Cambridge University Press.

_____ 1975a: *Accent, dialect and the school*. London: Edward Arnold.

_____ 1975b: Sex, covert prestige, and linguistic change in the urban British English of Norwich. In Thorne, B. and Henley, N., editors, *Language and Sex: Difference and dominance* (Rowley: Newbury House) 88–104.

_____ 1981: Linguistic accommodation: Sociolinguistic observations on a socio-psychological theory. In the *Proceedings of the Chicago Linguistic Circle* (Chicago: University of Chicago Press) in press.

Tsuzaki, S. 1971: Coexistent systems in language variation: The case of Hawaiian English. In Hymes, D., editor, *Pidginization and creolization of languages* (London: Cambridge University Press) 327–40.

Tucker, G. R. and Lambert, W. E. 1969: White and Negro listeners' reactions to various American-English dialects. *Social Forces* 47, 463–8.

_____ 1970: The effect on foreign language teachers of leadership training in a foreign setting. *Foreign Language Annals* 4, 68–83.

Turner, J. C. 1981a: Some considerations on generalizing experimental social psychology. In Stephenson, G. and Davies, J., editors, *Progress in applied social psychology*, Vol. 1 (Chichester: Wiley).

_____ 1981b: The experimental social psychology of intergroup behaviour. In Turner, J. C. and Giles, H., editors, *Intergroup behaviour* (Oxford: Pergamon) 66–101.

_____ 1982: Towards a cognitive redefinition of the social group. In Tajfel, H., editor, *Social identity and intergroup relations* (Cambridge: Cambridge University Press).

Turner, J. C. and Giles, H. 1981: *Intergroup Behaviour* Oxford: Blackwell.

Tversky, A. and Kahneman, D. 1980: Causal thinking in judgements under uncertainty. In Butts, B. and Hintikka, J., editors, *Logic, methodology and philosophy of science* (Dordrecht: D. Reidel).

Ulibarri, H. 1968: Bilingualism. In Birkmaier, E. M., editor, *The Britannica review of foreign languages* (New York: Britannica Publications) 229–58.

Ullrich, H. E. 1971: Linguistic aspects of antiquity: a dialect. *Anthropological Linguistics* 13, 106–13.

Unger, R. 1979: *Female and male: Psychological perspectives*. New York: Harper & Row.

US Bureau Of The Census 1981: *Persons of Spanish origin in the United States: March 1980 (Advance Report)*. Current Population Reports, Population

Characteristics Series P-20, No. 361. Washington: US Government Printing Office.

Valdes-Fallis, G. 1978: Code-switching among bilingual Mexican-American women: Towards an understanding of sex-related language alternation. *International Journal of the Sociology of Language* 17, 65–72.

Valdman, A. 1976a: Le statut du créole et les problèmes d'instruction primaire en Haiti. In Runte, H. R. and Valdman, A., editors, *Identité culturelle et francophonie dans les Amériques,* vol. 2 (Bloomington: Indiana University) 103–12.

_____ 1976b: Vers la standardisation du créole en Haiti. In Snyder, E. and Valdman, A., editors, *Identité culturelle et francophonie dans les Amériques,* vol. 1 (Quebec: Les presses de l'Université Laval) 166–201.

Van Eerde, J. 1979: Facets of the Breton Problem. *Language Problems and Language Planning* 3, 1–8.

Vaughan, G. 1978: Social categorization and intergroup behaviour in children. In Tajfel, H., editor, *Differentiation between social groups* (London: Academic Press) 129–47.

Veltman, C. J. 1979: New opportunities for the study of language shift: The anglicization of New England language minorities. *Language Problems and Language Planning* 3, 65–75.

Verdoodt, A. 1978: Belgium. *International Journal of the Sociology of Language* 15.

Viatte, A. 1969: *La francophonie*. Paris: Larousse.

Villegas, O. U. 1970: *Un mapa del monolinguisme y el bilinguismo de los indigenas de Mexico en 1960*. Mexico City: Instituto de Investigaciones Sociales, UNAM.

Vorster, J. and Proctor, L. 1976: Black attitudes to 'White' languages in South Africa: A pilot study. *Journal of Social Psychology* 92, 103–8.

Wachal, R. S. and Spreen, O. 1973: Some measures of lexical diversity in aphasic and normal language performance. *Language and Speech* 16, 169–81.

Watzlawick, P., Beavin, J. H. and Jackson, D. D. 1967: *Pragmatics of human communication*. New York: W. W. Norton & Company.

Weaver, R. 1953: *The ethics of rhetoric*. Chicago: H. Regnery Co.

Webb, E. J., Campbell, D. T., Schwarz, R. D. and Sechrest, L. 1966: *Unobtrusive measures: Nonreactive research in the social sciences*. Chicago: Rand McNally & Company.

Webb, J. T. 1970: Interview Synchrony. In Siegman, A. W. and Pope, B., editors, *Studies in dyadic communication* (Oxford: Pergamon Press) 115–34.

Weinreich, U. 1963: *Languages in contact*. The Hague: Mouton.

Weinstein, B. 1980: Language planning in francophone Africa. *Language Problems and Language Planning* 4, 56–75.

Welkowitz, J. and Feldstein, S. 1969: Dyadic interactions and induced differences in perceived similarity. *Proceedings of the 77th Annual Convention of the American Psychological Association* 4, 343.

_____ 1970: Relation of experimentally manupulated perception and psychological differentiation to the temporal patterning of conversation. *Proceedings*

of the 78th Annual Convention of the American Psychological Association
5, 387–8.

West, C. and Guiffre, L. 1980: *What is a medical interview? A preliminary
investigation of physician-patient interaction.* Paper presented at the meeting
of the American Sociological Association, New York.

Wheeler, C., Wilson, J. and Tarantola, C. 1976: An investigation of children's
social perception of child speakers with reference to verbal style. *Central
States Speech Journal* **27**, 31–5.

Wicker, A. W. 1969: Attitudes versus actions: The relationship of verbal and
overt behavioural responses to attitude objects. *Journal of Social Issues* **4**,
41–78.

Wiener, M. and Mehrabian, A. 1967: *Language within language: Immediacy, a
channel in verbal communication.* New York: Appleton-Century-Crofts.

Wilkinson, A. 1965: Spoken English. *Educational Review* **17** (supplement).

Williams, C. H. 1977: Ethnic perceptions of Acadia. *Cahiers de Géographie
de Québec* **21**, 243–68.

Williams, F. 1974: The identification of linguistic attitudes. *International
Journal of the Sociology of Language* **3**, 21–32.

Williams, F. et al 1976: *Explorations of the linguistic attitudes of teachers.*
Rowley; Newbury House.

Williams, F., Whitehead, J. L. and Miller, L. 1972: Relations between attitudes
and teacher expectancy. *American Educational Research Journal* **9**,
263–77.

Wilson, M. 1947: *The new etiquette: The modern code of social behaviour.* New
York: J. B. Lippincott.

Wish, M. 1978: Dimensions of dyadic communication. In Weitz, S., editor,
Nonverbal communication, second edition (New York: Oxford University
Press) 371–8.

Witan, K. U. 1940: *Lady Lore.* Lawrence: University of Kansas Press.

Wölck, W. 1973: Attitudes toward Spanish and Quechua in bilingual Peru. In
Shuy, R. W. and Fasold, R. W., editors, *Language attitudes: Current trends
and prospects* (Washington: Georgetown University Press) 148–73.

Wolff, H. 1959: Intelligibility and inter-ethnic attitudes. *Anthropological
Linguistics* **1**, 34–41.

Wolfram, W. 1974: *Sociolinguistic aspects of assimilation: Puerto Rican
English in New York City.* Arlington: Center for Applied Linguistics.

Woll, B. and Lawson, L. In press: British sign language. In Haugen, E.,
McCure, J. D. and Thomson, D. editors, *Minority languages.* (Edinburgh:
Edinburgh University Press.)

Woods, R. E. 1980: Language maintenance and external support: The case of
the French Flemings. *International Journal of the Sociology of Language* **25**,
107–19.

Woolard, K. A. 1980: *A formal measure of language attitudes in Barcelona: A
note from work in progress.* Unpublished manuscript, Department of
Anthropology, University of California, Berkeley.

Wright, M. 1936: *The art of conversation: And how to apply its technique.* New
York: McGraw-Hill.

Wyer, R. S. 1980: The acquisition and use of social knowledge: Basic postulates
and representative research. *Personality and Social Psychology Bulletin* **6**,
558–73.

Wyer, R. S, and Carlston, D. 1980: *Social cognition, inference and attribution*. Hillsdale: Lawrence Erlbaum Associates.

Yang, K. S. and Bond, M. 1980: Ethnic affiliation in Chinese bilinguals. *Journal of Cross-Cultural Psychology* 11, 411–25.

Yule, G. U. 1944: *The statistical study of literary vocabulary*. Cambridge: Cambridge University Press.

Zajonc, R. B. 1968: Attitudinal effects of mere exposure. *Journal of Personality and Social Psychology, Monograph Supplement* 9, 1–27.

Zimmerman, D. and West, C. 1975: Sex roles, interruptions and silences in conversation. In Thorne, B. and Henley, N., editors, *Language and sex: Differences and dominance* (Rowley: Newbury House) 105–29.

Index

273

Buss, A.R., 211
Butler, M., 84n.
Byrne, D., 142, 178

Cacioppo, J.T., 189, 190, 191, 197, 203, 204, 205, 206, 207, 212, 216
Cajuns, 53–4, 55
Calabrese, R.J., 111, 185
Calder, B.J., 204
California, 134
Calvet, L.J., 36, 37, 38, 40
Cambodia, French language in, 46–7
Campbell, D.T., 109, 168
Campbell, H.H., 191
Canada, attitudes and second language learning, 134, 136, 138, 139–40; Canadian official languages Act, 55–6; children's attitude towards language, 123, 124; convergence of speech style studies, 200; employment discrimination, 154; employment interviews, 157; French language in, 4, 5, 55–9; French language in Quebec, 57–9; group identity, 142; language recognition in children, 117–18; speech style evaluation, 179, 183
Canale, M., 56
Cantor, J.R., 109
Cantor, M., 84n.
Cantor, N., 177, 213
Capadano, 181
Caput, J.P., 37
Cardenas, G., 73
Carlston, D.E., 209
Carnegie, A., 170
Carr, E.B., 119
Carranza, M.A., 10, 25–6, 27, 30, 31, 73n., 74, 75, 77–8, 81, 82, 128, 143, 180, 184, 191, 221
Carroll, J.B., 21, 138
Carter, R.F., 203
Casanova, J.D., 53
Castaneda, A., 171
Castilian, 65–7, 165
Castillo, E.S., 218
Castonguay, C., 56
Catalan, 4, 5, 40, 41, 65–7
Cavanaugh, N.F., 134
Central African Republic, 49, 50
Centro de Estudios Puertorriquenos, New York, 71–2, 81
Césaire, Aimé, 52
Chad, 49
Chaiken, S., 200, 201, 206

Chantefort, P., 58
Chapanis, A., 198
Chapanis, N., 198
Charrow, R.P., 151, 162
Charrow, V.R., 150–1, 162
Chase, S., 103
Cheshire, J., 176, 212
Chetwynd, J., 217
Cheyne, W., 23, 64
Chiasson-Lavoie, M., 58
Chicago, 73
Chicanos, *see* Mexican-Americans
Chihara, R., 135
Child, P., 218
children, 116–31; acquisition of language attitudes, 118–26; communicative competence, 116–17; racial/ethnic attitudes and language attitudes, 126–8; recognition of language differences, 117–18; *see also* education
Chomsky, N., 99, 104, 164
Choy, S., 28
Chraibi, D., 45
Christian, C.C. Jr, 73
Christian, J., 73, 221
Cialdini, R.B., 204, 205, 206
Clarke, S., 10
Clément, R., 58, 134, 135, 137, 140, 142, 147, 179, 180, 214
Cockney accent, 23
codified norms, 3
cognitive dissonance theory, 197–8
cognitive processes studies, 212–16
Cohen, A.D., 63, 76
Cohen, A.R., 191
Cohen, C.E., 215
Cohen, S., 134
Cole, R.L., 41
Coltharp, L.H., 81
communicative competence, children, 116–17
concrete words, 101
conditioning, 190–1
Condor, S., 27, 94, 95
Congo-Brazzaville, 49, 50
congruity theory, 197
Connecticut, 53, 134
Conrad, A.W., 32
Conville, R., 106, 109
Conway, T., 109, 158, 210
Cook, T.D., 203
Cooper, J., 192
Cooper, R., 60, 72
Cooper, R.L., 7, 8, 12 and n., 20, 32, 63